Patterns of Political Participation in Italy

Patterns of Political Participation in Italy

by Giorgio Galli
and Alfonso Prandi

New Haven and London, Yale University Press, 1970

Library of Congress catalog card number: 78-99824
International standard book number: 0-300-01276-4
Designed by Helen Frisk Buzyna,
set in Baskerville type,
and printed in the United States of America by
Vail-Ballou Press, Inc., Binghamton, N. Y.
Distributed in Great Britain, Europe, and
Africa by Yale University Press Ltd., London; in
Canada by McGill-Queen's University Press, Montreal;
in Mexico by Centro Interamericano de Libros
Académicos, Mexico City; in Australasia by Australia
and New Zealand Book Co., Pty., Ltd., Artarmon, New South
Wales; in India by UBS Publishers' Distributors Pvt., Ltd.,
Delhi; in Japan by John Weatherhill, Inc., Tokyo.

Contents

List of Tables and Figures

Tables

Preface

In this book we have summarized the findings of an extensive study of Italian political life since World War II, carried out by a research team of the Carlo Cattaneo Institute of Bologna, Italy, between 1962 and 1966.* The project was sponsored by The Twentieth Century Fund.

The study, conducted with particular reference to the two major Italian political parties—the Communist Party and the Christian Democratic Party—was planned and directed by the authors, assisted by Giovanni Evangelisti, Gianfranco Poggi, and Giacomo Sani. Francesco Alberoni, Franco Ferrarotti, and Giovanni Sartori served as able consultants. Successive directors of the Institute during the period the study was under way were Fabio Luca Cavazza, Giovanni Evangelisti, and Agopik Manoukian.

Other members of the research team were: Silvia Adilardi Tozzi, Bianca Avanzini, Luigi Brunelli, Umberto Canullo, Vittorio Capecchi, Vittoria Cioni Polacchini, Franca Cervellati Cantelli, Gianluigi Degli Esposti, Paola de Vito Piscicelli, Stefania Guarino Cappello, Anna Lena, Franca Olivetti Manoukian, Sergio Pedroli, Luciana Pepa, Antonio Picchi, Alberto M. Rossi, Bruno Scatassa, Giordano Sivini, Ada Sivini Cavazzani, Antonio Tosi, Luigi Turco. Nicola Matteucci assisted in writing Chapter 1.

The detailed findings of the study are reported in several volumes published in Italian. These works and the methods and sources used in the various parts of the project are described in Appendix A of this book.

* The Institute is a private, nonprofit, research organization, associated with the monthly journal, *Il Mulino*. Its purpose is to study problems of Italian society and make the findings available to interested scholars.

This volume has the assets and liabilities characteristic of summaries: it presents, we hope, a useful overall view, but it does not explore in depth the problems considered.

The documentation is purposely weighted in favor of English language sources. The interested reader will find additional bibliographic references in the Italian volumes in which the results of this study have been fully reported.

The original Italian manuscript was translated into English by Mrs. Patricia Poggi. Joseph LaPalombara, Professor of Political Science at Yale University, read the several drafts of the text and made a number of useful suggestions for their improvement. The English manuscript was edited by Mrs. Louise Field and Mrs. Frances Klafter of the Twentieth Century Fund.

In our analysis of political developments in Italy from 1945 to 1963 we have tried to avoid biased terminology and political partisanship. Yet, in publishing the results of our research, we feel the need to lay aside for a few pages our dispassionate approach and to provide a judgment of the Italian political system from the point of view of scholars involved in Italian life.

We hope that the views expressed here by way of introduction to this book will help to temper the stereotyped views of Italy now in circulation. These include two views of the Italians and their characteristics that have been set forth in recent books by Italian as well as by British and American authors. In his book, *The Italians* (New York, Atheneum, 1964), for example, Luigi G. Barzini has revived the theme that while Italian names and official appearances may change with the passage of time, the recipe or formula for Italian political life is always the same: appearance rather than essence, form rather than content, theater rather than reality, spectacle rather than life, a façade rather than solid substance, a theme that another Italian, Giuseppe Antonio Borgese, skillfully treated in 1937 in his book, *Goliath: the March of Fascism* (New York, Viking). Studies by non-Italians, such as René Albrecht-Carrié in *Italy from Napoleon to Mussolini* (New York, Columbia University Press, 1950), and Denis Mack Smith in *Italy: A Modern History* (Ann Arbor, University of Michigan Press, 1959), have suggested that the continuity of Italian history is unbroken in both its liberal and fascist periods. They show Italian politicians as astute and clever diplomats who, when in power, have seized on existing forces and drawn them together into combinations tactically suitable for current exigencies, without bothering to offer solutions for problems that have long demanded attention. Although these two stereotypes of the Italian political character are contradictory, they imply a common criticism of Italian political life as lacking a solid base of ideals and of the Italian people as having an inherent inability to adjust to a free society.

There is no doubt that these stereotypes have been widely accepted in American and British cultural circles. That is why, in offering this sociological study of the Italian political system, we are worried lest these images of Italy and the Italians cloud the reader's interpretation of our tables and statistics, our empirical investigations and quantitative descriptions.

Since we do not believe that "the Italian" exists as a pure distillate of past ages, nor that a more malevolent force has been inherent in Italian history than in all other human history, we decided to begin our study of the postwar Italian political system with an examination of problems that Italians faced in 1945 and a brief review of the means by which they attempted to solve them. The picture is not complete, but it serves as an introduction to the Italians, whose experiences have produced the political system described in the chapters that follow, and whose participation has made that system function.

While the research was in progress, a precarious political balance was achieved by means of the Catholic and Socialist alliance in Aldo Moro's first three governments. Italian history was in the making, and we Italians were conscious of the choice before us: either the individualistic energies that inspired reconstruction and the economic miracle would become less antisocial and be put to work in a search for political solutions for the common good; or else the egoism of individuals, groups, and classes would finally prevail, thus compelling the state to assume all responsibility for individual security and prosperity.

It had become increasingly clear that Italians must break down the barriers between a dynamic society and a static political system by giving greater social and political effectiveness to the energy and drive that was felt throughout Italian society from 1945 to 1963. Social reforms must stimulate individual energy and voluntary effort and reinforce the freedom whose protection man entrusts to society.

Otherwise, a bureaucratic state awaits the Italians, and we will all end up as its employees, with all the threats to democratic government that such a change implies. But if the barriers are surmounted, we can anticipate a dynamic joining of forces in which individual egoism is mobilized by the state in the interests of national development, and the state itself is responsible for areas of human concern in which private initiative cannot function effectively.

Giorgio Galli
Alfonso Prandi

Istituto di Studi e Ricerche
Carlo Cattaneo
Bologna, May 1969

Italian Political Parties

Partito Socialista Italiano	PSI	Socialist Party, founded in 1892 and later split into various socialist groups, including the PSDI and the PSIUP. (See also PSIUP.)
Partito Comunista Italiano	PCI	Communist Party, founded January 21, 1921, after a split within the Socialist Party.
Partito Popolare Italiano	PPI	Popular Party, founded in 1919 by Catholic leaders. The Catholics had previously refused to participate in public life because of the conflicts between Church and State during the second part of the nineteenth century.
Democrazia Cristiana	DC	Christian Democratic Party, founded in 1942, was an outgrowth of the Italian Popular Party. It has been in power since 1945.
Partito Socialista Democratico Italiano	PSDI	Social Democratic Party, founded in 1947 after a split within the PSI.
Partito Socialista Italiano di Unità Proletaria	PSIUP	Socialist Party of Proletarian Unity, name assumed by the Socialist Party after World War I. The name was later changed to PSI. A new PSIUP emerged in 1963 as a splinter group from the PSI.

Partito Liberale Italiano	PLI	Liberal Party, conservative in orientation. Its origins can be traced to the process of the unification of the country in the mid-nineteenth century. Immediately after World War II the Liberals appeared on the electoral scene as the National Democratic Union (UND) and the Democratic Bloc (BN).
Movimento Sociale Italiano	MSI	Italian Social Movement, neofascist party founded in 1946.
Uomo Qualunque	UQ	Everyman's Party, right-wing, antiparliamentary. A "flash" party, successful in 1946, had already disappeared by 1948.
Partito Repubblicano Italiano	PRI	Republican Party, some 100 years old.
Partito Nazionale Monarchico	PNM	National Monarchist Party founded after the fall of the monarchy in Italy; has moderate right-wing tendencies.
Partito Monarchico Popolare	PMP	Popular Monarchist Party, broke away from the PNM in 1958.
Unione Socialista Indipendente	USI	Independent Socialist Union, formed by two ex-Communist leaders, Magnani and Cucchi, in 1951.
Alleanza Democratica Nazionale	ADN	National Democratic Alliance, formed by a group of Liberals for the election of 1953 and quickly dissolved.
Unità Popolare	UP	Popular Unity, moderate socialist group of dissidents from the Social Democratic Party. It achieved its maximum strength in the election of 1953, and was later absorbed by PSDI and PSI.

Patterns of Political Participation in Italy

I

Italy after World War II

On April 25, 1945, after a rapid advance beyond the Gothic Line [1] by the American Fifth Army and the British Eighth Army, the National Liberation Committees in northern Italy declared a general uprising. A few days later the whole of Italy rejoiced that the country was free and reunited at last. It was a day that had been anticipated with painful anxiety both in the North, which had toiled hard and sacrificed lives to achieve it, and in the Center and South, where Italians were anxiously waiting to be reunited with their northern compatriots. The rejoicing was short-lived, however, for Italians could not long ignore the tragic aftermath of the war and the urgent problems of reconstruction that confronted them.

Italy was a defeated country that had also experienced fierce fighting on its own soil; the line of battle had moved up the peninsula from Salerno to Cassino, Anzio, Florence, and the Gothic Line, crushing all before it like a gigantic steamroller. The slow liberation of their country, the partisan fighting, and the shelling and bombing had involved all Italians—had destroyed any distinction between fighting lines and dwelling places, soldiers and civilians.

Almost two years earlier, on the evening of September 8, 1943, Italians had spontaneously and ingenuously celebrated the "armistice" with bonfires that flared along the crest of the Apennines. Their yearning for peace had blunted their ability to be realistic about the fate that awaited them. The twenty months that ensued before Italy was completely liberated were in some ways harder for

1. The boundary (running in a line across the Apennines from Florence to Bologna) that separated central and southern Italy—both of which were liberated from the Germans after the armistice of September 1943—from northern Italy, which continued to be occupied by the Germans until April 1945.

3

the people than were the thirty-nine months during which Italy had fought as Germany's ally. During the earlier period—from June 10, 1940, to September 8, 1943—Italy's fighting forces had suffered losses of 68,000 dead and 146,000 missing. Following the armistice—from September 9, 1943, until the end of April 1945—losses among partisans, armed forces, and civilians amounted to some 65,000 dead, 33,000 wounded, and 20,000 missing.

THE AFTERMATH OF WAR

The economic situation at the end of the war was catastrophic. The national income had dropped to less than half its 1938 level and at least one fifth of the nation's assets had been destroyed. As much as 40 percent of railway property had been demolished (with the result that no trains ran between North and South until the autumn of 1945), as had 90 percent of dock equipment and 60 percent of the road system. This was the situation that confronted the Italian people at a time when those who had been separated from their families longed to return to their homes. With communications so difficult, it seemed as if distances had increased, and the extent of the disaster was thus magnified.

The feeling of uncertainty was intensified by the wrecked houses (containing three million rooms), the reduction of electrical plants to half their prewar capacity, the lack of regular employment, and the awaited return of prisoners of war (570,000 from the Western allies and 80,000—though only 20,000 in fact returned—from the Soviet Union). Furthermore, as the following index (1936=100) of the gold-exchange value of the lira shows, there was the frightening fall in the value of money, especially after April 1946: [2]

1936	100.0
1938	74.5
1943	74.5
1944	22.2
1945	14.2
1947	4.8
1948	2.4
1951	2.2
1961	2.2

2. *Il Valore della Lira nei primi cento anni della Unità d'Italia, 1861–1960* (Rome, Istituto Centrale di Statistica, 1961), p. 39.

After those joyous days of April 1945 when Italian soil was finally liberated, the people had to face the harsh reality of wreckage, bereavement, hunger, uncertainty, weak government, political clashes, and increasingly violent and inflamed social frictions.

Italians everywhere speedily set about clearing the wreckage. Everyone was involved, but involved as individuals, independent of any government program, without help from public authorities. In the face of increasing inflation, reconstruction was based on paper money, not on real savings. Everyone was conscious of the general effort and struggle toward reconstruction, but there were no clear directives from above. On the contrary, antifascist vendettas, strikes, and demonstrations constituted a serious obstacle to the development of a sound economy, for the factories and the countryside were the scenes of intense and sometimes violent class struggle.

It was reconstruction with an eye to the past, for the difficulties of everyday life so restricted the imagination that few possessed the public spirit and sense of discipline needed to work together toward the achievement of a new common objective. Political and social cohesion was, in fact, unthinkable in a country disrupted and divided as Italy was by the war. An austerity program such as that worked out by the British Labour Party would have met with stubborn resistance. The few who suggested such a program went unheeded and failed to give their ideas effective political force. Even the individual urge to reconstruct was rooted in nostalgia, and hence was concerned with putting the clock back to 1938.

Everything was to return to its rightful place in the old order of things, for that old order was at least more clearly understood and safer than anything new that might be put forward in the politically electric atmosphere of the time. In the work of reconstruction the feelings of many Italians were analogous to those that caused the disintegration of the Italian army in September 1943. Once the state had collapsed, and order with it, the only thing to do was to return home, for home represented the only remaining tangible reality. In 1945 private houses were rebuilt first; only later did work begin on workshops and schools, hospitals and state offices.

In the tense political atmosphere, involving the choice between the forces of conservatism and of socialism, Italians did not wait to see who would win. Each one began the work of reconstruction on his own. This work was dominated by a private, family view of things that pervaded all levels of society. This attitude was of advantage to the government, because it was indicative of an industrious and energetic spirit rather than of a resigned and passive acceptance. However, it did tend to inhibit economic and social innovation, as is clear from the delay in stemming inflation and from the long and fruitless discussions about the introduction of a new currency.

POLITICAL RECONSTRUCTION

Despite ideological differences, individuals could be recruited to work on coordinated projects to recover the material losses of war. But moral reconstruction, or building a new Italian society, was not so easy to achieve. The only past that could be looked back to with favor was the prefascist era of Giovanni Giolitti (who had served as Premier intermittently from 1892 to 1921). After twenty years of fascism, many knew of that era only from books or their fathers' recollections, not from personal experience.[3]

Foremost among the many obstacles Italians faced in reaching a common political philosophy was the division of Italy that had been created by the Gothic Line, which had effectively cut Italy in two, and furthered the development of two quite different political attitudes. Southern Italy had been rapidly liberated by the Allies, and a prefascist, parliamentary form of government was being reconstructed there. In German-occupied northern Italy, on the other hand, the activities of the partisans had led to the creation of new, revolutionary political institutions, such as the National Liberation Committees.

While the leading political parties in the South were the same as those represented on the National Liberation Committees, the southern and northern branches of these parties spoke very different languages. In southern Italy the state machine began slowly but surely to be reassembled around the monarchy; for the monarchy, attacked by Italian antifascists and defended by the Western allies, continued to be a source of power. At Brindisi and then at Salerno the central bureaucratic machines set up new offices. Though the

3. For a review of this historical background see D. Mack Smith, *Italy: A Modern History* (Ann Arbor, University of Michigan Press, 1959); and H. Stuart Hughes, *The United States and Italy*, rev. ed. (Cambridge, Harvard University Press, 1965).

On postwar Italian political life see G. Mammarella, *Italy after Fascism* (Notre Dame, University of Notre Dame Press, 1966); N. Kogan, *A Political History of Postwar Italy* (New York, Praeger, 1966); M. Grindrod: *The New Italy: Transition from War to Peace* (1947), and *The Rebuilding of Italy* (1955), (London, Royal Institute of International Affairs).

state bureaus were poor and provisional, they began to function and to assume control of that part of Italy that had been liberated, trying at the same time to refurbish the old administrative system.

Southern Italy also saw the formation of antifascist parties, whose opposition to Vittorio Emanuele III was upheld by such highly regarded former monarchists as the philosopher Benedetto Croce, and such notable political leaders as Vittorio Emanuele Orlando, Count Carlo Sforza, and Enrico de Nicola, Italy's first postwar provisional President. Thus behind a fairly quiescent social situation the allegiances of prefascist times began to reemerge within the political parties. Political argument was carried on in a fairly orderly way along old, established lines, in spite of the formidable moral problem implicit in the energetic and unflinching opposition to Vittorio Emanuele III by the antifascist parties. What looked like an inevitable clash was avoided, in part because after Palmiro Togliatti, the Communist leader, returned from the Soviet Union in 1944, he agreed to participation by the Communist Party in a government headed by Marshal Badoglio, the king's right-hand man. The conflict over the question of monarchy or republic had prevented the formation of an integrated national government for a long time, but in southern Italy the issue did not excite the population as it did in the North.

Everything was different in the North. During the twenty months when the partisans were fighting the Nazis and Fascists, hopes of revolution had sprung up and allegiances had become divided. For many Italians the goal was not just to free Italy from the Germans but to realize the ideals of the Resistance by creating a social revolution under the leadership of the National Liberation Committees, which had led the armed insurrection.

When representatives of these two Italys met, first in Rome and then in Milan in May 1945 they failed to understand each other, because their ideas of liberty and democracy had developed in different ways, The North maintained that all power should be vested in the National Liberation Committees, which expressed the vitality of Italian society and its need for self-government, in contrast to the central government, which was impotent and incompetent. The North also wanted a direct voice for the Liberation Committees in the form of a revolutionary assembly, which should be created at once and should immediately declare Italy a republic, reform the bureaucracy, and initiate a social revolution.

In Rome, however, representatives of the same six political parties that were represented on the National Liberation Committees preferred not to commit themselves. They decided to postpone all such decisions and, with the exception of the Socialist leader Pietro Nenni, all agreed to withstand these pressures from the North. Their thoughts turned not so much to revolution as to the establishment of the rule of democracy. They wanted to avoid clashes with the Western allied powers, and had no desire to stimulate the formation of revolutionary pockets that might result in a situation similar to that of Greece.

From the atmosphere of the public political meetings held immediately after the liberation of Italy it looked as though the wind from the North would sweep away all resistance and delay. But the wind slowly died down. It died down because the political experiences of northern and southern Italy had been so different, because the Western allies—whose prime concern was the maintenance of order—were still in Italy, and because no political leaders were really prepared to bring about a revolution. They preferred simply to call for one at political meetings.

When no revolution occurred, the power vacuum in the North was quietly but surely filled by the advancing bureaucratic state system. It worked silently. Few noticed how the bureaucracy's position was being consolidated, and its ability to carry out its old function of controlling social life gave it an unexpected strength. This became clear in 1946 when the Western allies handed over the North to the Italian administration. The prefects and police chiefs, who had been nominated by the National Liberation Committees in 1945 and hence directly represented party ideas, were forced to realize that they must either give up their positions or enter the ranks of the state bureaucracy—and that meant deriving their power from the central government, not from revolutionary institutions.

The reconstituted bureaucratic machine won the day, because it was the strongest guarantee of the continuity and preservation of the nation. Alcide de Gasperi, who had become Premier in December 1945, saw the logical necessity for this solution, and therefore gave it his support. He realized that Italy now required a government above party factions, which would safeguard the interests of the community, restore the prestige and authority of the state, and make the law effective and respected. As a staunch Catholic, De Gasperi had no time for pagan myths about the state. When he declared that the authority of the state must be reasserted, he was not speaking of "the state" as conceived in fascist mythology; he meant that the law must be equally respected by all, that the bureaucracy must be free from influence or corruption by the political parties, that the magistrates must be able to carry out their tasks with complete freedom of conscience, and that the political parties must function within the framework of a constitutional government and with complete respect for the law.

In other words, De Gasperi wanted to replace anarchy not with the omnipotent state but with the rule of law. He thus exhorted the political groups involved in the government to adopt a new attitude —to put service to the community before the interests of their own parties. This new emphasis on the community was vital, for, after all, the exaltation of the state during the fascist period—the strong feeling that the state was in effect a form of government above political parties and social classes—had failed to mold Italy into a cohesive nation-state. Though the old bureaucratic machine was consolidated, the fascist-induced habit of identifying party and government with the abstract "state" was so ingrained that the ideal of the rule of law—that is, government on the basis of laws rather than of men or parties—failed to become firmly established among the political parties.

De Gasperi's solution was a typically moderate compromise between fascist one-party rule and multiparty anarchy. The moderate solution was the logical one, for it represented the effective will of contemporary political forces. The greatness of De Gasperi as a political leader lay in his realizing this, and in his ability to adjust to it. However, the reconstruction of the political system was not accompanied by the formation of a ruling class that could visualize the polity as an instrument in the service of Italian citizens rather than of political parties. Politicians saw the political system as a source of personal power rather than as a source of individual rights.

The adoption of De Gasperi's solution meant only that it offered a powerful political instrument, not that the ideals behind it were accepted. Everyone realized the tremendous opportunities that a centralized governmental administration offered a victorious political party. De Gasperi had hoped to keep the administration of government free from political control. But the political parties began to move in exactly the opposite direction. As a result of exchanges of favors between politicians and bureaucrats, the administration gradually became more and more political in nature. It is impossible to say which side was more to blame. Politicians lost the authority that derived from their position as elected representatives of the people, and the bureaucrats lost the independence that derived from their position as impersonal administrators.

DEVELOPING CONCEPTS OF DEMOCRACY

Another problem the Italians had in adjusting to democracy was the profound difference between the experiences of the older and younger generations. Great reverence and respect were still felt for such leaders of prefascist Italy as Vittorio Emanuele Orlando, who had led Italians to victory in World War I; Francesco Saverio Nitti and Carlo Sforza, who were now returning from exile; Benedetto Croce, who, as a Senator, had been a lone opponent of the fascist regime; Ivanoe Bonomi, who had led a government of national solidarity after the liberation of Rome; Enrico de Nicola, who was to become provisional President of the Republic of Italy; and Luigi Einaudi, who was responsible for stemming inflation. But the reverence and esteem the Italians had for these men did not necessarily extend to the democratic, liberal, or radical parties with which they had been identified and which together had formed a constitutional majority before the advent of fascism. Not that the mass of Italians were factious or ungrateful to these democratic leaders; it was simply that fascism had nurtured new social forces and introduced the masses to new experiences that could not be reconciled or identified with these personalities. They represented a past whose ideas were associated with the era of Giolitti and a political system that was already in crisis before World War I.

There was also a certain diffidence and resentment toward the returning exiles who had abandoned Italy at a painful period in its life, and had returned from distant lands to offer formulas that were ill adapted to ideas Italians had formed from their experiences at home. Such political leaders as Giuseppe Saragat, Pietro Nenni, and Palmiro Togliatti succeeded in asserting their authority and prestige, but this was partly because they were the leaders of mass parties that had deep roots in Italian society. In Italian postwar politics the voices of émigrés and of prewar opponents of fascism who had stayed behind became progressively weaker, while the voice of the generation born under fascism, which moved more or less in good faith from fascism to antifascism, became increasingly powerful.

Though the older antifascists, whose opposition was based on moral intransigence and on their prefascist experience, commanded little political support, the attitude toward the Communist Party was quite different. Its antifascism and its desire to remain a mass party were evident, and throughout its history it had demonstrated its ability to adapt itself to the changing Italian scene. That is why so many of those who had traveled from fascism to antifascism ended up in the Communist Party.

These attitudes toward politics among the Italians had limiting effects. Preparation for democracy derives principally from experience in local administration and from a political tradition that is handed down from generation to generation. But Italians had had no such experience, since fascism had taken over the process of governing Italy after it had existed as a nation for barely fifty years. Consequently, Italian political leaders were inexperienced, and were not completely freed from the habits of the recent past. They had not acquired the confidence and spontaneity in democratic life enjoyed by the ruling parties in countries where the democratic process of selection of representatives had been going on for centuries.

Because of the exigencies of the political struggle to win over an electorate that in 1945 was still an unknown quantity, there was massive party propaganda, a strong tendency to treat each question on the basis of political theory, and attempts to simplify and adapt experience and to play on political consciousness for party ends. Intellectual and moral life was vigorous. A wealth of magazines and newspapers sprang up in every town, despite the scarcity of paper, and cultural lectures and debates filled the meeting halls and town squares.

Political discussions took place in street, square, and café. These were not the empty academic arguments of idlers; they were heated and even fierce at times, and sprang from a desire to make the most of the newly won right to state an opinion. These arguments reflected a passionate interest in ideas that is quite different from the feeling of curiosity about a sporting occasion that inspires millions today to watch the leader of their political party on television in order to see what sort of a showing he makes. The choice of political leaders represented a moral decision, not simply an opportunity for displaying one's colors.

In 1945 Italians knew that soon they would have to choose between the various parties. They knew, too, that the agreement on equal representation reached by the antifascist parties represented in the National Liberation Committees would have to give way to the principle of the democratic majority.

MODERATION VERSUS REVOLUTION

The importance of the pending political choices was heightened by the fact that Italy was being divided in a new way, which was to become clearly delineated in 1948. The new division was not geographical, nor was it based on different generations or experience. It was a division between a moderate Italy and a revolutionary Italy, and it was made deeper by international stresses. Consequently, Italian political life became rigidly simplified and regimented.

Even during the Resistance there had been disagreements within the National Liberation Committees and between bands of partisans, and these became more intense after the defeat of the common enemy. A lack of discipline and an atmosphere of anarchy persisted in the North, where the people had scant respect for the law. This was due partly to the difficulty experienced by partisans in returning to a law-abiding life; partly to the proliferation of the Liberation Committees, which laid down the law about everything to everybody at every level of society; partly to the many public appeals for mass action on political, economic, or trade union matters; partly to the fierce class struggle in field and factory; and partly to the so-called "antifascist purge," which affected only a few of those who were really blameworthy. This accounts for the unexpected success of the Uomo Qualunque (any man's) Party and newspaper, which violently opposed the National Liberation Committees.

Moderates wondered whether this could really be the democratic system for which they had fought, while the revolutionaries replied that if fascism were to be extirpated, power must be given to the masses. Behind the clash between moderate and revolutionary views, two different concepts of democracy were taking shape. Some held that democracy meant giving the popular mass parties a power that was above the law in the sense that the will of the people is law. This was called "popular democracy," as opposed to constitutional or liberal democracy, which holds that government of the people must coincide with the rule of law so that democratic liberties and minority rights will be respected.

The supporters of constitutional democracy were afraid that, as in the fascist period, well-organized public demonstrations at the behest of a revolutionary minority would result in the by-passing of the constitutional organs responsible for political decisions, that "emergency" measures would annul the separation of powers and threaten the autonomy of democratic institutions. They feared, in other words, another reign of tyranny in which the majority would be helplessly manipulated by the revolutionaries. The revolutionaries, on the other hand, feared that the rule of law was just an excuse to restore the old ruling classes to power, and that constitutionalism was an obstacle to social reform.

Who, then, was in a position to direct operations and lead the two opposing forces in 1945? Certainly not the traditional parties—the Liberals and the Democratic Socialists among the moderates and the Action Party and the Socialists on the left. In the end the clash turned out to be chiefly between two forces that represented much more than national groups. They were the Roman Catholic Church and the Italian Communist Party, the one inspired mainly by its universal religious mission and the other closely linked to the Soviet Union as the guiding power behind the socialist revolution. The political conflict in Italy thus became internationalized.

Why was it that the Catholic Church and the Communist Party were in effect the only forces capable of assuming a leading role in the struggle between the moderates and the revolutionaries? This is a fundamentally important question.

After the collapse of the fascist state there had been a void in northern and central Italy in the period 1943–45. It had been necessary for some organized group to take over at least the most elementary functions needed for the continuance of community life, especially since the fascist government had done little or nothing to prepare the masses of Italians for local political participation. For decades the Catholic Church had lived on the fringes of the official life of the conservative lay state, but now it displayed its deep-rooted vitality and its close links with Italian society through its dioceses and parishes. These had an administrative as well as social function, and also provided a basis for the powerful Catholic lay organizations within which the Christian Democratic Party was taking shape.

The Catholic Church had thus played an important role as a substitute for the state in German-occupied Italy, and had adopted a prudent but firm attitude toward both Germans and Fascists. At the political level the Church had been the only organization in a position to treat with the Germans (who often paid heed to what it had to say) and at the same time to support the Resistance movement by hiding political refugees and assisting with supplies for the partisans. The Church, with its far-reaching ramifications, had constituted a point of reference and of contact for Italians, who had no other authority to turn to except the Nazis and Fascists. Hence it had been a rallying point for working out ideas and attitudes. Moreover, Catholics, including members of the clergy, had been active in the armed Resistance, although they had constituted a small minority. To exemplify the prestige enjoyed by the Church in Italy, it is sufficient to recall that when Rome was liberated the entire populace (including Communists carrying red flags) flocked to the great square in front of St. Peter's to acclaim Pius XII as defender of the city. The Liberation Committees certainly had no such reception in central Italy at that time; and the return of the monarchy in the person of Umberto II took place unnoticed.

The Church's chief opponent, the Communist Party, with its flexible revolutionary structure and its strict discipline, was everywhere —in the bands of partisans, in the factories, in the poor and middle-class districts, in town and country. Its directives were clear and precise and were repeated (and sometimes adopted) everywhere. It cast itself in the role of the only genuine antifascist party, the only party that really intended to reform Italian society. Its self-assured and consistent behavior and its avoidance of provocative, inflated rhetoric gave many Italians an impression of confidence and orderliness. Behind the Italian Communist Party was the Red Army, with all the fascination and splendor of its great victories and spectacular advances. Many people thought of it as an army that achieved victory without pointlessly bombing defenseless cities and without having recourse to the atomic bomb. And then at the pinnacle was Joseph Stalin, the great sage who had come into the world to elevate the humiliated and downtrodden and who was now to banish injustice from the world and punish the powerful.

When Italians had to undertake the formidable task of reconciling their individual experiences within the nation, of amalgamating them into a common will, they thus found themselves faced with two vast supranational forces, each of which offered a guarantee of order and security, though in different ways. The Christian Democratic Party, whose most active and forceful leaders were supplied by the Catholic Church, represented tradition, or rather, evolution; the Communist Party bore a revolutionary message and, backed by disciplined and energetic forces, was ready to put theories into practice.

Ever since December 1944 Togliatti, as leader of the Communist Party, had rejected the possibility of gaining power by means of a revolutionary uprising, especially in view of events in Greece, where regular Greek troops and forces of the Western allies were fighting and defeating ELAS, the organization of left-wing Greek partisans. In 1945, however, this rejection of revolution was not fully accepted by either Communists or noncommunists. It was generally assumed to be a tactical measure designed to postpone the final reckoning.

THE CATHOLIC AND COMMUNIST PARTIES

In 1919–21 the Catholic movement had failed to persuade the moderate political leaders to help it create a moderate Catholic alliance benefiting Catholic political forces (as a similar alliance had benefited political moderates in 1913). In the years after 1945, especially in 1948, the reconstituted Catholic party—the Christian Democratic Party (Democrazia Cristiana, known as the "DC")—was largely successful in creating such an alliance. The local spring and autumn elections and the referendum and general election for the Constituent Assembly of June 2, 1946, had served as general rehearsals of the operation that was to be so successful in 1948.

During the period of the Resistance the Christian Democrats had reorganized, and in 1946 they were able to appear before the electorate as a potential governing party, especially since their leader, De Gasperi, was already Premier. This party, together with the parties of the socialist subculture, the Italian Communist Party (Partito Comunista Italiano, known as the "PCI"), and the Italian Socialist Party (Partito Socialista Italiano di Unità Proletaria, known as the "PSIUP," later "PSI") were the only mass parties organized on a national scale.[4]

---

4. Some of the complex circumstances that account for the successful reemergence of "political Catholicism" in Italy toward the end of the Second World War are discussed in G. Poggi, *Catholic Action in Italy: The Sociology of a Sponsored Organization* (Stanford, Stanford University Press, 1966), Chap. 2; R. Webster, *Christian Democracy in Italy, 1860–1960* (London, Oxford University Press, 1961).

On the socialist movement in Italy see W. Hilton-Young, *The Italian Left: A Short History of Political Socialism in Italy* (London, Longmans, Green, 1949); and R. Hostetter, *The Italian Socialist Movement* (Princeton, Van Nostrand, 1958).

On the Communist Party see A. Garosci, "The Italian Communist Party," in M. Einaudi, J. M. Domenach, and A. Garosci, *Communism in Western Europe* (Ithaca, Cornell University Press, 1951); and G. Galli, "Italian Communism," in W. E. Griffith, *Communism in Europe* (Cambridge, M.I.T. Press, 1964).

The Communists

The most important new element in the Italian political scene after the fall of fascism and the end of the Second World War was the transformation of the Italian Communist Party. It was no longer a small minority party. On the contrary, it had greater prestige and better organization within the left-wing movement than the Italian Socialist Party. (For a discussion of the organization and structure of the Communist Party, see Chapter 3.) The two parties had been engaged in open hostilities from 1921, when the Italian Communist Party was founded as a result of a split in the Socialist Party, until Hitler's rise to power in 1933. But the fight against European fascism and the change in policy when the Communist International supported the establishment of popular coalitions in 1935 and 1936 had brought about a reconciliation.[5] From 1934 on the Communists and the Socialists worked together in an alliance that became increasingly close, except during the crisis caused by the Russo-German Pact of 1939.

The Communists were the stronger partner in the alliance for a number of reasons. They enjoyed Soviet support at a time when the Soviet Union was recognized as the first socialist country in the world and had gained considerable prestige in the war against Hitler. Furthermore, Italian Communists had been in a majority both in the clandestine opposition to fascism before 1940 and during the period of the Resistance.[6] Also, the centralized and authoritarian Communist Party organization permitted the Communists to concentrate their attention on external policy, whereas much of the energy of the Socialist Party was wasted on ideological disputes and on internal clashes between individuals, groups, and factions.[7]

The Italian Communist Party therefore emerged after the war as the most positive, dynamic, and revolutionary element in the socialist movement. As Togliatti himself put it in a number of speeches in

5. For a discussion of the Communist International, see H. Seton-Watson, *From Lenin to Khrushchev* (New York, Praeger, 1960); and the documents collected in J. Degras, *The Communist International* (London, Royal Institute of International Affairs, 1953). For a summary treatment, see A. Meyer, *Communism* (New York, Random House, 1960), Chap. 7.

6. See C. Delzell, *Mussolini's Enemies: The Italian Anti-Fascist Resistance* (Princeton, Princeton University Press, 1961).

7. For a discussion of the similar situation in France, see E. D. Godfrey, Jr., *The Fate of the French Non-Communist Left* (New York, Random House, 1955).

1944, this was "the new type of party," whereas the Socialist Party was the old-fashioned party. The Communist Party succeeded in presenting itself as a positive force in the socialist tradition, invigorated by the revolutionary ideas of Lenin and Stalin, while the Socialist Party sometimes appeared to be the negative force among the socialists. Internal divisions had prevented the Socialist Party from opposing fascism effectively, and dissenting factions—revolutionary, reformist, and right-wing—still divided the party after the war ended.

The Christian Democrats

Another innovation in Italian politics was the preeminent position now gained by the Christian Democratic Party among the non-socialists. (For discussion of the organization and development of the Christian Democratic Party, see Chapter 3.) A fact of considerable significance is that De Gasperi was the first leader of a Catholic party to become Premier, when he took office after the ministerial crisis of December 1945, even before the electorate could express its support at the polls. The crisis had been caused when the Liberal Party withdrew its representatives from the National Liberation Committees, headed by Ferruccio Parri (leader of the non-Marxist radical Party of Action), because he favored the left.

Having caused the crisis, the Liberals were unable to resolve it, for the parties of the left would not tolerate a premier from the right. A compromise was therefore reached by which the premiership was given to the leader of the Christian Democrats. The aim of the Liberal Party in provoking the crisis had been to give greater political weight to the right, and this they did indeed achieve; but it was a Christian Democrat who became the Premier. The Christian Democrats were first sanctioned by the electorate in the local elections held in the spring of 1946, in which both parties of the left obtained large-scale electoral support, but the Christian Democratic Party was the only nonsocialist party to evoke a comparable response.

The results of the elections of 1946 reflected the decline of both traditional liberal and conservative strength. The same kind of decline had occurred in 1913–19, when the socialists and Catholics had formed monolithic parties, while the traditional liberal movement had been split into a number of local groups that were incapable of forming a large national party. In 1945–46, however, the decline was aggravated by the fact that the Communist, Christian Democratic, and Socialist parties, despite their organizational differences, were all mass parties on a national scale, with millions of members.

Regional Strength of the Two Parties

The relative increase in the Catholic vote between 1919 and 1946 is shown in Figure 1-1. (There were more provinces in 1946 than in 1919 because of a revision in administrative boundaries. This increase was taken into account in constructing the graph.) In the two provinces to the left of the diagonal—Brescia and Bergamo—the Catholic percentage of the vote in 1919 was higher than in 1946. The graph also shows that in one group of provinces in southern Italy the Christian Democrats succeeded in gaining between 30 and 47 percent of the votes in 1946, in spite of the fact that the Popular Party had obtained less than 15 percent in 1919. (See Appendix B for background tables on Italian electoral history from 1861 to 1921, and for bibliographic references to the political history of this period.) A key explanation for the leap forward of the Christian Democrats in the 1946 election was that suffrage had been extended to women in 1945.

In the South the parties of the right and those representing local interests were strong. Both of these groups depended on the influence, or sometimes coercion, exerted by local landowners, property owners, and wealthy professional men. The Resistance had been confined to central and northern Italy, and hence its politically emancipating effects were not felt in the South, which preserved a distinctive political culture characterized by political leaders supported by a network of personal followers.[8]

Segments of the ruling political group in southern Italy could see the value of courting the mass parties that formed the government coalition. They favored the Christian Democrats as being the most moderate and as having their moderation guaranteed by the Catholic Church. Many middle-class and moderate electors in northern

8. For specific references to political cultural patterns in the South, see J. LaPalombara, "Italian Political Culture: Fragmentation, Isolation, Alienation," in L. Pye and S. Verba, eds., *Political Culture and Political Development* (Princeton, Princeton University Press, 1965), Chap. 8. Cf. Sidney G. Tarrow, *Peasant Communism in Southern Italy* (New Haven, Yale University Press, 1967), especially Chaps. 3, 10, 11, 12, 13.

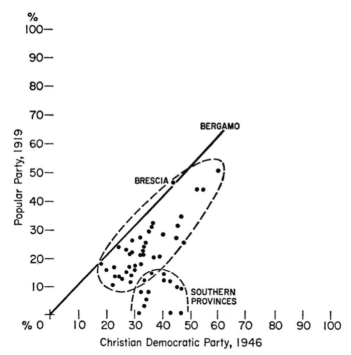

FIGURE 1-1. Percent of total vote cast for Popular Party, 1919, and Christian Democratic Party, 1946, by province or group of provinces.

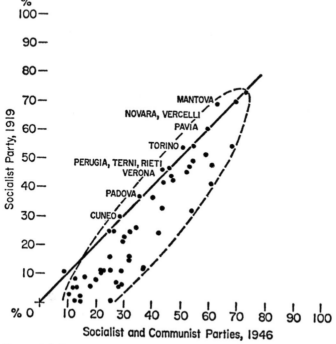

FIGURE 1-2. Percent of total vote cast for Socialist Party, 1919, and Communist and Socialist parties combined, 1946, by province or group of provinces.

Italy had similar feelings about this guaranteed moderation, and hence the Christian Democratic Party was the first party to attain a solid electoral following on a national scale. It was able to attract the masses and furnish guidance in the work of reconstruction without proposing any fundamental changes in the social structure.

The relationship between the share of the votes obtained by the Communist and Socialist parties in 1919 and in the elections for the Constituent Assembly in 1946 is shown in Figure 1-2. In most provinces their combined electoral strength in 1946 was closely related to their electoral strength in the prefascist period, although in a number of provinces their share of the poll was lower in 1946 than in 1919, particularly in Lombardy, Veneto, and Umbria. Between them they increased their share of the total vote from about one third in 1919 to nearly two fifths in 1946 (slightly more than two fifths, if the votes of the Party of Action, which also claimed to be socialist, are included). This increase reflected the radical trend in political viewpoints and a heightening of tensions resulting from a long, hard war—a civil war in the end—fought partly on Italy's own soil.

TABLE 1-1.   *Percent of valid votes cast for Christian Democratic, Socialist, and Communist parties, 1946 and 1921, by geographic area*

		Geographic area				
						All of
Party	*Year*	*North*	*Center*	*South*	*Islands*	*Italy*
Christian	1946	37.3	30.0	34.9	35.2	35.2
Democratic	1921	25.9	20.9	12.2	12.2	20.4
Socialist	1946	28.5	17.7	10.0	11.5	20.7
	1921	32.4	27.3	11.9	8.1	24.7
Communist	1946	22.4	24.7	10.9	8.8	19.0
	1921	5.7	7.1	1.4	0.9	4.6

Although the Communist Party was better organized in 1946 than the Socialist Party, its share was less than half of the total left-wing vote. (Table 1-1) However, votes cast for the Socialist Party were cast for a party that, though distinct from the Communist Party, was allied with it. The Christian Democratic Party, the only nonsocialist mass party, attracted both the voters belonging to the established Catholic tradition and the moderate middle-class liberals. The socialist and Catholic parties as a whole accounted for about three fourths of the votes in 1946, compared to less than half in 1921.

The new distribution of political strength produced a political system that could at least begin to function, for although Catholics and socialists had certain objections to the fairly classical framework of representative democracy that was emerging, they adopted a responsible and constructive attitude toward the system and its institutions. (See Chapter 3 for further discussion of this point.)

In the 1946 election each of the three mass parties was strong in the North, the area in which they had been building their strength over a long period. The Christian Democrats obtained more than a third of the vote in all areas except central Italy, where the Communist Party was particularly strong. The socialist parties were in general weak in the South, where the votes of the peasants and the middle-class townspeople tended to go to the parties of the right or to the Christian Democrats. The rightists had their only mass following in this part of Italy.

The Communist Party, however, was successful in organizing the working classes in the South, and even penetrated the peasantry. Just as fifty years earlier the Socialists had been responsible for giving electoral expression to wide disaffection among the masses and had established a trade union movement, so in 1946 the Communist Party, availing itself of an authoritarian party structure, attracted almost 11 percent of the voters in the South. In this sense it can be said that the Communist Party acted in Italy as a primary force in the process of "nationalization of politics," that is, of the progressive spreading throughout the country of national political agencies and issues.

The Christian Democratic Party also played an important part in this nationalization process—in the North, primarily by relying on the fairly efficient organizational network of the Catholic parishes and their laymen's associations; in the South, mainly by establishing a link with voters who traditionally had supported the parties of the right. The new Catholic party did much better in the South than had its predecessor, the Popular Party, after the First World War.

The Communist Party was much stronger than it had been immediately after its founding in 1921, particularly in the North, where nearly half of the socialist electorate voted for it. (Table 1-1)

Having established their positions in the North, both parties tried to gain strength in the South and began to penetrate low-income sections of the electorate that had been controlled by the right-wing parties. This development helped to make the electoral balance more homogeneous in the various parts of the country, accomplishing in the South what had taken place in the North before fascism.

The general pattern that emerged throughout Italy was a division of the electorate into two principal parties—a pattern similar to that in most representative democracies. From the point of view of the electorate—regardless of the actual policies of the parties concerned —this division can be seen as a polarization of left and right, progressive and conservative.[9]

1946 REFERENDUM—MONARCHY VERSUS REPUBLIC

The opposing orientations of the Christian Democratic and Communist parties were strengthened in 1946 when the elections for delegates to the Constituent Assembly were combined with a referendum in which the electorate was asked to choose between a monarchy and a republic. This was the principal issue in the electoral campaign. With the exception of the Liberal Party, all the chief parties declared themselves for a republic. Though the Liberals opted for the monarchy, in the elections they joined a coalition calling itself the "Unione Democratica Italiana," which refused to commit itself on this question. The only list of candidates that adopted the cause of the monarchy without reservation was the Blocco della Libertà, which obtained only 2.8 percent of the votes in the election for the Constituent Assembly. Still, some ten million votes (45.7 percent of the nationwide total) were cast in favor of the monarchy. On a regional basis the vote varied from over one third for the monarchy in the northern and central parts of Italy to around two thirds in the South and in the Islands.

While most parties, particularly those of the left, based their election programs on the cause of the republic, some candidates individually declared their support for the monarchy. Some parties tried to conceal their hostility to the monarchy from the electorate, especially in areas that supported the House of Savoy. There is no doubt that the Christian Democratic Party was one of these, though it did not behave in this way in all parts of the country.

9. On the persistent political significance of issues related to the traditional left-right conflict, see S. M. Lipset, *Political Man* (Garden City, Doubleday, 1960), especially Chap. 7.

At the communal level there was a close positive correlation between votes cast for a republic in the referendum and those cast for the Communist and Socialist parties in the national election, but there was a negative correlation between votes for a republic and votes for the Christian Democratic Party (and, generally, the parties of the right) and hence a positive one between votes for the monarchy and votes for the Christian Democrats. (Table 1-2)

TABLE 1-2. *Coefficient of correlation between party vote and vote for the Republic, elections of June 6, 1946, by zone* [a]

		Party		
Zone [a]	*Communist*	*Socialist (PSI)*	*Christian Democratic*	*"Rightist" Group*
Northwest	.59	.51	−.61	−.50
Northeast	.39	.55	−.52	−.44
Center	.68	.26	−.78	−.58
South	.58	.53	−.29	−.52
Sicily	.54	.63	−.32	−.48
Sardinia	.51	.21	−.54	−.37
All of Italy	.63	.64	−.35	−.63

a. See Figure 2-1 for delineation of zones.

The heavy vote for the monarchy in the South, reflecting the influence of the extreme right, the conservatives, and the moderates, shows clearly the different political situations in the two Italys, the North and Center on the one hand and the South on the other, at this early stage in postwar politics. The parties of the left, ranging from the Communist Party to the Republican Party, gained more than 55 percent of the votes in central and northern Italy, but less than 30 percent in the South.

THE POLITICAL BALANCE ON THE EVE OF THE 1948 ELECTIONS

In the voting for the Constituent Assembly in 1946 the Christian Democratic Party received 35.2 percent of the votes, the Socialist Party 20.7 percent, and the Communist Party 19 percent.

Although the Socialist Party received nearly five million votes, these votes carried little political weight because of the contradictions inherent both in party policies and the attitudes of its supporters. In 1945 the Socialist Party was highly regarded, even by other political parties. The Liberals (a right-wing party) were apparently willing to accept the Socialist Pietro Nenni as President. However, the Socialists had not learned from past mistakes and had not overcome the kind of internal stresses that reduced them to a state of impotence every time Italian society passed through a period of crisis.

Judging by their words, the Socialists were still a party of the left, even if theirs was to be a socialist rather than a communist revolution. But when it came to deeds, their democratic habits impeded direct action and led them to place their trust in abstract political discussion and in a hoped-for electoral majority for the left. Their disagreements—over theory; over external factors, such as the Marshall Plan and the beginning of the cold war; and over internal factors, such as the agreement between Socialists and Communists for combined action—resulted in the formation of several left and right wings within their own ranks and brought about a dramatic split within the party in January 1947 (known as the "Palazzo Barberini split," after the place to which the minority retired). This setting up of two socialist parties—the old Socialist Party and the new Social Democratic Party, which was subsequently joined by other splinter groups from the old party—showed that the Socialist Party was unable to function as a democratic and socialist party of the center, between the moderates and the Communists, despite the fact that it had reconstituted itself during the Resistance and had had considerable success in the 1946 elections.

On the eve of the 1948 elections the really powerful political forces were still the Catholic Church, which, through the Christian Democratic Party, represented the moderate point of view, and the Communist Party, which represented the revolutionary point of view. The other parties had little effect except as they could influence these two forces. Hope that the Socialist Party would be an effective political force capable of concerted action at government level proved illusory.

The Communist Party was involved in all the governments between 1943 and 1947—under Badoglio, Bonomi, Parri, and De Gasperi—and its political strategy was determined by two main objectives that it was unwilling or unable to abandon. On the one hand, it wanted to keep a foothold in the government at all costs, whatever compromise might be involved. On the other, it wanted to stir up popular discontent and resentment against the government in the hope that the elections for the first parliament would give the left an overwhelming majority. This subtle calculation proved wrong, however, because it failed to take into account the strength and resilience of the moderate parties under De Gasperi and the effect of international developments that were precipitating the cold war.

As each day passed, the moderates became increasingly aware of the need to take effective action in regard to Italy's problems of reconstruction—curbing inflation, making a real effort to balance the budget, cutting expenditures, halting wage rises, and returning to law and order. The political schism was getting deeper, but the presence of the Western allies in Italy guaranteed the democratic system. They stayed until December 15, 1947, when the provisional government set up under the armistice came to an end. In January 1947 De Gasperi was given a firm American promise of financial aid for the reconstruction of Italy. In the same year the left was weakened by the split in the Socialist Party. On February 10 the Peace Treaty was signed, and with Communist help the Concordat of 1929 between church and state was inserted into the Constitution.

At last De Gasperi had his hands free. He provoked a crisis on economic and financial policy, and on May 31, 1947, formed his fourth government, excluding the Communists and Socialists from participation. This was a government of the center and right, but before the year was out it had become a government of the center and left, when Giuseppe Saragat, leader of the Social Democratic Party, who had been at the forefront in the Socialist split, was given office.

The Socialist and Communist left was thus politically defeated, in part because it had previously sacrificed its views on domestic problems in favor of remaining in the government, and in part because its position on foreign policy was viewed by De Gasperi and others as dangerous. The wisdom of De Gasperi's choice was soon to be tested in the elections of April 1948.

2

Political Alignments in Four Elections, 1948-1963

The Constituent Assembly elected in 1946 having drafted the Constitution, elections for the first Parliament of the Republic of Italy were called for April 18, 1948. The electoral laws and procedures governing this and subsequent postwar elections were partly inherited from prefascist days and partly developed to meet postwar needs.

THE ELECTORAL SYSTEM [1]

Voting regulations enacted in 1919 and later repealed under fascism had been reinstated in 1944. These extended the franchise to all males 21 and over, provided for a list system of proportional representation, and required compilation of elector lists by local authorities without registration by the electors. In February 1945 the right to vote had been extended to women. The election for delegates to the Constituent Assembly and the referendum on the monarchy in 1946 had been governed by these electoral laws.

Article 48 of the Constitution reasserts the principle of universal suffrage for all Italians 21 years of age and over, declares that the vote shall be free and secret, and describes voting as a "civic duty." In accordance with a law of 1947 and later laws, the same electoral rolls are used for both local and national elections.

Article 56 of the Constitution provides that elections for the Chamber of Deputies shall be based on direct universal suffrage,

1. For a discussion of the electoral system of postwar Italy, see J. C. Adams and P. Barile, *The Government of Republican Italy* (Boston, Houghton Mifflin, 1961).

with one deputy for every 80,000 inhabitants. Article 57 provides that elections for the Senate (which under the prefascist Constitution was not an elective body but was appointed by the King) should be on a regional basis, with one senator for every 200,000 inhabitants. It restricts the right to vote in senatorial elections to those 25 years old and over.

The Constituent Assembly left it to the various legislatures to enact detailed electoral regulations for general and local elections. However, it enacted regulations for the 1948 elections to the Chamber of Deputies and the Senate. The electoral system it adopted for the Chamber of Deputies was similar to that used in 1946 for the Constituent Assembly.

According to regulations adopted for senatorial elections, each region was subdivided into single-member constituencies equal to the number of seats allotted to it by the Constitution on the basis of population. A candidate who received at least 65 percent of the votes cast was to be declared the winner. Electoral legislation for the Senate has never been modified, but in 1953 the electoral law affecting the Chamber of Deputies was changed by passage of the so-called "swindle law," discussed later in this chapter.

Local electoral procedures are similar to national procedures. Regulations for elections to communal councils in large communes, for example, resemble those for elections to the Chamber of Deputies. In small communes a majority system is used. From 1951 to 1956 a local electoral law much the same as the abortive national electoral law of 1953 was operative, but proportional representation was reintroduced in 1956, and recently it has been extended to all communes with more than 5,000 inhabitants. Elections for provincial councils were reestablished in 1951, with an electoral system similar to that used in elections to the Senate.

The Constitution provides for considerable legislative and administrative autonomy for each region. However, its provisions have been carried out only in Sicily, Sardinia, Valle d'Aosta, and Trentino-Alto Adige, the four regions that have a tradition of autonomy or have a homogeneous ethnic composition. Universal suffrage applies to elections held in these regions, but autonomy has resulted in a confusing array of electoral legislation that varies from essentially majority arrangements to various types of proportional representation.

HIGH TURNOUT AT THE POLLS

When the Italians voted in 1946, there had been a long period under fascism without elections. The novelty of this new means of expression plus the exhortations of political leaders to the voters helped greatly to increase voter participation. Furthermore, though demands to make voting compulsory had been rejected in 1945 and 1946, a law was passed in 1947 requiring that if a qualified elector did not vote in an election for which he was eligible, the words "Did not vote" would be entered on his identification papers (which all Italians are required to carry and present to public authorities when making a wide range of applications, from passports to applications for public employment.)

No specific penalties are attached to this entry on the certificate, and it is therefore not a legal sanction. But such a procedure in a country with a long tradition of bureaucratic control helps to spread a conviction that voting is not only a right but a public duty and that failure to exercise the right might have unfortunate consequences.

This feeling was already prevalent in 1946 and it was intensified in 1948 by the nature of the 1948 election campaign, when government, clergy, and Civic Committees used posters, the radio, and the press to stress the moral and political duty to vote.

TABLE 2-1. *Percent of qualified electors who voted in elections to the Chamber of Deputies, 1919 and 1948 to 1963, and to the Constituent Assembly, 1946, by zone* [a]

Zone [a]	1919	1946	1948	1953	1958	1963
I Northwest	66.6	89.8	93.2	94.8	95.6	95.5
II Northeast	58.5	91.3	93.1	93.7	93.6	94.3
III Center	70.1	92.1	95.0	96.3	96.3	96.1
IV South	79.6	86.7	90.4	92.6	91.9	90.0
V Sicily	47.9	85.5	88.0	89.8	90.1	86.0
VI Sardinia	56.6	85.9	90.0	91.7	92.0	88.0
All of Italy	56.6	89.1	92.2	93.8	93.8	92.9

a. See Figure 2-1 for delineation of zones.

The percentages of qualified voters participating in postwar elections are shown in Table 2-1, by geographic area. In the prefascist election of 1919 voter turnout for all of Italy was only 56.6 percent, ranging from a low of 47.9 percent in Sicily to a high of 79.6 percent in southern Italy. In the 1948 elections for the Republic of Italy's first parliament, more than 92 percent of the qualified voters participated, which indicates that the inducements to vote described above were remarkably effective. In Sicily, again with the lowest voting rate, 88 percent of the electorate voted. In central Italy the turnout was 95 percent. By 1963 almost 93 percent of the Italian electorate voted. Sicily, still with the lowest rate, had a turnout of 86 percent; central Italy, still with the highest, had a rate of 96.1.

Effect of Election Procedures

The complex administrative machinery dealing with elections tends to favor a high voter turnout. As already pointed out, the name of every Italian is automatically entered on the electoral rolls when he reaches the age of 21, and he is so informed by the local authority of his place of residence. In his adult life a certificate to the effect that he is a registered elector will often be required, especially if he applies for a post in the civil service.

Another factor in the high rate of voter participation in Italian elections is the extraordinary care taken to make it convenient to vote. Shortly before a local or general election a local authority messenger delivers to each elector at his residence an electoral certificate that tells him the date of the election, where to vote, and the hours when the polling places will be open.

The local authority is responsible for providing enough polling places to avoid overcrowding and distributing them over the commune in such a way as to make them easily accessible. Every district has its polling place. Even a cluster of houses may have one, if several hundred qualified electors live there. Certain categories of voters—seamen, members of the armed forces, and hospital patients, for example—may vote in a commune in which they do not reside. There are mobile voting booths within hospitals.

Although many Italian citizens live abroad, there are no provisions for absentee voting. Special arrangements are made to enable Italian citizens to come back to Italy to vote, however, and many voters take advantage of them. Inducements include reduced railway fares abroad and free return rail travel within Italy. Similarly, internal migrants are allowed substantial reductions in rail fares.

Election day is a public holiday. Polling places are open from

6:00 a.m. to 10:00 p.m. and are also open the following day—usually a weekday—from 7:00 a.m. to 2:00 p.m. A large number of organizations, such as the Civic Committees, the Red Cross, and the political parties and their supporting organizations, provide transportation to the polls for crippled and elderly voters. Furthermore, the large political parties arrange for their candidates to tour the polling places and note the names of likely supporters who have not yet voted. Party workers then seek out the nonvoters and try to persuade them to vote.

The voting rate is calculated on the basis of the number of qualified electors on the rolls, rather than on the basis of electoral certificates that are actually delivered. If the latter basis were adopted, the percentage of electors recorded as voting would be even higher. In 1946 the number of undelivered certificates was 5.4 percent of the qualified electors; in 1948 it was 3.5 percent; in 1953, 2.7 percent; in 1958, 2.8 percent; and in 1963, 3.0 percent.

The chief reason for failure to deliver electoral certificates is the elector's absence from his place of residence. Another reason is the failure of local authorities to keep their electoral rolls up-to-date, in spite of frequent reminders in ministerial circulars. This may result in a slightly inflated count of qualified electors.

Effect of Socioeconomic Factors

An examination of the successive increases in the percentage of qualified voters who voted in postwar elections reveals that there is a

TABLE 2-2. *Coefficient of correlation between percent of qualified electors who voted and selected socioeconomic indicators, elections of 1953 and 1963*

Indicator [a]	1953	1963
Employment		
Industry	.15	.21
Service	.11	.19
Agriculture	−.16	−.26
Illiteracy	−.14	−.40
Education		
Primary school	.07	.24
Junior high school	.24	.31
Radio and television licenses	—	.60

a. Data on indicators for 1953 and 1963 based on national censuses of 1951 and 1961, respectively, except for radio and television licenses, which are reported for 1962.

positive correlation between the percentage of the electorate voting and the percentage of the population engaged in nonagricultural employment, the standard of education of the population, and the percentage of the population with radio and television licenses. (Table 2-2) The figures in the table indicate that voter participation increases with a rise in industrialization and in the educational level of the population.

This was the setting for Italy's elections of 1948, 1953, 1958, and 1963—the first four elections after the establishment of the republic: an electoral system that encouraged widespread participation in the electoral process, a rising economic and educational level that further stimulated the interest of the electorate in voting, and an electorate that responded to these favorable factors with unprecedented turnouts at the polls.

THE 1948 CAMPAIGN

The situation on the eve of the 1948 election was radically different from that in 1946. The break between the countries of the West and the Soviet Union and the ensuing cold war had repercussions in Italy, as it did in other countries of Western Europe. The majority vote achieved in Rome in 1946 by the Uomo Qualunque Party, a right-wing movement with antiparliamentary tendencies, was a serious warning for the Christian Democratic Party. It suggested that if the Christian Democrats continued their convenient cooperation with the Communists, a strong conservative party might be formed on the right.

It was evident that De Gasperi was heeding this and other warnings. He had gone to the United States shortly after the election to obtain aid for Italy. On his return he reduced Communist participation in the government and he subsequently removed the Communist and Socialist ministers from their posts. He then formed a coalition with the Liberals and Independents that was extended in December 1947 to include the Republicans and the Social Democrats, who had refused to cooperate with either the Communists or the Socialists—now renamed Partito Socialista Italiano (PSI), having dropped the "di Unità Proletaria" of the PSIUP.

After the formation of the Cominform in late 1947 the Communists' pro-Russian attitude and their antagonism toward the Christian Democrats became more intense. In 1948 they joined with the Socialist Party to form the Popular Democratic Front.

Political tension was very high during the 1948 election campaign. The line-up of the parties involved was simplified by the clear-cut distinction between the attitudes of the opposing forces. On one side were the Christian Democrats and their allies: to the right, the National Bloc, consisting of the Liberals (conservative in orientation), the Monarchists, and the Italian Social Movement (Movimento Sociale Italiano), the first avowedly neofascist party to appear on the scene; and to the left, the Republicans and the Social Democrats, who, with other minority socialist groups formed the Unità Socialista. In opposition was the Popular Democratic Front, led by the Communists. The Christian Democratic coalition was defending democratic representative government; the popular front based its campaign on opposition to conservatism and clericalism and on implementation of the reforms provided for in the Constitution.

The election of 1948 was the first in which the Christian Democrats and the Communists were in direct opposition—a situation that has been repeated in all subsequent Italian elections. The Christian Democratic Party received 48.5 percent of the votes, and was particularly successful in making inroads on the right-wing vote. In fact the strength of the right was greatly reduced compared with 1946, particularly in southern Italy. The left as a whole polled a little less than its national total in 1946. Thanks to the support of conservative as well as Catholic voters, the Christian Democrats gained a larger share of the vote than ever before or since.

The Communist Party gained some ground by taking advantage of the lack of unity among the socialists. It achieved a more uniform distribution of votes over the country as a whole as a result of gains in the South, where socialist sentiment was manifested by votes for the Communists.

An important difference between the Christian Democratic and Communist campaigns was that the Christian Democratic campaign was not under the direct control of the party, a fact that led to policies that later caused difficulties for the Christian Democrats, as discussed below. During the campaign the bishops and the parish priests, Catholic Action and other lay religious organizations, and the Civic Committees (caucuses of clerical and lay Catholic leaders and activists formed for electoral purposes in each parish) played a decisive part in mobilizing Catholic electors and in creating the atmosphere of an anticommunist crusade. (For an extensive discussion of the activities of Catholic Action and related organizations, see Chapter 5.)

The result was that the moderate and conservative electorate delivered its vote to the Christian Democrats, although in the South the conservatives were unalterably opposed to the agrarian reforms that were an essential part of the Christian Democratic program. Thanks to their support, the Christian Democratic Party was able to withstand and overcome at the polls the strong Communist Party machine that was the main strength of the popular front. Both sides escorted their supporters to the polling stations, which, in districts where the electoral campaign was especially heated, were guarded by police in full battle dress. More than 92 percent of the electorate voted in the election.

Although the Communist Party increased its share of the vote compared with 1946, it was defeated on election day by the mass operations of the anticommunist forces. In addition to its electoral strength based on the Italian socialist tradition, the Communist Party had the prestige of the backing of the Soviet Union, which provided a model of the ideal society that the party advocated. The Communist electoral message was spread by a network of organizations—cooperatives, trade unions, and other mass associations—that under the guidance of Communist-trained personnel proved remarkably effective. Through this machinery for propaganda and agitation the Communist Party and the Socialist Party managed to attract 31 percent of the vote. Only the massive mobilization of the Catholic world under direct clerical guidance was able to hold Communist expansion to this percentage.

1953—The Christian Democratic Struggle for a Majority

In 1946 the central issue was the choice between a republic and a monarchy; in 1948 the issue was the choice between representative democracy and some kind of "popular democracy" under Communist leadership. The focus of the 1953 campaign was on the Christian Democratic Party's determined effort to achieve a two-thirds majority in the Chamber of Deputies.

This issue had its origins in the composition of the Christian Democratic electoral support in 1948, much of which had come from moderate and conservative ranks. Partly as a result, the Christian Democrats had serious difficulties in implementing their own program in parliament. The right wing of the party, led by Carmine De Martino, a southern member of parliament, particularly resisted the implementation of agrarian reform, with the result that as of the end of 1950 this reform had been brought into operation in only a few areas. Meanwhile the rightist forces were trying to gain control of the Cassa per il Mezzogiorno (Fund for the South), a financial agency for development that was set up in 1950 to boost the economy of southern Italy.

Their hopes frustrated, the right-wing parties decided to withdraw their support from the Christian Democratic Party and to organize as an independent political force around the Neapolitan shipowner, Achille Lauro, thus revitalizing the old monarchist movement throughout Italy. They succeeded in winning local elections in Naples, Bari, and a number of other southern cities. At the same time the small but active neofascist movement, the Movimento Sociale Italiano, was gaining strength on the extreme right, and the once powerful Liberal Party was preparing to run independently in the coming election.

The Christian Democrats sought to combat this pressure by passing a law, known as the "swindle law," intended to assure for themselves a two-thirds majority in the Chamber of Deputies. According to this law any party or combination of parties that received at least 50 percent of the total vote cast nationally would be awarded two thirds of the seats in the Chamber. The Christian Democrats' need for this law was particularly urgent, because, as a result of their failure to expedite reforms, their alliance with the Social Democrats was also crumbling. The left wing of the Social Democrats saw little purpose in collaborating with a government subject to pressure from the right.

A law similar to the new electoral law had been in effect in the local elections of 1951–52. The parties of both the right and the left were firmly opposed to its being used in the general election and compared it to the fascist electoral law of 1924. To obstructive tactics from the opposition the government countered with steps of doubtful legality.

Although the Social Democrats and the Liberals had withdrawn from the government coalition of Christian Democrats and Republicans, they allied themselves with it in the election in order to share in the reward, if the alliance should gain an absolute majority. The Partito Sardo di Azione and the Südtiroler Volkspartei—both limited to local lists of candidates—also joined this alliance

Important rifts occurred in the smaller parties supporting the goverment. A group left the Social Democratic Party to form the Unità

Popolare; another group had already left because they objected to the party's policy of supporting the Christian Democrats. They joined Valdo Magnani and Aldo Cucchi (two ex-Communist leaders of some prestige, who had left the Communist Party in 1951) to form the Independent Socialist Union, Unione Socialista Indipendènte (USI). There was also a group of Liberals, led by former Treasury Minister Epicarmio Corbino, who left the Liberal Party and, with the support of some independents, formed the Alleanza Democratica Nazionale (ADN). These three groups played an important part in defeating the Christian Democratic drive for an absolute majority and in thus rendering the new electoral law ineffective. The very fact that two minor parties that had supported the government had split over the question of the new electoral law served to give weight to the opposition.

In the local elections of 1952 the Communist Party had markedly increased its strength among the electorate in the South and in Sicily and Sardinia. In the 1953 election it further improved its position. It also succeeded in achieving more uniformity in its electoral strength throughout the country. (Appendix C) Its gains in the South offset a tendency toward stagnation in the North, caused by a slackening in the social tensions and revolutionary aspirations that had characterized the immediate postwar period. The Catholic organizations, which in 1948 had been the Communists' main opposition, in 1953 were compelled to fight on two fronts, since they had to defend the Christian Democratic Party against the attacks of the right as well, especially in the South, where even some of the clergy supported the Monarchists.

On the whole, the Communist Party increased its commanding position among the forces of the left, for it consolidated the lead it had gained in 1948 as part of the popular front. As Table 2-3 shows, Communist candidates for the Chamber of Deputies received 22.6 percent of the votes in 1953, compared with the Socialists' 12.7 percent, 4.5 percent for Social Democratic candidates, and less than 2 percent for the candidates of the minor parties of the left. The combined socialist vote was about the same as in 1946, about two fifths of the total, and slightly higher than in 1948.

Christian Democratic Party candidates, on the other hand, received a smaller percentage of the votes in 1953 than in 1948, especially in the South, where right-wing voters were particularly fickle, and the party was incapable of permanently controlling the heterogeneous forces that supported it from time to time. In the country as a whole the Christian Democrats received only 40.1 percent of the vote, compared with its 48.5 percent in 1948. In the same years the Monarchist share of the vote rose from 2.8 percent to 6.9 percent, and that of the neofascist Movimento Sociale Italiano from 2.0 percent to 5.9 percent. The Liberal Party obtained only 3.0 percent of the vote. (Table 2-3)

The Christian Democratic coalition failed by 57,000 votes, or 0.3 percent of the total, to receive 50 percent of the votes cast. The new electoral law therefore did not become operative. This contributed considerably to Communist prestige, because the Communists had centered their electoral campaign on defeat of the "swindle law," and had played the chief role, in terms of votes received, in thwarting the Christian Democrats' plan to use the law as a means of ob-

TABLE 2-3. *Results of elections to the Constituent Assembly, 1946, and to the Chamber of Deputies, 1948, 1953, 1958, and 1963* [a]

Voters and principal parties	1946	1948	1953	1958	1963
Size of electorate (thousands)	28,005	29,118	30,280	32,447	34,127
Voters					
Number (thousands)	24,947	26,854	28,410	30,438	31,714
Percent of electorate	89.1	92.2	93.8	93.8	92.9
Valid votes cast					
Number (thousands)	23,016	26,269	27,093	29,564	30,689
Percent of total votes	92.3	97.8	95.4	97.1	96.8
Percent of valid votes cast					
Right-wing parties	15.5	9.0	15.9	13.3	14.2
Neofascist (MSI and Uomo Qualunque)	5.3	2.0	5.9	4.8	5.1
Monarchist (PNM)	2.8	2.8	6.9	4.9	1.7
Liberal (PLI, UND, and BN) [b]	6.8	3.8	3.0	3.5	7.0
Other right-wing parties	0.6	0.4	0.1	0.1	0.4
Christian Democratic (DC)	35.2	48.5	40.1	42.3	38.3
DC plus right-wing parties	50.7	57.5	56.0	55.6	52.5
Left-wing parties	46.6	41.0	43.3	43.6	46.7
Republican (PRI)	4.4	2.5	1.6	1.4	1.4
Social Democratic (PSDI and US)	—	7.1	4.5	4.6	6.1
Socialist (PSIUP and PSI)	20.7	{31.0	12.7	14.3	13.9
Communist (PCI)	19.0		22.6	22.7	25.3
Other left-wing parties	2.5	0.4	1.9	0.6	—
Other national and local parties	2.7	1.5	0.7	0.8	0.8

a. Totals in this table do not coincide with aggregate totals of Zones I–VI in Appendix Tables C-1 to C-6, because of the exclusion in those tables of some provinces, as shown in the notes to the tables.

b. Includes the Liberal Party (PLI), the National Democratic Union (UND), and the National Bloc (BN).

taining two thirds of the delegates in the Chamber of Deputies against the wishes of the electorate.

STATUS OF THE PARTIES IN 1958

Five years later the various parties became involved in what proved to be the most diversified of the postwar election campaigns. Almost all the parties suffered from internal policy disagreements.

On the right the Monarchists had split: the Partito Monarchico Popolare had broken away from the Partito Nazionale Monarchico and shipowner Achille Lauro had turned it into an almost exclusively Neapolitan organization, which, despite great efforts, failed to gain adherents outside of southern Italy.

The Liberal Party was critical of the tendency of the Christian Democratic Party to support state intervention in economic affairs, but since future policies of the Christian Democrats were uncertain because of internal organizational changes, Liberal attacks on it were moderate. De Gasperi had been replaced as party secretary of the Christian Democrats by Amintore Fanfani, who had modernized and improved the party organization and had tried to strengthen its ties with Catholic lay organizations and other supporting associations. (See Chapter 5 for a description of these supporting groups.) His basic aim was to have at his disposal a political and electoral machine independent of the church hierarchy, the clergy, Catholic Action, and the Civic Committees.

The Communist Party was also facing organizational problems, as was its supporting union, the General Confederation of Italian Workers (CGIL), as a result of the disrupting effects of the de-Stalinization campaign, following the Twentieth Congress of the Soviet Communist Party, and the upheaval associated with the abortive Hungarian revolt. There had been many resignations from the party in 1956 as a result of these international developments.[2] The party was still faced with organizational problems in 1958, but the political crises besetting the communist world were by then largely over. By 1958 successes in the conquest of space were increasing Russian, hence communist, prestige and the American recession and the Algerian coup of May 13, 1958, which occurred just before the elec-

2. See documents collected in *The Anti-Stalinization Campaign and International Communism* (New York, Columbia University Press, 1957).

tion on May 25, offered the Communist Party effective grounds for attacking Western society.

The Socialist Party also was facing problems, as a result of its attempt to find a new position in the Italian political line-up. Its Congress in Venice in February 1957 had abrogated the unity of action pact with the Communist Party, which the Socialists had entered into during the period of fascism and war, when both parties were exiled in France. However, Pietro Nenni's independent line was strongly contested by the left wing of the party, which controlled the central committee and the party machine. Meanwhile, minor left-wing groups (the Unità Popolare and the Unione Socialista Indipendènte) had merged with the Socialist Party, whose unification negotiations with the Social Democratic Party had come to nothing. Thus the Socialist Party election campaign in 1958 was only partly distinct from that of the Communist Party, since the chief differences between the two parties—their attitudes toward the Soviet Union and toward relationships between socialism and democracy—remained in the background and were not openly attacked by either party.

Among the lesser parties of the left, the Republicans formed an alliance with a small radical group that had broken away from the Liberal Party, and based their election campaign on a criticism of Christian Democratic clericalism. The Social Democratic Party continued its anticommunist, social democratic policy, but with less effectiveness than in 1948, when the Socialists and Communists were more closely allied.

Thus the 1958 election campaign had no central theme. The situation in Italy and abroad, and the tendency of the electorate to hold to established positions, made the traditional struggle between Communists and Christian Democrats less dramatic than usual. (See later sections of this chapter for an extensive discussion of the stability of the electorate.)

The general picture of the distribution of votes in 1958 shown in Table 2-3 reflects the static nature of the political situation. The results differ little from those of the preceding election in 1953. The Christian Democrats and the Communists both increased their shares of the vote slightly. The percent of the vote cast for Socialist Party candidates also increased, as a result of support from other socialist groups. The Republican Party continued its slow decline, while the Monarchists and the neofascist Italian Social Movement also suffered losses, to the advantage of the Liberals and the Christian Democrats.

THE 1963 CAMPAIGN—THE CENTER-LEFT COALITION

The 1963 elections, like those of 1946, 1948, and 1953, had a central focus that pushed all other concerns to the background. But whereas the issues in the three earlier elections—monarchy or republic, democracy or communism, and an absolute majority for the Christian Democrats—had been clear-cut, the issue in 1963 was not. This time the controversial question was the alliance between left and center, inaugurated in March 1962 and preceded by the progressive moving away of the Socialists from the Communists.

The four parties involved in the center-left coalition (Christian Democrats, Social Democrats, Republicans, and Socialists) had already collaborated in nationalizing electricity, and together had embarked on another major, though less striking, reform aimed at creating uniform junior high schools for children from eleven to fourteen years of age. But they had failed to agree on the implementation of a third major reform, the establishment of autonomous regions, as required by the Constitution.

Despite their previous collaboration, the four parties were divided and uncertain in their attitudes when they faced the electorate. The government coalition consisted of Christian Democrats, Social Democrats, and Republicans, with support from the Socialists in parliament. The Socialists accused the Christian Democrats of trying to water down the political program of the coalition under pressure from moderate elements in the Christian Democratic Party, while the Christian Democrats accused the Socialists of failing to give energetic support to center-left policies, because of continuing ties with the Communist Party in local governments and in mass organizations. By these tactics the Christian Democratic Party was able to soften attacks from the Liberal Party on its right, while the Socialists were able to ward off attacks from the Communists on their left.

At the same time the Christian Democratic reform program was causing the resurgence of a conservative movement. The Liberal Party returned to the attack on state intervention in the economy that it had launched in 1958. It accused the Christian Democratic Party of allying itself with the Socialist Party—in turn allied to the Communists—in order to undermine the free economy and create an economy under central control, as exemplified by the nationalization of electricity and plans for legislation on town planning.

In order to retain their moderate and conservative support, the Christian Democrats played down the importance of the nationalization of electricity and reaffirmed both their belief in a free economy and their objections to communism. In short, they promised a program of cautious, nonadventurous reform for the future.

The Socialist Party, on the contrary, stressed in its platform the significance of the nationalization of electricity and the need for other programs of radical reform to be carried out by a strong center-left coalition. For the first time since the war the Socialists had to withstand an open attack from the Communists, who accused them of abandoning their principles, of becoming subservient allies of the Christian Democrats, and of favoring the consolidation of clerical influence. As for the nationalization of electricity, the Communists confined themselves to pointing to the excessive compensation paid to electrical concerns. They also stressed the failure of the government and the Socialist Party to set up the promised autonomous regions.

In their election campaign the Social Democrats and Republicans stressed the importance of the achievements of the center-left coalition, and promised to continue the alliance in order to achieve important, well-considered reforms. But the election programs of these two small parties could not counterbalance the contradictory attitudes of the two major parties in the alliance.

The Christian Democratic Party, in order not to be a target for the Liberals, attempted to create for itself a moderate image. This led to a Communist attack on the Socialists. The Socialists, in turn, tried to avoid this by presenting themselves as radical, anticapitalist reformers, thus giving the Liberals ammunition to use against the Christian Democrats. Cross fire of this sort proved useful to the opponents of the coalition parties.

More out of necessity than of conviction, largely as a result of the overriding issues in the elections of 1946 and 1948, moderate and conservative voters had accepted the Christian Democrats as upholders of order. But these groups had little in common with the Catholic subculture and little sympathy with its claim that it embodied the interests of large masses of the people. Among the moderates there had always been an undercurrent of diffidence toward the Christian Democratic Party, ready to come to the surface at a suitable opportunity. The somewhat half-hearted coalition of Christian Democrats and Socialists offered such an opportunity and the Liberal Party had only to paint the Socialists as the Socialists painted themselves in order to stir the disquiet of moderate electors about Christian Democratic policy.

The socialist subculture and movement had developed in clear opposition to conservative policies and to capitalism, and the Communist Party represented an authoritarianism that was implicit in all Italian forms of socialism. The Christian Democratic Party had been the chief defender of the capitalist system in the postwar period. Socialist participation in the government therefore ran counter to the tradition the Christian Democrats had established. This situation gave the Communists an opportunity to increase left-wing suspicion of a coalition built on such doubtful foundations.

In addition to the differences in the nature of the controversy in the 1963 election and in earlier elections, the conditions under which the 1963 campaign was conducted also differed.

The economic boom of the early 1960s brought about large-scale migration within Italy as well as emigration abroad. Young people, women, and farm workers, attracted by employment opportunities in industry, had flocked to industrial centers.[3] These developments modified the structure and the traditional make-up of Italian society, for they brought into contact with an evolving industrial society the social groups that had been the most attached to tradition—women, farm workers, and southerners. In general these changes favored the left rather than the right, since the left emphasized the need for progress. The best organized party of the left was the Communist Party, and the appearance of its leaders on the television screen undoubtedly had a considerable effect in enhancing its prestige and making it appear respectable.

Another new factor was that party propaganda had been restricted by mutual consent to a fixed number of posters and to controlled use of television—an experiment that had already been tried in the local elections of 1960.

Two significant events took place in Italy during the culminating phase of the 1963 campaign: the papal encyclical, "Pacem in Terris," and the audience that Pope John XXIII granted to Khrush-

3. S. B. Clough, *The Economic History of Modern Italy* (New York, Columbia University Press, 1964); also *A Century of Economic and Social Development in Italy, 1861–1961* (Rome, Istituto Centrale di Statistica, 1961).

chev's daughter and son-in-law. Both the encyclical and the audience were suggestive of the kind of dialogue between Catholics and Communists that the Communist Party had been mildly proposing for some time, and the party made the most of the propaganda value of this fact. Its task was made easier because the Catholic hierarchy and clergy played only a limited role in the election campaign, partly because the Pope tended to favor reducing the political involvement of the Church and partly because most church leaders viewed with suspicion the new center-left trend in Italian politics.

This combination of developments in the political climate increased both the Communist and the Liberal vote in 1963, while the share polled by the Christian Democratic Party—about 38 percent—was the lowest since 1946. Among the coalition parties only the Social Democrats made gains. The position of the Republicans remained stationary and the Socialist vote declined slightly. On the right the breakup of the monarchist movement slightly favored the neofascists and the Liberals. (Table 2-3)

GEOGRAPHIC VOTING PATTERNS

The broad outlines of national political alignments as they developed in postwar Italy from 1948 to 1963, described in the foregoing sections, obscure meaningful geographic differences.[4] In order to analyze these differences, Italy has been divided into six zones, historically homogeneous on the basis of the traditional strength and influence of the two major political forces, socialist and Catholic. (Figure 2-1) Various historical data, including pre-1921 election results and other evidences of the geographic strength of socialist and Catholic political or trade union organizations and other supporting groups, were used in delineating the zones. The boundaries are shown in Figure 2-1 and in the captions and notes to the tables in Appendix C. The percentages of the votes cast for the major parties and groups of parties in 1919 and in each of the postwar elections, by zone, are also shown in the tables in Appendix C, and the figures

---

4. Throughout this chapter the results of the research on electoral behavior in Italy made by the Carlo Cattaneo Institute and published in V. Capecchi, V. Cioni Polacchini, G. Galli, and G. Sivini, *Il comportamento elettorale in Italia* (Bologna, Società editrice il Mulino, 1968) have been used. See also the essay based on this research by V. Capecchi and G. Galli, "Determinants of Voting Behavior in Italy," in M. Dogan and S. Rokkan, eds., *Quantitative Ecological Analysis in the Social Sciences* (Cambridge, M.I.T. Press, 1969), pp. 235–83.

for the postwar period are shown graphically in Figure 2-2 and summarized briefly by zone below.

Zone I, Northwest

Here socialism took root when industrial development began in the late nineteenth century. The socialist group obtained about half the votes in 1919, and in 1946 the total left-wing vote reached a high point of 55 percent, but it dropped to 48.2 percent by 1963.

This area has experienced particularly intense industrial and urban development, accompanied by far-reaching cultural changes, including secularization, nationalization, and the emancipation of women from the conditioning influence of family and church as they entered the labor force. Within this new situation, the Communist Party—far better organized than the other two socialist parties—has achieved a modest increase in its share of the vote, while the other two socialist parties and the left as a whole have suffered a decline. The Christian Democrats in 1963 polled about the same share of the vote—about 35 percent—as it had in 1946.

Zone II, Northeast

In this zone the influence of the Catholic Church is very great and the Christian Democratic Party has received well over half the votes —almost two thirds in 1948—throughout the postwar period. The Communist Party's share of the vote has fluctuated within narrow limits from 12.5 percent in 1946 to 13.0 in 1963. Meanwhile, the share of the other socialist parties declined from 26.3 percent for the Socialist Party (PSIUP) in 1946 to 22.9 percent for the Socialist Party (PSI) and the Social Democratic Party (PSDI) in 1963.

Zone III, Center

Strongly anticlerical, anarchist, and socialist movements occurred in this zone in the nineteenth century and took root within a strictly agricultural society. The left had achieved a majority (54.6 percent) in 1919 and in 1946 received more than two thirds of the votes. Subsequently the left's share has been about 60 percent. Despite this decline in the left-wing vote, the Communist share of the vote increased from 33.5 percent in 1946 to 38 percent in 1963.

FIGURE 2-1. Italian regions and provinces and the six zones used in this study. For delineation of zones, see Appendix C.

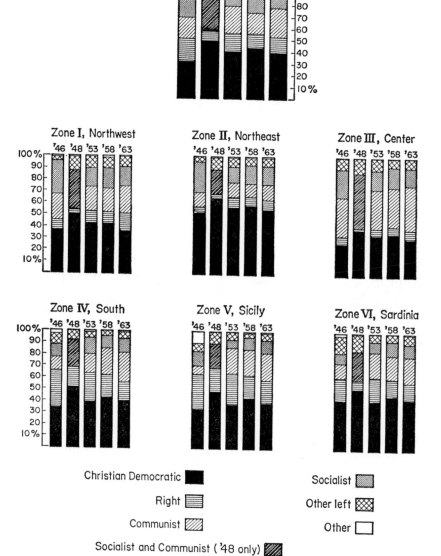

FIGURE 2-2. Percentage distribution of the vote by major party or group of parties, by zone, postwar elections, 1946–63 Sources: Appendix C and Table 2-3.

Though this is definitely a "red" zone, the Christian Democratic Party in 1953 received almost 30 percent of the vote, slightly more than in 1946, but down from the peak of 37 percent in 1948.

Zone IV, South

There was little or no widely established cultural, political, or trade union movement, either socialist or Catholic, in the South before the fascist period. In 1919 right-wing parties received almost 75 percent of the votes cast, but in the postwar period the right-wing vote gradually declined from 31.6 percent in 1946 to 17.1 percent in 1963, as the strength of the parties of the left and of the Christian Democrats increased. Only in this zone were Communist advances in 1946–63 accompanied by an increase in the total left-wing vote. The left-wing vote in the South rose from 11.8 percent in 1919 to 31.5 percent in 1946, and to 42.5 percent in 1963. Among the parties of the left the greatest gains were made by the Communists, who increased their vote from 11.5 percent in 1946 to 24.7 percent in 1963, mostly at the expense of the Republicans. The Socialists also made gains in the general left-wing expansion in the South, though their gains were smaller than those of the Communists.

The combined vote of the left did not equal the Christian Democratic vote in any year except 1963, when the Christian Democrats received 40 percent of the vote—down from their peak vote of 50.7 percent in 1948.

Zone V, Sicily—Zone VI, Sardinia

The postwar electoral experiences of Sicily and Sardinia, right-wing strongholds prior to the fascist regime, have been similar. The Christian Democratic Party was the leading party in these areas throughout the postwar period, though its share of the vote fluctuated somewhat from slightly less than half in Sicily in 1948 to less than two fifths in 1963. It reached a majority only in Sardinia in 1948, but had declined to a little over two fifths by 1963. The Communist Party increased its share of the vote from 7.9 percent to 23.7 percent in Sicily from 1946 to 1963 and in Sardinia from 12.5 to 22.4 percent. In both Sicily and Sardinia the parties of the right suffered a definite decline in the same period: their share of the poll fell from 29.6 to 19.8 percent in Sicily and from 20.7 to 15.3 percent in Sardinia.

The Communist Party made special organizational efforts in southern Italy and the Islands after the 1946 elections. These gains were largely complete by the early 1950s, considerable advances having been made in the 1948 elections.

STABILITY OF THE PARTY VOTE

A comparison of partisan voting trends on a geographic basis in 1919 and in five postwar elections leads to the conclusion that the generally accepted view of the stability of the partisan vote of the Italian electorate is subject to some qualification.

The long-term trend toward stability conceals fluctuations, as is typical in multiparty representative democracies. Furthermore, such stability is related to an initial process of settling down, and in some respects this process may not yet be complete in Italy. Over a period of a century two broad political currents, a socialist-inspired, left-wing subculture and a moderate-Catholic subculture, have been forming.

The Communists have advanced and gained a leading position within a left-wing movement that has made only modest progress, because its gains in the South have been counterbalanced by stagnation in the North.

Advances by the Christian Democrats have been determined by the inroads they have succeeded in making on moderates and conservatives and by their success in resisting pressures from the right. They are least successful when they are faced with an aggressive and articulate political organization on the right, as they were in 1946 by the neofascist Uomo Qualunque, in 1953 by the Monarchists, and in 1963 by the Liberals.

The competition for position by the Christian Democratic and Communist parties is a variant of the wider patterns of contrast between the socialist and the Catholic subcultures and of the right-left cleavage. Thus, the polarization of forces that has given the Christian Democrats and the Communists their positions of leadership is not entirely political.

Fluctuation in Voting at the Communal Level

To explore further the question of the stability of the electorate, a detailed examination was made of the electoral returns at the level of the commune,[5] the smallest administrative unit for which comparable data are available on a countrywide basis.

Of the more than 8,000 Italian communes, only 7,144 are included in the study, since in order to assure comparability over time it was necessary to include only communes that existed in 1946 and remained unchanged throughout the period covered.[6]

These 7,144 communes were grouped according to the six zones described in the preceding section and shown in Figure 2-1. They were first classified according to the percentage (using intervals of ten percentage points) of the votes received in the 1946 election by each major party or group of parties. They were then classified in the same manner on the basis of the 1963 election returns. The results in the two elections are correlated in Figures 2-3 to 2-6—for the Christian Democratic Party (Figure 2-3), the Communist Party (Figure 2-4), the Socialist Party (Figure 2-5), and the left-wing parties combined (Figure 2-6).

The graphs show the distribution in each zone of communes according to the percentage of the votes cast for the party indicated. The number of communes in each 10-percent interval in 1946 are shown in the columns and the number of communes in each 10-percent range in 1963 are shown in the horizontal rows. The numbers in the squares on the diagonals represent, for each party shown, those communes in which the fluctuation in the vote received in the two elections was 10 percent or less in either direction. If the percentage of the vote received in 1963 declined by more than 10 percent compared with 1946, the commune is included in the numbers to the left of the diagonal. A commune in which the 1963 vote exceeded the 1946 vote by more than 10 percent is included in the numbers to the right of the diagonal.

A few examples from Figure 2-3 will further clarify the meaning of the graphs. The numbers in the squares on the diagonal in Figure

---

5. On the communal structure see R. C. Fried, *The Italian Prefects: A Study in Administrative Politics* (New Haven, Yale University Press, 1963).

6. Some of the excluded communes are those whose boundaries were changed between 1946 and 1963; some were those added as the result of territorial settlements with Austria and Yugoslavia.

2-3 for Zone I, Northwest for the Christian Democratic Party show that in thirteen communes the Christian Democratic vote ranged from 20 to 30 percent in both years, etc., down the diagonal to three communes in which the Christian Democratic vote ranged from 90 to 100 percent in both years. To the left of the diagonal are the numbers of communes in which Christian Democratic losses occurred between 1946 and 1963. In three communes the Christian Democratic Party received 30 to 40 percent of the vote in 1946 and only 10 to 20 percent of the vote in 1963; in forty-five the party received 30 to 40 percent of the vote in 1946 and only 20 to 30 percent in 1963. To the right of the squares on the diagonal are the numbers of communes in which the Christian Democrats' percentage of the vote in 1963 was greater than in 1946. In two communes the party's share of the vote was 10 to 20 percent in 1963, compared with 10 percent or less in 1946; in two others it was 20 to 30 percent in 1963, compared with 10 percent or less in 1946.

"Absolute" and "Relative" Stability of Votes

This method of analysis, applied for the first time to an entire country, makes it possible to measure voting stability. The degrees of stability have been classified as "absolute" and "relative." "Absolute stability," as defined in this analysis, is the ratio between the total number of communes represented by the numbers in the squares on the diagonal and the total number of communes represented in the graph for each zone. Thus absolute stability is the percentage of the total communes in each zone in which a party's share of the vote did not fluctuate more than 10 percent. "Relative stability" is defined as the ratio between the number of communes represented by the numbers in the squares on the diagonal plus the total number of communes represented by the numbers immediately to the right and to the left of them and the total number of communes represented in the graph. "Relative stability," therefore, is the percentage of the total communes in each zone in which the fluctuation in the share of the vote did not exceed 30 percent.

Table 2-4 shows the absolute and relative stability of the vote at the communal level for the Christian Democratic, Socialist, and Communist parties and for the left-wing parties as a whole in the six zones between 1946 and 1963. The figures confirm the general conclusion that Italian partisan voting is relatively stable. Although

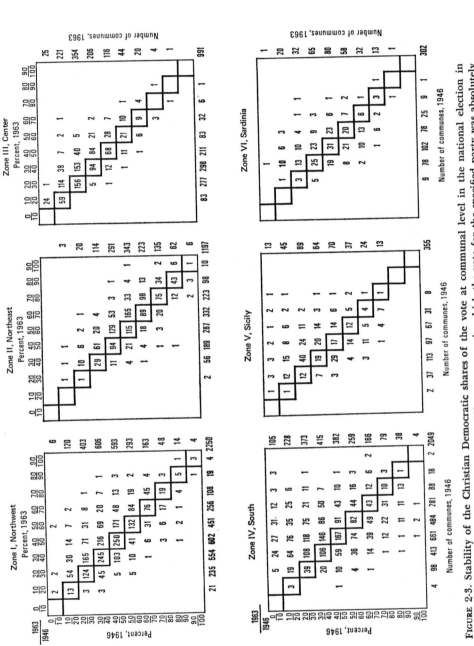

FIGURE 2-3. Stability of the Christian Democratic shares of the vote at communal level in the national election in 1963 compared with 1946, by zone. *Note:* The communes in which the vote for the specified party was absolutely stable fall within the squares on the diagonal: in these communes the party vote in 1963 compared with 1946 did

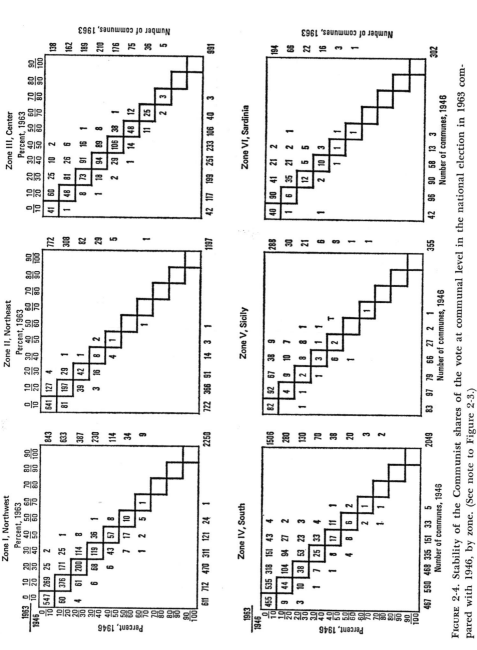

FIGURE 2-4. Stability of the Communist shares of the vote at communal level in the national election in 1963 compared with 1946, by zone. (See note to Figure 2-3.)

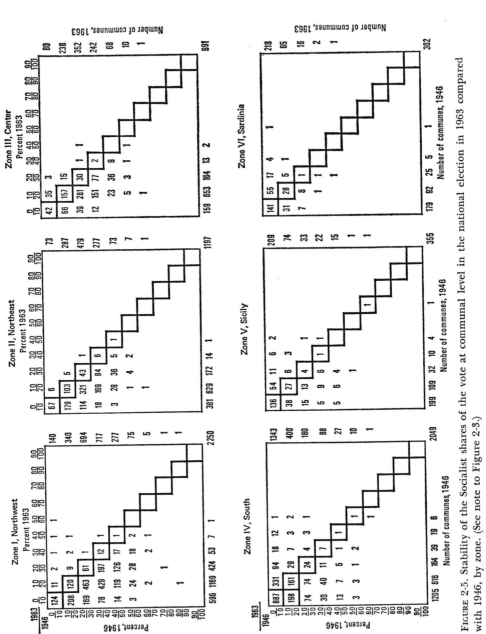

FIGURE 2-5. Stability of the Socialist shares of the vote at communal level in the national election in 1963 compared with 1946, by zone. (See note to Figure 2-3.)

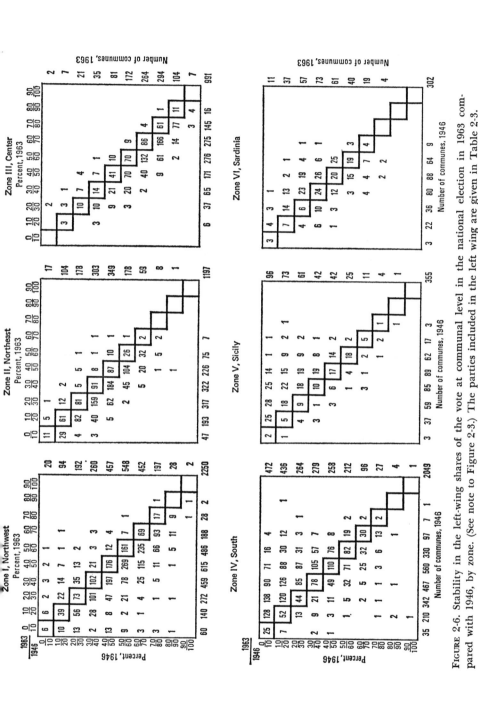

Figure 2-6. Stability in the left-wing shares of the vote at communal level in the national election in 1963 compared with 1946, by zone. (See note to Figure 2-3.) The parties included in the left wing are given in Table 2-3.

TABLE 2-4. *Percent of communes in which there was absolute* [a] *and relative* [b] *stability in the vote for major parties in elections to the Chamber of Deputies in 1963 compared with 1946, by zone*

Zone	Christian Democratic		Socialist (PSI)		Communist		Left-wing parties combined [c]	
	Absolutely stable	*Absolutely or relatively stable*	*Absolutely stable*	*Absolutely or relatively stable*	*Absolutely stable*	*Absolutely or relatively stable*	*Absolutely stable*	*Absolutely or relatively stable*
I Northwest	38.5	82.2	14.1	57.1	58.2	96.1	28.6	76.2
II Northeast	37.3	86.5	18.5	68.6	74.3	99.4	30.0	82.9
III Center	41.1	87.1	23.3	72.2	44.2	90.1	29.9	82.4
IV South	22.0	54.6	52.8	84.3	28.6	66.8	20.6	56.8
V Sicily	18.6	62.3	47.6	80.8	26.5	59.7	18.9	51.7
VI Sardinia	29.1	62.5	56.3	75.1	23.2	68.9	27.5	74.8

a. Absolute stability means that the party's share of the vote fluctuated no more than 10 percent in 1963 compared with 1946.
b. Relative stability means that the party's share of the vote fluctuated no more than 30 percent in 1963 compared with 1946.
c. For parties included see Table 2-3.

there was considerable fluctuation within some individual communes between the elections, the fluctuations within a zone were fairly modest. Both the Christian Democratic and the Communist shares of the vote were much more stable in the North and in the Center than in the South and the Islands. The Socialist vote, on the other hand, was more stable in southern than in northern Italy.

Another significant point brought out by this analysis is that the Communist Party on the whole tended to gain strength in 1963 where it had been particularly weak in 1946, and lose strength somewhat where it had been very strong. This supports the conclusion, based on the analysis of the vote by zone in Appendix C, that the Communist share of the vote tended to be more evenly distributed over the whole of Italy at the end of two postwar decades than it was in the first postwar elections.

In Zone I, for example, the Communist share of the vote was over 30 percent in 457 communes (about one fifth of the total) in 1946, but in only 387 communes in 1963. (Figure 2-4) In Zone III the Communist Party approached an overall majority, because it had full control of local government (a very important factor, as shown in Chapter 6), and it made steady gains. Here it had over 50 percent of the votes in 149 communes in 1946, but in only 116 in 1963. In the South, originally a weak spot for the Communists but later the focal point of expansion, the party obtained more than 30 percent of the votes in 524 communes in 1946, but in only 133 in 1963. However, the number of communes in which it obtained up to 20 percent of the votes rose from 1,057 to 1,786.

Over the whole of Italy the Christian Democratic share of the vote was absolutely stable between 1946 and 1963 in almost a third of the communes, increased in more than half, and decreased in the rest. The Communist share of the vote was stable in nearly half the communes, and increased or decreased in fewer communes than did the Christian Democratic share, though the Communists lost votes after 1946 in nearly 600 communes. The left as a whole lost votes in nearly half the communes and made advances in only a fourth of them, indicating that the left had already reached a high point in many localities in 1946. The communes in which the Socialist Party made gains are only slightly more numerous than those in which the Communist Party suffered losses.

FACTORS INFLUENCING ELECTORAL BEHAVIOR

In attempting to establish the determinants of the behavior of the Italian electorate, the reasons for the differences in party preference in the various parts of the country, and the factors that account for changes in party preference over time, the ecological rather than the survey approach was used.[7] The same 7,144 communes were included in this analysis as in the analysis of fluctuations in voting at the commune level. The data employed included official election returns and various indices of socioeconomic development derived from the census of 1951 and 1961. Some data were available only on a provincial basis. For comparability only 88 of the 92 Italian provinces could be included, since the provinces of Aosta, Bolzano, Gorizia, and Trieste were created after 1946.

Sex and Age and Party Preference

It proved very difficult to obtain valid results from comparative studies of the effect of sex and age on electoral behavior, as was done in Germany and France, for example, on the basis of experiments with separate ballot boxes for men and women.[8] Attempts to analyze the vote of those in the age group twenty-one to twenty-five, who are eligible to vote in elections for the Chamber of Deputies but not for the Senate, have produced doubtful and contradictory results.

The most interesting study of the voting preferences of Italian young people, based on sample surveys, was done by Joseph LaPalombara and Jerry Waters of Yale University.[9] LaPalombara and Waters came to the conclusion that the parties of the extreme left,

7. For a discussion of the strengths and weaknesses of the various approaches in studying electoral behavior, see P. H. Rossi, "Four Landmarks in Voting Research," in E. Burdick and A. Brodbeck, eds., *American Voting Behavior* (Glencoe, Free Press, 1959), pp. 5–54. The factors influencing electoral behavior are examined in detail in the second and third parts of *Il comportamento elettorale in Italia*, pp. 119–213, based on an ecological analysis. The present study, however, took into account results of the few studies made in Italy utilizing the survey method. On this subject see the secondary analysis made by Gianfranco Poggi, "Le preferenze politiche degli italiani: Analisi di alcuni sondaggi elettorali," *Quaderni dell'Istituto di Studi e Ricerche Carlo Cattaneo* (Bologna, Società editrice il Mulino, 1968), No. 2.

8. W. Hirsch-Weber and K. Schutz, *Waehler und Gewaehlte, Eine Untersuchung der Bundestagswahlen 1953* (Berlin-Frankfurt, Institut für Politische Wissenschaft, 1957).

9. Joseph LaPalombara and Jerry Waters, "Values, Expectations, and Political Predispositions of Italian Youth," *Midwest Journal of Political Science, 1* (1961), 39 ff.

the Communists and Socialists, draw less support from young voters than from old. Other surveys conducted in 1958 (the same year examined by LaPalombara and Waters) and in 1963 suggested that this hypothesis might well be valid but they did not completely confirm it.

Professor Mattei Dogan, in a study of the electoral behavior of women based on sample surveys, concluded that women may account for more than 60 percent of the Christian Democratic vote, and that the Christian Democratic Party is practically the only party that receives a sizable number of women's votes.[10] He suggested, therefore, that if women did not have the vote, the two Marxist parties together would become—all other conditions being unchanged —the principal political force in Italy.

Influence of Income on Voting

Since the most important economic change in Italy in the postwar period was the doubling of national income during the 1950s, net per capita income provides the best index of the effect of the general economic situation on election results. The relationship between this variable and party choice in the elections of 1953, 1958, and 1963 is shown in Table 2-5. In general, the increase in per capita income seems to have been advantageous to left-wing parties.

TABLE 2-5. *Coefficient of correlation between per capita income and party vote in elections for Chamber of Deputies at provincial level, 1953, 1958, and 1963*

Party or party group	1953	1958	1963
Right	—.45	—.28	—.09
Right (excluding MSI)	—.37	—.38	.20
Christian Democratic	—.08	—.30	—.44
Left	.39	.41	.43
Left (excluding Communist)	.54	.63	.54
Communist and Socialist (PSI)	.32	.27	.36
Communist	.12	.11	.21

The tendency indicated by the figures in the table refutes the popular view that the Communist vote is closely related to poverty.[11] In fact, the increase in incomes since the beginning of the industrial

---

10. See Mattei Dogan, "Le Donne Italiane tra Cattolicesimo e Marxismo," Spreafico and LaPalombara, eds., *Elezioni e Comportamento Politico*, pp. 39 ff.

11. See H. Cantril, *The Politics of Despair* (New York, Basic Books, 1958).

revolution has worked to the advantage of the socialist left in most of Europe. In Italy this tendency has been particularly marked for the noncommunist left. (Table 2-5)

The experience of the Christian Democratic Party has been quite different, for its strength has been greatest in those provinces where income is lowest, and the strength of this relationship has increased considerably with the passage of time. The trend in the relationship between income and party vote for the Christian Democrats has been almost exactly the opposite of the trend in the relationship between these variables for the parties of the right. A major reason for this is probably that in 1953, when the right achieved its highest vote since 1946, its success in the underdeveloped zones was based on a demagogic, monarchist, or even neofascist appeal. In 1963, however, the main support for the right was for the conservative Liberal Party, which was strongest in the more highly developed zones.

Type of Employment and Party Preference

Another outstanding economic characteristic of the 1950s was the mass movement of workers out of agriculture into industrial and service activities. In 1951, 42 percent of the working population was employed in agriculture, compared with barely 28 percent ten years later.

The influence on electoral behavior of this mass abandonment of agriculture and of the associated phenomenon of internal migration from South to North, from country to city, and from the mountains to the plains is shown in Table 2-6. In all six zones both in 1953 and in 1963 there was a negative correlation between the Christian Democratic vote and the percentage of workers in nonagricultural activities, and conversely, a positive correlation between the Christian Democratic vote and agricultural employment.

The vote for the Communist Party on the other hand, showed a negative correlation with agricultural employment throughout Italy both at the beginning and the end of the period 1953 to 1963, but the relationship at the communal level was less consistent than for the Christian Democratic Party. (Table 2-6) There was a parallel positive correlation between the Communist vote and industrial employment.

The correlation between votes for the right-wing parties and employment in both agriculture and industry was generally negative,

TABLE 2-6. *Coefficient of correlation between type of employment* [a] *and party vote for Chamber of Deputies at communal level, 1953 and 1963, by zone*

		I	II	III	IV	V	VI
Party group and type of employment [a]	Year	North-west	North-east	Center	South	Sicily	Sardinia
Right							
Agriculture	1953	.32	—.11	—.05	.06	—.04	—.03
	1963	.18	—.21	—.10	.06	—.07	.05
Industry [b]	1953	—.36	—.01	—.04	—.07	—.06	—.10
	1963	—.25	—.02	—.13	—.15	—.04	—.17
Service	1953	.01	.27	.17	—.03	.14	.19
	1963	.16	.44	.39	—.10	.18	.14
Christian Democratic							
Agriculture	1953	.07	.19	.03	.15	.12	.42
	1963	.22	.24	.18	.20	.08	.29
Industry [b]	1953	—.07	—.13	—.04	—.12	—.14	—.44
	1963	—.19	—.13	—.21	—.16	—.08	—.30
Service	1953	—.02	—.20	—.01	—.13	—.06	—.21
	1963	—.12	—.22	—.04	—.17	—.06	—.14
Left							
Agriculture	1953	—.24	—.17	—.01	—.17	—.06	—.32
	1963	—.29	—.20	—.14	—.21	—.03	—.27
Industry [b]	1953	.26	.15	.05	.16	.18	.43
	1963	.30	.16	.23	.24	.10	.35
Service	1953	.01	.11	—.05	.13	—.08	.04
	1963	.02	.10	—.07	.09	—.07	.04
Communist and Socialist							
Agriculture	1953	—.51	—.14	—.01	—.19	—.02	—.40
	1963	—.35	—.17	—.13	—.21	—.01	—.28
Industry [b]	1953	.29	.14	.07	.18	.15	.51
	1963	.36	.14	.24	.24	.12	.36
Service	1953	.01	.05	—.07	.14	—.12	.09
	1963	.03	.07	—.10	.07	—.13	.04
Communist							
Agriculture	1953	—.05	—.13	—.05	—.12	—.06	—.28
	1963	—.16	—.10	—.12	—.17	—.01	—.16
Industry [b]	1953	.06	.11	.10	.12	.15	.38
	1963	.17	.08	.23	.21	.08	.24
Service	1953	—.02	.10	—.04	.08	—.05	.02
	1963	.00	.05	—.10	.05	—.07	—.01

a. Data on employment based on censuses of 1951 and 1961.
b. Includes workmen, employees, and managers.

while the correlation between right-wing votes and employment in
service activities was positive in all parts of Italy except the South.

This analysis indicates the sectors of society from which the various political parties obtain their chief support: the Christian Democratic Party is above all the party of rural Italy; the parties of the
left, including the Communist Party, are the parties of industry; and
the right represents the middle classes employed in service activities,
especially in northern and central Italy.

TABLE 2-7. *Provinces in which there was a positive correlation at communal
level between the Communist Party vote in 1963 and the percent of
population employed in agriculture in 1961 and 1951*

Province	Coefficient of correlation at communal level, 1963	Percent of population employed in agriculture, 1961	Percent of population employed in agriculture, 1951		
			Farm owners	Tenant farmers	Farm laborers
Brindisi	.41	63.6	13.7	1.6	67.3
Ferrara	.33	46.6	6.2	1.7	70.3
Leghorn	.33	13.3	13.8	17.8	13.5
Cremona	.25	29.3	18.2	1.1	60.4
Milan	.22	3.6	37.7	0.4	44.4
Catania	.19	39.2	13.5	5.6	68.6
Ragusa	.18	46.3	20.5	5.8	58.2
Agrigento	.17	49.8	21.2	8.1	52.3
Pistoia	.16	22.0	17.2	23.1	12.7
Messina	.13	42.5	12.5	8.4	57.9
Foggia	.13	54.8	18.3	1.3	52.9
Potenza	.12	58.6	25.1	2.3	30.0

The situation varied, of course, in different provinces. (Table
2-7) At the provincial level, for example, the traditional hold of the
left on sharecroppers and farm laborers is evident. The fact that the
negative correlation between the vote and agricultural employment
was higher for the left as a whole than for the Communist Party suggests that the Communist Party has been more successful than the
other parties of the left in penetrating rural areas, though this pene-
tration generally slowed down in 1963.

The specific provinces in which there was a positive correlation
between the Communist vote and the percentage of the labor force
employed in agriculture are shown in Table 2-7. With a few exceptions these are provinces in which heavy proportions of the agricultural workers are day laborers or, as in Leghorn and Pistoia, the in-

cidence of sharecroppers is exceptionally high. The explanation for the positive correlation in the provinces of Brindisi, Ferrara, Leghorn, Cremona, and Milan is probably that in these provinces there is a very strong and enduring historical relationship between the political left and the poor. The trend in provinces such as these might lead one to the conclusion (as one might also infer from Table 2-8) that there was a positive correlation between the vote of the left and agricultural employment in all zones of Italy except Sicily and Sardinia. The relationships indicated in Table 2-6 are more generally applicable, however, and it would be incorrect to

TABLE 2-8. *Coefficient of correlation between occupation and party vote at communal level, 1953, by zone*

Party and occupation [a]	I North-west	II North-east	III Center	IV South	V Sicily	VI Sardinia
Right						
Peasant farmers	.39	—.16	.24	.06	—.13	—.07
Farm laborers	—.20	—.01	.02	—.04	.02	—.00
Industrial and service workers	—.36	.02	.03	—.06	.02	—.01
Christian Democratic						
Peasant farmers	.19	.40	.45	.17	.04	.35
Farm laborers	—.18	—.09	—.21	—.05	.09	.10
Industrial and service workers	—.06	—.08	—.04	—.14	—.14	—.46
Left						
Peasant farmers	—.38	—.39	—.47	—.19	.09	—.24
Farm laborers	.27	.10	.16	.07	—.10	—.08
Industrial and service workers	.25	.15	.03	.16	.10	.39
Communist and Socialist (PSI)						
Peasant farmers	—.48	—.43	—.43	—.22	.10	—.32
Farm laborers	.37	.16	.13	.09	—.07	—.11
Industrial and service workers	.28	.14	.04	.18	.06	.47
Communist						
Peasant farmers	—.30	—.34	—.38	—.17	.01	—.23
Farm laborers	.41	.13	.11	.09	—.03	—.06
Industrial and service workers	.05	.10	.08	.12	.08	.35

a. Occupational data from 1951 census.

conclude that the parties of the left are agricultural rather than industrial parties. This is true despite the attraction of the left, particularly the Communist Party, for agricultural day laborers and sharecroppers. (See Table 2-9)

TABLE 2-9. *Coefficient of correlation between*
incidence of sharecroppers in labor force [a]
and party vote, 1953

Party	Coefficient of Correlation
Right	−.20
Right (excluding MSI)	−.31
Christian Democratic	−.32
Left	.39
Left (excluding Communist)	.14
Communist and Socialist (PSI)	.38
Communist	.43

a. Based on 1961 census, at the provincial level, as the incidence of sharecroppers at the communal level was not reported.

The rise of the industrial working class has favored the left-wing parties and the Communist Party has benefited from the general trend. During the transition from an agricultural society to an industrial society, the parties whose support is mainly agricultural usually suffer. In Italy, however, because the Christian Democratic Party has been, and still continues to be to some extent, the party of the working classes under the influence of the clergy, and has also become the party favored by the moderate sectors of the urban population, it has not suffered as much as it would have otherwise. This has tended to reduce the electoral influence of the right, which in Italy is generally conservative but not reactionary. The right has, however, gained some strength in Italy from the development of employment in service activities, as a result of the well-known tendency of service workers, because of the individualistic nature of their work, to favor the parties of the moderate right. Service industries have not yet acquired the importance they have in more advanced societies.

Industrial Development and Political Stability

The foregoing analysis suggests that political alignments in Italy changed less between 1946 and 1963 than might have been expected on the basis of the socioeconomic changes that occurred during the period. The industrial left maintained in general the level of support it attracted in 1946 on the crest of the left-wing wave of the immediate postwar period, while the Christian Democratic Party consolidated its position by attracting the moderate urban voter.

The effect of industrialization on the stability of party vote at the communal level is analyzed in Appendix Table D-1. The figures indicate that the level of industrialization had little effect in changing party fortunes at elections. The stability of the Communist vote in the North and its increase in the South, as well as the decline of the left-wing vote as a whole in two thirds of the communes in the highly industrialized northern and central zones took place without regard to the degree of industrialization. Similarly, figures for the Christian Democratic Party show no consistent relationship between changes in patterns of industrialization and the party vote, though there is some indication that the party loses support when industrialization is rapid.

Agricultural Occupations and Voting Stability

This general picture of the limited effect of economic development on electoral stability is confirmed by the analysis of the relationship between type of agricultural employment and stability of party vote at the communal level, summarized in Appendix Table D-2. This analysis includes only those communes in which at least 50 percent of the working population was engaged in agriculture— about double the national average. There were 4,824 of these agricultural communes, more than half the approximately 8,000 communes in Italy. When the overall vote of these communes is examined, it is found that between 1946 and 1963 the stability of the vote for the Christian Democrats, the Communists, and the left as a whole was almost exactly the same as that shown in Appendix D-1 for communes that were the most highly industrialized:

	Percent of communes		
Stability of vote	*Christian Democratic Party vote*	*Communist Party vote*	*Vote for left*
Stable	28.2	45.6	24.2
Increased	57.3	47.4	31.8
Decreased	14.5	7.0	44.0

The chief areas of increasing Communist Party influence in these predominantly agricultural communes were in central and southern Italy, Sicily, and Sardinia, where a majority of the agricultural workers are noncasual farm laborers. In Sicily Communist influence also increased in communes where peasant farmers were in the majority, a type of commune in which the Christian Democratic vote increased in almost all parts of Italy.

Education and Voting Stability

Along with the increase in the national income and the development of industry, the 1950s were also marked by the spread of education and mass culture in Italy, as indicated by the following figures on the decline from 1951 to 1961 in the percentages of the population 6 years old and over that were illiterate:[12]

	1951	1961
Male	10.5	6.6
Female	15.2	10.1
Total	12.9	8.4

This increase in the general level of education in Italy is especially significant because of the strong cultural heritage both of the Catholic movement and the socialist movement, from which the Communist Party sprang. In general, these two subcultures were strongest among groups who had less education than the liberal and anticlerical middle classes.

In examining the effects of education on electoral behavior between the years 1953 and 1963, the completion of junior high school was selected as the upper educational limit, because in Italy only a small proportion of the population completes senior high school and a smaller proportion goes on to university. Some general conclusions can be drawn from the figures shown in Table 2-10, which is based on an analysis of findings at the communal level. The findings, however, were not conclusive and indicate the need for further investiga-

12. *Dati Riassuntivi Comunali e Provinciali su Alcune Principali Caratteristiche della Popolazione, 10 Censimento Generale della Popolazione, 15 Ottobre 1951* (Rome, Istituto Centrale di Statistica, 1963), p. 9. On the political significance of trends in education and mass culture, see two collective works in the series *Studies in Political Development* (Princeton, Princeton University Press): J. S. Coleman, ed., *Education and Political Development* (1965); and L. Pye, ed., *Communications and Political Development* (1963).

tion. The Christian Democratic Party apparently gained a greater advantage from the diffusion of elementary education, while the Communist Party seemed to profit more from the diffusion of mass culture, chiefly through radio and television, during the period studied.

TABLE 2-10. *Coefficient of correlation between educational level and party vote at the communal level, 1953 and 1963*

Party and educational and literacy level [a]	Year	I North-west	II North-east	III Center	IV South	V Sicily	VI Sardinia
Right							
Illiterate voters	1953	−.16	.08	.03	.01	−.19	−.21
	1963	−.08	−.12	−.11	−.08	−.17	−.03
Literate voters with or without primary education	1953	.12	−.30	−.06	−.02	.11	.15
	1963	−.24	−.45	−.14	−.01	−.01	−.14
Voters with at least junior high school education	1953	−.03	.28	.05	.02	.18	.24
	1963	.27	.53	.28	.16	.22	.22
Christian Democratic							
Illiterate voters	1953	−.20	−.35	−.07	−.06	−.10	−.18
	1963	−.22	−.24	−.03	−.03	−.18	−.22
Literate voters with or without primary education	1953	.29	.49	.16	.10	.17	.25
	1963	.44	.47	.24	.17	.30	.28
Voters with at least junior high school education	1953	−.18	−.26	−.15	−.14	−.14	−.14
	1963	−.37	−.37	−.25	−.22	−.17	−.07
Left							
Illiterate voters	1953	.27	.36	.05	.04	.26	.30
	1963	.27	.30	.05	.08	.27	.21
Literate voters with or without primary education	1953	−.32	−.42	−.11	−.07	−.24	−.31
	1963	−.31	−.37	−.18	−.14	−.25	−.16
Voters with at least junior high school education	1953	.18	.16	.11	.09	−.60	−.05
	1963	.23	.24	.16	.09	−.00	−.08
Communist and Socialist							
Illiterate voters	1953	.30	.40	.09	.04	.29	.27
	1963	.30	.37	.10	.08	.32	.23
Literate voters with or without primary education	1953	−.32	−.41	−.12	−.07	−.25	−.29
	1963	−.31	−.35	−.16	−.13	−.26	−.19

(Continued)

TABLE 2-10.—*Continued*

		I	II	III	IV	V	VI
Party and educational and literacy level [a]	*Year*	*North-west*	*North-east*	*Center*	*South*	*Sicily*	*Sardinia*
Voters with at least	1953	.15	.11	.05	.10	−.09	−.01
junior high school education	1963	.12	.18	.09	.07	−.06	−.07
Communist							
Illiterate voters	1953	.39	.36	.07	.05	.26	.22
	1963	.39	.41	.13	.05	.28	.27
Literate voters with	1953	−.32	−.39	−.11	−.07	−.25	−.23
or without primary education	1963	−.29	−.32	−.17	−.08	−.28	−.23
Voters with at least	1953	.10	.13	.07	.05	−.03	−.04
junior high school education	1963	.17	.14	.07	.04	.01	−.07

a. Educational level and literacy status is based on data from the censuses of 1951 and 1961, with calculations based on members of the resident population aged 6 years or more.

At the communal level there was a positive correlation between illiteracy and the Communist Party vote and a negative correlation between the party's vote and percent of the population with a primary education. In the North, however, the Communist Party tended to gain from an increase in education beyond the primary level.

For the Christian Democratic Party, on the other hand, the correlation between voting strength and education was highest at the primary educational level. Primary education is broadly Catholic in nature, partly because of the influence of Catholic Action, as discussed in Chapter 5. Hence primary education in Italy tends to reinforce the Catholic cultural tradition.

Conversely, there was a negative correlation between the vote for the Christian Democratic Party and percent of illiteracy as well as percent of the population with a junior high school education. Illiterate voters tended to favor the left, and especially the Communist Party; those voters with a junior high school education tended to favor the right.

A higher degree of education among voters, then, seemed to detract from the Catholic vote and partly to favor the left, particularly in the North, but in general to favor the right in all parts of the country.

Radio and Television and the Party Vote

Television was introduced into Italy in 1954, so it was possible to establish coefficients of correlation between party voting and the increase in radio and television broadcasting for the elections of 1958 and 1963. As Table 2-11 shows, the correlation was negative for the Christian Democratic Party and positive for the Communist Party, the left as a whole, and the right (with minor exceptions).

TABLE 2-11. *Coefficient of correlation between number of radio and television licenses, 1957 and 1962, and party vote for Chamber of Deputies, at communal level, 1958 and 1963*

		I	II	III	IV	V	VI
Party	*Year*	*North-west*	*North-east*	*Center*	*South*	*Sicily*	*Sardinia*
Right	1958	—.01	.35	.07	.03	.18	.00
	1963	.10	.36	.14	.02	.22	.20
Christian Democratic	1958	—.42	—.41	—.33	—.26	—.18	—.10
	1963	—.47	—.40	—.38	—.22	—.18	—.32
Left	1958	.42	.32	.27	.20	.02	.08
	1963	.42	.32	.31	.18	.01	.15
Communist and Socialist	1958	.47	.29	.22	.18	—.01	.12
	1963	.47	.37	.26	.16	—.05	.23
Communist	1958	.38	.25	.18	.14	.06	.09
	1963	.40	.30	.19	.16	.01	.20

These figures seem to be a refutation of the argument that Christian Democratic control of television gives the party an electoral advantage. The figures also seem to lend support to the view that the Communist Party adapts to mass culture much more effectively than does the Catholic movement. However, only tentative conclusions can be drawn from these correlations. While they suggest (on the basis of the increases in the positive correlations in 1963, when television was more developed than in 1958) that television may be even more effective than radio in breaking down cultural barriers and spreading new patterns of political behavior, other forces also may have affected the coefficients of correlation. The spread of television began in the economically more advanced zones, those with a socialist political tradition, where the segments of the population whose living standards were rising also tended to be the first to accept radio and television.

The negative correlation between television licenses and the Christian Democratic vote was so constant and general and showed such a tendency to increase, however, that it must be significant. And although the distribution of Christian Democratic votes remained fairly stable in the whole postwar period, a period of great change in Italian life, the spread of mass culture through television and other means does not appear to have been of particular benefit to the Christian Democratic Party.

Organizational Influences on the Party Vote

Political parties are not merely receivers of influences flowing from the socioeconomic characteristics of the electorate. They stand, in fact, in a much more dialectical relationship to those characteristics. This has been pointed out by, among others, Maurice Duverger, in his discussion of the relationship between political parties and public opinion.[13]

TABLE 2-12. *Coefficient of correlation between party vote at the provincial level, 1953 and 1963, and membership in political parties and trade union organizations of adult population,*[a] *1951 and 1961*

			Party or organization belonged to			
Party or group voted for	Year	Christian Democratic Party	Catholic-oriented trade union (CISL) [b]	Catholic-oriented interest group (ACLI) [c]	Communist Party	Socialist-oriented trade union (CGIL) [d]
Right	1953	.44		−.10	−.56	−.62
	1963	.21	.01	−.39	−.46	−.41
Christian	1953	.32		.36	−.61	−.54
Democratic	1963	.50	.31	.29	−.69	−.70
Left	1953	−.56		−.19	.85	.84
	1963	−.54	−.28	−.10	.81	.80
Left (excluding	1953	−.57		.04	.45	.59
Communist)	1963	−.58	.06	.21	.05	.26
Communist and	1953	−.47		−.20	.85	.82
Socialist	1963	−.45	−.26	−.08	.81	.80
Communist	1953	−.33		−.29	.84	.72
	1963	−.31	−.31	−.17	.82	.72

a. 21 years of age and over.
b. Italian Confederation of Free Unions.
c. Italian Association of Christian Workers.
d. General Confederation of Italian Workers.

13. Maurice Duverger, *Political Parties: Their Organization and Activity in the Modern State*, 2nd English edition, translated by Barbara and Robert North (New York, Wiley, 1959), pp. 378 ff.

The success of a political party depends not merely on its acting as the receiver of public opinion, but also on its serving as a processor and to some extent as a molder of it. The ability to do so in turn depends on the extent to which the party can avail itself of influences other than its own organization, such as a newspaper, a network of sponsored or allied organizations, or its control of local government agencies. (The sources of the organizational strength of the leading parties is discussed in detail in Chapter 5.)

The correlation between membership in political parties and trade unions and the vote for the two major parties in 1953 and 1963 is shown in Table 2-12. For the Christian Democratic Party the correlation between party vote and party membership increased considerably between 1953 and 1963, but it still was not so close as that between membership in the Communist Party and the party's electoral support, despite a slight decline in the latter between 1953 and 1963.

The relationship between membership in General Confederation of Italian Workers and the Communist Party was almost as close as the relationship between party membership itself and the party vote. The correlation was well over twice that between membership in the Italian Confederation of Free Unions, the Catholic-oriented trade union, and the Christian Democratic vote. This difference was due to the differences in the relationships between the two trade unions and the respective parties, which is discussed in detail in Chapter 5.

TABLE 2-13. *Coefficient of correlation between party vote at the provincial level, 1953 and 1963,* **and** *the circulation of the Communist daily newspaper,* L'Unità, *1951 and 1962*

	Average sales			
Party or group voted for	*Daily*		*Sunday, 1962*	*Special issues, 1962*
	1951	*1962*		
Right	−.54	−.32	−.38	−.43
Christian Democratic	−.47	−.68	−.71	−.72
Left	.74	.74	.80	.83
Left (excluding Communist)	.51	.31	.30	.32
Communist and Socialist	.67	.69	.75	.78
Communist	.63	.64	.69	.72

The Communist Vote and Circulation of L'Unità

L'Unità, the Communist daily newspaper, has no rival as a political daily of national significance. No other Italian political party has at its disposal a daily newspaper with a wide circulation. Consequently, *L'Unità* has exerted a strong influence on the whole of the left, although the correlation between the Communist vote in 1953 and 1963 and the daily circulation of *L'Unità* was stronger than the correlation between the paper's circulation and the vote for the noncommunist left. (Table 2-13)

Summary of Factors Influencing the Party Vote

The tables in this chapter present figures indicating the relationships during a decade of various social and economic factors (income, type of employment, education, and the spread of radio and television) and organizational factors (political parties, trade unions, and the press) on the percentage of the vote received by the leading parties. The data suggest that for the Communist Party the correlation between voting strength and support from sympathetic organizations is much higher than the correlation between the voting strength and social and economic conditions, whereas for the Christian Democratic Party the correlations between both groups of factors are roughly the same.

The data further indicate that the emergence of the Christian Democratic Party and the Communist Party as the dominant parties in Italy cannot be explained solely in socioeconomic terms. Other factors involved include the strength of the Catholic and socialist subcultures, the organizational structure that increases the effectiveness of a political party "in proportion as the party is more centralized, better organized, more firmly based on a complete and coherent doctrine which enables it to act upon opinion instead of registering it and to organize the masses instead of following them," as Maurice Duverger has expressed it.[14]

These remarks apply not so much to the Christian Democratic Party itself as to all Catholic organizations taken together. For the Catholic world since 1946 has had a form and structure capable of influencing moderate and conservative as well as Catholic opinion, at a time when Italy had no tradition or activating force on which

14. Ibid., p. 380.

to build an influential secular party to represent the moderate and conservative points of view.

Duverger's remarks are true of the Communist Party as well, although its expansion within the left has been subject to the limits expressed in two statements made by Communist leaders, one in 1946 and one in 1963. A resolution voted by the Communist Party leadership on July 19, 1946, reads as follows:

> Our aim was that the Socialist Party and the Communist Party should together poll sufficient votes for us to have half the deputies in the Constituent Assembly. This aim was not achieved. Our aim was also to gain sufficient votes to establish ourselves as the strongest party representing the working classes and the second strongest party in the country. This aim was not achieved either.

Yet, seventeen years later, on May 5, 1963, following the national elections, the Communist Party Secretary said, "Our party has gained a great victory, beyond our hopes and expectations."

In 1946 the Communist Party leaders had hoped to translate support from the socialist subculture into a combined Socialist-Communist vote of about half the total vote; and they had hoped that the Communists would receive more than half of that vote. But in 1963 the same party leaders considered the just over 25 percent of the total vote the party had obtained a victory beyond their hopes and expectations. The socialist parties together now had 45 percent of the votes, as compared with 41 percent in 1946, but the Socialist Party vote had declined, while the vote for the Communist Party was rising, so that the electoral increase for the left as a whole between 1946 and 1963 was very slight.

The Communist Party made use of the most efficient party machine in Italy to turn into votes the influence of the socialist subculture, which it had thought to command as early as 1946. The party did not modify or overturn the basic trends in electoral behavior in the twentieth century in Italy; it simply rode with the tide. Communist successes were achieved by an authoritarian internal organization that permitted more energy to be concentrated on influencing those outside the party than could be generated by the other parties, some of whose energies were used up in internal struggles.

This combination of organization and ideology enabled the Communist Party rather than the divided and much more poorly organized socialist parties to mold left-wing opinion and to translate into votes for the party a variety of tendencies and tensions.

3

The Structure of the
Two Leading Parties

The Christian Democratic and Communist parties have clearly been
the dominant forces in Italian politics since the Second World War.
Together they have received about two thirds of the popular vote in
elections since the war, and through party memberships have organized an even greater share of the Italian electorate.

Among Italian political parties only the Christian Democrats and
the Communists have avoided major schisms in the postwar period.
These two parties are alone in possessing permanent organizations
throughout the country. They are unique as well in their close relationship with a network of organizations operating in all spheres of
social life, as described in Chapter 5. Each of these parties is heir to
one of the two political subcultures that since the 1920s have progressively established dominant positions in the political process. In
the postwar period the Communist Party has given expression to the
more dynamic segments of the socialist subculture; the Christian
Democratic Party, while solidly based in the Catholic subculture,
owes much of its success to its ability to win the support of groups
previously identified with moderate secular interests. These two parties, similar in so many respects, represent the two poles of political
thought in Italy. It might even be said that the Christian Democrats
and the Communists alone act out the drama of Italian politics, that
through their interaction Italy's apparent multiparty system functions somewhat as a two-party system.

Methodological as well as substantive considerations guided the
decision to concentrate in this study on these two parties. They were
not only the most researchworthy, they were also the most researcha-
ble. The Communist Party's vast literature, as well as its habit of

scrutinizing itself in its provincial and national meetings, offered promise that a focused research effort would bring results. While the Christian Democratic Party is not nearly so self-conscious a party, and an analysis of its press was expected to prove less rewarding, it was assumed that easy access to information from party sources would be granted to researchers on a privileged basis. Neither expectation was disappointed; in fact, the Communist Party proved most cooperative, and on some subjects provided the study staff with more information than did the Christian Democrats.

ORIGINS OF THE COMMUNIST PARTY [1]

The Italian Communist Party was organized in January 1921 by the left wing that had seceded from the Socialist Party. Its formation was a response to the revolutionary pronouncements of the Third (Communist) International, which maintained that the First World War had opened the way for the proletarian conquest of power. Interpreting the economic crises and the dissension among the bourgeoisie as the death throes of capitalism, heralded by Marx a half century earlier, the Communists opposed any further collaboration with the bourgeoisie. They condemned the socialist parties for having joined the bourgeoisie in its "imperialist" war, and interpreted this collaboration as evidence that the socialist parties were no longer interested in the seizure of power by the proletariat.

In an early official document the Italian Communist Party described its revolutionary mission as follows: "The World War has ushered in the disintegration of capitalism, and the class struggle is bound to lead to armed conflict between the working masses and the power of the bourgeois states. The proletariat can neither destroy nor change the capitalist system of production . . . without the violent overthrow of bourgeois power." [2]

But the months that followed saw the offensive not of the Communists but of the Fascists. Instead of the violent overthrow of bour-

1. On the Italian Communist Party, see Aldo Garosci's essay in Mario Einaudi, Jean-Marie Domenach, and Aldo Garosci, *Communism in Western Europe* (Ithaca, Cornell University Press, 1952); for postwar history in particular see G. Galli, "Italian Communism," in W. E. Griffith, ed., *Communism in Western Europe* (Cambridge, M.I.T. Press, 1964); S. G. Tarrow, *Peasant Communism in Southern Italy* (New Haven, Yale University Press, 1967); and D. L. M. Blackmer, *Unity in Diversity: Italian Communism and the Communist World* (Cambridge, M.I.T. Press, 1968).

2. From a collection of documents, known as *Come si costitui' il Partito Comunista d'Italia*, relating to the birth of the Communist Party in 1921, as quoted in Giorgio Galli, *Storia del Partito Comunista Italiano* (Milan, Schwartz, 1958), p. 47.

geois power there occurred within a few years the violent establishment of an authoritarian regime.

The Italian Communist Party of these years, particularly after 1926, was primarily a party in exile. Only a cadre functioned in Italy, where political parties other than the Fascist Party were illegal. Most of the activities of the Italian Communists were carried on in France, Switzerland, and Belgium, where there were many Italian émigrés. The party's official position was made known through *Lo Stato Operaio,* a periodical published in Paris.

The party was directly affected by the internal struggles of the Bolshevik Party and the Third International that followed the death of Lenin.[3] At the Third Congress of the Italian Communist Party, held at Lyons, France, in 1926, those members who shared the views of Trotsky and Zinoviev were replaced by the followers of Antonio Gramsci,[4] who had the support of Stalin and the Bolshevik majority. But in November 1926 Gramsci was arrested in Italy, and the leadership of the party was taken over by his trusted collaborator, Palmiro Togliatti.

The official position of the Italian Communist Party was that capitalism's brief recovery would soon be followed by a revolution, particularly after the 1929 crisis. Some of the most active of the underground leaders disagreed with these predictions and criticized Togliatti for believing them. But Togliatti, in order to demonstrate his solidarity with Stalin, continued to predict an Italian revolution. Those who dissented were in the minority and were finally expelled from the party.

But if revolution had been an illusion in 1920, in the early thirties it was even more so. Fascism gained strength, and the underground Communist organization suffered severe blows. Many leaders were arrested and some were not freed until 1943. Under Stalin's leadership the Third International had taken the position that socialists and fascists similarly represented the bourgeoisie's fight against the proletariat. In the 1960s Togliatti was to characterize this theory of "social-fascism" as a "countertruth." But in the 1930s he accepted it, and in France the Italian Communists carried on a violent campaign against the exiled Italian Socialists.

3. L. Schapiro, *The Communist Party of the Soviet Union* (New York, Random House, 1960), Chaps. 15, 16, 20–22.
4. On Gramsci see H. S. Hughes, *Consciousness and Society* (New York, Knopf, 1959), pp. 99–104. Some of Gramsci's writings have been translated in A. Gramsci, *The Modern Prince* (London, Lawrence & Wishart, 1957).

With the advent of nazism the communist movement under Stalin renounced the theory of social-fascism and adopted the new strategy of the popular front.[5] The communist parties were to formulate political objectives and form coalitions with those parties hostile to fascism and willing to pursue through constitutional means a policy of limited social reform, coalitions that would include the social democrats and some left-wing "bourgeois" parties.

Through this strategy the Italian Communists' ideology underwent a deep and perhaps irreversible transformation. Within the framework of the popular front, the party committed itself to the image of a democratic, representative political system in which the underprivileged sections of the population (not only workers, but peasants and the urban petite bourgeoisie), by fully exploiting the franchise and by means of legislation enacted by a freely elected parliament, could counteract the preponderance of the wealthy. Through collaboration with all parties interested in the same objectives, but primarily with those of socialist inspiration, and with a base in the working class, the Communists committed themselves to defend this system against fascism and to work for its establishment in countries where fascism could be forced to give way.

A communist party that adopts this strategy makes room in its own ideological makeup, side by side with Marxism-Leninism, for traits that go back to the reformist, continental socialist parties of the Second International in the last decade of the nineteenth century.[6] The two aspects of these dual objectives are distinguished as "maximum" and "minimum" programs. The objective of the maximum program is a Leninist revolution leading to the dictatorship of the proletariat; the minimum program aims at limited reform through constitutional means within a popular front. With the Italian Communist Party, as with some socialist movements during the Second International, the minimum program has progressively become central, while the maximum program has lost significance.

In the 1930s, of course, the Italian Communist Party was forced to carry out its popular front policy in exile: first, by a unity of action pact with the Socialist Party in Paris in 1934, and later by giving

5. For an account of the most important popular front experience, that of France, see D. Thomson, *Democracy in France: The Third and Fourth Republics* (New York, Oxford University Press, 1952).

6. The best documented experience is probably that of German Social Democracy. See G. Roth, *The Social Democrats in Imperial Germany* (Totowa, New Jersey, Bedminster, 1964).

support to the formation of the French and the Spanish popular fronts. The electoral success of the latter in the February 1936 elections was challenged in July of that year by Franco's military coup. The Italian Communists formed an important group among the foreign volunteers who fought in defense of the Spanish Republic. Togliatti became the Comintern representative in Spain in 1937, while Luigi Longo and Giuseppe Di Vittorio were among the most important leaders of the International Brigades.[7]

From the mid-1930s on, the ultimate objective of the Italian Communist Party—the proletarian revolution and the creation of the socialist state—receded more and more into the background. The primary goal became the reduction of the power of the capitalists and the large landowners (whom the Communists held responsible for fascism's rise to power) by the creation in Italy of a representative, democratic system, incorporating strong government control over the economy.

This orientation was strengthened during the Second World War, when in 1942–43 the Italian Communist Party began once again to engage in large-scale underground operations in Italy. The Communists confirmed their unity of action pact with the Socialists; cosponsored, with the other antifascist parties, the Committees of National Liberation; and, when Togliatti returned to Italy in March 1944, were the first to withdraw the demand (previously voiced with other parties) for the abdication of King Vittorio Emanuele III. Thus the Italian Communist Party declared itself willing to postpone the question of the monarchy versus the republic, and put forth a program of social reform to be enacted after the war, within a democratic system and with the cooperation of other antifascist forces.

The party remained, however, markedly authoritarian, reflecting Stalin's interpretation of Leninism and, even more, the totalitarian nature of the Soviet Union under Stalin. This characterizes particularly the Italian party's internal structure, with its emphasis on uniformity, its lack of organized competition between alternative tendencies and leaders, its intolerance of dissent in the ranks, and its refusal to allow democratic political processes within the party. The Leninist-Stalinist heritage is reflected further in an emphasis on the voluntary element in politics, in a distrust of spontaneity, in the occasionally violent and contemptuous way in which adversaries are

7. On the role of the communist parties in the Spanish Civil War, see D. Cattell, *Communism and the Spanish Civil War* (Berkeley, University of California Press, 1955).

addressed, and in a certain toughness and militancy in political style. The party's Leninist-Stalinist heritage is also expressed in its ritualistic attachment to doctrinal interpretations of political realities and in a compulsive refusal to recognize the extent to which the party itself deviates from such orthodoxy and adopts a basically revisionist posture. To these characteristics should be added the party's complete acceptance of the Soviet Union as a source of guidance and inspiration and as a model of the good society and political system. These organizational and ideological features make the Communist Party quite unlike the social democratic parties, despite the apparent similarities in the evolution of their policies.

ORIGINS OF THE CHRISTIAN DEMOCRATIC PARTY

The Christian Democratic Party is a much younger party than the Communist Party, having been founded in 1942,[8] although it might be considered a descendant of the Popular Party of 1919–24, from which it drew its earliest leaders. When it was organized as an underground party in Milan, the possibility of its assuming the name of its predecessor was considered and rejected; the name adopted instead was "Party of Christian Democracy," although today it is called the "Christian Democratic Party."

The naming of the Italian Catholic party marked a reconciliation between Catholicism and democracy, at least in principle, since for many decades the term "democracy" had negative connotations among European Catholics because of its association with the liberals and the socialists, both with a history of hostility to the Church.[9] Furthermore, the first Catholic movement in Italy to call itself "Christian Democracy," although led by a priest, had been disowned by the Church and its leader had been defrocked. At the beginning of the 1940s the war against fascism was being carried on in the name of democracy, a term that had then been accepted, in its essential aspects, by the Italian Communists. The adjective "Christian" stresses the party's religious and confessional inspiration, which

8. For further background on the Christian Democratic Party see R. Webster, *Christian Democracy in Italy, 1860–1960* (London, Oxford University Press, 1962); M. Einaudi and F. Goguel, *Christian Democracy in Italy and France* (Notre Dame, University of Notre Dame Press, 1952); and H. S. Hughes, *The United States and Italy*, rev. ed. (Cambridge, Harvard University Press, 1965), Chaps. 7 and 9.

9. One of the best sources on the doctrinal evolution of this complex question is a book by a liberal Catholic scholar, F. Rommen, *The State in Catholic Thought* (St. Louis, Herder, 1945).

causes it to view political and social values, including democracy, as basically instrumental, however useful and immediately necessary they may be.

In addition to the religious difference, two other characteristics separate the Christian Democratic Party from the European (and Italian) liberal tradition. The Christian Democrats favor increased participation in public life of the workers and low-income groups in society and the nation, with a corresponding limitation or elimination of privilege conferred by wealth. Public intervention in the economy is seen as a means of limiting these privileges, affecting the formation of national income, and of insuring a more just income distribution.

Thus in a sense both the Communist and Christian Democratic parties have an ambivalent attitude toward the political institutions originally identified with liberalism in Italy. They accept them as a framework for political action, but their respective ideological heritages lead them to differ both with one another and with traditional liberal values. What is more, their political strategy, which has made them the two dominant mass parties, has been based to a large extent on an appeal to political subcultures that were traditionally hostile to the liberal view of democracy.

ORGANIZATIONAL DEVELOPMENT OF THE TWO PARTIES

The two leading parties experienced three roughly parallel phases of organizational development in the postwar period to 1962.[10] For the Christian Democratic Party the first, the De Gasperi phase, lasted from 1945 to 1953; the second, while Amintore Fanfani was Secretary-General of the party, lasted from 1954 to 1958; and the third, under Aldo Moro's leadership, from 1959 to 1962. For the Communist Party the period from 1945 to 1950, which marked the establishment of Togliatti's "new type of party," operating within a framework of constitutional democracy, constituted the first phase; the period of consolidation and further development from 1951 to 1955 was the second phase, while the third phase was the period of de-Stalinization from 1956 to 1962.

10. This section is a synthesis of the findings published in F. Cervellati Cantelli, V. Cioni Polacchini, P. de Vito Piscicelli, S. Guarino Cappello, G. Poggi, G. Sani, G. Sivini, and A. Sivini Cavazzani, *L'organizzazione partitica del PCI e della DC* (Bologna, Società editrice il Mulino, 1968), pp. 23–316.

The De Gasperi Phase

The dependence of the Christian Democratic Party on Catholic organizations and structure was most marked in the early years of its existence, under De Gasperi's leadership. Between 1945 and 1947 two thirds of the party's 12,000 sections were set up either on the direct initiative of the clergy, or through the Catholic Action organizations.

This organizational dependence on the clergy and on Catholic Action became stronger after 1947, when the Christian Democratic Party became the cornerstone of the "bloc for order" against the popular front. The requirements of a difficult electoral campaign forced the party to avail itself of the mass organizational support of the Catholic world under the leadership of the Civic Committees. (See Chapter 5 for detailed discussion of this support.) This dependence and the party's alliances with conservative groups in the South set serious limits to its autonomy.

De Gasperi, the leader of the Christian Democrats, governed as the head of the center coalition, an interparty anticommunist movement for representative democracy. As Premier and party chief, he followed a policy of moderation and compromise.

The Dossettians

Within the party a new group, with reform goals, was forming. It was led by Giuseppe Dossetti, a young, distinguished legal scholar and a deputy from Reggio-Emilia. The Dossettians were a left-wing group who relied on the theories of Keynes and Beveridge to support a policy of government intervention in the economy. This group asserted that as long as the party was dependent on conservatively oriented Catholic organizations, it would be unable to develop its own policy of reform.

At the party's 1949 congress the Dossettians controlled 30 percent of the votes, but the party remained organizationally dependent on Catholic Action and the clergy, which selected the leaders, influenced the distribution of "preferential votes" [11] in local and na-

11. In Italian elections for Chamber of Deputies, for example, the voter casts his ballot for a party "list," which generally includes the names of as many candidates as there are deputies to be elected from the district. The percentage of the vote cast for

tional elections, and even turned the party sections into organizational props for the parish.

Dossetti and his friends were, however, able to build up a circle of young leaders who recognized that organizational autonomy was a condition of the party's political autonomy. Ten years later the members of this circle, which included Aldo Moro, Mariano Rumor, Benigno Zaccagnini, Luigi Gui, and Emilio Colombo, were to dominate the Christian Democratic Party and the Italian political scene.

In 1950 Dossetti became vice-secretary of the party and began to work for the passage of the party's reform platform into law. He made decisive contributions to the passage of the agrarian reform law and to the creation of a financial agency for economic development in the South, the Cassa per il Mezzogiorno, or Fund for the South. But his attempts to increase government intervention in the economy met with little success, and, conscious of a lack of support from the Catholic world, he retired from political life at the end of 1951.

Fanfani's Secretaryship

After the 1953 elections, in which popular support for the Christian Democratic Party declined and the so-called "swindle law" sponsored by the Christian Democrats was defeated, Amintore Fanfani took over the leadership of the Dossettian group. This group now called itself "Iniziativa Democratica" and became the first organized faction within the Christian Democratic Party.[12] With Fanfani as its leader and many of the "second generation" Christian Democratic leaders as members, it became a party within a party, with its own organization and its own apparatus. Thanks to these resources, it obtained a majority at the Naples party congress in 1954, and Fanfani became the new party secretary.

Drawing on the experience of Roosevelt's New Deal and the postwar British Labour government, Giuseppe Dossetti had proposed an

---

each party determines how many deputies each party is entitled to. The deputies are selected from the party list in the order in which their names appear on the ballot (which is decided initially by the party), unless this order has been changed by the preferential votes of the voters. Each voter may indicate three (sometimes four) preferences among the names on the party list.

12. On intraparty conflict within the Christian Democratic Party, see R. Zariski, "Intra-party Conflict in a Dominant Party: The Experience of Italian Christian Democracy," *Journal of Politics*, 27 (1965), 3–34.

economic policy in which the state would be strongly supported by mass organizations, such as the unions, and would aim at broad popular participation in economic decision-making. Fanfani, instead, stressed Christian Democratic control of public economic agencies, such as the National Hydrocarbons Trust, the Institute for Industrial Reconstruction, the agrarian reform agencies, the Cassa per il Mezzogiorno. He attempted to create a party organization that would not have to ask for help from the Catholic hierarchy or from the moderates or the business world. This attempt, which characterized the second phase of the organizational life of the Christian Democratic Party, was carried on under somewhat favorable conditions, since its beginning (1954–55) coincided with a crisis in the Communist Party.

Fanfani increased the size of the Party's National Council and included representatives of the Catholic world, which he hoped to make subordinate to the party. He saw the party as the center of a constellation of front organizations. (See Chapter 5 for a discussion of the relationship between the parties and allied nonparty organizations.) At the periphery he increased the number of party sections and attempted to give rank-and-file members responsible positions in the party and in public office, replacing personnel loaned by Catholic Action, imposed by the clergy, or suggested by moderates, industrialists, and landowners who financed the party.

Public firms offered positions to faithful party officials and otherwise financially supported the party, thus reducing its dependence on conservative and moderate businessmen.[13] Alarmed by these developments, the great employers' organizations (Confindustria, Confagricoltura, Confcommercio) joined together in the Confintesa in February 1956 to maintain and build up their political influence. Their efforts were in vain. Fanfani's apparatus greatly reduced the number of their representatives on the local election ballots in 1956.

Fanfani's leadership, confirmed by the Trento congress of 1956, was authoritarian. He proposed to isolate within the party or squeeze out of it the dissenters on the left who would not be assimilated, and to isolate and keep out of key positions such important figures on the right as Mario Scelba, Guido Gonella, and Giuseppe Pella. He introduced into the party the same type of petty bossism that was so severely criticized in the Communist Party. But he gave

---

13. On the obscure matter of party financing in Italy, see S. Passigli, "Comparative Party Finance: Italy," *Journal of Politics*, 25 (1963), 718–36.

new life and effectiveness to the Christian Democratic Party, provided it with a sense of functional autonomy, and allowed a new
body of leaders to rise from the ranks. The favorable results of the
1956 and 1958 elections can be attributed to this organizational renewal as well as to the decline of the Communist Party during that
period.

In 1958 Pius XII died and Cardinal Roncalli succeeded him on
Peter's throne under the name of John XXIII. His vigorous policy
of innovations was to have wide repercussions in the Church.[14] His
effort to disentangle the Church from political affairs by establishing
a clearer demarcation between the religious and the political commitments of Catholics was in keeping with Fanfani's design of an
autonomous Christian Democratic Party. However, another aspect
of Pope John's policy—greater autonomy for the bishops of the individual nations in relation to the Holy See itself—indirectly caused
difficulties for Fanfani.

Most of the church hierarchy was less willing than the Pope to accord greater autonomy to the Catholic party. Most Italian bishops
were quite concerned about Fanfani's plans to make the party less
dependent on the Catholic world and they questioned the general
direction of the government's policies as well.[15]

Fanfani became Premier after the 1958 elections, and there were
reasons to believe that in this capacity he intended to increase the
government's intervention in economic affairs and to reduce private
economic privilege. This prospect appeared threatening not only to
the Italian bishops but even more to the Italian business world,
which also was losing control over the Christian Democratic Party.
Industrial leaders, in particular, feared a strengthening of the de-
tested publicly owned oil firm, National Hydrocarbons Trust, and
of the publicly owned giant holding company, the Institute for Industrial Reconstruction. They also feared the plans for establishing
party units in factories, as advocated by one of Fanfani's allies, Giulio Pastore, the leader of the Catholic trade union organization, the
Italian Confederation of Free Unions, and minister in charge of
the Cassa per il Mezzogiorno in the Fanfani government.

It is difficult to say how successful Fanfani might have been in his
plans if his only opposition had been the Italian industrialists and

14. The most significant and best documented aspect of John XXIII's policy was the
calling of the second Vatican Council. See X. Rynne, *Letters from Vatican City* (New
York, Farrar, Straus & Giroux, 1963). (X. Rynne is a pseudonym, probably concealing
one or more American Jesuits.)
15. See H. S. Hughes, *The United States and Italy,* rev. ed., Chap. 9.

the Italian bishops, led by the redoubtable Cardinal Siri, the Archbishop of Genoa. But resistance also grew within the party among leaders who had previously been associated with Fanfani in Iniziativa Democratica and had formed the party majority.

Until 1958 Fanfani had been able to get the support of all members of Iniziativa Democratica, largely because he had underplayed the Dossettian inheritance and had represented himself as the heir of the moderate policy of De Gasperi's center. He had never clearly disclosed the direction of his policies, and the wide following he had gained was thus based largely on ambiguous plans and on the benefits all those identified with him thought to gain from his energetic, capable leadership.

After the elections of 1958, however, as Fanfani seemed to follow De Gasperi's moderate policies less and less and to become increasingly a proponent of a technocratic variant of Dossetti's design for social and economic reform, criticisms arose even in the ranks of his own collaborators and followers. The most faithful of these collaborators (Colombo, Taviani, Rumor, Gui) were not opposed to the strengthening of the party, to an increase in its autonomy with respect to the Catholic world, or to an extension of political power into the economic field. But they wished to see these programs carried out with caution and moderation and by means of compromises rather than head-on collisions with groups who might feel their interests threatened. This is the basic reason for the conflict that arose between Fanfani and his youngest, or "third generation" followers— among them Arnaldo Forlani, Franco Maria Malfatti, and Luciano Radi—on the one hand, and the "second generation," on the other, a conflict that was to lead most of the latter to split off from Iniziativa Democratica and form the so-called *"dorotei"* center group.

In short, Fanfani had maintained his leadership of the Christian Democrats, carried out his plans for strengthening the party, and attained the direction of the government, because it had been assumed by his collaborators and allies that support, not hostility, would be forthcoming from the Catholic and the business worlds. But when a clash with these two groups developed, the organization faltered, and some of its former supporters broke with Fanfani, who then withdrew from the government and resigned as party secretary. Aldo Moro was elected to fill his party post in March 1959. His election was confirmed by a narrow majority (thanks to the alliance of the *dorotei* with the right) at the party congress in Florence in October 1959.

The Moro Regime

The unity of command within the Christian Democratic Party
that Fanfani had been able to maintain as party secretary, Premier,
and Foreign Minister was broken by a compromise by which Segni
(a party leader of the older generation, and a promoter of agrarian reform) became Premier and Moro party secretary, a post which he
held until 1962.[16]

Moro as party secretary faced the task of attempting to bring the
warring party factions under organizational control. At the party
congresses in 1959 and 1961 he stressed the need for ideological reform within the party and restructuring of the party organization to
make it more representative and more responsive to its constituency.
On both these counts, however, his efforts were halfhearted and not
very sucessful. He emphasized the importance of the party—rather
than of Parliament—as the policymaking body.

Moro managed to strengthen the alliance with the Socialists—the
"opening to the left"—of which Fanfani had, to some extent, been
the architect. Although the Socialists had abrogated their postwar alliance with the Communists in February 1957, the major shift in
Italian politics that this move had heralded was not formalized until
1962, when the Socialist Party supported in Parliament (but without participation in the Cabinet) the government coalition of Christian Democrats, Social Democrats (PSDI), and Republicans
(PRI).[17] This move had already been preceded by the formation of
center-left governments in a number of central and northern Italian
cities in the spring of 1961, despite Cardinal Siri's warning to Moro
against such coalitions.

While strengthening the center-left coalition, Moro attempted
also to maintain the party's moderate image and thus protect it from
attack by the Church hierarchy and conservative political groups led
by the Liberals.

Though the Christian Democratic Party itself was torn with internal factional struggles and harassed by external attacks, the overall
effect of the Moro leadership during the early 1960s was to reinforce

16. Moro served as Premier from December 1963 to June 1968, a period not covered
by the present study.

17. The Socialists entered the Cabinet in 1964, when Pietro Nenni accepted the post
of Vice-premier in the coalition government headed by Moro. Other Socialists accepted
ministerial portfolios.

the center-left coalition and give it a certain amount of stability. Perhaps the most important result was that the Communist Party was confronted with a new situation which was to have important bearing on its later evolution.

The Communist Party's First Postwar Phase

After 1945 the Italian Communist Party was a "new type of party," according to Togliatti's definition: [18]

The new party is a party of the working class and the people which does not limit itself only to criticism and to propaganda, but which positively and constructively intervenes in the life of the country. The working class has abandoned the position of single-minded opposition and criticism which it has held in the past, and today it intends to assume, along with the other democratic forces, a position of leadership. The new party is the party which, through its policy and its activity, is able to put into action this new position of the working class, and which, to this end, transforms its organization.[19]

While in opposition to the capitalist system, the party continued to function within it by virtue of its popular strength in the nation and in parliament. This dualism was emphasized in 1945–47, when the Communist Party presented itself to the masses both as a partner of the Christian Democrats in government and as a potential alternative to that party and to bourgeois power. After the 1948 electoral defeat, Togliatti wrote:

It is a serious error to think that a program of profound social reform could only be realized by means of the government's action. Small democratic and socialist minorities have, in the past, pushed through important reforms under reactionary governments. We want social reform because liberating the nation from its backwardness and facilitating the progress of the working masses would create the best conditions for our policy.[20]

The goal, then, was a party which, thanks to its organized presence in the country and in local governments and parliament, could

18. The organizational features of this new type of party are discussed at length in F. Cervellati Cantelli and others, *L'organnizzazione partitica del PCI e della DC*, pp. 31 ff.
19. "Che Cosa è Il Partito Nuovo," *Rinascita*, August–September 1944, p. 2.
20. *Rinascita*, April–May 1948, p. 4.

exercise leadership and push through reforms even though it represented the opposition. To this end the pre-1945 structure of the party was transformed from a small party of cadres into a great mass party. The first postwar congress thanked Togliatti "for having brought the party . . . to that imposing numerical strength which makes it a decisive factor in the national life."

But this "imposing numerical strength" was a consequence of the immediate postwar situation; it was still necessary to consolidate it and to make it permanent. This task was given to Pietro Secchia, together with Togliatti and Luigi Longo, a member of the secretariat responsible for organization since 1946, and vice-secretary of the party since 1948. It was to Longo's ability and zeal that the party owed the fine organizational network that by the early 1950s was becoming established throughout the country.

The political significance of this organizational drive was subject to two different interpretations. While the top party leadership stressed "the new party," a concept compatible with the acceptance of the democratic framework, a good part of the rank and file and of the intermediate leaders believed this powerful organization was meant to prepare the "second wave," that is, a Communist bid for power through revolutionary means.

It is impossible to review all of the evidence of the existence of this belief. As late as 1956 Togliatti repeatedly acknowledged and criticized the "duplicity" of the intermediate leaders of the party in interpreting the legalistic reformist strategy as a mere covering tactic for the true strategy of preparing for the revolution. Probably those most guilty of such "duplicity" were the most active Communists, the former partisans, the workers' cadres, who throughout this early phase patiently dedicated themselves to recruiting members for the party and its supporting organizations. They went from house to house collecting party dues and distributing Communist publications and during the electoral campaigns soliciting votes for the party. These workers were often motivated by the hope that once the party had gained a strong mass following, it would undertake the conquest of power.

The electoral defeat of April 18, 1948, and the obvious unwillingness of the leaders to engage in serious mass action in July (when a nearly successful attempt on Togliatti's life set off a general strike and local subversive activity) reduced the hopes for an imminent "second wave." With the beginning of the 1950s the concept of the "new party" had also tarnished, as it became increasingly clear that the party did not in fact "lead." Instead it reacted to the initiatives of the party in control of the government, while the industrialists and landowners, having overcome their fears of the immediate postwar years, were now reasserting the privileges they derived from control of the factories and the countryside.

The growing disillusionment within the party was to a great extent offset by the holding power of the socialist tradition, the organizational efficiency of the Italian Communists, the prestige of the Soviet Union, and in some areas, by the sense of belonging to an integrated community. These influences helped to keep the party strong and unified, but participation in party life could no longer be stimulated by the prospect of an imminent revolution. Rather, revolution became associated with the expectation of a future triumph of the Soviet Union over the West, and thus became largely independent of the action of individuals and even of the initiatives of the Italian Communist Party itself.

Hundreds of party pronouncements demonstrate this. A statement by Valdo Magnani, the secretary of the Reggio Emilia Federation, to the 1951 federal congress is representative:

> . . . The leadership takes on the character of a petty boss system, and the internal party life goes on between the two poles of mass enthusiasm and of intimidation of individual members. There is an opinion rather diffuse among our comrades according to which only war will assure the progress of the revolution, and we should say that this opinion is fairly well tolerated in our party. But we are not here to make predictions about the "great day of victory," as our comrades say. How and when that will come no one can honestly say. We are here to discuss the function of our party in the national community of today.[21]

This is an accurate portrait of the Stalinist-oriented Italian party of 1948–51; its organization could function as a "petty boss system" with the "intimidation of individual members," because in the

21. Valdo Magnani used to be called "Togliattino" (little Togliatti), because of his manner of speech and his remarkable intellectual gifts. He left the party in 1951 and for some time headed a small, strongly anticommunist political movement from which he dissociated himself after a few years. In 1962, however, he again joined the Italian Communist Party and immediately regained a position of leadership. This unique venture gives a feeling of the complexity of the political experience of the man whose words are reported here.

collective ceremonies there was "mass enthusiasm," and in the daily life of the members hope for the "great day of victory."

Second Phase of Communist Party Organization

From 1951 until 1955 the party's organizational and propaganda machinery functioned more from inertia than because of any clear commitment to an immediate task. The number of members and cells grew under the continued momentum of past exertions. Signatures were collected in peace drives, and the local election campaigns of 1951 and 1952 and the general election campaign of 1953 represented fairly precise goals. The Stalinist line became less important because the party's organizational machinery had become an end in itself, oriented toward distant and uncertain political goals. The crisis became evident during the winter of 1953–54 with the first beginnings of de-Stalinization—the purging of Beria and the establishment of collective leadership in the USSR.

While Fanfani was trying to make the Christian Democrats aware of the importance of organization, the limitations of party organization were becoming increasingly evident in the Communist Party. Secchia, who had put the Communist Party machinery on its feet, was the first to realize that it was running idle for lack of political targets. Some of his collaborators on the national organization commission shared his conviction and attempted to do something about it. In the summer of 1954, while plans were being made for the fourth national organizational conference, they circulated a "Letter to the Comrades of Communist Action" which criticized the party for, among other things, having become a machine for the collection of membership cards, dues stamps, and signatures, a party without any political prospects.

Secchia was held indirectly responsible for this "provocation" and was removed from the secretariat. But a serious organizational crisis was already underway: the factory cells had lost their vigor; the Communist-controlled unions were doing poorly in the factory elections; and the number of members and territorial cells had begun to decline.

Third Phase of Communist Organization

In 1959, as the Christian Democratic Party was slowing down its organizational drive but still maintaining close connections with public firms, the Communist Party was coming out of its 1951–56 crisis. The most damaging element of the crisis had been the refusal of the party leadership to establish a new relationship with the intermediate cadres and the rank and file, although they were aware of the failures and limitations of the line pursued so far.

In 1956 the whole international communist movement had been involved in the repercussions of the Hungarian rebellion, and this forced the Italian leaders to face the crisis in their own party.[22] The slogan of the eighth congress in 1956 expressed dedication not only to the strengthening of the party but to its rejuvenation.

The rejuvenation of the party consisted mainly of removing some of the old Stalinist elements and curbing the petty bossism and the intimidation of the individual members, by setting up a somewhat more liberal framework in the Khrushchev style. Just as the secretary of the Soviet party had continued the de-Stalinization program after the bloody Hungarian revolution, so the leaders of the Italian Communist Party, after their invectives against the "shadowy figures" and the "defectors" of 1956, now permitted criticism of the party. Members had formerly been expelled from the party for what they thought or for what the leaders thought they thought. But now members could withdraw from the party; one was no longer liable to expulsion for his thoughts, but only for his actions—that is, for acts that might endanger the formal unanimity of "democratic centralism."

In spite of the internal crisis, the Communist Party was able to hold its ground in Italian politics between 1956 and 1962 for a number of reasons. In the first place, the main anticommunist forces —Catholics and the business interests—and the party's two most important political rivals—the Christian Democrats and the Socialists— were too busy with their own internal factional struggles to take advantage of the Communist reverses. Second, the public image of the Soviet Union under Khrushchev's leadership was improving. Third, the Communist leaders were willing and able to effect significant changes within the party itself.

Thanks to these circumstances, although the circle of its supporters was reduced, the Communist Party was able to maintain its close

22. As discussed in a selection of documents compiled by the Russian Institute of Columbia University, *The Anti-Stalin Campaign and International Communism* (New York, Columbia University Press, 1956), which contains also a translation of important statements on the significance of the Twentieth Congress of the Communist Party of the Soviet Union, made by Togliatti during an interview.

contacts with Italian society and through these contacts to increase its voting support. It behaved with sufficient elasticity to face the challenge of a time of rapid and extensive social change.

ORGANIZATIONAL STRUCTURE OF THE TWO PARTIES [23]

These two leading Italian political parties are structurally more different than they are alike. They have certain features in common, however, and these similarities have increased since 1945. Even in 1945 the two parties shared certain characteristics. Both were direct membership parties whose members held individual membership cards, [24] and both were mass parties that counted their members in the millions. At the beginning of 1946 the membership of the two parties combined was about 2.5 million, of whom 1.8 million belonged to the Communist Party. As with the figures on voter turnout, however, some caution must be used in interpreting these figures. They do not necessarily indicate a high degree of political participation. The 1946 membership figure of four million for all Italian parties was to some extent the effect of twenty years of compulsory mass participation in party organizations under fascism.

Before 1922 membership in Italian political parties was rather low. The Socialist Party, the first modern party in Italy, had a membership in the tens of thousands at the end of World War I. By 1921, after the Communist Party had split away from it, the Socialist Party membership reached 216,000. But in the spring of 1943, on the eve of the regime's crisis, the Fascist Party had 4.5 million members, 10 percent of the entire Italian population. These figures indicate that the idea of party membership as a natural part of civic life began to be accepted with fascism, and remained a component of the political culture when the major antifascist parties became mass organizations.

Maurice Duverger has suggested the significance of this mass membership in terms of political commitment and of supporters:

Three concentric circles of participation can be distinguished. The widest comprises the electors who vote for the candidates put forward by the parties at local and national elections . . . The second circle is made up of supporters, a vague term for a vague

23. For a more detailed description and analysis see F. Cervellati Cantelli and others, *L'organizzazione partitica del PCI e della DC.*
24. On the significance of the question of direct or indirect party membership, see Maurice Duverger, *Political Parties* (London, Methuen, 1954), Part I.

concept corresponding nonetheless to a reality. . . . Finally the third, the inmost circle, is composed of the militants; they consider themselves to be members of the party, elements in the party community; they see to its organization and its operation; they direct its propaganda and its general activities . . . .

Whence therefore this refusal to enter the ranks of the party, this desire to remain outside the real party community when agreement with the party is acknowledged? . . . Sometimes the supporter is confronted by some material obstacle. . . . The supporter may refuse to become a member because he dislikes regimentation, because he refuses to give up his personal independence.[25]

Adopting this terminology, one might suggest that the objective of the campaigns carried on by the Christian Democrats and the Communists since 1945 has been the transformation into card-carrying members of those hundreds of thousands of individuals who in other historical or social contexts would have remained only supporters. The primary objective of the structural changes in the parties since 1945 and the diffusion of local party units throughout the nation has been to provide the parties with recruiting centers in all corners of Italian society.

The Communist Party, thanks to its cellular organization, has been more successful in recruiting than has the Christian Democratic Party. At the time of its greatest expansion the Communists had over 57,000 cells grouped in about 11,000 sections. The Christian Democratic Party, which does not have units as small as cells, had over 12,000 sections at its point of maximum expansion. The Communist Party's cellular structure assures it a greater growth, even though it lacks the reinforcing organizations that the Christian Democrats find in organized Catholicism. Conversely, the major cause of the organizational stagnation and decline of the Communists was the mid-1950 crisis in the cells, the most peripheral and the smallest of its recruiting offices.

Communist Party Structure

Figure 3-1 shows the organizational structure of the Communist Party. Since the 1920s the cell has been the basic organizational

25. Ibid., pp. 90 and 102–03.

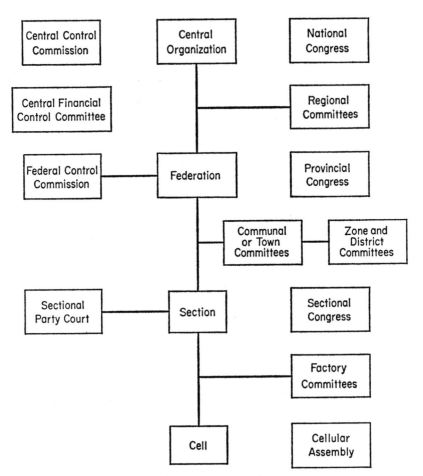

FIGURE 3-1. Organizational structure of the Communist Party.

unit.[26] A minimum of five members is necessary for the creation of a new cell. Throughout the period under study the Communist cells have been of two basic types: those organized in places of work and those organized geographically. In some periods there have also been youth cells (1947–49), and a party statute in 1962 provided for the creation of cells within many types of voluntary associations as well as in various professional groups.

TABLE 3-1. *Number of Communist Party cells, by type, 1945–63*

Year	Total	Geographical	Factory	Women's
1945	29,250	—	—	—
1946	35,637	—	—	—
1947	50,033	41,286	8,747	8,877
1948	52,235	43,135	9,100	9,581
1949	51,726	42,598	9,128	10,184
1950	52,418	41,209	11,272	12,226
1951	54,352	43,602	10,750	12,732
1952	55,598	44,333	11,265	13,065
1953	56,401	44,851	11,550	13,547
1954	56,934	45,439	11,495	14,043
1955	57,519	46,083	11,436	13,853
1956	56,044	45,312	10,732	13,169
1957	—	—	—	—
1958	—	—	—	—
1959	39,852	32,737	7,155	8,564
1960	41,100	34,818	6,282	8,680
1961	40,894	34,202	6,692	8,085
1962	37,994	32,077	5,917	5,701
1963	33,646	—	—	4,536

Until 1962 there were separate cells for women, but the statute passed in 1962 provided that the cells be mixed, except in unusual circumstances. In the mid-1950s, at the height of the party's expansion, women's cells accounted for about 25 percent of the total, while in 1963 they represented only about 13 percent. (Table 3-1) Cells associated with places of work had for a long time a preferential status as the "normal form of party organization." In 1956, however, they lost this status. The two types of cells—geographical and factory—were given equal importance, a decision long overdue, since the geographical cell had always been numerically dominant.

By the mid-1950s the Communist Party had as many geographical

26. For a discussion of the significance of this type of organizational unit, see P. Selznick, *The Organizational Weapon* (New York, McGraw-Hill, 1952), passim.

cells as there were voting precincts, but not necessarily a cell in each precinct. Most of these cells did not have permanent premises, which limited their effectiveness in recruitment and propaganda. Cell meetings were held in rooms loaned by cooperatives, unions, clubs, or party sections or in the homes of the members themselves.

Until the mid-1950s the number of cells and the number of members increased at about the same rate, except in 1947 and 1950, when an increase in the number of cells was accompanied by a small drop in membership. The average number of members in each cell fell from fifty-nine in 1945 to thirty-six in 1955 and 1956. After the 1957–58 crisis, however, the number began to rise again, finally reaching forty-nine in 1963.

Throughout the period under study the cell—a small, easily controlled group—represented the only place where party members met as members. At the cellular assembly cell officers and delegates to the section congress are chosen. Electors named by the cells elect both the section leaders and the delegates from the sections to the federation congress. This procedure is fundamental to the so-called "democratic centralism" of the party's internal organization.

The number of Communist cells declined markedly during the second half of the 1950s. The decline took place during a crisis brought about by the way the cells functioned. One of the essential functions of the cell is to hold an assembly in preparation for the national party congress. According to official party data, almost all cells (56,000 out of 56,044) held their assemblies in 1956. But in 1959 only 60 percent did so, and in 1962 only 13 percent. This falling off in the activity of the cells can be attributed to several factors, but the most important factor is the nature of the cells themselves. The members of the cell not only share a common organizational link, but they also belong to the same socioeconomic group. The smooth functioning of the cell is dependent on members who are motivated to participate, tasks to be performed, and a social environment within which it can operate.

The crisis in the cells in the late 1950s occurred because there were too many cells that did not meet these requirements. Absenteeism and a decline in active participation during that period indicated a decrease in the number of members "motivated to participate." Also, the party was having difficulty in setting goals for the cells that the rank and file were capable of achieving. The party's external activities, intensified during election campaigns, tended to include only generalized opposition tactics that had no precise objectives, while its internal action had come to be increasingly concerned with routine membership campaigns.

Finally, because of discrimination against Communist workers, factories had become less viable settings for the establishment and operation of cells. The increasing amount of leisure time spent away from the place of residence (due to the greater frequency of commuting and the spread of motor vehicles) also affected the vitality of geographical units.

In spite of these problems, the Communist cell generally fulfilled its function of creating a network of intimate links between the party and Italian society. The Communist Party itself recognized that a fairly large number of cells existed in name only and not as actual centers of organizational life, and that a functional decline had taken place in all of the cells. Still the existence of tens of thousands of cells, and the feeling of belonging and of having a concrete job to do that these cells gave to hundreds of thousands of Communists greatly helped to maintain the active interest and support of the party members.

This critical function was effectively performed during the late 1940s and the early 1950s, when the Communist Party was first establishing permanent roots in Italian society. Later this network became less vital, as the sections began to take over the tasks of socialization and of activating and guiding the rank and file.

The section, which is composed of a group of cells within a specified area, "should have permanent premises which represent a meeting place and the center of Communist activity and of the political, cultural, educational, recreational, and welfare activities of all of the workers in the area" (as stated in Article II of the by-laws adopted at the tenth party congress in 1963). The activity of the section, as well as of the cell, is mainly oriented toward electoral goals. This was made clear in 1946 at the fifth party congress:

> In the next general and local elections we must be able to present our candidates in every Italian commune. . . . In order to do this it is absolutely essential to create and set into motion, at the earliest possible moment, Communist sections in every commune. . . . We advise you to construct the organizational network as much as possible on the basis of electoral districts . . . so that every cell, every section, of the party will have the task of working

on voters of the electoral districts corresponding to their own territories.[27]

During the first half of the 1950s, when there were still many areas where cells did not exist, the section often became the basic unit of the party. Of the 9,936 sections in 1950 more than 44 percent were not divided into cells. A third of the 11,147 sections in 1954 were not so divided. Thus, even during the period of the party's maximum expansion, a third of the sections were the basic units of membership. The goal of having a section in every commune was only partially realized. The number of sections has varied during the 1950s, when at least 1,500 of the 8,000 communes in Italy were without sections.

At the beginning of the 1960s, when the sections were progressively taking over the functions of the cells, less than two thirds of the more than 11,000 sections had regular premises, according to data supplied by the party:

	Percent	
	1960	*1961*
Sections with permanent premises	7.8	8.0
Sections occupying premises in common with some union, cooperative, or other mass organization	18.2	15.0
Sections renting premises	38.0	34.0
Sections without regular premises	35.8	42.0

The number of Communist sections and their distribution in selected years, 1950 to 1961, are shown in Table 3-2. Sections of from 20 to 99 members were the most numerous. The next most numerous were sections of from 100 to 449 members.

TABLE 3-2. *Membership in Communist Party sections, 1950–61*

Number and size of sections	1950	1954	1956	1960	1961
Number of sections	9,938	11,148	11,262	11,076	11,140
Less than 20 members per section	1,163	1,579	1,854	1,996	2,105
20–99	4,071	4,350	4,349	4,254	4,296
100–499	3,636	4,135	4,038	4,002	3,973
500–999	739	801	779	674	648
1,000 and over	329	283	242	150	118

27. *La politica dei comunisti dal V and VI Congresso: Risoluzioni e Documenti* (Rome, La Stampa Moderna, no date), p. 51.

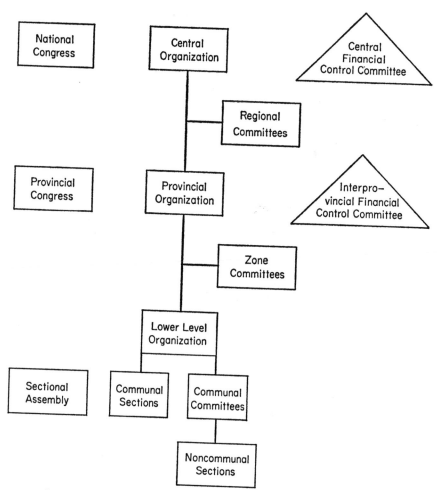

Figure 3-2. Organizational structure of the Christian Democratic Party.

Christian Democratic Sections

In the Christian Democratic Party the section is the lowest unit of organization. (Figure 3-2) There are two types of sections: communal, with a territorial jurisdiction of one commune and minimum of twelve members, and noncommunal, set up in electoral precincts or districts that have particular requirements, with a minimum of twenty-five members. For the Christian Democrats as for the Communists the electoral function of the section is the essential one.

This function was considered so important that during Fanfani's leadership of the party in 1954–58 the Christian Democratic Party attempted to create units in precincts and factories below the section level, equivalent to and partly modeled after the Communist cells. This attempt to create more intimate links between the Christian Democratic Party and Italian society was abandoned, however, and the section again became the basic organizational unit of the party. The section is headed by a board of directors, the members of which are elected by the general assembly of section members, as are the delegates to the provincial congresses. Each board of directors has a permanent secretary. The number and geographical distribution of Christian Democratic sections in 1959–62 are shown in Table 3-3.

Intermediate Party Organizations

One step above the sections are the intermediate party organizations—for the Communists, the federation; for the Christian Democrats, the provincial committee. (Figures 3-1 and 3-2) They have generally as their territorial base one of the ninety-two Italian provinces.

In the Communist Party organization a single province may be the seat of two federations, for particular geographical or organizational reasons. In 1961 there were 114 such federations; in 1962 there were 113. While cells and sections are organized and staffed by volunteers who dedicate their leisure time to this activity, the intermediate organizations generally have full-time paid staffs. The Communist federation secretaries usually have no occupational commitments other than political ones, while the intermediate leaders of

TABLE 3-3. Distribution of Christian Democratic Party sections, 1959–62, by geographical area

Year	North		Center		South		Islands		Total	
	Number	Percent	Number	Percent	Number	Percent	Number	Percent	Number	Percent
1959	6,217	53.9	1,700	14.6	2,509	21.7	1,119	9.8	11,545 [a]	100.0
1960	6,140	51.0	2,361	19.5	2,469	20.4	1,102	9.1	12,072	100.0
1961	6,266	51.9	2,375	18.4	2,498	20.4	1,131	9.3	12,270	100.0
1962	6,246	53.0	2,252	19.1	2,172	18.5	1,109	9.4	11,779	100.0

a. This figure and the figure shown for number of sections in Table 4-4 differ because of inconsistencies in the figures in party sources used.

the Christian Democrats are apt to have extrapolitical careers as well. In both parties, however, the difference between the leadership at the section and the intermediate levels is rather marked. The member who is a leader at the section level is a citizen who is also active in politics; while the member who is a leader at a higher level is, or tends to become, a citizen whose professional commitments are almost exclusively political.

The organization of the intermediate organs of the two parties is quite similar. The Communist federation has a federal control commission, a board of directors (called the executive until 1956), a secretary, a secretariat, and various commissions. The provincial committee of the Christian Democratic Party includes an executive board, a provincial secretary, and provincial offices and commissions.

The federal and provincial committees, elected by federal and provincial congresses, are large bodies whose official function is to direct the intermediate organizations. The Christian Democratic provincial committees vary in size from fifty-one members in provinces of over two million inhabitants to thirty in provinces of less than one million. The Communist Party statutes do not regulate the size of the federal committees: in 1956 there were 3,563 members in the 99 federal committees, an average of 37 members to each committee; but some committees had as many as 70 members. Because these federal committees may be so large, there is usually a board of directors restricted to eight to ten members. The Christian Democratic statutes expressly provide for a provincial board of seven to eleven members. These boards meet periodically, one of their tasks being to appoint the members of the federal or provincial secretariat and the secretary who directs them.

The permanent officeholders are the real leaders of the intermediate organizations. They have the task of coordinating party activities, including the designation of the candidates who will appear on the party tickets, in the territories under their jurisdiction. In this way they exercise their influence on the national government and on local governments. This power is limited, however, by the fact that the national leadership must be in agreement with their selection of candidates, at least in the more important posts. In size and number of personnel the provincial headquarters bear a resemblance to important public agencies. They bear very little physical resemblance to the premises occupied by the sections, which are apt to have the air of clubs or meeting rooms.

The Central Party Organizations

The National Council of the Christian Democratic Party and the Central Committee of the Communist Party are structurally very similar. Both are elected by party congresses and represent the supreme power of the party between the annual congresses. They appoint the party directorate and secretariat, which is a permanent organ built around the figure of the party secretary.

The Central Committee of the Communist Party has been steadily increasing in size. From 57 members in 1946–47, it rose to 98 in 1966–69, and had 140 at the tenth party congress in 1962. The membership of the directorate, on the other hand, has remained about the same, with nineteen members in 1962. According to the party statutes, the Central Committee is to meet once every two months; but in fact before 1956 it rarely met more than three times a year. After 1956 it usually met four to five times annually. The secretariat, which in practice is the true executive organ of the Communists and forms the core of the directorate, meets about twice a month. From 1954 until the end of the period under study it had seven members.

The Central Committee's tasks are generally limited to consultation and the ratification of decisions taken at other levels. This can be seen from the following table, which classifies all important policy statements issued by the party between 1955 and 1959 by the party units making them:

	1955–56	*1957*	*1958*	*1959*	*Total*
Central Committee	17	12	8	2	39
Directorate	31	16	26	16	89
Secretariat	28	7	7	5	47
Total	76	35	41	23	195

The National Council of the Christian Democratic Party is also elected by the national party congress, but its members are selected with a view to ensuring the representation of specific categories of members, such as: members of parliament; a nonparliamentary representative for every region; mayors; presidents of provincial administrations; delegates from the women's movement, the youth move-

ment, the factory groups, the veterans' groups, and recreation organizations; all members who have served as political secretaries, presidents of the council, or the editor of the party daily. The National
Council had 165 members in 1962, compared with 61 in 1946 (the
first congress). The directorate, however, has remained stable with
between fifteen and twenty members.

According to statute, the National Council is to meet at least four
times a year. Between 1945 and 1961 there were, in fact, sixty-four
meetings, an average of four annually. During the same period the
directorate met 344 times, an average of 21 meetings annually.
These figures are similar to those for the Communist Party Central
Committee and secretariat. According to the Christian Democratic
Party statute the National Council must meet under two special circumstances: within twenty days of the formation of a new government, in order to review the work of the directorate and the parliamentary groups; and within fifteen days of the proclamation of the
results of the general elections, in order to review the new parliamentary balance of forces.

The direction of both parties is actually in the hands of the secretariat. But the Christian Democratic secretariat is somewhat less stable than the Communist secretariat. In the period under examination the Communists had only one secretary-general (Togliatti) and
only two vice-secretaries (Longo, for the entire period, and Secchia
between 1948 and 1954), while the Christian Democrats had seven
secretaries and twelve vice-secretaries.

The Coordinating Structures

Certain organized bodies or committees at various levels in each
party have no directive functions. Their members are generally
party officials or public officeholders, whose influence on the functioning of the party organization is limited. In the Communist Party
these units are factory committees, communal or town committees,
sectional and regional committees. In the Christian Democratic
Party they are the same, with the exception of the factory and sectional committees. The most important of these are the communal
committees (called town committees in cities of over 50,000 inhabitants) and the regional committees, set up where regional governments have been established. They are important because of their
power to influence the selection of party candidates for public office,

and may sometimes possess, in addition to their coordinating functions, some political influence.

Control Structures

The function of certain control organs is to protect the statutory rights of individual members and the organizational units, and to serve as judicial bodies that deliberate on members' violations of party statutes. In the Christian Democratic Party this mechanism is rather simple, for "party courts" exist only at the provincial and national levels. It is more complicated in the Communist Party, where there are sectional courts, control commissions at the federal and central levels, and the central financial control committee. The Communist sectional and federal organs were created in 1956, when a discussion of "socialist legality" was going on in the party. They were intended to increase the statutory rights of the members, who that year were given the right to withdraw from the party. Prior to that time the only way to leave the party was to be expelled from it.

But even with the new norms the possibility of an effective "watchdog" commission is limited by several factors: repeated warnings from above that controlling organs ought to collaborate with the political organs in fostering unity in the party; the participation of control bodies in certain deliberations and decisions of the directive organs; and overlapping officials of the control and directive groups. For example, the president of the Communist federal control commission is also a member of the federal committee; while the chairman of the central control commission is a member of the party directorate.

Party Assemblies

The differences between the two parties are most marked in the assemblies. Here the authoritarian nature of Communist "democratic centralism" can be seen most clearly, while the Christian Democratic Party is revealed as a pluralistic party of organized factions.

In the Communist Party the cell is the assembly in which all party members have the right to participate. Delegates to the sectional and national congresses are elected at these assemblies. The functions of the assemblies and congresses are to discuss the activity of the directive organs, to debate the agenda, and to elect members of the directive organs and delegates to higher assemblies. The third function is in reality a ceremonial one, for in fact the assembly merely sanctions the choices made by an electoral commission.

The Central Committee determines the topics the assemblies will discuss and prepares a document around which the discussion is to be oriented. In fact, most of the preparation is carried out by the directorate and especially by the federation secretary.

Until 1956 the cellular and sectional meetings were viewed primarily as a means of contact between the party and the public, through such devices as arranging dances and lotteries. The national and federal congresses of 1956, however, which took place after the Twentieth Congress of the Communist Party of the Soviet Union and the Hungarian revolts, were more in the nature of a debate and internal discussion. But this atmosphere became less marked in the two successive congresses.

Procedures at Communist Congresses

The typical program of a federal or national Communist congress, which has remained unchanged throughout the period covered by this study, begins with invitations to distinguished party members to participate in presiding over the proceedings. The opening meeting starts with a report by the secretary (of the federation or party), which takes up a great part of the first day. Federation congresses meet for two or three days and national congresses for five or six. Then the work goes on in the assembly and in committees, which include policy, organization, and electoral committees and a committee for the modification of the party statutes.

The following tabulation indicates the extent of delegate participation in the Communist Party's national congresses in the 1950s and the early 1960s.

In general about 5 percent of the delegates speak at these national congresses. However, an exceptionally large number spoke at the 1956 assembly, which followed the twentieth Soviet party congress and the Hungarian revolt. But even at this congress the only two speeches that were openly critical of the party's policies were those of Antonio Giolitti, who left the party the following year, and Valerio Bertini, a rank-and-file delegate.

In the 113 federal congresses held by the Italian party before

Communist national congress	Number of delegates present	Delegates speaking Number	Percent
1951	750	44	5.5
1955 *	1,142	49	4.0
1956	1,054	80	8.0
1960	934	48	5.0
1962	874	50	5.0

* Fourth organizational congress.

1960, the vote for candidates for office was public in 69 and private in 44. Innovations made in 1956 did not materially alter the assembly's usual voting procedure of approving a list of candidates previously drawn up by the electoral commission. Before 1956 the list prepared by the commission was considered final. In 1956 the rule was changed to permit delegates to add or withdraw names. But even though the delegates were given this opportunity in 1956, no use has been made of it in any subsequent federal congress.

The extent to which the outcome of the elections is predetermined can be judged by comparing the lowest number of votes going to an elected candidate with the highest number of votes going to a nonelected candidate. In the absence of pressure on the delegates to vote for particular candidates these numbers would presumably be fairly close together, rather than very far apart, as in the 1956, 1960, and 1962 congresses:

	Number of votes received		
Communist national congress	Maximum by any candidate	Minimum by any elected candidate	Maximum by a nonelected candidate
1956	1,029	884	25
1960	913	809	—
1962	837	654	7

The Communist assemblies have a strong ceremonial component. The assembly's function is to build morale and to strengthen the sense of belonging to a great movement. This function, which was primary in the first congresses, is still quite important. The preparatory work provides an occasion to transmit themes and directives to lower levels of the party. The assembly merely echoes these themes and directives, thus making it appear that they have originated from the party ranks. Reports and debates are oriented to sanctioning the policy decisions already made. Even the electoral mechanism ensures that the party leaders chosen in higher circles will be elected. The decisions made at higher levels are not offered to the assemblies as debatable, but as directives that they are to approve. This is a fundamental difference between the Communist Party and the other Italian parties.

Procedures at Christian Democratic Congresses

The lowest unit of participation in the Christian Democratic Party is the section assembly—the only meeting in which every party member may participate. Provincial and national congresses are the intermediate and the highest levels of party participation. Their function is to set the general outlines of party policy and, more important, to elect the members of the directive organs.

The short duration of the assemblies, the discussion themes that are submitted to them from above, the fact that some national congresses have closed without even holding a vote on motions—these are indications that a political orientation is arrived at mainly through the selection of the top leaders. The overriding importance of the assemblies' electoral functions is also confirmed by the existence of an enormous body of regulations governing the electoral mechanism. These statutes and regulations control in a precise—indeed pedantic—way the manner in which the elections are carried out.

The most important debates on internal party affairs have centered around the electoral system, particularly the struggles between a majority of the party members who favored the majority system and a minority who favored the proportional system. In fact, for the entire period under examination the internal electoral system of the Christian Democratic Party was based on three elements: a limited number of lists of candidates; a majority electoral system that gave to the list receiving the greatest number of votes a large majority in the directive and executive bodies (for example, until the sixth congress in 1956 the majority received four fifths of the seats in the National Council; after the sixth congress this majority was reduced to two thirds); a second ballot or runoff election (*panachage*) in which electors could combine names on different lists.

Although this system leads to underrepresentation of minorities, its use was based on the argument that adoption of the proportional system would not only allow but encourage the formation of organized factions, which are forbidden by the party statutes, and that this would lead to a decrease in the efficiency of the various directorates.

A proposal to adopt the proportional system was rejected at the fifth party congress in 1954 by a close vote of 594,300 to 543,000, and at the sixth congress in 1956 by a vote of 895,100 to 412,100. The proposal was made again at the two successive party congresses, but did not come to a vote. (In 1964, after the conclusion of the present study, the proportional system was finally adopted.)

The use of the majority electoral system has had a decisive influence on the composition of the directive bodies. The *panachage,* or runoff voting system, in turn had the effect of softening the party's internal divisions by restricting the control from above over the actual selection of party leaders.

Organizational Differences Between the Two Parties

But whether the electoral system is based on the majority or the proportional principle, it is the presentation of a number of lists of candidates that constitutes the important difference between the Christian Democratic and Communist parties and makes their assemblies profoundly different. At the Christian Democratic assemblies, although delegates cannot discuss adequately the general orientation of the party, they can influence the party's course of action by voting for party leaders whose programs they approve. Unfortunately, alternative courses of action are not always made clear to the assemblies, especially the sectional assemblies. This is particularly true when only two alternatives are offered and the party factions are more numerous. But despite these limitations on the delegates' freedom of choice, the Christian Democratic assemblies have a much less ceremonial character than Communist Party assemblies. What is said at the Christian Democratic assemblies has some bearing on decisions. A national congress of the Christian Democratic Party presents the outside observer with the image not of a united party, as does a Communist congress, but of one that is divided, often rather markedly. It is often characterized by a sequence of speakers who present divergent views in aggressive or violent language. This picture is strikingly different from that of a Communist national congress, where discussions of differences that may exist are characterized by subtle exchanges that at first appear to be much alike.

This analysis of the organizational structures of the two parties indicates that they were as markedly dissimilar in 1962 as in 1945, even though their development throughout this period brought them closer together in many ways. The analysis further indicates that although the vitality of the Communist Party cells seems to be declining, the party's organization brings it in intimate contact with the Italian environment; the Communist Party is autonomous while the Christian Democratic Party, despite its attempts to increase its autonomy, especially between 1954 and 1958, is but one of the many expressions of the Catholic world; the Communist Party is an authoritarian and centralized party whose organizational structure contributes to reducing internal divisions to a minimum; the Christian Democratic Party, on the other hand, is a pluralistic party whose organizational structure permits the expression of the internal tensions through organized factions; the capacity of the Communists to act as a unit toward the outside world is much greater than that of the Christian Democrats.

4

Party Rank and File and
Party Leaders

The organizational structures described in the preceding chapter enabled both the Christian Democrats and the Communists to take advantage of the Italian population's avid interest in politics in the years immediately following the war, and to keep their memberships at high levels after this mass interest had lost its initial strength. Both parties derive their strength from large supporter-member circles.

PARTY MEMBERSHIP

Membership figures for the two parties from 1945 through 1952, shown in Table 4-1, were supplied by the parties themselves, since no independent data on membership are available.[1] For different reasons, both parties may have somewhat exaggerated their membership figures. The desire of the Communist Party leadership to give the best possible image of the party's strength may have led to some inflation of its figures, while party factions within the Christian Democratic Party may have altered its membership records, in order to modify the balance of forces within the party. While it is impossible to judge the extent of these possible distortions, they are most likely to have occurred in the South. However, on the basis of conversations with party officials and with rank-and-file activists, the data appear to be reasonably reliable.

As the table shows, membership of the Christian Democrats in-

1. On membership in the Communist and Christian Democratic parties see F. Cervellati Cantelli, V. Cioni Polacchini, P. de Vito Piscicelli, S. Guarino Cappello, G. Poggi, G. Sani, G. Sivini, and A. Sivini Cavazzani, *L'organizzazione partitica del PCI e della DC* (Bologna, Società editrice il Mulino, 1968), pp. 319–473.

TABLE 4-1. *Christian Democratic and Italian Communist membership, Italian adult population, and average per capita income, 1945–62*

Year	National per capita income (lire) [a]	Population 21 years of age and over (thousands) [b]	Party membership			
			Christian Democratic		Communist	
			Total (thousands)	Percent of adult population	Total (thousands)	Percent of adult population
1945	—	—	537.6	—	1,370.9	—
1946	—	28,005.4	608.0	2.2	1,603.5	5.7
1947	—	—	800.4	—	1,817.2	—
1948	—	29,056.5	1,127.2	3.9	1,922.3	6.6
1949	—	—	762.9	—	2,027.3	—
1950	—	—	885.3	—	2,134.1	—
1951	159.8	30,224.4	920.1	3.0	2,097.8	6.9
1952	165.4	—	960.8	—	2,093.5	—
1953	182.2	—	1,146.7	—	2,134.3	—
1954	190.1	—	1,255.5	—	2,145.3	—
1955	205.9	31,642.9	1,189.3	3.8	2,090.0	6.6
1956	216.9	31,974.8	1,377.3	4.3	2,035.4	6.4
1957	231.3	32,356.8	1,295.0	4.0	1,825.2	5.6
1958	245.2	—	1,410.2	—	1,818.6	—
1959	256.6	—	1,602.7	—	1,787.3	—
1960	295.0	—	1,470.8	—	1,793.0	—
1961	319.2	33,615.1	1,447.6	4.3	1,728.6	5.1
1962	—	—	1,446.5	—	1,630.6	—

a. May be converted to dollars at the approximate rate of 602 lire to the dollar in the 1960s.
b. Based on number of membership cards issued by the national headquarters of the two parties.

creased steadily throughout most of the period 1946–62, while Communist Party membership remained fairly constant. From a low of 2.2 percent of the adult population included in its membership in 1946, the Christian Democratic Party increased its percentage of the adult population to about 4.3 in both 1956 and 1961. The Communist Party's percentages were higher in all three years: it had already organized about 5.7 percent of the adult population in 1946; its membership then rose to a peak for the period of 6.9 percent in 1951; and dropped back to 6.4 percent in 1956 and to 5.1 percent in 1961.

Although the Christian Democratic Party accounted for most of the marked increase in the total membership of the two parties from 1946 to 1962 as can be seen from the foregoing figures, it had fewer members than the Communist Party throughout the period. On the other hand, the Christian Democrats had much greater electoral strength, as shown in Figure 4-1 and Appendix E. The Communist Party was more successful in organizing the electorate, while the Christian Democratic Party did a better job of getting the vote of the large majority of the electorate that did not belong to either party.

The strength of these parties in 1946 and 1961, by geographical area, is compared in Table 4-2. In the North Communist Party

TABLE 4-2. *Organizational strength of the two parties, by geographical area,*[a] *1946 and 1961*

Party membership	North	Center	South	Islands	All of Italy
Communist					
Percentage distribution					
1946	41.4	41.4	12.5	4.8	100.0
1961	27.8	51.5	14.4	6.4	100.0
As percent of adult population					
1946	6.1	8.5	3.4	2.5	5.7
1961	3.6	9.5	3.5	3.0	5.1
Christian Democratic					
Percentage distribution					
1946	54.3	20.3	18.4	7.0	100.0
1961	29.8	23.8	29.8	16.6	100.0
As percent of adult population					
1946	3.0	1.6	1.7	1.4	2.2
1961	2.8	3.9	6.7	6.0	4.3

a. The regional classification in this table differs from the standard classification in the following respects: Emilia is classed with the Center and Sicily and Sardinia are not included with the South.

a. Christian Democratic Party membership as percent of adult population, 1951.

FIGURE 4-1 (a-h). Comparison of Communist and Christian Democratic membership strength and voting strength, early 1950s and 1960s. See key on page 120. *Source:* Appendix Tables E-1 and E-2.

b. Christian Democratic Party vote as percent of total vote, 1953.

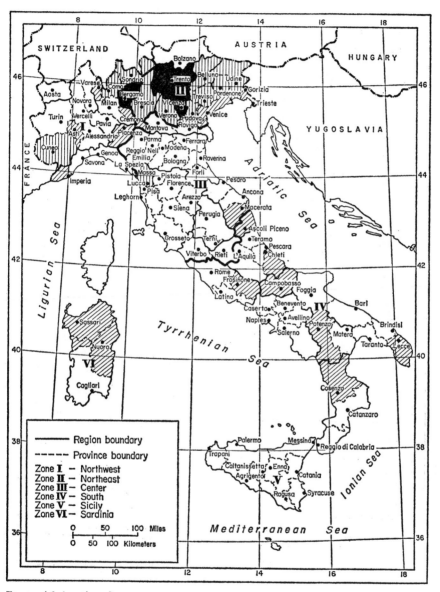

FIGURE 4-1 (continued).

c. Christian Democratic Party membership as percent of adult population, 1961.

FIGURE 4-1 (continued).

d. Christian Democratic Party vote as percent of total vote, 1963.

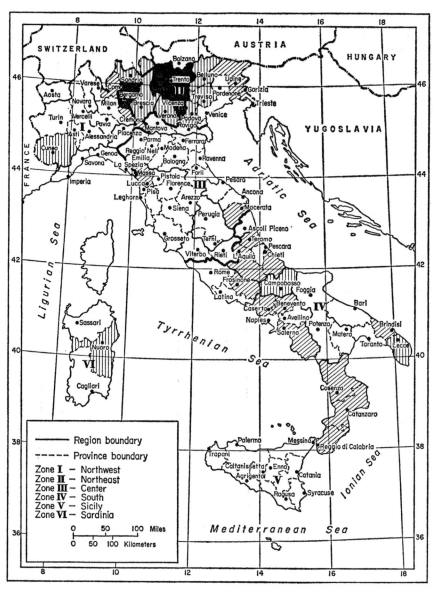

FIGURE 4-1 (continued).

e. Communist Party membership as percent of adult population, 1951.

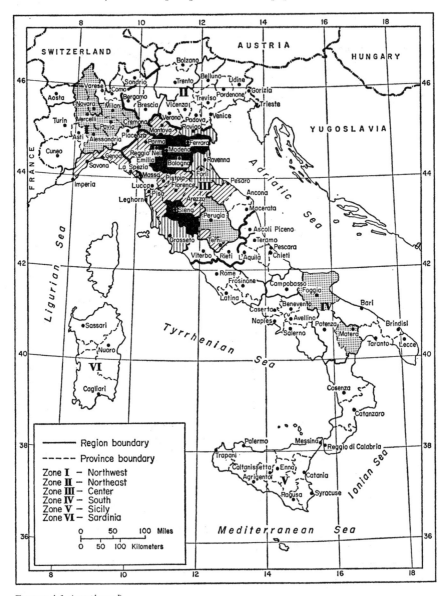

FIGURE 4-1 (continued).

f. Communist Party vote as percent of total vote, 1953.

FIGURE 4-1 (continued).

g. Communist Party membership as percent of adult population, 1961.

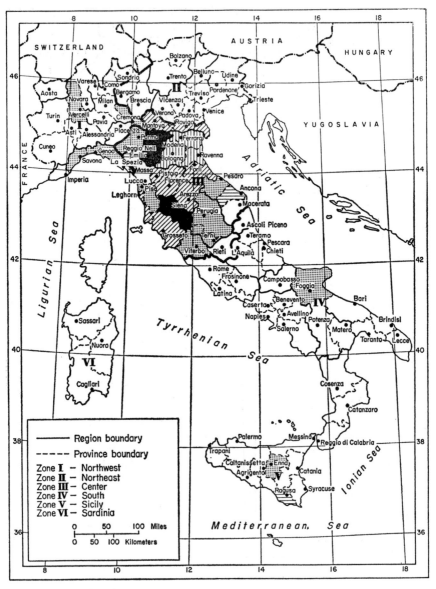

FIGURE 4-1 (continued).

h. Communist Party vote as percent of total vote, 1963.

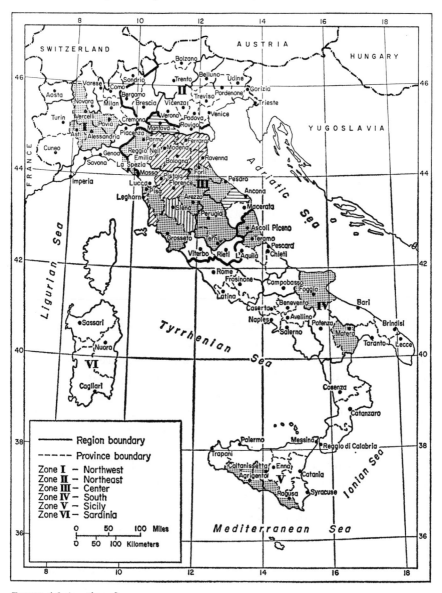

FIGURE 4-1 (continued).

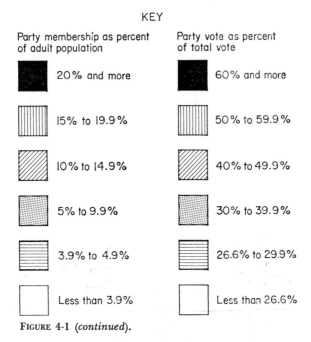

FIGURE 4-1 *(continued)*.

members continued to constitute a larger percentage of the adult population than did the Christian Democratic membership of that area, even though the Communist percentage declined sharply between 1946 and 1961, while the Christian Democratic share remained almost stable. At the same time the Communist Party continued to increase its hold in central Italy, where it had its greatest strength in 1961. It also gained some ground in Sicily and Sardinia. It should be pointed out that these comparisons of figures for the first and last year of a fifteen-year span conceal fluctuations that occurred in the intervening years. For instance, the Communist Party reached its maximum strength—in terms of the ratio of membership to adult population—in 1948 in the North and in 1953 in all other areas.

Membership growth in the Christian Democratic Party between 1946 and 1961 took place exclusively in areas south of the Po. The bulk of the increase was in the South and the Islands. The membership figures for the southern section of the party, particularly, may be inflated, as exaggerated membership claims have been a favorite weapon in the factional intraparty struggles in that part of the country.

The success of the Christian Democratic organizational drive in the central region was confined almost entirely to Rome and nearby provinces. Both here and in the South the Christian Democratic gains were due largely to the party's ability to present itself as the "party of the government," that is, as a party with a recognized claim to the exercise of power. In the political culture of the South, becoming a member of such a party often is insurance against unemployment or gives one an advantage in the competition for a desirable position in a public office or in a private firm. A similar situation existed under fascism, when Fascist Party membership came to be called "the bread card." To some extent the same can be said of Communist membership in the central region, in view of the party's power to dispense patronage in a number of local administrations and in cooperative organizations.

It is not surprising that both parties exert a stronger attraction where membership in the appropriate party not only opens the door to political participation but may also lead to some personal material advantage. This would not be an acceptable basis for recruitment to a party whose main objective is to make its members committed agents for political deployment, but the two leading Italian parties are mainly oriented to attracting votes, and their recruitment policies are therefore designed primarily to create a solid link with their members, so that they can count on their votes at election time.

Such policies can have serious consequences (especially when an inflated membership is used as a weapon in intraparty struggles). That the result can be a lack of correspondence between areas of organizational strength and areas of electoral strength can be seen in Figure 4-1 and Appendix E, which show for each party the provinces in which it was organizationally strongest in the census years 1951 and 1961 (as indicated by the ratio of membership to adult population in each province in those years) and the provinces in which it received its highest percentage of electoral support (votes cast for the party out of total votes cast) in the general elections of 1953 and 1963. In both the early 1950s and the early 1960s there was a high degree of correspondence for the Communist Party and a low degree of correspondence for the Christian Democratic Party between party organizational strength and electoral strength.

Between 1951 and 1961 the pattern of organizational strength was much more stable for the Communist Party than for the Christian Democratic Party. In its organizational strongholds the Communist Party was stronger organizationally than was the Christian Democratic Party in the thirty provinces where it had its greatest organizational strength. On the other hand, the Christian Democratic Party, where it was electorally strong, was stronger than was the Communist Party in its electoral strongholds. The high degree of correspondence the Communists achieved between organizational and electoral strength in some provinces was generally due to their solid control of local governments, sometimes alone, mostly in a coalition with the Socialists, during most of the period under study.[2] Many of the provinces where the Christian Democrats made a good organizational but not a good electoral showing were in areas of serious factionalism, as in some Sicilian provinces, or in areas controlled by a major leader who was using his local position as a steppingstone to a position of national power, as in Latium (Giulio Andreotti's territory), Avellino (Fiorentino Sullo's), Matera (Emilio Colombo's), Cagliari and Nuoro (Antonio Segni's). The Christian Democrats' electoral strength was heightened where the traditional Catholic subculture and network of organizations was still very strong.

CHARACTERISTICS OF PARTY MEMBERS

Despite their lack of adequate records, the Italian Communist and Christian Democratic parties are well aware of the significance of the socioeconomic composition of their membership.[3]

For the Communist Party, which has traditionally assumed the role of a workers' party, this awareness may take the form of concern over the extent to which the party has actually organized the workers. The data collected in the course of the present survey suggest that although industrial workers constituted the largest single occupational category of the party's membership they were in the majority only in the immediate postwar years. By 1954 nearly three fifths of the members were industrial or farm wage earners, but by the early 1960s these groups combined constituted only a little more than half of the total party membership. How-

2. In these areas the Communist Party is at the center of a complex network of organizations, and takes on the aspect of S. Neumann's "party of social integration." See the concluding chapter in S. Neumann, ed., *Modern Political Parties* (Chicago, University of Chicago Press, 1954).
3. On the question of social and economic status and political participation, see, for example, R. Bendix, "Social Stratification and Political Power," in Seymour Martin Lipset and Reinhard Bendix, eds., *Class, Status and Power* (Glencoe, Free Press, 1953), pp. 596–608.

ever, the party could be considered predominantly proletarian, since, with the addition of working-class retirees and housewives to the industrial and farm wage earners, the combined group accounted for nearly three quarters of the total membership in 1963, as it had in 1954. (Table 4-3)

TABLE 4-3. *Percentage distribution of Communist Party membership, 1946, 1954, and 1963, and Christian Democratic Party membership, 1955 and 1961, by occupational group*

Occupational group	Communists			Christian Democrats	
	1946 a	1954	1963	1955	1961 b
Industrial worker	52.7	39.9	40.2	19.4	21.2
Agricultural worker					
Farm wage earner	11.9	17.8	11.3	6.0	5.5
Sharecropper	10.9	12.2	9.9	2.2	2.0
Small farmer	4.9	3.9	5.7	14.8	12.4
Housewife	9.4	13.5	13.4	24.0	25.5
Retired person	—	4.4	9.8	2.9	4.5
Student	0.6	0.3	0.4	2.5	2.5
Artisan or shopkeeper	5.2	5.2	6.4	11.3	9.2
Professional	0.7	0.6	0.7	4.8	5.3
White-collar worker	3.7	2.2	2.2	9.4	9.2
Other	—	—	—	2.7	1.5

a. The data cover only 53 percent of party members. However, the distribution is probably fairly representative of the total membership.

b. The data do not include members from the provinces of Bergamo, Brescia, Avellino, and Agrigento.

Sharecroppers and small farmers comprised about 16 percent of the Communist Party membership from 1946 to 1963. The rest of the membership was made up of members of the urban middle classes: artisans and shopkeepers, white-collar workers, and professional workers and students.

Information about the composition of the membership of the Christian Democratic Party is quite fragmentary. Some general characteristics of the party membership based on 1955 and 1961 data suggest that more than a fourth of its members were engaged in urban middle-class types of employment described above. For example, 9.2 percent of the members were artisans or shopkeepers, 5.3 percent were professionals, 9.2 percent were white-collar workers and 2.5 percent students in 1916. Another quarter of the party's 1961 members were housewives. A good many of these housewives, as well as the retired members of the party, probably also belonged to the urban middle classes. Petit bourgeois rural groups comprised 14.4 percent of the membership, with small farmers outnumbering the sharecroppers (the reverse of the situation in the Communist Party). Wage earners employed in industry and agriculture made up 26.7 percent of the membership. Four out of five of these were industrial workers. Industrial workers, who accounted for slightly more than one fifth of the membership, were the strongest single occupational category, except for housewives. These figures suggest that the Christian Democratic Party membership fits the party's claim of being an "interclass" party.

WOMEN'S PLACE IN THE TWO PARTIES

Women constituted about a fourth of the membership of the Communist Party during the 1950s and early 1960s, compared with 14 percent in 1945. The increase in the employment of women in industry was probably not the primary reason for this increase, but rather the fact that the Communist Party has tended to become the party of proletarian families rather than of workers only.

The size and importance of women's share in Communist Party membership has varied in different parts of the country. In the northern industrial cities, such as Alessandria and Vercelli, which do not have a strong Catholic tradition, women accounted for 20 to 30 percent of the total party membership in 1951. The proportion has since decreased slightly. In most of the northern industrial provinces with a strong Catholic tradition women members of the Communist Party have comprised only 10 to 20 percent of the membership. The proportion has slowly decreased. Although in the southern provinces women have generally made up only 5 to 10 percent of the membership, in the province of Foggia, where there is a strong tradition of labor militancy among seasonal farm workers, such as olive pickers, most of whom are women, 38 percent of the members of the Communist Party were women in 1951 and 32.5 percent in 1961.

In the Christian Democratic Party women accounted for about a third of the total membership in the 1950s and early 1960s, but there were significant regional differences. In the northern province of Trento, for instance, women made up a narrow majority of all Christian Democratic members in 1961. In addition to the expectedly high percentages of women members in the northern provinces, where organized Catholicism has always been very strong, the percentages of women members in a number of provinces in the South, particularly in Sicily and Sardinia, were also high.

RANK-AND-FILE PARTICIPATION [4]

Members of political parties vary in the degree of their commitment and active participation in party affairs. Participation in the two leading Italian parties varied from presence, to active, to decisional influence.

"Presence," as used in this survey, consists merely of passive or receptive attendance at meetings and party assemblies. "Active" involves organizing meetings, campaigning for new members, sponsoring small rallies, distributing party publications. "Decisional influence" is exercised when the member is called upon to make a choice between alternative policies or courses of action or to choose the members of directive bodies.

Decisional influence operates in markedly different ways in the two mass parties in Italy. At crucial moments in the development of the Christian Democratic Party the rank and file have been able to choose between alternative lines of action and policy, as, for example, between De Gasperi's centrism and the Dossetti "left" in 1949, or the moderation of the *dorotei* and the Fanfani "left" in 1959. But rank-and-file members of the Communist Party have never made a decision of this kind.

Presence at Christian Democratic assemblies, where policies and leaders are chosen, may involve some degree of decisional influence, whereas Communist Party rank-and-file members do not participate in discussions that lead to policy decisions.

Throughout the period under study the number of both the members who merely attended meetings and the activists has decreased somewhat in both parties, thus reducing total political

4. See. B. Barber, "Participation and Mass Apathy in Associations," in A. Gouldner, ed., *Studies in Leadership* (New York, Harper, 1950), pp. 477–504; Seymour Martin Lipset, Martin A. Trow, and James S. Coleman, *Union Democracy* (Glencoe, Free Press, 1956), passim; R. Mayntz, "Oligarchic Problems in a German Party District," in Dwaine Marvick, ed., *Political Decision-Makers* (Glencoe, Free Press, 1961), pp. 138–92.

participation in the country. But the efforts of the two parties, especially the Communist Party, to increase their members' interest and participation in party work have borne fruit. Because they are mass parties, both the Communist and Christian Democratic parties have been able to establish the intimate contacts with Italian society that have made them the two strongest parties in the country today.

Attendance at Communist Meetings [5]

Examination of data from Communist Party sources indicates that participation in the party through presence at meetings has never involved more than 25 percent of the total membership, even in years of strong support, as in 1948 to 1951, and that after 1956 such involvement dropped to between 10 and 15 percent of the membership.

Rank-and-file attendance was apparently relatively high in 1945 to 1947, immediately after the war. This may have been a reaction to the sudden return of democratic political life in Italy. As soon as the situation began to stabilize, member participation fell rather sharply. Information on participation trends is fairly easy to obtain for the Communist Party, which is both better organized and more organization conscious than the Christian Democratic Party.[6] A few quotations from the party press serve to illustrate the party's preoccupation with poor attendance at meetings from the late 1940s on. For example, as early as 1948 the Communist daily, L'Unità, reported that party members had stopped coming to the section meetings, which were now deserted or semideserted.

Membership apathy was apparent, also, in the South, where the party was still establishing itself. Even in an industrial zone such as Taranto, the able organizer and later national leader, Giannini, stated in 1949 that there was "a very low attendance at cell meetings, with a maximum of 25 percent." [7]

Two years later the party's great organizational effort in Rome had not changed the general picture. In the most efficient cells at-

5. The main sources for this section were the following Communist publications: the daily L'Unità, the weekly Vie Nuove, the bimonthly Il Quaderno dell'Attivista, and the monthly Rinascita.
6. Il Quaderno dell'Attivista, September 15, 1948.
7. Ibid., March 1, 1949.

tendance averaged 25 percent with a maximum of 40 percent in cells in the Ponte Parione section.[8] The strongly Communist San Lorenzo railway workers' section recorded an average attendance of only 5 percent for 1949–50, and thought its efforts quite successful when it managed to increase this average to 10 to 15 percent in 1962.[9]

Even in Bologna, a Communist stronghold, two thirds of the cells did not meet regularly in 1953, a key election year. Even in active cells, 30 to 40 percent of the members failed to participate.

Similarly, in Naples, the center of the Communist Party's organizational effort in the South: "of the nine cells of the Chiaia section, only three meet, and those only irregularly. . . . at least 50 percent of the members live completely cut off from national politics." In the North, in the modern Necchi sewing machine plant at Pavia, there was "low attendance at the cell meetings. . . . Of 700 members, only about 70 engage in party activity with any degree of constancy." [10]

Congresses preceding the party's fourth organizational conference in January 1955 were held at all party levels, but at the lower party levels no more than 400,000 out of more than 2 million members participated.[11] During this important period in the party's development the average attendance at party meetings was less than 20 percent of its membership.

Fewer attendance records are available for the third phase of the Communist Party's development, beginning in 1956. One of the main sources of information for the earlier phases, *Il Quaderno dell'Attivista,* ceased publication and was replaced by the more specialized *Problemi di Organizzazione,* which was issued irregularly and not widely distributed. The available data suggest a further decline in attendance. In Modena, for instance, where the Communist Party was very strong: ". . . attendance at cell meetings varies between 15 percent and 45 percent of the members; about 40 percent of the cells meet only once a year, and their only activity is the collection of dues and the distribution of literature." [12]

The decline in attendance was particularly marked in the cells op-

8. Ibid., September and July 1950.
9. Ibid., January 1953.
10. Ibid., January 1953, pp. 42 and 154.
11. *IV Conferenza Nazionale del Partito Comunista Italiano, Resoconto* (Rome, Edizioni di Cultura Sociale, 1955), p. 7.
12. *Problemi di Organizzazione,* July 1961.

erating in factories. The influx of new elements into the working class, and the simultaneous loss of some hard-core militants, had a negative effect on the Communist factory cells. While the militants had joined the party in times of struggle and tension, most of the newcomers were introduced to industrial work and politics after 1948, in a much more relaxed atmosphere. Throughout the 1950s the management of most Italian firms used a strong-arm strategy in order to keep the factories free of political activity and to break down the organizational network of the Communist factory movement. Pressure, transfers, and dismissals were used quite freely.

Changes in working conditions, such as an increase in mechanization, a speedup in the work flow, variations in work shifts, and new training requirements made it difficult to organize meetings and maintain continuous contact between the members. Also the increasing distance between the worker's home and place of work and the consequent increase in travel time reduced the time and energy available for political activity.

Attendance at Christian Democratic Meetings

Attendance records of Christian Democratic meetings prior to 1959 are sparse. Since that date party leaders have estimated that about 30 percent of the membership attends section meetings, which occur two or three times a year, usually coinciding with special events, such as a party congress or an electoral campaign. Section leaders interviewed indicated that in general the same members are present at most meetings.

Attempts to gather information comparable to that for the Communist Party on member participation trends from Christian Democratic literature were largely unsuccessful. But, with the cooperation of the Christian Democratic Youth Movement, local leaders were questioned. Some 250 local leaders active in the Christian Democratic Youth Movement were contacted throughout the country. (No systematic sampling plan was adopted. The sample was based exclusively on suggestions from the Youth Movement's national leadership.) These local youth leaders were asked to submit detailed accounts of the organization and activity of their respective sections in the years 1960–62. Unfortunately, only sixty-seven reports were received, despite a number of follow-up requests.

While a quantitative analysis could not be made from these rather disappointing returns, some typical observations emerged. The reports received included comments about the lack of activities in the sections, failure of leaders to call meetings, poor attendance at the meetings that were called, the apathy of the party members, and their lack of concern with public affairs.

While some of the replies indicated that as many as four or five meetings were held during the year and that attendance by party members occasionally was as high as 40 percent, most of the informants said that meetings were called only when absolutely necessary or during electoral campaigns.

Communist Activists

The active member is one who assumes responsibility for a definite task within the party or the mass organizations or both. Typical tasks within the party are recruiting new members, sponsoring meetings, collecting dues, and distributing publications; tasks outside the party organization include engaging in propaganda activities, organizing demonstrations, and campaigning. Very few Communist Party members are active party workers. Before 1951 a maximum of 10 percent were active; in recent years the percentage has fallen to around 5.

Examination of the party literature shows that activism was at a peak during 1953, an election year, and in an area where the Communist Party, together with the definitely subordinate Socialist Party, obtained 86 percent of the votes. In 1953 the organizational decline of the Communist Party had already begun. But in areas where the Communists were a party of "social integration," as in the Irma Bandiera section in Bologna, where 28 percent of the party members were activists,[13] the maximum levels of participation were maintained.

In a neighboring area of Communist hegemony, the situation was described as follows in 1955:

Of more than 68,000 comrades in Reggio Emilia, about 25,000 belong to the party cadres; 14,000 of these work within the party, 11,000 in mass organizations. Not all of these 25,000, however, are

13. *Il Quaderno dell'Attivista*, 1953, p. 210.

active . . . From an examination of about 30 sections, it was found that attendance at meetings was rather good—about 80 percent of the activists. And they were really meetings of activists.[14]

In a major effort to activate its members in the immediate postwar years the Communist Party created the position of "collector," an experiment that had been tried in Alessandria in 1946 and which was described as follows to the first organizational conference in May 1947:

he is the comrade who goes into the factory or from house to house . . . [who] not only can collect the dues, but can also check on why Tom doesn't come to the meetings any longer and why Dick and Harry have deserted the cell or the section.[15]

The position of collector was institutionalized at the sixth congress in January 1948, when Pietro Secchia asserted:

In order to facilitate the activation of the comrades, we think it would be helpful to adopt a form of organization which is already in use in the Communist Party in Czechoslovakia, and that is to subdivide the members of the cells into groups of eight or ten. At the head of each of these small groups should be the collector whose job it is to explain to his ten comrades the most important political questions of the day, to invite them to cell meetings, to see to it that every comrade has a job to do, and to see to it that this job is done. The collector should furthermore see to it that the comrades in his group are enrolled and active in the unions and the other mass organizations, that they pay their dues, that they study, that they read the party publications.[16]

Thus, in addition to his original job of collecting dues, the collector was also the supervisor of the members' activities.

Further information suggests that in 1949 less than 15 percent of the members of the Communist Party had any kind of party responsibility,[17] although some of the more active members no doubt had more than one organizational responsibility either in the party or in a mass organization. It was therefore difficult to determine the total

14. Ibid., 1955, p. 168.
15. Pietro Secchia, *Il Partito della Rinascita* (Rome, UESISA, 1947), p. 52.
16. Pietro Secchia, *Piu' forti i quadri migliore l'organizzazione* (Rome, Intervento al VI Congresso del PCI, 1948) .
17. *Rinascita*, March 1949.

number of party members who were active in any one year, but because of overlapping, the number of active members in the Communist Party was probably no greater than 200,000 between 1950 and 1954—that is, no more than 10 percent of the party membership.

The period 1955–57 was one of organizational crisis for the Communists. In 1957 the position of dues collector was abolished and the crisis in the cells led to the elimination of other posts. The motivation to participate in party activities was adversely affected by political and social developments both within the party and without. The number of members who held posts at the local level was about 80,000, or about 5 percent of the total Communist Party membership. This included about 18,000 to 20,000 members active in the cells (an average of 2 per cell) plus some 55,000 active in the sections (an average of 5 per section), plus perhaps 5,000 people active in the 2,000 plants where the Communists maintained an organization.

Active Members of the Christian Democrats

While the active Communist works both within the party itself (in membership campaigns, distribution of literature, calling of meetings) and outside the party (in propaganda activities and electoral campaigns), the active Christian Democrat tends to work on behalf of the faction of the party to which he belongs. Within the party he takes part in the factional struggle; outside of it, he campaigns for the candidate his faction prefers.

Except during the period of Amintore Fanfani's leadership, when efforts were made to increase the points of contact between the Christian Democratic Party and Italian society at large, the active members of the party have generally been the leaders or officers of the sections. The number of sections, section leaders, and leaders per section from 1947 to 1959 are shown in Table 4-4. Since the number of leaders increased faster than the number of sections, the average number of leaders per section increased over the period—from four in 1947–54 to more than six in 1959. In anticipation of the 1958 electoral campaigns, the party statutes were revised to increase the number of members in the sectional directorate to a minimum of nine. During the same period the party attempted to set up an electoral network at the precinct level. (Table 4-5) The organizational changes reflect the efforts made to activate the members by giving them special tasks in the 1958 election campaign.

TABLE 4-4. *Number of Christian Democratic sections and leaders, 1947–59*

Year	Sections	Sectional leaders	Average number of leaders per section
1947	8,495	33,980	4.00
1951	9,443	37,772	3.99
1954	10,510	42,240	4.00
1956	11,525	50,637	4.30
1957	12,137	67,973	5.60
1958	12,454	74,631	5.99
1959	12,672 [a]	82,843	6.28

a. This figure and the total shown for 1959 in Table 3-3 differ because of inconsistencies in the figures in party sources used.

TABLE 4-5. *Number of Christian Democratic precinct leaders, 1957–59*

Type of precinct organization	1957	1958	1959
General	32,857	48,097	47,346
Women's	14,049	34,355	34,520
Youth	9,617	30,048	30,480
Total	56,523	112,500	112,346

The percentage of the Christian Democratic membership active either in the sectional leadership or the precinct network was 9.5 in 1957, 12.5 in 1958, and 12.0 in 1959. Since there was a great deal of duplication, it is probably correct to conclude that the Christian Democrats were not able to activate more than 10 percent of their members, even during the organizational drive under Fanfani in the late 1950s. After 1959 the precinct network ceased to function, and only the sections continued to operate. By the early 1960s slightly more than 60,000 members—only about 4 percent of the total membership—were active.

Rank-and-File Activists

A survey of some psychological aspects of active party participation at the local level was undertaken in 1963 in connection with this study.[18] The survey was conducted in 6 towns of from 20,000 to 60,000 inhabitants each: two industrialized communities in Lombardy, an agricultural center in Veneto, an agricultural community in Emilia-Romagna, a recently industrialized community in Campania, and an agricultural community in Apulia. These towns were selected on the basis of the importance of the Communist and Christian Democratic parties to the communities, the degree of their industrialization and economic development, and their geographic location.

In each of these 6 communities 9 well-known active members of each party—a total of 108 activists—were interviewed. Care was taken to ensure that the activists interviewed had been recruited in different periods, spanning the years since the end of the war. Each interview was conducted in a nondirective manner on the basis of an extensive check list of topics. Thus the answers were obtained during interviews that often totaled several hours in length.

For a description of the sample of communities and of activists and of the methods used in this survey, see Appendix A. The statistical results of the interviews are summarized briefly in Table 4-6 and in detail in Appendix F.

Socioeconomic Environment and Political Participation

In response to questions about the effect of a particular social and economic environment on the degree of active participation in the work of the parties in local communities the local activists interviewed said they thought there was no significant difference between northern and southern activists in the Communist Party, that commitment to the party leads to a kind of cultural homogeneity among the party members. In the Christian Democratic Party, however, the activists thought there were differences between northern and southern active workers. For example, they suggested that party activity as a means to personal advantage is found more often in the South than in the North.

Party structure, and thus organizational support of party activists,

18. The results of the research have been published in F. Alberoni, V. Capecchi, A. Manoukian, F. Olivetti, and A. Tosi, *L'attivista di partito* (Bologna, Società editrice il Mulino, 1967).

TABLE 4-6.   *Profile of party activists* [a]

Indicator of background and attitudes	Christian Democratic activists	Communist activists
Social position in relation to average family in the community	Average or above average; reported gradual improvement in socioeconomic position of family	Average or below average; reported gradual improvement or no change in family status
Occupation	Large majority either white-collar or professional and managerial workers	Largest percentage industrial workers; white-collar workers next largest category
Degree of education of parents of activists and of activists themselves	Parents' educational status about equally average or below average; almost half the activists completed high school; one fifth went to university	Parents' educational level mostly low; majority of activists finished only elementary school
Political agreement between activists and parents	Fairly close to close political agreement with father; majority in agreement on political questions with parents	Majority in fairly close to close political agreement with parents but more than one third do not agree politically with father
Positions held in local government	About half had held the posts of magistrate or other executive, communal councillor, or member of communal board; more than half had held no political post	Large majority had held no political post; the most frequently held position was that of communal councillor
Influences determining choice of party and decision to take active role	Most became interested through gradual conviction; the principal actuating influences were Catholic associations, friendships, and family	Joined party mostly through gradual conviction, but in a number of cases because of critical episodes; chief actuating influences were family and friendships, coworkers, and decisive movements
Chief indoctrinating influence	Party and Catholic associations	Party
Frequency of reading party press	Only a few read party papers; most never did	Almost all were constant readers
Frequency and direction of proselyting efforts by activists	Almost half proselytized "mostly during elections" but almost a third reported that they did so more frequently, and about an	Almost all engaged constantly in these activities, particularly among "adversaries," with some effort directed toward "neutrals"

TABLE 4-6.—*Continued*

Indicator of back-ground and attitudes	Christian Democratic activists	Communist activists
	equal number never did. These activities were about equally directed toward "adversaries," "neutrals," and "like-minded people"	
Attitude toward party leaders	Majority admired some, were critical of others	Almost all approved of the party leaders, with few exceptions
Expectation of party's growth	About equally divided in expecting party gains and not expecting party to grow	Almost all believed party would gain in strength

a. For a description of the survey of 108 party activists—54 from the Christian Democratic Party and 54 from the Communist Party—on which this information is based, see accompanying text and Appendix A. For detailed tables presenting the findings of the study, see Appendix F.

is apparently stronger in areas where one of the parties is in control of the local government. For example, the Communist activists were more committed and optimistic in the two areas (a community in Lombardy and one in Emilia-Romagna) where the party had the majority in the local government; in these same areas the Christian Democratic activists appeared to be more or less resigned. The reverse was true where the Christian Democrats were strong.

There was more marked variation between Christian Democrats in the different towns than between Communists. The Christian Democratic Party tends to project a different image in each community, depending on the party faction that is in power there. Communist loyalties are more uniform, although the party may stress local problems and interests in order to fit more easily into the life of the community.

Particularly in communities where the Communists are in control of the local government they are apt to present a different image of themselves to different local audiences. When confronting the electorate at large, especially the economically powerful sectors of the population, Communist activists stress that Communists are able administrators, devoted to the public interest. But at the same time the Communist Party is presented to its own members as a force that must build socialism and exploit every opportunity offered by a capitalist society controlled by a capitalist central government.

In the six communities in which the survey activists lived, the two parties were the only mass parties with an articulate organization and with active programs not limited to electoral campaigns.

Three distinct types of socioeconomic situations were found in the communities studied. Some of them had undergone rapid social transformation, accompanied by sudden demographic and economic development that had destroyed the traditional structures. Political commitment was a means of identification with an idealized future and of participation in the attempt to direct and control the changes taking place. The activists in such communities were likely to be youthful party members, critical of the official party line.

Some of the communities, on the other hand, had experienced slower and better integrated development. In these communities the role of the parties was to champion modernization. The dynamic activist who avoided extremism and was committed to civic improvement could, through his party work, help to introduce innovations in these communities.

While the general economic development had caused some improvement in the local standard of living, the rest of the communities had undergone no marked structural change, and the traditional forms of the distribution and administration of power prevailed. In these communities active participation in a party meant attempting to benefit from that power to increase one's personal prestige and social position.

Socioeconomic Background of Active Participants

In an effort to determine the socioeconomic level of the Christian Democratic and Communist activists, information was obtained about their economic, social, educational and family backgrounds, compared with those of the average families in each community. Although the sample was limited, it provided a general picture of the differences between the activists in the two parties.

In their own opinions the majority of the families of the Communist activists occupied a social and economic position below average and none of the activists were from families who were above average according to the measurements used. Among the Christian Democratic activists the majority came from families whose socioeconomic level was average, but there were more from above-average backgrounds than from families who measured below average. (Table 4-6 and Appendix Tables F-1 to F-3)

Almost all of the Christian Democratic activists had completed elementary school, almost half had been through high school, and some had been to the university. Among the Communists, however, an elementary school education was the general rule. Their political education had been acquired through intensive study as Communist Party activists and was almost exclusively along party lines. Workers formed the nucleus of Communist activists, with a good representation of white-collar workers. The Christian Democratic activists tended to be white-collar workers, teachers, and professionals. There was no indication that political engagement could be interpreted as a response to dissatisfaction with occupational status. The occupations of most of the respondents were a source of satisfaction to them and represented the central values in their lives. Furthermore, many of the activists in both parties asserted that their economic situation had improved over the course of time. Somewhat more marked differences between the activists of the two parties were found when they were questioned on their socioeconomic aspirations, which in general were higher for the Christian Democratic activists. Both groups wanted to be in a position to own more consumer goods, especially electrical appliances.

The impression that the activists of both parties were basically well-adjusted and socially integrated was confirmed by their attitudes toward their families. The families that the activists were a part of or had formed or wanted to form represented a central value for both of the groups and very few felt any serious conflict between their family duties and interests and their obligations to the party.

Factors Influencing Choice of Party

The influence of the family was felt not only in regard to social and economic status but also in the political orientation of the activist.[19] (Table 4-6 and Appendix Tables F-4 and F-5) The majority of the activists interviewed came from politically conscious families. There was a high degree of correspondence between the political allegiances of the respondents of both parties and the political orientation of their fathers (Catholic, socialist, or communist). The Catholic or socialist orientation was shared by mothers of a majority of the activists.

19. On the relation of family influences and political loyalties, see H. Hyman, *Political Socialization* (Glencoe, Free Press, 1959), pp. 69–91.

On the whole the conditioning of the activist to an ideological orientation apparently took place primarily in the family. Here are some typical quotations from the interviews with the activists:

from Campania:

My father was a Communist activist . . . every night at home he sort of gave us lessons about what the Communist Party does for the working people and how we can be helped by the party's struggles.

from Lombardy community (1):

My father is still a member of the Christian Democratic Party, and until a few years ago he was very active in the union. . . . When my mother was young she was in Catholic Action, and although she's not a member of the party, she has worked in the Civic Committees.

from Lombardy community (2):

My father was one of the first members of the Communist youth movement before fascism. All his brothers were with the Reds except one who was a Christian. . . . I remember that he used to whistle "The Red Flag" a lot and that he was always antifascist. I think it was because the Fascists had hurt him.

from Campania:

All my family are solid Christian Democrats. There are about a hundred of us all together. In the local elections my father voted for the Christian Democrats, but in the national elections he voted for the monarchists, since he came from a family of *carabinieri*. But after 1953 he voted for the Christian Democrats in the national elections too. Before the fall of fascism he was an officer in the local fascist section. Everybody in my family belongs to Catholic Action. . . . My brother-in-law is president of it.

from Lombardy community (2):

My father's decision to be a Communist didn't have any reasons, he just did it because he's always contradicting. I don't think he really thinks like a Communist. My mother is the one who kept the family going. She doesn't say who she votes for, but I'm sure she votes for the Communists because she knows we're right.

Thanks to these family influences, the development of a personal political commitment was found to have taken place in most cases gradually, not as a result of a crisis.[20] Exceptions to this were more frequent among the Communist than among the Christian Democratic activists.

For the Communist activist the social forces of greatest influence were apparently the work group, the Resistance, and the family. For the Christian Democratic activist, however, the decision to work actively for the party had its center in Catholic associations. Friendships formed in childhood, more often than not on the parish playground, had obviously exerted a strong pull toward one or the other of the parties.

Thus, while party membership itself had been determined largely by family influences, the decision to take an active part in the work of the party had developed either in the family or had been fostered by membership in religious associations (for the Christian Democrats) or the work group (for the Communists). But simple membership, and sometimes the decision to be active as well, had often been the result of vague convictions.

While occupational environment and co-workers had been important influences in making political choices, the unions had been less influential on the political development of Communists than on that of Christian Democrats. Party schools had had an important role in indoctrinating Communist activists. Eleven of the fifty-four Communist respondents attended the central party school, while all the rest of them took brief sectional courses or instruction offered at the national level. But only two of the fifty-four Christian Democrats interviewed attended the three-week course at the Christian Democratic study center at Camilluccia. For the Communist Party worker the party press had been an even more important influence in his political education. For his Christian Democratic opposite number, however, the party press apparently had been of very little importance. (Appendix Table F-6)

20. Personal influences have been stressed by Harold Lasswell, for example, in *Power and Personality* (New York, Norton, 1948). Some of the concepts developed in G. Almond, *The Appeals of Communism* (Princeton, Princeton University Press, 1954), are related to this approach.

Differing Images of Society [21]

Although the survey did not reveal great differences in the activists' acceptance of life in contemporary society, a marked difference was found in the Christian Democratic and the Communist images of society. The Communists' general acceptance of modern conveniences was accompanied, in fact, by an equally general criticism of the principles of the social system as a whole.

Some of the comments of the activists recorded during the interviews reflect the differences between the Communist and the Christian Democratic views of contemporary Italian society and government policy. Here are some typical comments of the Communists:

from Campania:

We see that the one who gives the orders is a capitalist, not us. But this isn't right, because capital is created by labor, and thus capital should be controlled by labor. Certainly the capitalists now have all the power, and they won't easily give up. But it is just for this reason that we must use all our strength and remain united, because the whole nation suffers from capitalism.

from Lombardy community (1):

Little by little we begin to understand that we must rebel, using the legal means at our disposal, because we don't want violence. But we are able to explain the causes of the evil.

from Apulia:

There are people who lead the governments into war, who ruin the world, just to have a monopoly. They don't give a damn if the whole world dies, if the whole world is massacred, if the world is drowned in blood, provided that financial capital comes out on top.

from Emilia-Romagna:

I want to change things because the society I live in doesn't satisfy my needs as a member of a class of workers, peasants, farm la-

21. The term "image of society" as used by the social scientist encompasses the comprehensive view of the social world that often forms the implicit framework of the discreet judgments and attitudes of social theorists and activists. Most of the literature on the image of society held by activists (the perspective adopted here) is in German. Perhaps the most important reference in English, focused on the British working class, is R. Hoggart, *The Uses of Literacy* (London, Chatto & Windus, 1957).

borers, intellectuals, students. I want to improve, to create . . . a society in which one man is equal to another.

from Veneto:

There has been an economic miracle, but it has happened for only a part of the Italians. If we look at the question seriously we will find that the beneficiaries have been the big people, the capitalists, in short, the monopolists of Italian commerce and industry. They have also profited from the state. For example, the new factories which they have built have been put up in places where they could find cheap labor—like here.

And here are some typical statements on Italian society and government policy from Christian Democratic activists. Of particular interest is the wide difference of opinion on the nationalization of the electric industry that occurred in 1962.

from Apulia:

I think this about the Common Market: that it ought to be correlated with the currency, with monetary value. Because if the Americans give me a dollar for 672, 673, or 674 lire, then they are certainly not allowing me to trade. There ought to be monetary equality, and then you can call the Common Market the "common market," that is, I spend the same as you. I think it can happen among the European nations.

from Campania:

I feel it was wrong for the state to nationalize electric power, especially doing it in such a hurry—in two months. I saw no reason for such hurry, and if there were not a strong right wing in the Christian Democratic Party, certainly they would have also passed the law for the regional governments. Moro held it up in order to keep the Socialists under control.

from Emilia-Romagna:

Nationalization is a great mistake in economic terms. Purely political considerations have prevailed . . . It won't have any economic results, rather it will be more a burden than anything else. I'm not a Liberal, but I can't deny that their economic doctrine knows how to create wealth, but that is its limit, it doesn't know how to distribute it.

from Lombardy community (1):

> About the nationalization—I'm for it. In spite of all these alarms
> which have been raised, I don't think it's such an upset . . . I
> think the state did well to do it, because under private manage-
> ment all sorts of problems had been overlooked. . . . Nationaliza-
> tion in itself does nobody any harm.

from Veneto:

> I feel nationalization was right, although, of course, it isn't per-
> fect because the capitalists have lost an important controlling
> lever which allowed them to control all sorts of things. They must
> truly make reforms in electric power, and this will be a positive
> fact for everybody and brings benefits to the workers.

On the basis of a detailed analysis of the views and criticisms of
Italian society expressed by the two groups of party workers, it was
found that the Communist image of society was very much the same
regardless of when the activist was recruited, except that the Soviet
Union tended to be less often considered a positive point of reference for those recruited more recently. The Christian Democratic
activists tended to have a more dynamic concept of society. On the
whole the majority of the Communist activists exhibited an oversim-
plified class concept of social phenomena, while only a small minority of the Christian Democratic activists accepted the class view of
society.

The various ways in which the activists interpreted Italian social
structure and its organization revealed to what extent they saw social and human reality as a struggle between two—and only two—opposing positions, one good and the other evil, without any possibility
of mediation and compromise, unless it is provisional or instrumental. This is an important problem, given the strong ideological and
subcultural components of the two political movements. For the
Christian Democratic theorist the dichotomy between good and evil,
from the religious point of view, is fundamental; while for the Communist theorist the Marxist polarization between proletariat and
bourgeoisie and between socialism and capitalism is equally fundamental. However, such marked polarization was not characteristic of
the views of the majority of the Christian Democratic activists, and
even the Communist activists, despite the marked centralization of
party ideology, exhibited a diversity of opinion and points of view.

Relations with the Party

Most of the activists who joined either party in the first ten years after the Second World War, and who had not been members of the Communist Party or the Popular Party in prefascist times, became party members between the ages of twenty-five and thirty-five without having first belonged to the youth movement of either party. But two thirds of those who joined later came up through their party's youth movement, which they had joined before the age of twenty. Of thirty-two activists (nineteen Communists and thirteen Christian Democrats) who had been members of one or the other of the youth movements, twenty-five Communists and nine Christian Democrats had held some sort of office in one of the youth organizations.

A majority of the Communist and Christian Democratic workers were active in the unions, mostly as office holders, while as many as fifty of the fifty-four Christian Democrats and thirty-eight of the fifty-four Communist activists interviewed were also members of one or more social associations outside the party. For the Communists the great majority of these associations were party front organizations, while for the Christian Democrats they were Catholic organizations.

The main party activities of the activists were concerned with propaganda and recruitment, trying to make members out of supporters and activists out of members, sponsoring meetings and demonstrations, and making speeches to publicize party principles and stands on public issues. (Appendix Table F-6) But while the Communist Party workers continuously carried on these activities, the survey revealed that the Christian Democratic activists engaged in such efforts much less often, perhaps only during elections.

Many of the activists also occupied positions such as magistrates or communal councillors in local government administrations. (Appendix Table F-7)

The party leadership enjoyed much more confidence and admiration among the Communist activists than among the Christian Democrats. (Appendix Table F-6) Almost all of the Communist activists said that they approved of the party's leaders, although there was indication of a growing realization of the autocratic nature of the party. Acceptance of democratic means of achieving change and the expectation of a gradual rather than a violent defeat of capitalism were attitudes found more frequently among the recently recruited activists.

ATTITUDES TOWARD COMMUNISM AND CAPITALISM

While "evolution versus revolution" remained the basic issue of Communist strategy, for the Christian Democratic activists the major issues were apparently their attitudes toward communism and the relations between the Church and the party. (Appendix Table F-8) There was evidence of a mellowing of attitudes in the two parties—of the Communist attitude toward democracy and capitalism in Italy and of the Christian Democratic attitude toward communism. There also was evidence of a decreasing willingness to subordinate the party to religious authority.

On the whole the interviews with the activists of the two parties seemed to indicate that changes of direction were taking place in both parties. Among these were the markedly different expectations for the future of the two parties. (Appendix Table F-6) The Communists evidenced much greater optimism and confidence in their party's future than did the Christian Democrats. Here are some comments from the Christian Democratic activists—first, from two middle-aged respondents from the South:

> I've always liked this party, but it isn't what it used to be. Now I'm unhappy about it because, you see, I feel the need, the duty, to size up the leaders, to figure out what they're thinking about, where they're trying to go. In fact, unfortunately, ever since the first big election when we got an absolute majority, we have been doing worse and worse—so much worse that we can't have a stable government.

> The drift of things is very dangerous. . . . Italians—I want you to write this down—are not mature enough to enjoy freedom . . . The Socialists were to blame for a lot of things; even now if they go along with the Communists, the Christian Democrats will be knocked out. If the Communists take over power, all the leaders of Christian Democracy are done for.

More optimistic was the comment of a young Christian Democratic activist from Lombardy community (2):

> I think that in the next ten years the Christian Democrats will become a modern party, more and more disassociated from the organized Catholic world, because a new generation of leaders is forming and maturing now at the local level.

And another activist from the same community:

> I think that the party could legitimize its existence if it would really act as a sort of filter to insure that the best citizens are the ones who arrive at positions of responsibility.

Even in the language used, the first two and the second two respondents represent two completely different worlds, with very little in common.

Reflecting the attitude of the Communists a respondent from Lombardy community (2) said:

> I am convinced that the Communist Party will within, I don't know, five or six years, ten years, have a much more important role than it does now. Maybe that's the only thing that will change, but maybe it will be the other parties and not the Communist Party.

General optimism was voiced by a Communist from Campania:

> The Communists here in Italy have made and are making at this moment a great advance. But we need to advance more, and the Christian Democratic movement will lose other votes. . . . the Christian Democratic Party plays its little games, but at a certain moment the people will decide its fate.

This electoral optimism is much more cautiously expressed by a worker from Lombardy:

> The fact itself of the Communist Party's advances, even if only small ones, or its maintenance of its position, never losing ground —this shows that with time . . . All you need to do is add it up— 1.5 percent gain every five years—within fifty years we'll be in power.

Often, among the communists, faith is inspired more by national than by local leaders, as indicated by this respondent from Veneto:

> The national leadership is aware of all the national and international problems. I believe that they are capable, that they know

how to govern even if they aren't the government. The local leadership still feels the effects of the years of defeat . . . of the past. They were very sectarian, very divided, and had lots of problems. And even now there are difficulties which hamper political action.

In spite of some doubts, however, many Communists think they can win, while many Christian Democrats think they can survive. Here are two typical expressions of these attitudes, the first from a Communist from Campania, the second from a Venetian Christian Democrat:

We are determined to beat the Christian Democrats. Then we can really control power. And if we win the elections and they don't let us take over the power, what will happen? If we win and they don't give us the power we'll kill.

I think that if the Christian Democrats got rid of certain people whom I like to call "ballast," Christian Democracy would be able to survive . . . because Christian Democracy in Italy is an eminently Catholic party and then because it is a party which can govern as well as and better than the Socialists. And even better than the Communists. The only thing is that there are those people who are mainly looking out for their own interests.

The Political Elite of the Two Leading Parties [22]

It is generally agreed by writers on this subject that the Italian political elite, particularly in the major mass parties, is composed increasingly of party leaders and functionaries—professional politicians who devote full time to political activity and have no other employment or occupation. To some extent this assertion is contradicted by some of the findings of the present study,[23] which is based on the concept of political "class," or elite, as part of the ruling class. Giovanni Sartori explains this concept as follows:

By ruling class I mean all of the ruling minorities, political, economic, social, religious, intellectual, technological, military, bureaucratic. . . . The political class is then a subclass of the rul-

---

22. For specific empirical research with reference to political elites see D. Marvick, ed., *Political Decision-Makers* (Glencoe, Free Press, 1961).

23. The full results of this survey, conducted by the Carlo Cattaneo Institute in Bologna, appear in F. Cervellati Cantelli and others, *L'organizzazione partitica del PCI e della DC*, pp. 479–570.

ing class: that part of the ruling class whose concern is the exercise of political power.[24]

In studying the members of the Chamber of Deputies of all parties Sartori used the same method used in the present study (a questionnaire, supplemented by data from other sources).

The present study was broadened to include not only those who had represented the Communist and Christian Democratic parties in parliament (either in the Constituent Assembly, the Chamber, or the Senate) but also those who were elected between 1946 and 1963 to the two highest party organs: the Central Committee of the Communist Party and the National Council of the Christian Democrats. Of the 966 Christian Democrats included in the questionnaire survey, 798 were members of parliament at some time between 1946–63; of the 599 Communists, 465 were at some time members of parliament.

Middle-Class Dominance

The information on the political careers of the national party leaders suggests that the most significant step in the rise to national leadership, especially for the Communists, was to hold a party post at the provincial level. Many members of parliament or holders of national party offices had previously held provincial offices or were still holding them. According to the survey findings, less than a third of them (in both parties) had held positions at the sectional or communal level, more than 84 percent of the Communists and about 70 percent of the Christian Democrats had been members of federal or provincial organs. This is the level at which the party "machine" or, as the Communists say, the party "apparatus" operates, that is, the network of offices, clerks, and bureaucratic and propaganda agencies.

This apparatus has often been described in Italy and elsewhere as one of the reasons for the strength and success of the Communists. It is probably true of all national parties with a well-developed organization. While the Christian Democratic organization is not much different from that of the Communists, the continual factional struggle within it lowers its level of performance. As mentioned earlier in this chapter, the Communists owe their more efficient performance

24. Giovanni Sartori, Luigi Lotti, Stefano Somogyi, Alberto Predieri, *Il Parlamento Italiano* (Naples, Edizioni Scientifiche Italiane, 1963), p. 281.

to their centralized leadership, the absence of factions, and access to positions of power at the local level. To this list should be added considerable financial resources invested in the organization. A comparably developed and efficient organization can be found only in the Catholic world as a whole, as a result of the operation within it of a number of associational groups and other types of unit. (This point is discussed further in Chapter 5.)

Information about the background of the political leadership at the provincial level (from sources other than the questionnaire— largely the parties themselves), indicated a strong bias in their selection in favor of members of middle-class occupational groups. This was particularly true of the Christian Democratic provincial leadership in which the manual occupations, already somewhat underrepresented in the sectional committees, were hardly represented at all: not one of the 494 Christian Democratic provincial secretaries who held office between 1945 and 1962 was an unskilled worker, farm worker, or peasant. But nearly one quarter were lawyers and another quarter were teachers. Other professionals and white-collar workers accounted for more than one third of the provincial secretaries during this period. This illustrates how the proletarian and peasant components of the Christian Democratic Party disappeared as the party became concerned with wider issues. A political career in the Christian Democratic Party was clearly not a vehicle for social mobility for workers and peasants, but almost exclusively for the middle status groups.

TABLE 4-7. *Occupation of Communist Party national leaders,* [a] *selected years, 1947–54*

Occupation	1947	1950	1951	1954
Industrial workers	1,029	1,116	1,557	1,725
Farm workers	23	73	177	211
Peasants	191	210	326	359
White-collar workers and technicians	542	564	641	670
Students	104	167	150	114
Intellectuals and professionals	699	572	637	709
Other	266	174	260	246
Unknown	107	66	0	0
Total	2,925	3,075	3,930	4,246

a. For paid party officials the occupations shown are those engaged in before they became professional politicians.

Comparable figures are not available for the Communist Party leadership at the provincial level, but the representation of different occupational groups in the party leadership is illustrated by the figures in Table 4-7, showing occupational backgrounds of Communist national leaders during the first postwar decade. Although well over two fifths of the leaders in 1947 and 1950, and more than a third in 1951 and 1954 had middle-class occupational backgrounds, they were outnumbered in all years from 1951 on by leaders with backgrounds as industrial or farm workers or peasants, who comprised well over half the national leadership by 1954. In the following distribution of national leaders in 1957 the number of paid party functionaries is compared with party leaders employed elsewhere:

	Number	Percent
Paid officials of the Communist Party and mass organizations	1,574	44
Leaders employed elsewhere or self-employed	1,738	48
Other	251	8

Data on the members of the national directorates elected in the same year reveal a still greater incidence of this professional element. Of the 1,047 members elected in 1957, the externally employed represented less than a quarter of the total, while those employed by the party and supporting organizations made up more than three quarters of all the members.

Although no comparable data are available for the Christian Democratic Party, it can be assumed that many reported as teachers and lawyers were, at the time of reporting, full-time professional politicians. In this respect, there was probably little difference between the occupational backgrounds of the leaders of the two parties. An essential difference between the two groups, however, was that only in the Communist Party were national positions open to party members who had manual occupations.

Sex Composition

The responses to the questionnaires revealed marked underrepresentation of women among the national party leaders. (Table 4-8)

From 1946 to 1963 women constituted from 2.3 percent (1961) to 4.4 percent (1946) of the national leadership of the Christian Democratic Party and from 6.7 percent (1961) to 10.8 percent (1950) of the Communist Party's national leaders. These figures contrast with a Christian Democratic membership that was 33 percent women and a Communist membership that was 27.5 percent women in 1962.

TABLE 4-8. *Percent of women among national leaders in the two parties, 1946–63*

Year	Communist	Christian Democratic
1946	9.4	4.4
1950	10.8	3.1
1953	8.1	2.8
1957	8.6	2.6
1961	6.7	2.3
1963	7.0	2.9

Of the twenty-six women who had served on the Christian Democratic National Council, only two had never been members of parliament. Of the fifty-two Communist women who had been members of the Central Committee, fourteen had never been members of parliament. While in both parties women have had difficulty gaining access to the top circles, this has been more true of the Catholic than of the Marxist party. In the Christian Democratic Party nearly the only chance of getting to the top has apparently been to receive sizable support from the voters. A strictly party avenue to political achievement has been open to women only in the Communist Party.

This trend toward the underrepresentation of women in party leadership positions, shown in Table 4-8, places in question the extent of the commitment of leading Italian parties to women's emancipation. Some apparently promotional moves, such as the election of a female Communist deputy to the vice-presidency of the Chamber and the appointment of some Christian Democratic women as under-secretaries in some of the postwar cabinets have not been enough to offset the doubts.

Date of Birth

To speak of the age composition of the two groups of national party officials would be inappropriate, since all who had been national party leaders since the Second World War were included.

Quite a few of these had died as of the date of the survey, had left political activity, or were no longer in positions of national leadership.

The percentage distribution by date of birth (within ten-year intervals) of those leaders whose dates of birth were known (590 out of 599 Communists, 901 out of 966 Christian Democrats) is shown in Table 4-9. As of 1963, according to the table, nearly 50 percent of the Communist leaders, as against 30 percent of the Christian Democrats, were less than fifty years old (or, if they were dead in 1963, would have been less than fifty years old).

TABLE 4-9. *Percentage distribution of Communist and Christian Democratic national party leaders by date of birth*

Birth date	Communist	Christian Democratic
Before 1879	0.7	1.9
1880–89	2.4	9.7
1890–99	14.6	21.1
1900–09	22.6	26.4
1910–19	23.4	20.8
1920–29	35.1	19.4
After 1929	1.1	0.7

A comparison of the percentages of individuals in the national leaderships born before 1900 in the first and the last years of the period covered by the survey shows that in 1946 they accounted for 53.4 percent of the Christian Democratic and 45.2 percent of the Communist leadership; nearly twenty years later, in 1963, the percentage had declined less sharply for the Christian Democratic leaders (to 14.6 percent) than for the Communist leaders (to 4.9 percent).

While it could not be said that either party's leadership was very youthful, the younger average age of the Communist Party leadership is probably one of the reasons, in addition to its tight organization and control, for the party's political flexibility. The ability to adjust to changed circumstances was particularly apparent in the party's handling of the tensions induced by Khrushchev's policies.

Social Background

In his study of the Italian Chamber of Deputies, Sartori, the foremost student of Italian national political leaders, concluded that the proportion of national leaders of the democratic mass parties from the upper social classes had progressively decreased in favor of representatives of the middle and lower social strata.[25] This conclusion was also indicated by the findings in the present inquiry, and applied to the leadership of both of the parties. More political representatives were drawn from the middle classes than from the lower economic groups, however, and the Christian Democratic Party, particularly, appears to have been a vehicle for political promotion almost exclusively from the middle classes.

TABLE 4-10. *Percentage distribution of national party leaders by socioeconomic status of families*

Socioeconomic status of families	Communist	Christian Democratic
Socioeconomic status of parents		
Lower	30.5	9.8
Lower middle	19.9	17.9
Middle	21.8	33.0
Upper middle	8.9	9.4
Upper	14.4	24.4
Not stated	4.5	5.8
Economic condition of families during adolescence of leader		
Very poor	16.5	7.3
Poor	37.8	24.1
Average	37.4	52.0
Wealthy	8.8	14.2
Other	2.5	2.4

The Communist national leadership included a larger proportion of the poor and of the poorly educated than did the Christian Democratic national leadership. (Tables 4-10 and 4-11) This fact was brought out by S. Somogyi in his statistical analysis of the composition of the Chamber of Deputies:

The lower stratum has a significant weight only in the Communist Party where it accounts for a little over a fourth of the cases, 25.9 percent. For the other parties, representatives of this stratum are very few or not to be found at all . . . The level of formal education is radically different only with respect to the Communist group inasmuch as—contrary to the other parties where university

25. Ibid., pp. 321–22.

graduates predominate—a university degree is held by only a few more than a third of the representatives. Those having only elementary educations and those who are entirely self-taught represent almost one fourth of the Communist group, 24.5 percent; while among the Socialists . . . the corresponding figure is only 5.6 percent. Also the percentage of Communist deputies having gone no further than junior high school, 12.3 percent, is almost double . . . that of the Socialists at 6.6 percent.[26]

TABLE 4-11. *Percentage distribution of national party leaders by educational level*

Degree of education	Communist	Christian Democratic
No formal education or self-educated	4.9	0.3
Elementary school or vocational school	25.0	2.8
High school	30.5	11.5
University	39.6	85.4

Education

While 70 percent of the Communist Party leaders surveyed had a high school or university education, many more Christian Democratic leaders (85 percent) had gone to a university. (Table 4-11) The percentage of university graduates in the Communist national leadership increased between 1946 and 1963 (from 33.0 to 43.5), while the Christian Democratic leadership had a large but decreasing percentage (from 88.5 to 85.5) of university graduates in its ranks. (Table 4-12)

TABLE 4-12. *Percent of national party leaders who were university graduates, Communist and Christian Democratic parties, 1946–63*

Year	Communist	Christian Democratic
1946	33.0	88.5
1950	36.9	87.5
1953	32.9	86.7
1957	34.7	85.9
1961	42.5	85.0
1963	43.5	85.5

26. Ibid., pp. 93–96.

The rising number of graduates among the Communist Party leaders may be explained by the growing desire of industrial workers and middle-class families to send their children to the university. These two economic groups have been increasingly represented in the political leadership of the Communist Party (at the expense of leaders drawn from the farming class).

Political Activity and Professional Alternatives

An attempt to ascertain how many of the political leaders surveyed were engaged in occupations other than politics did not produce very reliable results. Many of the Christian Democratic leaders who had held cabinet posts for years claimed that they were engaged in nonpolitical occupations, although professional politics was clearly their main occupation. Similarly many Communist Party leaders declared that they were "workers" or "white-collar employees," although their employer was the party.

Members of parliament or members of national party organs are often engaged in full-time political activity. This is true for both parties: for the Communist Party because of the many demands it places on its leaders, and for the Christian Democratic Party because its officials often have responsibilities in public bodies and other organizations.

The answers on occupations other than politics are interesting when viewed either as indications of the levels of educational-occupational attainment achieved previous to engaging in full-time politics or of the kinds of occupations these officials could fall back on if or when their political careers ended or were interrupted. The tabulation below shows the percentage distribution of Communists and Christian Democrats according to socioeconomic status normally associated with the occupations they gave as their usual ones:

	Socioeconomic status of occupation			
	Lower and lower middle	*Middle and upper middle*	*Upper*	*Politicians*
Communists	25.3	29.2	32.9	12.6
Christian Democrats	2.2	29.9	66.7	1.2

This occupational breakdown shows that Communist Party leaders surveyed differed significantly from the Christian Democratic leaders in that more of them claimed no occupation other than political, or claimed occupations that fell in the lower income groups. The increasing "professionalization" of the leadership of the two mass parties indicated by the survey does not necessarily imply that most of the leaders were so committed to politics that they lacked an alternative way of making a respectable living. Most of the Christian Democratic leaders surveyed, and a majority of the Communist leaders since 1960, held university degrees. Among the Communist Party leaders who had left the party, quite a few had moved to professional and managerial occupations. These facts indicate that the profession of politics may in many cases have been a favorite calling rather than that it was chosen simply as a means of preserving one's social status. The incidence of political professionalism among the leaders surveyed also indicates a response to objective demands of contemporary party politics as well as to other needs of a modern, industrial, mass society.

Furthermore, in Italy as elsewhere, the constraints acting upon political leaders are not necessarily due to professionalism, especially if one is classified as a professional merely because he devotes full time to his party activity and expects it to extend over much of his adult life. There are other constraints under which political leaders operate: for example, their objective qualifications for leadership and the extent to which they are overloaded with commitments.

Political Activity and Competence

Sartori suggests that political activity is not accompanied by the development of specific skills or competence.[27] And Luigi Barzini, the author of *The Italians* and a Liberal Party deputy in the last two legislatures, asserts that the professional organizers so common in the parties today are experts in only one thing: getting themselves reelected.[28] One need not be so pessimistic as Mr. Barzini to recognize that the conditions under which most political careers develop do not make the politician particularly responsive to the changing demands of society.

27. Ibid., pp. 323 ff., especially p. 328.
28. New York, Atheneum, 1964.

A political career often begins at the provincial level, with entrance into the offices of the provincial directorate, where clerks are engaged mostly in paper work. Yet what might be called "the living party," that of the ordinary people of varied social backgrounds and interests, of political and cultural debate, finds expression in the party section, with which those launched on political careers in the provincial offices have little contact. The provincial directorate offers political support, alliances, and opportunities to become known to the electorate.

As the party official advances in the party hierarchy an increasing amount of his time is divided between the provincial and the central offices of the party or of parliament. He seldom sees the rank-and-file party members; he seldom engages in conversation with them; he arrives in a rush at the section to deliver a speech, and then as quickly departs for the provincial or national capital. As he becomes increasingly committed to the party apparatus, he loses contact with the party as an expression of social needs.

In this way the political leader's competence in terms of input—his capacity to sense, understand, and interpret the needs of the rank and file—tends to disappear. At the same time his competence in terms of output, that is, his ability to translate social needs into action, is progressively reduced by the overcommitment of his time and energy.[29] He is besieged by things that he must do to keep or improve his position.

Since the party politician increasingly represents the party machine rather than its rank-and-file electorate, he is continually in the company of party and front-organization functionaries or representatives of specific sectional or local interests. He needs them; they need him; and this reciprocal dependence is transformed into tasks and responsibilities that the leader assumes in order to maintain this relationship.

He is beset with the same overlapping of responsibilities that characterizes many activists at the local level. And like the activist who is committed to too many tasks, the party official never refuses any task that offers him more and better control over the machine. In this manner he prevents others from having access to positions of leadership; and since he can devote too little energy to each of his

29. The terms "input" and "output" have recently been used in attempts to systematize the functional analysis of political systems. See, for example, Gabriel Abraham Almond, "Introduction," in G. A. Almond and James Smoot Coleman, eds., *The Politics of the Developing Areas* (Princeton, Princeton University Press, 1960).

multiple commitments, the party as a whole loses its capacity for political initiative and for reacting to social needs. This pattern of overcommitment is particularly characteristic of leaders of the Christian Democratic Party, and it therefore has serious consequences, because of the cabinet responsibilities that the party bears.

TABLE 4-13. *Percent of Communist and Christian Democratic national party leaders who had held specified party positions, 1946–63*

Position	Communist	Christian Democratic
Sectional secretary	21.0	24.1
Secretary of city or commune committee	6.1	8.3
Member of national or provincial committee	84.4	69.8
Member of regional committee	38.4	31.5

The party leaders covered by the survey were asked which of a list of specific positions they had held in their respective party organizations. (Table 4-13) There was a remarkable parallelism between the two parties in the kinds of party positions the leaders reported that they had held. Political careers were likely to have been launched at the provincial level. The rather low percentage of national party leaders who had served the party at the city or commune level is understandable, when it is remembered that both party organizations had been set up throughout the country on very short notice no more than twenty years before the survey was made, and that the establishment of the grass-roots organization had rarely predated that of the provincial organization.

TABLE 4-14. *Percent of national party leaders who held one or more specified positions* a *in party, 1946–63*

Number of specified positions held a	Communist	Christian Democratic
One	43.8	44.4
Two	43.1	39.6
Three	12.3	12.9
Four	0.8	3.1

a. See Table 4-13 for list of specified positions.

The party leaders surveyed were asked how many of the positions in the party they had held. The results, as shown in Table 4-14, again revealed a striking similarity for the Communists and Christian Democrats in the number of party positions held.

TABLE 4-15. *Percent of party officials who occupied or had occupied selected public offices*

Public office	Communist	Christian Democratic
Communal councillor	69.2	48.9
Communal magistrate (assessor)	14.1	17.8
Mayor	20.2	22.6
Provincial councillor	29.7	17.5
Provincial magistrate	6.4	7.7
Provincial chairman	3.1	6.3

The percentage of the party officials surveyed who had held public offices, as opposed to party posts, is shown in Table 4-15. A larger percentage of Communist than of Christian Democratic national leaders had held positions in local councils, but more Christian Democratic leaders had held posts on local executive boards, as mayors in the communes, or chairmen in the provinces. (Party participation in local government is discussed in detail in Chapter 6.) Although national offices are not shown in the table, almost 7 percent of the Christian Democratic leaders had held ministerial posts, and almost 16 percent had held junior cabinet posts.

The party leaders were also questioned about positions held in party-related organizations, and whether they had held such positions before becoming national party leaders. (Table 4-16)

Apparently the organizations in which posts had been held most frequently were, for the Communists, the General Confederation of Italian Workers; for the Christian Democrats, the youth sections of Catholic Action. It is also significant that while in the General Confederation of Italian Workers the national leadership posts had generally been held after the leaders had become members of the Communist Party's national leadership, comparable positions had generally been held in Catholic Action before the leaders had achieved leadership status in the Christian Democratic Party.

This analysis gives some idea of the extent to which supporting organizations either supply leadership personnel to the two parties or offer party leaders additional props for the maintenance of their positions. A further analysis of trends from 1946 to 1963 indicated

TABLE 4-16. *Percent of national leaders who held offices in party-related organizations before or after they became party officials, 1946–63*

Organization and level	After	Before
Communist officials		
Communist Youth Federation		
Provincial	11.9	88.7
National	8.0	89.6
General Confederation of Italian Workers		
Provincial	28.7	67.5
National	14.2	30.6
Peasants' Alliance		
Provincial	10.0	20.0
National	4.5	18.5
Cooperative League		
Provincial	11.7	30.0
National	3.8	34.8
Christian Democratic officials		
Catholic Action (youth sections)		
Local	26.6	75.9
National	5.4	76.9
Catholic University Students' Federation		
Local	9.9	70.8
National	3.1	86.7
Catholic Action (men's and women's union)		
Local	12.6	56.6
National	2.5	54.2
Catholic Action (university graduates' movement)		
Local	6.7	56.9
National	1.3	61.5
Italian Association of Christian Workers		
Local	14.1	53.0
National	6.0	53.5
Confederation of Small Farmers		
Local	7.2	21.7
National	4.7	20.0
Italian Confederation of Free Unions		
Provincial	6.9	55.2
National	5.8	32.1
Confederation of Italian Cooperatives		
Provincial	4.4	42.9
National	3.5	11.8

that the percentage of Communist leaders who had held positions in the organizations at provincial level tended to increase. An exception was the Communist-dominated Cooperative League, in which positions have increasingly gone to business-trained managers rather than to political leaders.

In line with the Christian Democratic Party effort to preserve an interclass image, the percentage of its leaders who held provincial positions in workers' and peasants' organizations and in the cooperatives also tended to increase over the period surveyed. The percentages of those holding posts in organizations having more markedly Catholic characteristics, however, tended to remain stationary or to decline slightly.

Since the data on the social backgrounds of the Christian Democratic national leaders indicated that the middle class was dominant both in 1946 and in 1963, the trade unions and related organizations were probably the main avenues of political promotion for leaders from petit bourgeois and white-collar backgrounds.

The Public Managers

The Christian Democratic Party has promoted growth in the public sector of the economy. One result of this has been an overlap of political and managerial personnel.

In 1945 the new representative democracy inherited from fascism the Institute for Industrial Reconstruction, a financial holding company created to overcome the consequences of the 1929 crisis; and the General Italian Petroleum Agency, which was to have furnished Italian, African, and Albanian fuel to Mussolini's empire. Also in 1945 the elected local governments, which replaced the fascist governments, were given the right to appoint their representatives to local banks and municipally owned utility companies. Some of these institutions were of national importance, as, for example, the Cassa di Risparmio in Lombardy, with its headquarters in Milan, a Christian Democratic stronghold; and the Monte dei Paschi, with headquarters in Siena, where the Communist Party is quite strong.

At the same time the parties appointed representatives to the national workers' social security and welfare institutes: National Institute for Social Security, National Institute for Workers' Compensation, and National Health Insurance Institute. These agencies have built up enormous financial resources through the dues paid by subscribing workers.

These agencies were only the first centers of economic power that were opened to the party leadership, especially that of the Christian Democratic Party. In 1950 the Cassa per il Mezzogiorno (Fund for the South) and the agencies for agrarian reform were added to them. In 1953 the powerful National Hydrocarbons Trust was created out of the General Italian Petroleum Agency and other companies, and in 1957 the firms belonging to the Institute for Industrial Reconstruction withdrew from the national manufacturers' association and formed an association of their own. In 1962 the center-left government nationalized the electric industry, and the National Agency for Electrical Energy was formed.

Between 1945 and 1950 the Christian Democrats were already well represented in the municipal companies and in the credit and welfare institutes. In 1950 many Christian Democratic leaders took positions in the Institute for Industrial Reconstruction, the Cassa per il Mezzogiorno, the agrarian reform agencies, and, later, in the National Hydrocarbons Trust. The public agencies became the battlegrounds and weapons in the party's factional struggles. Giovanni Gronchi, a Christian Democrat and President of the Italian Republic, became president of the Institute for Industrial Reconstruction, and the welfare institutes provided positions for members of the unionist faction. While Amintore Fanfani was Minister of Agriculture, with Mariano Rumor and Luigi Gui as undersecretaries, the agrarian reform agencies provided the nursery for Fanfani's Iniziativa Democratica movement, as they later did for other groups. The reform agencies in Apulia and Lucania became the strongholds of Aldo Moro and Emilio Colombo. The political connections of the managerial staff of the National Hydrocarbons Trust are well known.

This overlapping of political and managerial responsibilities is time-consuming and adds substantially to the many tasks assumed by Christian Democratic leaders. Answers to the survey questions suggest that as many as half of the 800 Christian Democratic leaders who replied may have held posts in various public economic agencies.

Unlike most of the data previously presented on positions held in other organizations, which tend to indicate the backgrounds from which these political leaders came, the figures in Table 4-17 suggest the extent to which rewards arising from growing governmental economic intervention accrue to party leaders. While the data are not sufficient to constitute proof, there is reason to believe that the majority of the Christian Democratic political leaders have had access

to these public posts after achieving positions of political promi-
nence. This suggests a qualification to Giovanni Sartori's generaliza-
tion that positions of political leadership are increasingly held by
people who do not have a solid, previously acquired, economic
position.[30] Modern political figures often seek a position of economic power on the basis of public managerial functions rather
than on the basis of ownership of property.

TABLE 4-17. *Percent of Christian Democratic
political leaders who held posts in various
public economic agencies, 1946–63*

Type of agency	Percent
Social security or welfare	34.3
Financial	12.4
Municipally owned utilities, transport, etc.	3.2
Publicly owned firms	8.8

This addition of managerial functions to all of the other commitments of the national party leaders results in increasing paralysis in
the political sphere. Although this type of overlap is particularly a
problem of the Christian Democrats, Communist leaders have opportunities, in areas where they are locally in power, to enter the
municipal agencies, the banks, and other economic agencies that are
controlled by the commune and the province.

Regional Representation in the National Leadership

In both parties the distribution of the leadership by region of
origin reflects to some extent the increase in importance of the central and southern regions of the country during the period studied.
For example, the Christian Democratic leaders of southern and island origin constituted more than a third of the national Christian
Democratic leadership—36.6 percent in 1946 and 38.5 percent in
1963. The changes in the regional composition of the Communist
leadership in the same period were more marked: the number of
leaders from the South and the Islands increased from 22.4 percent
to 33.1 percent. The North, which had claimed about half of the national leaders of both of the leading parties at the beginning of the
period under study, had lost its numerical supremacy by the end of
the period, when it could claim only about 40 percent.

30. Sartori et al., p. 329.

A striking fact about the national leadership of the Communist Party has been the constant underrepresentation of Emilia-Romagna, the home of more than a fourth of the members of the party. Here the Communists have had local control and have transformed their front organizations into mass associations. And yet this region, so important to the Communists, accounted for only 14.6 percent of the national party leaders from 1945 to 1963. This is significant because Emilia, including Romagna, has always been one of Italy's major sources of political leaders, both in quality and quantity. This was true of the socialist and fascist movements and, to a lesser extent, of the Catholic movement itself. The Communist Party inherited much of the old socialist tradition, especially in Emilia-Romagna. But the party did not equally inherit the Emilian tradition of socialist leadership; no top national Communist leader came from this region between 1945 and 1963.

A somewhat similar relationship exists between Communist Party membership in Tuscany and its representation in the national party leadership, although Tuscany, with 16 percent of the Communist Party members and 12 percent of its national leadership, was not so badly underrepresented in 1963 as was Emilia-Romagna. Tuscany is another region that, since the war, has contributed Christian Democratic leaders of great national importance (Amintore Fanfani, Gronchi, La Pira), but it has not been the home of a single top Communist leader. During the de-Stalinization crisis and the fears aroused by the possibility of a break with the Socialist Party, the Tuscan Communist leaders, like those in Emilia-Romagna, had no spokesman to express their preference for a more active and daring party policy. In order to defend their positions of local power, they turned to the leadership of Giorgio Amendola, a Neapolitan. In these regions that are highly politicized and have always been a source of Italian political leaders, an entire generation passed without the appearance of a single top national Communist leader. Only a strongly centralized direction at the top with tight control over the party apparatus and with authoritarian discipline could account for the lack of representation from regions of Communist strength.

In the Christian Democratic Party the situation is quite the reverse. Almost every local leader has autonomous power, independent of the central apparatus, and almost every region has supplied its quota of top national leaders.

The Catholic Hierarchy and the
Christian Democratic Leaders

The wide geographical representation in the national leadership of the Christian Democratic Party, when added to the diverse situations caused by the many factions within the party, has increased the fragmentation that pervades the party from top to bottom. But at the highest level one fact is largely responsible for holding the party together: most of the Christian Democratic leaders have had leadership experience, either locally or nationally, in the Catholic Action organizations. In fact they owe their access to party leadership in large part to these Catholic associations. But since the organizations in turn are directly and tightly controlled by the Catholic hierarchy, which in Italy is a highly unified body, it is ultimately the hierarchy, either directly or through the organizations of the Catholic world, that counteracts the potentially disruptive heterogeneity of the Christian Democratic leadership.

When the Church leaders do not intervene, factional struggles often carry the party to the point of schism. Because of the habits of obedience inculcated in the party leaders by their experience in the Catholic organizations, as well as the threat that the organizations might withdraw their support of the party, when the hierarchy does intervene, in the name and the defense of the political unity of Catholics, its influence is decisive.

During December 1964, when the new President of the Republic was being elected, the Christian Democratic Party came close to a breaking point. Pressure was then brought to bear on the party factions by the Vatican and also on the members of parliament in Rome by the peripheral hierarchy, through the pages of *L'Italia,* a daily published by the Curia of Milan. This publication made it clear that those who turned a deaf ear to the Church's exhortation to unity in such a difficult and important moment could no longer count on the support of the hierarchy. Independent of reasons of conscience, there are practical reasons why the Christian Democratic leaders cannot ignore such admonishments.

When necessary this cohesive force exercised by the Church can keep the Christian Democratic political leaders united. But it cannot make of these men—most of whom are advanced in age, lack contact with whole classes of society, are busy with too many functions, and worried about too many things—a broad, dynamic political class, able to understand and resolve the many serious problems of social development faced by the government of Italy today.

These and other inadequacies of the Christian Democrats, together with the fact that they have to carry on the onerous and often controversial task of governing the nation, make the opposition of the younger and more broadly based Communist political leadership much easier and more effective.

5

The Parties and Their Mass Support

By establishing organizations of many types—from those with local interests to those concerned with culture and leisure—or by acquiring some measure of control over already existing organizations, the Communist and the Christian Democratic parties, as mass parties, seek to give political direction to social actions of all kinds, at all levels of society.[1]

While the Communist Party is the center of a number of associations and special groups that revolve around it, the Christian Democratic Party represents just one activity among the many clusters of organized activity that center around the hierarchy of the Italian Catholic Church. Thus it is the Church rather than the Christian Democratic Party that holds the dominant position in the organizational activity of the Catholic subculture in Italy. This has important consequences for the Christian Democratic Party, since the political goals of the many Catholic organizations differ. For instance, two important Catholic movements, the Italian Association of Christian Workers and the Confederation of Small Farmers (Coldiretti) are allied with factions to the left and to the right of the Christian Democrats and attempt to pull it in opposite directions.

For political parties to assume responsibility for action in various spheres of social life has a number of unfortunate consequences. From the standpoint of society at large, it leads to a distorted kind of pluralistic development, with poor boundaries between interest

1. For American sources of information, see Joseph LaPalombara, *Interest Groups in Italian Politics* (Princeton, Princeton University Press, 1964); and "Italy: Fragmentation, Isolation, Alienation," in L. Pye and S. Verba, eds., *Political Culture and Political Development* (Princeton, Princeton University Press, 1965), pp. 282 ff.

groups and political parties,[2] and to the duplication of effort in the pursuit of single social goals. It thwarts the development of a social solidarity that could cut across political cleavages.[3] It thus tends to reinforce the kind of social structure already implicit in a society historically divided into two major politico-ideological groupings or subcultures.

The nonparty organizations themselves suffer under these circumstances. Their programs are inspired not by particular social demands or by the needs of a sector of the population, but by the requirements of the parties. Their leaders and activists, already overworked in similar capacities in the political field, can give them only scraps of their time, energy, and dedication. The result is a rhythm of operations in which periods of nearly total inertia are broken occasionally by fits and spurts of activity in response to sudden calls for action from the outside.

It is at times difficult to see what advantages, if any, the parties derive from their sponsorship of some of these organizations. This applies particularly to the Communist Party in its relation to organized groups other than the unions and cooperatives. These organizations do little to widen the party's sphere of influence; in fact, their membership largely coincides with sectors of society and with geographical areas already under party control. Nor do the organizations supply cadres to the party. In fact they are mostly manned by already committed Communists whose energies the party could well use elsewhere.

The same cannot be said of the relationship between the Christian Democratic Party and the Catholic organizations. With the exception of the economic organizations, such as unions and cooperatives, the Catholic organizations bring to the Christian Democrats the support of sectors of society that would otherwise be outside the party's reach. Throughout the postwar period (although decreasingly so since the middle 1950s) these organizations have supplied activists, cadres, and leaders to the party.

The relationship between the parties and the supporting unions and cooperatives is different for the two parties. The economic organizations connected with the Communist Party constitute one of

2. See the essay by G. A. Almond in G. A. Almond and J. S. Coleman, *The Politics of the Developing Areas* (Princeton, Princeton University Press, 1960).

3. The critical significance of "overlapping memberships" in organizations outside the parties has been stressed by many authors. In recent American literature, see David Truman, *The Governmental Process* (New York, Knopf, 1951).

the main bases of the party's strength, while those with leanings toward the Christian Democratic Party tend to support factions of that party rather than the party as a whole.

The Catholic organizations based on noneconomic interests are more vital than their Communist-dominated counterparts and have a more significant relationship with the Christian Democratic Party. In fact, the Communist-oriented organizations of this kind arose largely in response to the clearly effective performance of the Catholic organizations, and they tend to be largely imitative and defensive.

The opposite is generally true of the organizations of employees and consumers. The first unions and cooperatives to become established were associated with the socialist subculture, and the present dominance of those controlled by the Communists reflects this priority. The Catholic economic organizations developed later and largely in response to the Communist-controlled organizations.

THE CHRISTIAN DEMOCRATIC PARTY AND THE CATHOLIC ORGANIZATIONS

Confronted by a large Communist Party after the Second World War, the Roman Catholic Church felt itself threatened by a movement that transcended politics and was guided by a philosophy directly opposed to the ideals, traditions, and philosophy of the Church. Although the Church was not itself the founder of the Christian Democratic Party, it saw in it a political instrument for defending Christian ideals and traditions. The Church therefore threw its support behind the party, reasoning that the unity of Catholics is necessary in every field in the battle against communism, that since the battle against communism is waged on the political plane, Catholics must be politically united. As the political party of Christian inspiration, the Christian Democratic Party came to be regarded by the hierarchy—the Pope and the bishops (including the Cardinals, all of whom are also bishops)—as the organization of the Catholic world that specialized in the conduct of political activity.

Religious-Political Directives of the Church

The intervention of the ecclesiastical hierarchy in Italian political life since 1945 has been constant, and has taken on the aspect of a continuous religious education. To Pius XII and the Italian bishops the existence of a strong Communist Party in Italy meant that a normal political interchange could not apply, since the two parties shared no underlying system of values. The Church's violently anticommunist position rested on its belief that from the Communists and their allies a complete reversal of the social order could be expected. This expectation explains the insistence of the Church that Christian principles are the proper foundation for the institutional edifice of the state and the proper inspiration for its laws and customs, and that it is the duty of every Catholic to be active, as a Catholic, in public life.

The situation between the young Italian democracy and the Church in 1945 did not seem to augur a peaceful settlement. Even the Concordat and the Lateran Treaty (which in 1929 had ended the sixty-year-old conflict between the Church and the Italian state)[4] seemed subject to possible change. Therefore the Church, through its bishops and the Pope, appealed to the faithful, alerting them to the growing Communist threat to religion. It thus became its principal objective to see that all Catholics voted and that they all voted for the same party. Absenteeism at the polls, apathy, the indifference of the faithful to imminent religious-political dangers were what the Church feared most.

Electoral campaigns provided the best occasion for such appeals from the Church authorities. The basic document of hierarchical intervention is the circular of the Consistorial Congregation addressed to all Italian bishops in August 1945. It contained the following instructions:

(a) In consideration of the dangers to which religion and the public well-being are exposed and whose gravity requires the unanimous collaboration of all honest men, all those who have the right to vote, of every condition, sex, and age, with no exceptions, are, in conscience, strictly obliged to avail themselves of that right.

(b) Catholics may give their vote only to those candidates or those lists of candidates of whom one has the certainty that they

---

4. The best source in English on the Concordat and the Lateran Treaty, and the relations between the Holy See and the fascist regime, is D. A. Binchy, *Church and State in Fascist Italy* (London, Royal Institute of International Affairs, 1941). See also A. C. Jemolo, *Church and State in Italy* (Oxford, Blackwell, 1960).

will respect and defend the observance of the divine law and the rights of religion and the Church in private and in public life.[5]

This language is explicit that the candidates who should have the votes of honest men (Catholics) can be only those of the Christian Democratic Party.

In the 1946 elections for the Constituent Assembly Catholics were admonished to vote as a bloc "to ensure to the present and future generations the blessing of a fundamental law of the nation which is not opposed to sound religious and moral principles, but rather takes from them vigorous inspiration and proclaims them and wisely follows their lofty ends." [6]

During the general elections of 1948, in the face of the threat from the Communist and Socialist popular front, the appeals from the Church became more fervent, as if there were taking place in Italy an all-out battle that would decide the future of the Church itself. The Pope and bishops joined the fray, repeatedly admonishing Catholics, under penalty of sin, to vote against the Socialist-Communist enemy. It being perfectly clear that the mass support of the Church was going to the Christian Democrats, the other political parties (not only the Communist Party) violently contested the Church's intervention.

While the warnings and teachings of the Pope and the bishops were always prefaced by statements of the reasons justifying such intervention, symptoms of disturbance and perplexity began to appear even among Catholics. Especially between 1945 and 1948, a number of Catholic militants in the Christian Democratic Party wished to keep the Church out of the political contest. Others failed to understand the reasons for the anticommunist alarm. There was even a movement (the "Christian Left") that expressly favored an alliance between Catholics and Communists. When this movement was quickly condemned by the Church and disbanded, some of its followers joined the Communist Party.

5. Circular of the Sacra Congregazione Concistoriale of August 29, 1945, "Sull'uso del diritto di voto." See the text in *Civiltà Cattolica*, Notebook 2286 of September 15, 1945. The results of the research on the interventions of the Catholic hierarchy in Italian politics have been fully reported in Alfonso Prandi, *Chiesa e politica: La Gerarchia e l'impegno politico dei cattolici italiani* (Bologna, Società editrice il Mulino, 1968).
6. Excerpt from a letter written by Pius XII to Cardinal Lavitrano on the occasion of the Nineteenth Italian Catholic Social Week, held in Florence from October 23 to October 28, 1945. The theme of the meeting was "Constitution and Constituency." See *L'Osservatore Romano* of October 22, 1945.

Catholic criticism of ecclesiastical intervention became especially strong from 1953 on, as the Church began to take sides in intraparty disputes. The bishops themselves began to speak of an increasing indifference to their warnings. But criticism of its political role did not cause the Church to abstain from politics. The fact is that the hierarchy, which had earlier limited itself to strong recommendations to Catholics to cast united votes for the Christian Democratic Party, began to have other worries. The growing factional strife within the Christian Democratic Party and questions of the party's goals and strategy threatened the very basis of the Church's support for the party.

When the results of the 1953 general elections proved a disappointment, the Church felt even more called upon to devote its attention to what was going on within the party. Catholic unity was no longer enough if the Church-supported political party was divided in its aims and lacked a solid organizational foundation, such as characterized the Communist Party. It seemed necessary for the "best" Catholics (that is, the members of Catholic Action, discussed later in this chapter) to devote themselves more closely to strengthening the Christian Democratic Party and making it more sensitive to the warnings of the Church. Beginning in 1954, when Amintore Fanfani became party secretary, the party began to transform itself from a merely electoral party into a mass party. This move implied the beginning of a rigorous discipline that the bishops at first viewed with favor.

But consideration by the Christian Democratic Party of an "opening to the left" as a possible policy alternative immediately brought the hierarchy into opposition. This policy proposed a government based on a Christian Democratic-Socialist alliance that would transfer the Socialists from the Communist camp into the "democratic area." A government based on this majority would have the votes necessary to carry out a policy of reform, which, its advocates believed, was the only decisive answer to the Communist challenge.

The bishops did not hide their alarm over the possibility that certain Catholic factions might consider a dialogue or collaboration with Marxist forces. It seemed to them that the new movement, which was making progress in the guise of social reform, actually represented Marxist infiltration and engendered a feeling of rebellion against the ecclesiastical authority. Pius XII remained firm in his anticommunist denunciations, and the bishops, in their turn, denounced the illusion, the falsity, and the impossibility of such a co-existence.

The hierarchy took the opportunity offered by the 1958 general elections to remind Catholics that the Church's position concerning political commitment had undergone no change. The Catholics must be and remain united. Ten years earlier the hierarchy had simply endorsed the Christian Democratic Party. Now, however, this endorsement was qualified—Catholics were expected to vote for those Christian Democratic candidates who specifically opposed the daring designs of the "leftists."

Tension between the Italian episcopate and the Christian Democratic Party was at its peak from 1958 to 1961. Growing numbers of party members favored opening a dialogue with the Socialists in order to accelerate their separation from the Communists; but the hierarchy, in ever stronger terms, denounced the Christian Democrats' wooing of the Socialists as the most serious of threats to Catholic unity. The pressures that were regularly brought to bear on the party were explicit and sometimes openly provocative. Cardinal Siri, Archbishop of Genoa and President of the Italian Episcopal Conference, wrote to Aldo Moro, the Secretary of the Christian Democratic Party, to dissuade him from continuing the policy of trying to form a parliamentary majority that would include the Socialists. At times the bishops even threatened to withdraw Catholic support from the party.

In the autumn of 1958 John XXIII succeeded Pius XII. Pope John appeared not to share the burning concern of his predecessors for events on the Italian political scene. The episcopate, which previously had only to repeat, amplify, and adapt the position of the Pope, was now left to its own discretion. While on the surface nothing seemed changed, in fact Rome either left politics alone or suggested that such matters should not be too much discussed.

In spite of the warnings and threats of the most alarmed and most vocal of the bishops, the first center-left alliances were cautiously formed in the governments of such large cities as Milan, Genoa, and Florence after the local elections of November 1960. While this caused serious concern among the episcopate, the lack of a pontifical pronouncement weakened the bishops' position. The Christian Democratic Party meanwhile did not seem to fear that the united hierarchy would go so far as to excommunicate the party and advise the Catholics to withdraw their electoral support.

Many bishops, in fact most of them, were silent. Only Cardinal Montini (the future Pope Paul VI, then Archbishop of Milan) expressed himself as being willing to reconsider his position. In May 1960 he wrote that although he did not favor the "so-called 'opening to the left' at the present moment and in the manner now being considered," he could not exclude the possibility of guarantees that would be sufficient to permit a change in the Church's negative attitude.[7] The Bishop of Pesaro, who had most strongly denounced the "opening to the left" as going against religious teachings, wrote: "We have concerned ourselves too much with politics, to the detriment of our ministry." [8]

In reality, John XXIII had induced the episcopate to give more attention to general problems of humanity and the Catholic world. The calling of the Ecumenical Council and the encyclicals *Mater et Magistra* and *Pacem in Terris* created an atmosphere in which the politico-religious themes of the first fifteen years sounded a jarring note. At last the bishops were silenced.

At its Naples Congress at the end of 1961 the Christian Democratic Party initiated the "opening to the left" by starting a program of collaboration with the Socialists, and in 1962 the Socialist Party pledged itself to support the government, although it did not form part of the Cabinet. The bishops still refrained from comment; in fact, many of them seemed to be worried lest their earlier thunderous pronouncements against the operation would not be used to justify a break in the united Catholic front. To the extent that they discussed political questions at all, they returned to the theme of Catholic unity. That unity was said to be a blessing superior to the contingent decisions of the party and the various orientations of its factions. Cardinal Siri, one of the most explicit adversaries of the "opening to the left," limited himself in 1962 to encouraging the "coherence" of Catholics even "in the face of most dangerous and perplexing facts." [9]

The official organ of the Italian episcopate advised Catholics to vote united during the 1963 electoral campaign and "make their choices with a watchful Christian conscience, knowing, if necessary,

7. Letter to the clergy of the Diocese of Milan, dated May 21, 1960. The letter was not supposed to have been released to the public, but through an indiscretion it came to the attention of the press. See *L'Italia*, June 4, 1960.
8. Pastoral letter for Lent, 1961. See *Lettere Pastorali di Vescovi Italiani, 1961* (Padua, Cittadella, 1961), pp. 422–42.
9. Pastoral letter to the faithful of the Diocese of Genoa for Lent, 1962. See *Lettere Pastorali 1962–63* (Padua, Cittadella, 1964), pp. 771–811.

174

Patterns of Political Participation in Italy

how to put their faithfulness to essential Christian principles and the requirements of the common good before personal opinions and particular interests." [10] The communication contained not a word about the center-left; in fact, it was fairly clear that "faithfulness to essential Christian principles and the requirements of the common good" consisted of voting for the Christian Democratic Party. Residual objections to agreements with the Socialists were brushed aside as merely "personal opinions and particular interests."

It is not known whether the Italian bishops had merely resigned themselves to their new role as guardians of Catholic unity or had felt the impact of John XXIII and the significance of the Council, but a process of disengagement had clearly taken place and it was reflected in the Catholic Action organizations, which are directly controlled by the hierarchy.

The Party and Catholic Action [11]

Italian Catholic Action is an organization of Catholic laymen associated with the Church hierarchy in its apostolic mission. It has historical roots in the Catholic subculture formed within the newly constituted Italian state, in which political and religious motivation were inextricably entwined.

Later developments led to a degree of differentiation between political and religious organizations. In 1919 the Popular Party was formed as autonomous from the hierarchy, and Catholic Action was assigned specifically religious goals, such as training the young and conducting apostolic work. During the fascist period Catholic Action was preserved from the Gleichschaltung (incorporation into the state) only by stressing its religious motives and by making its organization clearly dependent on the Church. The parish and the diocese, under the control of the priest and the bishop, respectively, were the main local levels of activity, while the national organs were

10. Communication of the Conferenza Episcopale Italiana of March 12, 1963. See Civiltà Cattolica, Notebook 2707 of April 4, 1963. See the clarification of the meaning of the Communication in L'Osservatore Romano, April 7, 1963.
11. See Joseph LaPalombara, Interest Groups in Italian Politics, passim; and G. Poggi, Italian Catholic Action (Stanford, Stanford University Press, 1966). The latter study, however, is not specifically concerned with the political action of Catholic Action. See also Luigi Brunelli, Umberto Canullo, Gianluigi Degli Esposti, Giorgio Galli, Anna Lena, Luciana Pepa, Antonio Picchi, Alfonso Prandi, Alberto Mario Rossi, Bruno Scatassa, Ada Sivini Cavazzani, Luigi Turco, La presenza sociale del PCI e della DC (Bologna, Società editrice il Mulino, 1969), pp. 329–616.

directly controlled by the Holy See. This form of organization has continued.

Before the war Catholic Action consisted of four separate groups: Unione Uomini, the men's union; Unione Donne, the women's union; Gioventù Femminile Italiana, the young women's branch; and Gioventù Italiana di Azione Cattolica, the young men's branch. In 1946 the Holy See issued new statutes establishing within Catholic Action, in addition, Federazione Universitari Cattolici Italiani, the university students' movement; Movimento Laureati, the university graduates' movement; and Movimento Maestri, the elementary school teachers' movement. According to the directives, each of the four branches and movements was to have a national organization and a local organization in every diocese and parish.

At the national level and executive organ, the General Presidency of Catholic Action, and a deliberative organ, the Central Junta, were created. All of the officers of the General Presidency, as well as of the various national executive organs, are appointed by ecclesiastical authority.

At the diocesan level the organizational structure is identical, except that the diocesan president and the branch presidents are chosen by the local bishop. The same structure is used in the parishes, where the priest selects the leaders. Although all of the leaders are laymen, each level has an ecclesiastical assistant representing the hierarchy. In short, the hierarchy and the clergy maintain a tight control over Catholic Action, which is their devoted army and instrument.

During the 1950s Catholic Action had nearly a million members in the adult branches and almost two million in the youth branches (which include children), with additional members in the specialized movements.

Catholic Action is present in all areas of the country and reflects the level of political development of the Catholics more clearly than does the Catholic-oriented political party. In the central and northern regions it is Catholic Action and not the Christian Democratic Party that is the mass political and social organization of Italian Catholics. For example, about 15 to 20 percent of Catholic Action's membership is in Veneto, where the Party is electorally much stronger than its organizational strength would lead one to expect. (See Figure 4-1) This suggests that the party's electoral support is largely due to the votes delivered by this laymen's organization. In the South, where the political development lags behind that of the North, Catholic Action organization and membership are weak.

In the North, in fact, Catholic Action was the instrument of fusion between the Catholic electorate and the liberal-moderate electorate, and its influence has been the reason for the continued support of Christian Democracy by these disparate groups. In the South, where the fusion of these two groups took place more recently, the party plays a more independent role, but it still has close ties to Catholic Action.

Catholic Action, after announcing its unwillingness to engage in political activity, defended its intervention in the electoral campaigns with the same arguments advanced by the hierarchy—that Catholic unity was the best weapon in the struggle against communism. Thus justifying its political commitment, the organization set out to defend, promulgate, and practice Christian principles in public life. Its spirit of militancy made Catholic Action one of the most active forces on the Italian political scene.

During 1947 and 1948, particularly, when opposition between the anticommunist forces and the Communist and Socialist popular front was the central theme of Italian political life, Catholic Action was among the most energetic and conspicuous protagonists of the battle.

ROLE OF THE CIVIC COMMITTEES [12]

In preparation for the April 1948 elections a new organization, the Civic Committees, was created to sponsor and manage the "Christian crusade against communism" by channeling votes to the Christian Democratic Party. Although purportedly autonomous, this organization was in fact a cover for Catholic Action and was manned entirely by Catholic Action personnel. After the 1948 election Catholic Action did not hesitate to take credit for the Christian Democratic Party's electoral success, and no one contradicted these assertions.

Organized in 1948 under the leadership of Luigi Gedda, in the political climate of a struggle between the forces of "good" and "evil," the goal of the Civic Committees was the mobilization of the cadres of every type of nonpolitical Catholic organization in the

12. See LaPalombara, Interest Groups, especially pp. 334 ff.; Poggi, Italian Catholic Action, Chaps. 13 and 14.

struggle against communism and the establishment of a Christian political and social order.[13] Since the tight discipline of the Communists was considered the greatest asset of the forces of evil, the Civic Committees was meant to evoke a similarly disciplined response among all the adversaries of communism.

Although Catholic Action's members were the backbone of the Civic Committees, it was thought inadvisable to subject Catholic Action to a charge of political intervention and possible violation of the Concordat, which the Holy See was anxious to have respected by the state. The Civic Committees was created as a separate entity, therefore, for the purpose of joining the political fray.

One stated difference between the two organizations was that Catholic Action considered itself directly responsible to the hierarchy, while the Civic Committees offered itself to the hierarchy to be used as the Church thought best. The Civic Committees thus did not depend directly on the ecclesiastical authority; it had not been created by the hierarchy, nor were its leaders officially appointed by the Church.

More openly than Catholic Action, the Civic Committees supported the Christian Democratic Party, working to gain electoral support for it, but, at the same time, also hoping to exercise some amount of influence over it.

The ideas that the Civic Committees sought to instill in the minds of the public were rather simple. Although it believed that certain urgent social reforms had to be undertaken before much ground could be gained against the Communists, the Civic Committees continued to harp on the theme that communism was a program of deceit and falsehood. As Ugo Sciascia was to say in 1955:

> The Communists are prisoners of untruth, and we wish to liberate them. Let us reveal the positive significance of our mission. Before laying the foundations of a better world we simply wish to clear away the materialistic mud in order to build on the rock of spiritual value.[14]

13. The significant financial contribution made by the American Catholics to the setting up of the Committees in 1948 was privately acknowledged by the organization's leaders. In fact, powerful overseas backing, particularly in the early phase, was suggested both by the scale of financial resources available and by the remarkable resourcefulness of the propaganda techniques adopted.
14. *Collegamento,* February 1955, 8, 2, 1.

CRITICISM OF THE PARTY

Accompanying these attempts to "unmask" communism before the eyes of public opinion was the constant demand that the Christian Democrats, as the governing party, engage in action against the Italian Communist Party with all the means at their disposal. This demand was made so often and so strongly that the feeling grew that if the spread of communism was not arrested the main fault would lie with the Christian Democratic Party. This sort of logic, which saw the Catholic party both as an object of hope and of guilt in disappointments, was typical of the hierarchy, of Catholic Action, and thus of the Civic Committees.

Although Catholic Action took as active a part in the local elections of 1951 and the general elections of 1953, as it had in 1948, most of its campaigning was carried out behind the facade of the Civic Committees. But although in 1948 Catholic Action had claimed most of the credit for the Christian Democratic Party's success, in 1953 it refused to share the blame for its losses. It had done its part, it claimed, by encouraging and maintaining Catholic unity; the party, on the other hand, had not properly administered the support delivered to it. Above all, the Christian Democratic Party's scruples had prevented it from dealing the Communist Party a blow, as it could have, for instance, through special legislation. In short, the party had not done its part in the crusade. It had asserted its autonomy, put too much emphasis on democratic values, rejected alliances with nondemocratic but anticommunist political forces, and had made exaggerated antifascist pronouncements, thus alienating possible allies from the right.

From this disagreement over the political orientation of the party, there emerged a second phase in the history of Catholic Action's political commitment. It began in 1952 when Luigi Gedda, General Vice-President, and later President of Catholic Action, with the consent of the Vatican, sought to bring about an alliance between the Christian Democratic Party and extreme right-wing forces in order to ensure an electoral victory in the commune of Rome. The operation did not succeed, and Gedda suffered a considerable loss of prestige.

But Catholic Action had taken the position that it was entitled to a voice in the Christian Democratic Party's policy decisions. And once Catholic Action began to concern itself with party policy, it was to find more and more reasons for concern over developments within the party. If the solidarity of Catholic Action was due to its devotion to the Church, the many factions in the party—it was hinted —were the result of religious immaturity, of human weakness, of the attention given to outdated polemics (fascism versus antifascism), which had no place among Catholics engaged in the defense of the Church.

Catholic Action seemed to feel that once the cadres and militants it supplied to the party became established, they would merely carry out the directives of the hierarchy, behave in the disciplined manner in which they had been trained in the organization, and thus carry on enormous weight in determining party policy. In fact, however, the influx of Catholic Action members into the party did not bring the factional struggles to a halt. Instead, dissension within the party became more bitter, and even the leaders trained in Catholic Action became involved in the disputes on every side.

Since Catholic Action, and particularly its President, Luigi Gedda, wished to see the formation of political alliances between the Christian Democrats and the extreme right-wing, anticommunist, and antidemocratic forces, it began to support those men and factions who also favored such alliances. It maintained this attitude from 1953 to 1958 and even later, which strongly suggests that the political preferences of at least a sizable sector of organized Catholicism (as well as of the hierarchy) leaned toward a confessional, authoritarian state, led by a strong man like Franco or Salazar. When the conflict between the Christian Democratic Party, the bishops, and the Catholic Action leaders over the "opening to the left" was at its height, it was even suggested that Catholic Action was considering the creation of a new Catholic political party that would be much farther to the right.

Catholic Action was fully supported in its attacks on party policy by the Civic Committees. Criticism also led to veiled threats at times, as during the general elections of 1958. Observing that at the Twentieth Congress of the Communist Party of the Soviet Union, communism had unmasked itself and revealed its true face to many of the simple souls who had swelled its ranks, the Civic Committees declared:

We offer to the Christian Democrats a second great opportunity
(the first was in 1948): if they should fail to take full advantage
of it—but we are sure they will not—then Italy will surely seek another solution.[15]

DECLINE OF POLITICAL INFLUENCE OF CATHOLIC ACTION AND THE CIVIC COMMITTEES

Within Catholic Action itself there was opposition to the Gedda
policy among the top leaders and the rank and file, especially in the
most active branches, such as the youth branches and the university
movements.[16] Although the most outspoken critics of the Gedda
line were severely reprimanded by the clergy and sometimes expelled, the organization did not suffer membership losses. However,
because of these tensions, the Gedda group within the organization
never fully recovered its vigor. As Catholic Action became more bitterly critical of the Christian Democratic Party, it also began to lose
its influence. Even the clergy became dissatisfied, or at least divided
in opinion.

With the pontificate of John XXIII, Catholic Action seemed to
withdraw into its old limits of an organization dedicated to the religious training of the laity, and increasingly avoided becoming engaged in political conflicts, although it continued to be the chief organizational support of the Christian Democratic Party. It is strong
in those areas of the country with a strong Catholic tradition. Its
membership is not artificially inflated as a weapon in factional
struggles, as the membership of the Christian Democratic Party
often is. Unlike most of the Communist Party's supporting organizations, whose membership is strongly concentrated in Emilia-Romagna and Tuscany, Catholic Action has achieved a satisfactory level
of organization throughout most of the country.

With the slow withdrawal of Catholic Action from the political
scene, the political influence of the Civic Committees also began to
decline. Partly responsible for this decline was the decreasing effectiveness of the flashy propaganda techniques that the Civic Committees had used so successfully in earlier years. While the Civic Committees had carried out its original mission of mobilizing the widest
possible consensus behind the Christian Democratic Party and of es-

15. *Collegamento*, May 1956, 9, 7, 1.
16. See Poggi, Chaps. 8, 10, and 13.

tablishing a tight control over the party, the organization as a whole had failed in the task and in justifying its own survival.

The strategy of the Civic Committees, as well as of Catholic Action itself, was based on the assumption that Italy was a "Christian" country and that therefore the overwhelming majority of Italians could be relied upon to respond to the anticommunist call. After years of unsuccessful attempts to call forth such a majority, the danger of basing its strategy on this assumption became ominously clear to the Civic Committees. The Church in Italy could no longer insist on a political expression of the religious loyalties of the people.

To the extent that the hierarchy was led, during John XXIII's pontificate, to question itself in these terms, the Civic Committees could only reveal its limitations and the perhaps spurious nature of its early success. But the Civic Committees is not necessarily a thing of the past, especially if the ecclesiastical authority should again view it as a valid instrument of its pastoral activity.

The key aspect of the activity of the Civic Committees was always its propaganda support of the Christian Democratic Party during electoral campaigns. In 1948 and 1953 the contribution of the organization was obvious, because of its gaudiness and flashiness, but even after that it maintained a close propaganda collaboration with the party. The ways in which the Civic Committees sought to influence the Christian Democratic Party also reflect its electoral orientation. While Catholic Action had hoped to saturate the party with its own members, the Civic Committees tried to exercise some control over the composition of the party's parliamentary group in order to influence the direction of the party and the policy of the government. It did this by becoming involved in the selection of Christian Democratic candidates at the local level and by trying to channel the preferential votes to its favorite candidates.

These were the tactics used in 1958, when the threat of the "opening to the left" seemed most urgently to require intervention in party affairs. At this point, however, the party itself, as well as a number of its factions, was sufficiently well organized to keep the Civic Committees from having a serious impact on the contest for preferential votes. The national Civic Committees also had only limited control over the extent, character, and direction of electoral activities at the local level, since all Catholic organizations represented in the local Civic Committees are primarily dependent on the local bishop. In the late 1950s and early 1960s this meant that the national Civic Committees could count less and less on its local organs to adopt a uniform line of action. All of these developments gave a decided downward turn to the influence of the Civic Committees on the party.

Movimento Maestri and the Italian Catholic Teachers' Association

One of the major guarantees of lasting Catholic influence in Italy is the predominance of Catholics among elementary school teachers. The state system of elementary education has a religious base that the Church has declared its intention to preserve. In order to ensure the continuation of this hegemony, the elementary teachers' movement, the Movimento Maestri, in 1945 sponsored the formation of the Italian Catholic Teachers' Association, a professional association that could claim formal autonomy.

The structure of the Catholic Teachers' Association is formally democratic. However, its connection with Catholic Action (through the Movimento Maestri) is unmistakable, since its basic territorial units at the intermediate level are diocesan—a fact that ensures its control by the Movimento Maestri. In 1946 the association had 20,-316 members; by 1948 its membership had doubled to 41,717; in 1950 it had 50,671 members; in 1960, 62,151; and in 1961, 59,733. Its membership of 63,030 in 1962 was nearly a third of all the elementary teachers in Italy.

In 1963 the association had the same national president, Maria Badaloni, a Christian Democratic member of parliament, that it had in 1947; the same vice-president, Carlo Buzzi, also a Christian Democratic member of parliament, that it had in 1953.

The association's original plans did not include an active role in politics. Until 1953 it limited itself to participating in the general mobilization of Italian Catholics under the direction of the Civic Committees, along lines suggested by the Catholic hierarchy and Catholic Action. (The president of the association was vice-president of the Civic Committees in 1948).

Beginning in 1953, however, the Teachers' Association began to strengthen its connections with the Christian Democrats. The principal leaders of the association were also members of the party's national political group. In 1963 there were seven members of parliament who were also high level leaders in the Teachers' Association, and innumerable association members were the Christian Democratic representatives in local governments. The national president of the Teachers' Association has for many years been a member of the National Council of the party, an influential member of its parliamentary group, and, as Undersecretary of Public Instruction in charge of elementary schools, a junior member of the Cabinet itself. This means that the association does not limit itself to putting pressure on the party in order to have its preferred policies carried out; it can, through its own top leaders, directly activate them. Perhaps no other Catholic organization can claim such success for its own activities.

The Catholic Teachers' Association does not officially participate or take positions in the factional struggles of the Catholic political party. In fact, none of the association members of parliament has been known to attach himself to a minority Christian Democratic faction.

Catholic Action in the Labor World

Immediately after the allied liberation of Rome the Holy See sought to combat the danger of a total domination of the working masses by the forces of the Marxist left. This problem posed itself in very different terms for the rural and the industrial working classes. As the few available data on the social composition of Catholic Action indicate, the Catholic organizations were already strongly established in rural areas and particularly among the *coltivatori diretti,* that is, the small, self-employed farmers. The Communist danger was considered much more threatening among urban industrial workers. In any case, although the points of departure were different in the two sectors, a serious organizational effort was needed in both.

This effort was not made directly by Catholic Action, but by related organizations in whose creation it was deeply involved. The two most important of these were the Italian Small Farmers' Confederation (Coldiretti), specifically directed to the self-employed rural workers; and the Italian Association of Christian Workers, directed to the urban and rural manual employees.

The Italian Confederation of Small Farmers (Coldiretti)

The Italian Confederation of Small Farmers (usually referred to as "Coldiretti") was founded in October 1944 in Rome by Paolo Bonomi. Its constitution, which describes it as "an apolitical organization inspired by the principles of the Christian school of social thought," represented the victory of a group led by Bonomi, advocating an organization qualified as Catholic, over a group that thought that Catholic peasants should be channeled into the rural workers' federation associated with the Italian General Confederation of Labor. Its goal was to be the defense and betterment of the economic situation of the small farmer, including the sharecropper,[17] both through political pressure on parliament and the government and by economic and other activities to increase farm production.

The confederation has an intricate organizational structure that starts with the membership unit, the small farm family, continues up through the communal section to the council of the provincial federation, with elected representatives and officials at each level. At an intermediate level called the "zone," as well as at the provincial level, there are also full-time professional officials who are appointed and paid by the central organization of the confederation. Delegates are elected to the National Assembly which, in turn, elects the National Council, the president, three vice-presidents, and the College of Auditors. In its turn the National Council elects the National Executive Board. (Ten of the thirty-six members who make up the National Council of Coldiretti are elected by the young Farmers' Group and the Rural Women's Group.) [18]

Despite the apparently democratic structure, there is little rank-and-file participation. The top leaders, who feel themselves able to interpret the will of the rank and file without consulting them, merely ask the members for their consent to already formed decisions. The life of the confederation follows the paternalistic pattern typical of a large number of Catholic associations. The easily manipulated rank and file behave as a disciplined mass. The confederation press, entirely controlled from the top, is designed to foster this characteristic docility of the Italian small farmer, who is often only too glad to have someone think and act for him.

17. The term "sharecropper," which has here been adopted as a translation of the Italian *mezzadro*, can be somewhat misleading if it is interpreted to mean a poor, isolated, exploited peasant dealing with a powerful capitalist landowner. While this description may sometimes apply, the typical *mezzadro* is by no means at the lowest economic level among farmers. The usual relationship is between a rural household and a landowner, who relinquishes the day-to-day management of the farm to the *mezzadro*, and who often is not a large-scale farmer.

18. On the structure of the confederation, see also LaPalombara, *Interest Groups*, pp. 238–39. LaPalombara adopts a literal translation of the term *coltivatore diretto*, "direct cultivator."

During its early years this small farmers' association was remarkably successful in its organizational efforts, and was able to consolidate and increase its early gains. Its membership grew rapidly until the 1960s. (Table 5-1) Between 1945 and 1953, when the farming community accounted for a third of the country's labor force, most of the small landowners and tenant farmers were associated with Coldiretti, although the Communist Party controlled most of the sharecroppers. This allowed the confederation to present itself as a powerful pressure group and to join its efforts with those of other groups whose purpose was to consolidate (as well as to exploit) the political preeminence of the Catholic Party.

TABLE 5-1. *Growth of the Italian Confederation of Small Farmers, 1944–62*

Year	Associated families	Workers represented	Communal sections [a]
1944	70,925	100,388	399
1946	504,803	807,684	4,798
1948	711,230	1,620,460	6,132
1953	1,156,821	2,326,163	9,846
1958	1,702,349	3,423,640	13,825
1960	1,728,320	3,531,446	13,974
1962	1,773,618	3,561,711	14,360

a. Units composed of heads of families at the communal level.

The political position of this small farmers' association is characterized by its particularly bitter anticommunism, an attitude arising both from its ideological principles and from its view of the interests of its rank-and-file members. Its strong anticommunist attitude reflects the reluctance of the small farmer to consider his interests in the light of the socialist-communist class logic.[19]

But while Coldiretti is the most bitterly anticommunist of the Catholic organizations, it takes the form of a struggle not so much against the enemies of the faith as against the enemies of property. The religious aspect is tacitly connected with the defense of the socioeconomic status of the small landowner, the ideal type of productive unit cherished by "the Christian school of social thought." In the confederation's propaganda the small landowning family is constantly extolled as the healthy force in the nation, the champion of business honesty, of virtuous labor, and of wise judgment. Private

19. The small farmer, in turn, has been for decades a favorite whipping boy of Marxian economic and political writing. See D. Mitrany, *Marx against the Peasant* (London, Weidenfeld & Nicolson, 1951).

property is lauded as a uniquely beneficial institution, important for social equilibrium.

These ideas are proposed to the membership not merely in order to stimulate their self-esteem. They have been put forward by the confederation as the principles that the Christian Democratic Party was expected to pursue as the party in power. In fact, unlike other organizations, Coldiretti's political activity is not merely concerned with mobilizing strong electoral support for the Christian Democrats. In exchange for its contribution to the party's success Coldiretti has claimed and achieved a virtually exclusive right to speak politically, socially, and economically for its membership. It has asserted this monopoly against other Catholic organizations, such as the Confederation of Free Unions and the Association of Christian Workers. Coldiretti has greatly influenced the government's agrarian program, especially until the late 1950s.

The privileged position of Coldiretti with respect to the governing party in Italy began to deteriorate when, as a result of rapid industrialization and emigration from the countryside and the increasing European economic integration, the entire Italian agrarian system began to show increasing signs of serious disarray. The general orientation of Coldiretti's policy has been antagonism toward developments associated with modernization of the economy.

The agrarian situation has become so serious, however, that the confederation's petty reformism and single-minded exaltation of the virtues of small landownership appear more and more pointless, and its capacity to "inspire" Christian Democratic policy has been correspondingly impaired. By the early 1960s Coldiretti was no longer able to impose its own policy either on the party and its parliamentary group or on the government.

This development altered the nature of the relationship between Coldiretti and the Christian Democratic Party. Until the 1960s the confederation had been a loyal and powerful supporter of the party as a whole; all of the members of parliament connected with Coldiretti had been elected on Christian Democratic ballots; in the electoral campaigns it was clear that the confederation supported the party. While it could not avoid some involvement in the intraparty struggles, on the whole it had managed to keep on good terms with the party majority and therefore with the government.

This strategy was clearly threatened by the increasing demand within the party for an "opening to the left," an operation bound to result in an alliance with groups to which the confederation was deeply hostile and an abandonment of the agricultural policy that had so far been followed. Coldiretti found itself compelled to jettison its traditional policy of supporting the party majority, and to become much more involved in the factional struggle by aligning itself with the forces that resisted the "opening to the left," which at first it was able to forestall. In 1959, for example, Bonomi and his collaborators helped to vote down the left-wing Fanfani line at the party congress in Florence. Then, when the opening to the left was finally endorsed by the party majority at Naples in 1961, Coldiretti made its misgivings obvious, without, however, coming into open conflict with the party's leading group and thus endangering its influence within the parliamentary group and the government. But there was a clear divergence between Coldiretti's politico-economic orientation and that of the party, which was leaning away from an agricultural policy aimed at protecting the weakest and least productive type of farm management.

The effects of this lack of harmony became apparent also in the elections of the early 1960s, when many candidates favored by the confederation made a bad showing in the competition for preferential votes—a result probably of the party's increasing control of the distribution of the votes. Coldiretti's decreasing prestige in the party may make it difficult for the Christian Democrats to get the small farmers' vote. Coldiretti still has considerable strength in the countryside, thanks partly to its control of two important economic institutions for peasants, the Federation of Agrarian Syndicates and the Small Farmers' Health Insurance Agency.

The Federation of Agrarian Syndicates is a national federation of cooperatives compulsorily established among the small farmers of a single province. Created in 1948, its official goal is to strengthen the farmer's position in the market, both as buyer and as seller, through bulk purchases of equipment and fertilizers, haulage pools, credit facilities, and so forth. In the course of fifteen years, the federation has become a powerful financial holding, controlled by Bonomi and a narrow circle of collaborators. It now constitutes one of the pillars of Catholic hegemony (mediated by Coldiretti) in rural Italy.

Another such pillar is the Small Farmers' Health Insurance Agency, created in 1955 in response to the long-standing demand of small landowners for free sickness and accident benefits similar to those enjoyed by industrial workers since the beginning of the century. The agency was to have been locally managed by representatives of the peasants themselves, who would be elected for a three-year term. In practice, however, the majority of these representatives are tightly controlled by Coldiretti, which, through its strong organization, manages almost everywhere to win most of the peasant vote for its own list of candidates, competing with the candidates of the Communist-controlled Peasants' Alliance. The overwhelming victory of Coldiretti candidates in three of these elections is shown in the following percentages of the total votes cast for local boards of the Small Farmers' Health Insurance Agency:

	Coldiretti	Peasants' Alliance
1951	87.50	11.30
1958	89.83	9.18
1961	91.45	7.54

These results, the fruit of a massive and ruthless organization, allow Coldiretti to present itself as the "unshakable wall," to use Bonomi's metaphor, which blocks the road to communism in the countryside.

Thus, although its influence has been declining, Coldiretti's control was still strong at the end of the period under study. Furthermore, no other instrument seemed to replace it in its task of maintaining Catholic influence among the peasants.

Italian Association of Christian Workers

After the fall of fascism Catholic labor leaders, in an attempt to help to unify the labor movement, agreed to channel their followers into the General Confederation of Italian Workers, strongly supported by Socialists and Communists. But in keeping with a previously established policy of the Holy See, this decision was soon followed by one establishing the Italian Association of Christian Workers. (Officially the decision was made by the highest national organ of Catholic Action.) This action was taken to safeguard the moral and religious development of Catholic workers, and thus to minimize the danger implicit in their association in union activities with Communist and Socialist workers.[20]

20. The official statement of the national directive organs of Catholic Action relating to the founding of the Italian Association of Christian Workers is reprinted in Poggi, *Italian Catholic Action,* Chap. 12. In general, on the role played by the asso-

The Association of Christian Workers was not intended to duplicate the union activity of the General Confederation of Italian Workers (discussed later in this chapter), but rather to support and direct the Catholic workers within the movement. Catholic workers as such were to be instructed in their rights and duties as employees and union members and encouraged to be active in the Communist-inspired union in counteracting the predominance of its Marxist leaders and in upholding the principles of Catholic social doctrine. As long as the experiment in labor unity seemed worthy of Catholic support, the Association of Christian Workers paid particular attention to the objective of promulgating and defending Christian social doctrine.

But the politicization of the unity movement was inevitable. The General Confederation of Italian Workers became an obvious front and instrument for the Communist and Socialist parties. The ecclesiastical authorities became increasingly alarmed and less and less willing to permit the involvement of the Catholic working masses in union policies apparently inspired by the Marxist parties. Given the situation in 1948, a split was a foregone conclusion.

The Association of Christian Workers took the initiative. At a specially called congress in September 1948, Christian workers were informed of their duty to transfer their loyalties to a new union organization, the Italian Confederation of Free Unions (discussed in a subsequent section of this chapter). Although the new union (like the Christian Democratic Party) defined itself in its charter as "a confessional," not committed to a particular political party or government, it became, in fact, the Catholic union, with obvious ties to the Catholic-oriented party.

With the formation of this new union, the association's function as the guardian of Catholic workers was no longer needed. In the following years, instead, the Association of Christian Workers intensified its activity in the political field, not only through the Civic Committees, but also as an organization committed to a non-Marxist view of the workers' rights. Between 1948 and 1959 it sponsored welfare, cooperative, recreational, and educational programs.

In the course of this development the association acquired such close party ties that some of its members began to feel that it was be-

___

ciation in recent developments within the Italian labor movement, see the well-documented study by D. L. Horowitz, *The Italian Labor Movement* (Cambridge, Harvard University Press, 1963), Chaps. 6 and 8.

coming too committed to party politics. Until 1959, in fact, the leaders of the Association of Christian Workers were influential members of the Christian Democratic Party at all levels and of its parliamentary group. This close relationship of the party and the association entangled the association in the party's factional struggles, and may have prevented the association from undertaking a fully autonomous activity.

In 1959, in opposition to the national leadership, the Association of Christian Workers of Milan (where the organization was particularly strong) proposed a change in policy. After a series of debates the Milanese view prevailed; the central association leaders would no longer be permitted to be Christian Democratic leaders or members of parliament. While the president of the association was to be a member of the Christian Democratic National Council, any interference by the party in association policy or activities was not to be permitted. Many of the lower level cadres, however, continued to operate in the left-wing factions of the party. The association wished to remain in touch with the party but as a pressure group on it rather than an active force within it.

Since it drew its cadres and members from among the more fervent Catholics, the Association of Christian Workers became a rival of other Catholic associations. The covert rivalry between it and various branches of Catholic Action was intensified by the fact that the parish clergy often gave preference to the workers' association, seeing it as a more modern and efficient instrument of organized religious activity.

One reason for the effectiveness of the workers' association may perhaps be its democratic structure. While its constitution provides for the appointment by the hierarchy of ecclesiastical assistants to the various association units, its leaders have all been laymen elected by the members. The members of the association in a given province hold an annual congress at which they elect provincial presidents and delegates to the national congress. These delegates, in turn, elect the national president.

The organization rests on two types of groups at the grassroots level—the workers' clubs and the factory groups. The workers' clubs have jurisdiction over communes or parts of communes. From 250 in 1945 these clubs grew rapidly to 3,823 in 1948, 5,766 in 1953, 7,500 in 1959, and 7,649 in 1963. The clubs are educational and recreational centers. Especially in the smaller communes they are popular meeting places, where political propaganda activity is carried on in much the same way as Communist propaganda is taught in the cooperative shops. The factory groups are based on the cell principle and organize members of the Association of Christian Workers in factories to carry on apostolic efforts directed toward nonmembers. Not many of these groups are in actual operation.

TABLE 5-2. *Percentage distribution of membership of Italian Association of Christian Workers, by age and sex, selected years, 1955–61*

Year	Male		Female	
	Under 25	25 and over	Under 25	25 and over
1955	15.9	52.5	10.1	21.5
1957	16.6	53.3	9.4	20.7
1959 a	15.9	54.7	8.8	20.3
1961 a	16.6	55.0	8.4	19.8

a. Components total less than 100.0 because of rounding.

Membership in the Association of Christian Workers has steadily increased. In 1949 there were 390,323 members, 808,655 in 1953, 986,000 in 1958, and 1,015,400 in 1963. Men of twenty-five years of age and over have made up more than half of the membership. The age and sex composition of the membership changed very little from 1955 to 1961. (Table 5-2) More than a third of the association's members in 1955 and 1961 came from the ranks of industry and a little less than a third from agriculture. (Table 5-3) The association is quite strong in some areas where the Communists get the majority of the electoral support and control the local governments, such as Emilia-Romagna and Tuscany. Like other national social and political associations, it is stronger in the North than in the Center and the South.

TABLE 5-3. *Percentage distribution of membership of Italian Association of Christian Workers, by type of employment, 1955 and 1961*

Type of employment	1955	1961
Industry	37.7	38.0
Agriculture	31.0	30.0
Civil service	8.5	8.0
White-collar	2.4	3.0
Other	20.5	21.0

While the members of the Association of Christian Workers can be counted on to support the Christian Democrats, a majority of them may not even be members of the party. There is undoubtedly a good deal of overlapping of the two memberships, especially among the top leaders. Except for a brief period in 1960–1961, the president of the association had always been a Christian Democrat, and until 1960 he was also a member of parliament. Of the 118 national councillors of the Association of Christian Workers from 1946 to 1963, 30 were Christian Democratic members of parliament and 24 were national councillors of the Christian Democratic Party.

From this evidence it is clear that the Association of Christian Workers is a supporting organization of the Catholic party. Together with the rest of the Catholic world it has always supported the political unity of Catholics centered in the Christian Democratic Party, and during elections it was its policy until 1958 to make known publicly which of the party's candidates it favored. In the 1958 elections its leaders, who were also party leaders, tried to involve it in factional disputes within the party. Even after 1958 this orientation was not substantially modified and the association even retained some of its factional characteristics, at least at the lower levels. In 1963 the association supported the policies of the center-left, which were, in fact, in keeping with the spirit of the organization's ideology and particularly with its insistence on the necessity for competition with the Communist Party among the Italian workers.

Italian Women's Center

The associations described in the foregoing sections were patterned on the Italian Catholic Action model, which predated the fall of fascism and the appearance of the Italian Communist Party as a mass party on the political scene. The Italian Women's Center (Centro Italiano Femminile), founded in 1945, is of a different character. Unlike Catholic Action, it is not directly under the control of the hierarchy and can thus more openly and directly engage in political activity. It is composed of various preexisting Catholic women's associations and was organized in response to its previously established Communist counterpart, the Union of Italian Women. Since the size of all component organizations is not known, it is not possible to determine the center's dimensions. But the organization includes individual members as well as affiliated women's organizations.

The Women's Center set itself the goal of "regrouping and coordinating openly and actively Catholic women's organizations in view of the serious moral, social, and civic responsibilities" that a democratic order imposes on women.[21] It appealed to all women devoted to the Church and willing to work for the equality of women in occupational and civic activities and in every field of social life, especially that of public administration, and for the moral protection and education of children and young people.

The Communist Union of Italian Women was seeking the support of all women by denouncing the condition of social inferiority of women in Italy, and the Catholic Italian Women's Center began to compete with it on the same grounds. Just as the Union of Italian Women sometimes subordinated the special problems of women to the objectives of Communist propaganda, the Italian Women's Center accompanied or subordinated its discussion of problems of particular interest to women to the defense of the Church and democracy and thus committed itself to the support of the Christian Democratic Party. The center has always been strongly dependent on the support of the two women's branches of Catholic Action.

The center is not, however, a part of Catholic Action and is not subject to ecclesiastical control. This independence is reflected in its structure and its methods of operation. It has ecclesiastical consultants only to guarantee its doctrinal orthodoxy and not to act as agents of the hierarchy. The structure of the center is democratic and all offices are elective. Majority rule is respected at all levels, from the communal council and its presidency to the provincial council and presidency (elected by a provincial congress), to the national council and presidency (elected by the national congress).

This type of structure would seem to favor a working unity among the various Catholic women's associations. But this has turned out to be a difficult goal to achieve. The main interest of the associated Catholic groups in dealing with the Women's Center seems to have been to get women from their own ranks elected to positions of authority and to keep them there. As a result, the democratically elected leadership of the Women's Center has usually con-

---

21. See Paola Gaiotti de Biase, *Noi Donne* (Rome, Oggi, 1961); and *Atti dei Congressi del Centro Italiano Femminile dal 1953 al 1962* (*Acts of the Congresses of the Italian Women's Center from 1953 to 1962*) (Rome, Italian Women's Center, no date).

sisted of a small group of Catholic Action leaders who as such are appointees of the hierarchy.

On the national level the Women's Center has always come out in support of the Christian Democratic Party, particularly in voting for its women candidates for positions in parliament and in local governments and the party organs. Otherwise it has kept aloof from the factional struggles within the party and has never officially supported any one faction. Since the center is predominantly a federation of associations, it has taken the position that each affiliate may have its own independent political orientation. This general rule has not always been adhered to locally, however, if the bishop, the local clergy, and Catholic Action have favored a particular faction.

At the national level the Women's Center has tended to seek a close relationship with the Christian Democratic women's movement. Particularly since 1958, the women's branch of the party has tried to establish control over the center's leaders and to use the center as its own channel of communication with the Catholic women's organizations. The first goal has been much more fully realized than the second, because of the lack of effective control by the center's national leadership over its federated associations and over its regional units. For instance, the national leadership of the Women's Center took a neutral attitude toward the center-left movement, while some of its affiliated groups have expressed strong misgivings over the "opening to the left."

The returns of a questionnaire concerning activity during the 1963 electoral campaign, sent to members of the Italian Women's Center, showed that some of the federated associations (generally charity groups of well-to-do women, such as the Ladies of Charity, the Maria Cristina Circles, and the St. Vincent de Paul Group) were in complete opposition to the directives of the national office of the center.

At its 1962 national congress the center had attempted to go back to its original goals—to be a federation expressing the unity of women in a democratic society. Partly because of internal developments of Italian Catholicism and partly because it is difficult to establish among federated associations a uniform policy and the will and discipline to enforce it, the center's influence on the Christian Democratic Party has declined. The party, which owes so much of its success to the women's vote, presumably feels that support from

Catholic movements in general will never be seriously challenged on the basis of its attention to the specific problems of Italian women.

THE COMMUNIST PARTY AND ITS MASS ORGANIZATIONS [22]

In organizing mass supporting organizations, the Italian Communist Party has had to compete with the powerful Catholic organizational network—described in the foregoing sections—that supports the Christian Democratic Party. It set up a Communist counterpart to a large artisans' confederation controlled by the Catholics. It also has representatives in important veterans' organizations, and in disabled workers' associations. Furthermore, the party has sponsored associations of the most varied types, ranging from an organization of lawyers to the Italian-Russian Association, organized to promote friendship with the Soviet Union. This latter association sponsors trips, meetings, and Russian language courses, and is the center of a constellation of sister organizations—the Italian-Hungarian, the Italian-Polish, the Italian-Rumanian, and others—designed to promote friendship with the countries of Eastern Europe.

In 1946 the party founded an association for tenants and the homeless because of the postwar housing crisis, it was a mass association with 300,000 members and was thus a strong pressure group. When the housing shortage eased in the 1950s and the association had lost its original usefulness, its Communist representatives remained on the various commissions involved in assigning tenants to housing units constructed with public funds. In the 1960s, when urbanization and land speculation caused another housing crisis, the association again became active sponsoring new mass action. This is an example of the way the party adjusts the activity of its specialized organizations to changing conditions.

By its variety of organizational efforts, the Communist Party has been able to influence spheres of society in which it is not directly active as a political party. However, some of the organized groups that it sponsors seem not to yield returns to the party proportionate to the effort required to organize and maintain them.

It might be said that the Italian Communist Party is its own mass

22. The organizations discussed briefly in this chapter are analyzed at length in Luigi Brunelli and others, *La presenza sociale del PCI e della DC*, pp. 177–325. A number of these organizations are also discussed in Joseph LaPalombara, *Interest Groups*, especially Chap. 5.

organization—at least for the traditional functions of supporting organizations to widen the party's sphere of influence and rally voter support. This is the function that the Catholic organizations have performed for the Christian Democratic Party. The function of the Communist organizations, on the other hand, is to strengthen the integration of party supporters and to create areas of organized activity.

As suggested in Chapter 3, to the extent that the Communist Party has managed to transform its supporters into party members, it has deprived its mass organizations of their proper supporting role. For example, it makes a direct effort to enroll hundreds of thousands of women in the party itself, and thus detracts from the activities of the Union of Italian Women. It makes a point of organizing the small peasant proprietors, thereby limiting the operation of the National Peasants' Alliance. In making the "struggle for peace" one of its own major commitments and in mobilizing many of its resources to this end, the party deprives the Peace Partisans of dedicated manpower. In short, it is questionable how much the Communist Party has accomplished in terms of widening its area of influence, through the flanking organizations sponsored and directed by it according to the traditional communist model. The intense organizational drives that took place between 1948 and 1951 did not extend the party's supporting movements beyond the front lines to which the party had already advanced. And when the organizational decline of the party set in, its supporting associations went into a semiparalysis, declining earlier and more rapidly than the party itself. Only after 1956 did some organizations, such as the Union of Italian Women, the Italian Union of Popular Sport, and the Italian Recreational and Cultural Association, show signs of renewed vigor.

The Union of Italian Women

During the Resistance period, the problem of assuring women the status of politically active citizens became the subject of lively discussion, and all parties involved in the Resistance manifested their intention of establishing in the new Italian democracy the principle of equal civic rights for both sexes. The principle was first put into practice by granting the vote to women in local and national elections and by further recognizing their right to run as candidates for political office. The political parties and unions then opened their doors to women.

But the realization of equal rights for women required more than the enunciation of general principles, especially in the face of the many strong obstacles inherent in Italian culture. Thus there arose the idea of an organization that would aim at real equality for women and would, at the same time, educate women to a mature awareness of their rights.

There seemed to be some reason to hope that a broad, unified, nonpartisan, nonconfessional organization could be set up, since both the Catholics and the socialists, as well as large sections of the conservative bourgeoisie, were to some extent committed to the idea of women's emancipation. But this hope was not realized; instead two national women's movements were established: the Catholic Italian Women's Center, already discussed, and the Communist-Socialist Union of Italian Women.

After the fall of fascism the need for a women's movement was immediately felt within the Marxist left, and in Rome in October 1944 a group of Communist and Socialist leaders, together with some supporters of other leftist parties, organized the Union of Italian Women. The union described itself as an organization of all Italian women, without regard to religious or political affiliation. But, because of its Communist sponsorship and the influx of members who supported the Marxist parties, it soon came to be recognized as a supporter of the left and particularly of the Italian Communist Party.

The decisive factor in so classifying this women's organization, and one that has remained unchanged since it was founded, was the political composition of its leadership. From 1947 to 1956 the union president was a Communist member of parliament, Maria Maddalena Rossi, and its secretary was a Socialist member of parliament, Rosetta Longo. In 1956 the presidency was taken over by Marisa Cinciari Rodano, one of the movement's founders and a former member of the Christian left who joined the Communist Party and later became Vice-President of the Chamber of Deputies.

The statutes and organizational structure of the Union of Italian Women have been modified from time to time to increase its flexibility. In 1959, for example, it was decided that the national congress would elect a twenty-four-member national committee and a national council. The lower units consist of provincial committees, which may be divided into sections or subcommittees according to their locations and individual requirements. The delegates to the national congress are chosen from the provincial committees.

In 1959 the executive organ of the union became more broadly representative: its membership consisted of six Communists (members of parliament or high-ranking party members), five Socialists, and three independents. Actually, however, Communist control over the union was greater than the composition of this body would suggest, in part because of the great prestige of the Communist leaders and the fact that they had for the most part held high party office for a long time. Of the twenty women who as of 1959 had served on the organization's national council without interruption since the war, twelve were Communists, seven Socialists, and one independent.

Furthermore, until 1962, *Noi Donne,* the official publication of the Union of Italian Women, was edited by a militant Communist. Still, when an independent nonparty editor took over in 1962 the paper's editorial policy was not significantly altered. Her selection was probably due to the political tension between the Communist and Socialist parties, which the independents were, at least formally, called upon to mediate.

As in all of the organizations discussed in this section, Communist Party leaders tend to be more prevalent in the top echelons of the union than in its lower units. Local leadership of the union and the leadership of women's activities in the party organization apparently overlap a great deal. Communist leaders themselves have been critical of the fact that membership in the lower units of the women's union too often coincides with that of the women's cells of the party. The party lends members to and withdraws them from the women's union according to its own current needs for activists and cadres. Under these circumstances, Communist women are apt to conceive of their work in the Union of Italian Women only as party work. Communist Party sponsorship and control have undoubtedly limited the organization's effectiveness in attempting to carry out programs that would gain it support from areas not already under Communist influence, and have inhibited its efforts to promote women's emancipation.

As long as the Communist Party continued to grow (until 1953) the union's membership also continued to grow, but when the party was no longer able to increase its membership, the Union of Italian

Women found itself in the same situation. Actually, except in 1948 and 1949, the membership of the union was smaller than the female membership of the Communist Party alone. The geographical distribution of the union's membership, according to figures supplied by the organization, bears out its close relationship to the Communist Party. Following the pattern of party membership, the bulk of its members are in Emilia-Romagna and Tuscany: 42 percent in 1946, 46 percent in 1949 and 1950, and 70 percent in 1962.

The welfare activities of the union—nurseries, summer camps, after-school play groups, courses for illiterates—are largely oriented to sections of society that have traditionally supported the Marxist left. But the union's primary activity has always been political. It has consistently echoed the party's slogans and taken part in its campaigns—such as the popular front, the struggle against the Atlantic Pact, collaboration with the Peace Partisans, support of the left-wing labor unions, anti-Franco protests. The women's union was especially active politically during the 1950s, when it took part in all Communist mass demonstrations—against monopolies, for agrarian reform, for the nationalization of power sources, against the "swindle law."

During electoral campaigns the union has been particularly active in supporting the Communist Party and its allies. Between elections its press as well as its small body of active rank-and-file members have generally followed the party line on political issues. In 1953, when the Italian Communists were fighting the "swindle law" and carrying on a violently anti-American campaign, the women's union press faithfully repeated their slogans. It also kept in step with the Italian party's support of the Soviet Union and of Stalin. The events of 1956 made its press more cautious. In fact, *Noi Donne* was reluctant to discuss anything that might damage or embarrass the party.

Women's emancipation had become only a formal propaganda slogan. The failure to commit itself to the solution of the specific problems of Italian women caused a serious crisis in the organization—so serious that its very usefulness as a party instrument became impaired. Near the end of the 1950s the more politically sensitive of the union's top leaders proposed to rejuvenate it by loosening its ideological and political ties with the Communist Party. This was no easy task, with a membership long accustomed to identifying itself with the activities of the party. In the early 1960s, however, the union began to show new vitality. While it still supported the party, it no longer merely duplicated its efforts. Instead, it began to address itself to the current problems of women in contemporary society and to give its members, through conferences, study groups, and lobbying activities, a nonideological solution to their problems. By pursuing the policy of a weakening Communist control in favor of giving a greater voice to women of other political persuasions, the union may be able to broaden its support among all Italian women. The loosening of Communist control in this as well as in other Communist-oriented organizations discussed in this section may result in the expansion of the Communist Party's field of activity by decreasing its isolation.

The National Peasants' Alliance [23]

After the war the Italian Communist Party was faced with the problem of how to organize its activity among the peasants. At first it decided that its policy on agricultural problems (centering on the demand for extensive agrarian reform) could be satisfactorily carried out by a peasants' union called "Federterra," acting within the framework of the General Confederation of Italian Workers, which was then being formed. This decision was consistent with the principle preached by Gramsci, the founder of the Italian Communist Party, of the necessity of forming a popular alliance between the rural and the industrial proletariat. However, this policy did not foresee that the bulk of the Italian peasantry would remain outside the Workers' Confederation and would be organized by the Catholic Coldiretti. While the rural arm of the workers' confederation was having satisfactory results in organizing farm laborers, it was able to appeal to only a limited section of the Italian peasant farmers, particularly the Emilian and Tuscan sharecroppers.

Faced with the growing success of Coldiretti, the Communist Party at first reacted by sponsoring a number of small local associations; but in 1955 it decided that the adversary had to be confronted through a new and broader based organizational effort, the National Peasants' Alliance. The alliance is a union organization that might properly have been discussed in the following section of this chapter on the labor movement. It is being discussed here, however, because

23. This organization, the object of a closely focused study conducted as part of a wider research project, is discussed in S. Tarrow, *Peasant Communism in Southern Italy* (New Haven, Yale University Press, 1967).

much of its significance lies in the party's realization that the peasant element had to be represented by an organization not too closely identified with a labor confederation, and that an open attempt should be made to oppose the Catholic-dominated Coldiretti on its own terrain.

COMMUNIST CONTROL OF THE ALLIANCE

The party considered the new organization of such importance that it appointed two of its top men to be its directors—first, Ruggiero Grieco (until his death in 1956) and then Emilio Sereni, an agricultural economist. Both men had previously held high positions in the party and were also acknowledged experts on rural problems. Although the alliance also included Socialists, they were greatly outnumbered by Communists and, furthermore, were fully committed to a close collaboration with the Communists.

A look at the leaders who were elected at the first congress of the National Peasants' Alliance is sufficient to show the Communist Party's hegemony. A directive council of forty-one members included twenty-six Communists and fifteen Socialists. A five-member presidium included three Communists and two Socialists. The presidents of the economic organizations represented in the alliance—the National Association of Farm Cooperatives and the National Association of Sugar Beet Growers—were also Communists. Also holding office in the alliance and acting in a liaison capacity between the organization and the legislature have been a number of Communist members of parliament. Socialists who have occupied positions of responsibility below the top ranks have generally been chosen from among those well-disposed toward the Communist Party. At the eighth Communist Party congress in December 1956 Sereni remarked that the party had supplied the alliance with personnel to man its whole structure.

In seeking a mass following, the alliance has met with two major difficulties: the peasantry's traditional antagonism toward socialist ideology, and the narrowness of its organizational base. As pointed out earlier, in spite of the difficulties faced by agricultural workers and small farmers in Italy—the failure of their incomes to keep pace with those of industrial workers, the burden of taxation relative to income, and the low level of mechanization in agriculture—only the sharecroppers of Emilia-Romagna, Tuscany, and Umbria gave any

sizable support to the rural organizations affiliated with the Communist-dominated General Confederation of Italian Workers.

EFFORTS TO ORGANIZE THE FARMERS

The alliance undertook a serious effort to remedy this situation. It
admitted not only individuals but also cooperative farms to membership and sought to recruit, in addition to farm laborers, farm
owners, tenant farmers, farmers who had been assigned land made
available by the agrarian reform, and sharecroppers. Like the Catholic confederation it encouraged the membership of entire families.
Thanks to this policy, the alliance reported it had organized more
than 175,000 families by 1963. Of these, 33 percent were in Emilia-
Romagna and Tuscany and 15 percent in Sicily. The comparative
strength of the Peasants' Alliance and of Coldiretti is indicated by
the results of elections of representatives to the governing body of
the Small Farmers' Health Insurance Agency (discussed earlier in
this chapter). Only in Emilia-Romagna have alliance candidates for
positions on local boards of that agency received more than a fourth
of the peasant vote. In Tuscany alliance candidates have received
only 20 percent of the votes, while in no other region has its vote exceeded 10 percent.

Another measure of the support of the alliance is the 30,000 sub-
scriptions in 1963 to its official publication, *Il Giornale dei Contad-
ini,* sold only by subscription. That meant that the paper went to
less than a fifth of the 175,000 farm families claimed as members by
the alliance. Emilian families accounted for about half of the sub-
scriptions.

PROGRAM AND POLICIES OF THE ALLIANCE

The alliance acts as a pressure group to promote the Communist
Party's interests in the field of agrarian politics. Christian Democratic measures and proposals, as advanced by the government or in
parliament, have been systematically opposed by the Communists
and the alliance has echoed this opposition or has tried to strengthen
it. In 1960, for example, a five-year plan for the development of
agriculture" (the "Green Plan") was proposed. It provided for
government financial assistance for agricultural investment and
modernization of equipment. The alliance rejected the plan, alleg-

ing that it would merely "reinforce the economic and political strength of the monopolies." In June and July of 1961 the government, under Fanfani, organized a national agricultural conference. All interested organizations were invited to send representatives to express their opinions on the solution of agricultural problems. The alliance sent its minority representatives to the conference, but disparaged both its efforts and results. It took the position that the conference favored the dominance of agriculture by capitalistic interests.

The alliance took a similar position on the European Common Market, denouncing its monopolistic spirit and warning that it would only increase the Italian farmer's precarious economic situation. This paralleled the position taken by the Communist Party, which declared that the Common Market would only strengthen capitalism and its interests.

Thus, through the alliance the Communist Party organized its opposition to the agricultural policies of the government, the parliamentary majority, and the associations supporting the government. At the same time the party sought to convince the peasants that agricultural problems could not be resolved gradually or by patchwork local programs. It claimed that only complete political and social change could guarantee to the farmer, as to the worker, the end of exploitation and the real solution to his problems. However, because of Soviet agricultural reverses, the party was forced to modify its propaganda about the marvels of socialist agriculture in the Soviet Union.

National Association of Italian Partisans [24]

Another organization through which the Communist Party has sought to widen its influence is the National Association of Italian Partisans, created in June 1945 by partisans of all political movements that had contributed to the efforts of the Resistance.

The Communist Party, which was the most important group in organizing, developing, and coordinating the antifascist Resistance, has always sought to enhance its position by taking credit for all resistance activity. It has depicted the Resistance not only as a force opposing fascism but as an attempt to build a society along the lines of Marxist ideology. One of the party's constant themes has been to

24. See LaPalombara, *Interest Groups,* pp. 150 ff.

measure its own efforts and those of others against the standard of the "ideals of the Resistance," complimenting itself on its faithfulness to these ideals, while deploring the infidelity of other groups in the Resistance.

As one means of establishing this claim, the party has maintained firm control over the National Association of Italian Partisans. In the beginning the association had no ideological and political platform, unless it was the generic one of antifascism. Its original goal, too, was a general one—to help strengthen the reborn Italian democracy and to oppose every attempt to revive fascist totalitarianism. It also aimed to publicize the contributions made by Resistance workers and partisans to the cause of democracy. Like veterans' associations in other countries, the partisans' association proposed to offer moral and material assistance to its members, their families, and the families of those who had been killed during the Resistance.

At its 1947 congress, the association's national council already showed signs of strong Communist influence. Of the more than fifty members of that decision-making body, twenty-six were Communists and six were Socialists. Furthermore, the Secretary-General, who in practice is the executive officer, was Arrigo Boldrini, a Communist member of parliament, noted for his almost legendary record of courage in the Resistance and his personal dynamism and fidelity to the party.

Following the 1947 congress, the Christian Democratic partisans withdrew from the Association of Italian Partisans in order to found their own association, the Federation of Freedom Volunteers, headed by Enrico Mattei as president. The reason given for this move was that the original association had become an instrument of the Communist Party. In 1948 the Social Democratic and Republican partisans also withdrew and formed the Italian Federation of Partisan Associations, with Ferruccio Parri as president, leaving the National Association of Italian Partisans with only Communist and Socialist members. By 1949 the association had thus suffered the same fate as the unions and other organized groups that had initially included members of different political parties who had withdrawn because of the domination of the Socialist-Communist majority. Among the remaining members the Communists greatly outnumbered the Socialists and held most of the leadership posts. Although some prestige positions were filled by independents, these were of a purely symbolic nature.

The association has a very simple structure that exists mostly on paper, except at the national level. By securing an association endorsement of its own views on current political events, the Communist Party can claim that those judgments represent a valid interpretation of the significance of the Resistance movement. Thus the association, in its role of custodian of the spirit of the Resistance, followed the Communist Party in condemning the Atlantic Pact, American "aggression" in Korea, and Tito's "betrayal." It continues also to denounce the dictatorships of the right, in Spain and Portugal, for example, and the subordination of other countries to the United States—thus encouraging a certain kind of nationalism. It rages against West Germany, picturing it as the heir of nazism. In domestic politics the association never ceases to oppose the Christian Democratic regime and to accuse it of betraying the Resistance and the Constitution.

These positions are proclaimed with particular vigor during electoral campaigns. In 1948, in a desperate effort to prevent the withdrawal of the noncommunist groups, the association declared that it would not support any political party. But since 1953 the association's support of the Communist Party has been unequivocal.

After reaching a 300,000 member peak in 1952, the association's membership declined, and it no longer provides fresh support for the Communist Party. It has become a symbolic and ceremonial organization, serving to unite the men of an older generation with bonds that are half political and half sentimental. But the Communist Party still attaches a certain importance and prestige to having its slogans repeated under the by-line of the National Association of Italian Partisans.

Leisure-time Organizations

The Communist Party, whose ideology offers a complete interpretation of all aspects of human society and historical events, seeks to bring all areas of community life within the orbit of Communist influence and inspiration. Like Catholic Action, the Communists do not consider as neutral ground even such spheres of human activity as the use of leisure. The party fears that the workers, because of the general economic development and the increase in the amount of leisure time and available money, might devote less of their time to political activities. Furthermore, religious or employees' recreational associations not controlled by the party might lure the workers away from the traditional meeting places of the Italian left, the *case del popolo* and the cooperative clubs.

To counteract these dangers the Communist Party sponsors leisure-time activities in its own name or through front organizations that are formally autonomous. Representatives of these are the Italian Union of Popular Sport, which was created in 1948 and is clearly a party organization, and the Italian Recreational and Cultural Association organized in 1957. These organizations are intended both to insure that the leisure activities of party members will be conducted in an "appropriate" setting (rather than in one provided by Catholic organizations or by employers) and to provide propaganda channels to reach people outside of the party's direct sphere of influence.

ITALIAN UNION OF POPULAR SPORT

The organizational structure of the Italian Union of Popular Sport resembles that of the other organizations already described, except that intermingled with local, provincial, and national officials are staff officers concerned with specific sports. Membership is open both to individual sportsmen and to sport societies.

Throughout this structure Communist personnel are in control, even though, especially among the top leaders, there are also Socialists. But the national executive body, which is responsible for policy decisions, always has a Communist majority, and all of the national staff organs are headed by Communists. This phenomenon is even more marked at the lower levels, where only Communist Party militants and activists man the branches.

The sports union had 671 local units with 14,500 members in 1949. The number of units had risen to 1,620 and the membership to 59,327 by 1960. Most of the affiliated units are in Emilia-Romagna and Tuscany. The organization's press carries continuous praise of Soviet sports life and, indeed, of Soviet society as a whole and attacks on the government-controlled agencies dealing with sports activity in Italy. Only toward the end of the period under study did the Italian Union of Popular Sport start to respond to its members' interests by putting less emphasis on political themes and more emphasis on sports.

ITALIAN RECREATIONAL AND CULTURAL ASSOCIATION

The founding of the Italian Recreational and Cultural Association in 1957 was an attempt to unite within an organized national framework the many circles and clubs that both the Socialist and the Communist parties had organized since the end of the war. The fact that the attempt was not made earlier suggests that this was a defensive move on the part of the Communists to counter the growing initiative taken by the Italian Association of Christian Workers.

Not only individuals but also cultural, recreational, sporting, and tourist associations and clubs may hold membership in the association. Its task is to help its affiliates to grow and to acquire prestige, as well as to coordinate their activities so that their resources will be used more efficiently. In 1962 the recreational association had about 3,000 affiliated clubs, 600 of which were in the province of Florence and 200 in the province of Bologna.

Communist control of the Recreational and Cultural Association is indisputable: all of the full-time leaders are Communists, though some of the national leaders are Socialists. Among the provincial leaders the Communists have a definite majority.

The political concerns of the Recreational and Cultural Association are almost exclusively domestic. It regularly criticizes the bureaucracy of government-sponsored recreational agencies, the taxation of recreational and sports equipment, censorship of entertainment, and the police. Communist propaganda themes are frequently echoed by the association's press organ, *Le Ore Libere*. Its articles criticize the negative aspects of mass culture and attack religious obscurantism and dogmatism. They discuss the problems of youth, promote equal rights for women, and extol science and the emancipating forces of history.

At the National Cultural Conference in Florence in 1961 a new program was put into effect. Attending the conference were members of the central Communist leadership, and the keynote address was given by Mario Alicata, a top Italian Communist. It was decided that the Recreational and Cultural Association, in planning the activities of the clubs, should promote the widest possible debate on the major problems of national culture. The Communist Party, which suggested this course, presented itself as the driving force of a coalition of all cultural forces working for the progresss of the nation. At the same time the association's action was expected to help the party break out of its isolation and extend its influence over wider spheres of the cultural world.

The Peace Partisans

Of all the Communist movements the Peace Partisans movement reveals most clearly the party's desire to appear as the moral leader of society, the champion of a universal society founded on justice. In an age in which humanity has passed from tragedy to tragedy, the desire for peace gave the party a theme upon which to base this claim.

By waving the banner of peace the Communists intend, on the one hand, to profit from a widely shared human desire and, on the other, to give to the idea of peace a content that conforms to their own ideology. Peace can be gained, they suggest, only through a constant struggle against the capitalist classes and the forces that serve them and are controlled by them. During the cold war, in particular, the threats to peace were said to be the fault of international capitalism, and especially of the United States and its allies.

The Italian peace movement, sponsored by the Communist Party, was a part of an international program launched by the First World Peace Conference held in Paris in April 1949. At this conference the international movement (clearly inspired by the Eastern European bloc) assigned itself the task of mobilizing, in the defense of peace, as many men and women as possible, without regard to their religious or political affiliation. After the Paris conference the Italians became among the most active participants in the movement. When the World Peace Council was formed after the Second World Peace Congress in Warsaw in November 1950, thirty-two Italians were elected to membership and three of these were also on the executive board (Pietro Nenni, Riccardo Lombardi, and Emilio Sereni).

In Italy the National Committee of the Peace Partisans, as a section of the World Congress, elected the Socialist leader, Pietro Nenni, as its president and the Communist, Emilio Sereni, as its vice-president. The real leadership of the organization, however, was in the hands of Sereni. After the mid-1950s, Socialist Party personnel ceased to occupy conspicuous positions either at the top or on the periphery.

Basically, the Peace Partisans movement was intended as an instrument for the diffusion and proliferation of the Communist position on foreign policy. For example, it opposed the proposed European army (European Defense Community), the entrance of the German Federal Republic into the North Atlantic Treaty Organization, and the American "aggression" in Guatemala, Korea, and Indochina. It took the orthodox Communist position that war is an evil inherent in capitalism and inevitable under it. The United States, a capitalist nation, was therefore a supporter of war—along with its ally, Italy's Christian Democratic government. The Christian Democrats were therefore responsible for voting armaments expenditures that worsened Italy's economic situation and increased unemployment. Their war politics reflected, as well, a servile dependence on the United States.

On these grounds the Peace Partisans could denounce every act of the government as preparatory or leading to war. For example, the majority electoral law (the "swindle law") which was in effect for the 1953 general elections, was interpreted by the Peace movement as part of a joint maneuver by "reactionary" European governments to ratify the European Defense Community against the will of the majority of their peoples.

Paradoxically, after trying to create a sounder organizational base, the movement declined—a setback attributable both to the change in the international atmosphere and to the post-1950 crisis in the Italian Communist Party itself. Since its only signs of activity in the early 1960s were sporadic demonstrations against the establishment of missile bases in Italy, the Peace Partisans movement no longer seems to be an active and influential aid to the Communist cause. Perhaps the very modest impact this peace movement was able to achieve most clearly demonstrates the limitations of Communist-sponsored mass associations. In the first place, the only response to its initiatives were within that section of public opinion already in sympathy with the Communist Party. In the second place, it achieved even this result only by overtaxing the energies of the relatively small and diminishing pool of Communist activists.

THE ITALIAN LABOR MOVEMENT AND THE POLITICAL PARTIES [25]

Italian labor unions have always been characterized by a high degree of political orientation. The major unions and their national confederations have customarily been closely identified with a political party. Furthermore, because of the chronic financial weakness of the unions and because the labor movement as a whole has traditionally viewed itself as one part of a broader movement attempting to shape the whole society, the union confederation has always played a subordinate role to the political party with which they are associated.

For the socialist-oriented unions, which have always dominated the Italian labor movement, this kind of relationship is explained by their adherence to Marxist ideology, which stresses the primacy of political action to achieve a better society. The explanation for the political subordination of the Catholic unions was different. Since there was no Catholic party proper when unions began to organize at the turn of the century, the Catholic unions were at first controlled by Catholic Action, and through it by the hierarchy itself.

Although the Fascists used this pattern of subordination of labor to political forces as a pretext for wrecking both the socialist and the Catholic labor movements in the early 1920s, their labor legislation, clearly putting the Fascist unions at the service of the one-party regime, strengthened the general pattern.[26]

Attempt to Establish a Unitary Labor Confederation

When, immediately after the allied liberation of Rome, an attempt was made to set up a unitary labor movement, headed by a single General Confederation of Italian Workers, it seemed a bold experiment. Actually, the attempt carried the seeds of its own fail-

25. The best sources in English on the Italian labor movement are: Joseph LaPalombara, *The Italian Labor Movement: Problems and Prospects* (Ithaca, Cornell University Press, 1957); and Horowitz, *The Italian Labor Movement*. There are also multiple references to the historical development of the movement in M. Neufeld, *Italy: School for Awakening Countries* (Ithaca, New York State School of Industrial and Labor Relations, 1961). See also J. Raffaele, *Labor Leadership in Italy and Denmark* (Madison, University of Wisconsin Press, 1962) .

26. On Italian unions under fascism, see G. Salvemini, *Under the Axe of Fascism* (New York, Viking, 1937).

ure. The agreement setting up the confederation was signed by the "syndical representatives" of the three major antifascist parties, the Communists, the Christian Democrats, and the Socialists, which supplied the leaders of the confederation from their own ranks. Since it was the Communists who enjoyed the strongest support among the labor masses and who rapidly established the firmest hold on the commanding positions in all levels of the organization, the confederation became a "transmission belt" for the party itself. Furthermore, the majority of the Socialist union leaders, who were fewer, less prepared and less efficient than the Communists, were willing to go along with subordination of the confederation to the Communists, since such subordination was in keeping with the prefascist tradition.

Thus, even before the Catholics broke away from the General Confederation of Italian Workers in 1948, the language spoken by this unitary labor organization was almost exclusively Marxist and emphasized the concept of class struggle. By an aggressive interpretation of antifascism, to which all three parties were committed, the confederation was clearly denouncing the whole capitalist socioeconomic system. What was perhaps even more damaging, particularly from the standpoint of the Catholic section of the labor movement, was the suspicion that the Communist Party, through its near control of the confederation, was trying to establish hegemony over the Catholic working masses as well, by playing down the atheistic component of Marxism.

Communist control of the confederation can be gauged by the composition of its national congress held in Florence in June 1947. Of the delegates present, 52 percent had been elected on Communist tickets in the provincial congresses, compared with 30 percent on Socialist, and 12 percent on Catholic tickets. As a result, eleven of the twenty-one members of the national executive body elected at that congress were members of the Communist Party.

The 1948–49 Split in the Labor Movement

This Communist hegemony could lead only to a split in the labor movement. The year 1947 saw the expulsion of Communists and Socialists from the national Cabinet and a critical year in the emergence of the cold war. Even apart from these political events in Italy, the Catholics in the labor movement could not indefinitely tolerate their position of marked inferiority to the Communists and their Socialist allies. The Catholic leaders in the confederation had inherited a tradition of Catholic unionism that had developed in opposition to the earlier socialist tradition. The Christian Democratic Party, furthermore, could not favor Catholic participation in a labor movement that consistently and viciously attacked the social and economic policy of the government which it headed. Finally, the Catholic world as a whole, engaged at the time in an all-out attack on the Socialist-Communist coalition, was obviously committed to breaking up a united labor movement that seemed to benefit only the enemy coalition.

The Catholic faction left the General Confederation in 1948 and set up the Italian Association of Christian Workers, discussed earlier in this chapter. After a number of false starts the Italian Confederation of Free Unions was founded in 1950. The workers who were sympathetic to the policies of the Social Democratic and Republican parties had also left the General Confederation and later founded a third confederation, the Italian Union of Labor.

TABLE 5-4. *Membership of the General Confederation of Italian Workers (CGIL) and of the Italian Confederation of Free Unions (CISL), 1946–62*

Year	CGIL	CISL
1946	4,680,987	—
1947	5,958,722	—
1948	5,306,632	—
1949	5,109,089	1,221,523
1950	4,782,090	1,489,682
1951		1,812,501
1952	4,938,142	2,800,000
1953		2,000,000
1954	4,625,000	2,045,642
1955	4,622,343	
1956		2,138,300
1957	4,078,000	
1958	3,678,000	2,316,896
1959	3,600,000	
1960	3,745,000	2,334,002
1961	3,673,430	2,425,262
1962	3,495,971	

The Two Major Confederations

On the basis of data supplied by the confederations themselves,[27] Table 5-4 shows the annual membership of the two principal confederations from 1946 to 1962. This table indicates the relative and absolute decline of the General Confederation of Italian Workers and the growth of the Confederation of Free Unions. The General Confederation appears to have lost fewer members as a result of the 1948 split than might have been expected, probably because of the energy with which it undertook to organize the laboring masses in the South. The General Confederation's organizing drive in those regions parallels, in fact, the drive of the Communist Party in the same years.

TABLE 5-5. *Geographical distribution of membership of the General Confederation of Italian Workers, selected years, 1946–62*

Region	1946	1947	1948	1949	1950	1962
Piedmont	417,682	600,628	605,091	525,776	503,120	237,176
Lombardy	1,153,699	1,153,687	1,382,211	1,063,402	937,809	639,438
Veneto	505,719	658,968	550,162	428,442	383,266	301,733
Liguria	416,196	300,550	287,462	290,391	286,130	182,117
Emilia-Romagna	734,852	881,119	875,427	908,412	965,360	675,377
Tuscany	341,404	436,060	471,853	550,995	547,458	386,786
Marches	85,830	115,783	91,926	121,239	132,281	87,061
Umbria	56,858	62,951	66,674	72,204	71,522	61,159
Latium	277,818	328,637	233,832	219,629	198,010	158,928
Abruzzi e Molise	48,822	71,425	35,138	53,349	51,189	46,823
Campania	174,283	209,230	170,766	181,167	170,233	136,715
Apulia	288,689	382,595	284,701	263,429	239,575	201,816
Basilicata	14,832	23,319	14,661	17,257	15,334	22,152
Calabria	57,776	106,740	45,113	66,738	57,673	60,639
Sicily	166,899	247,100	152,505	206,096	172,060	242,751
Sardinia	65,691	85,600	39,110	68,563	51,070	55,290

The figures shown in Table 5-5 suggest that the General Confederation greatly increased its membership in the 1940s but that the

27. Membership figures supplied by the unions are undoubtedly exaggerated, and are used in this analysis only because of the absence of other figures. The following examples illustrate the caution with which the union-supplied membership data must be used: in the early 1960s the total membership claimed by all unions active in Italy was 9 million, almost twice the 4.5 million estimated by informed sources outside the unions. Of the 4.5 million members, 2.5 million were said to be affiliated with the General Confederation; 1.5 million with the Confederation of Free Unions; and 500,000 with other unions.

membership in most regions declined in the 1950s and early 1960s. Confederation members seem to have been more evenly distributed over the whole of Italy in the early 1960s than were the members of most of the Communist front organizations previously discussed in this chapter. This may suggest that a labor movement, as such, can develop somewhat independently within the broad area of influence of the socialist parties. The figures do not reflect any marked expansion in membership in the industrial sectors of Italy, centering mainly in the North. The geographical distribution of the membership of the Confederation of Free Unions, as it developed from 1953 to 1961, is shown in Table 5-6.

TABLE 5-6. *Geographical distribution of membership of the Italian Confederation of Free Unions, 1953, 1956, 1958, and 1961*

Region	1953	1956	1958	1961
Piedmont	125,596	156,523	173,008	151,890
Lombardy	395,812	404,994	433,567	457,874
Veneto	300,081	319,248	331,429	345,061
Liguria	69,139	78,903	91,021	101,849
Emilia-Romagna	135,210	141,769	150,774	149,130
Tuscany	118,436	118,436	122,983	132,519
Marches	52,774	52,774	72,722	72,929
Umbria	24,751	24,571	133,404	42,268
Latium	104,118	106,915	55,584	160,273
Abruzzi e Molise	53,779	53,885	55,584	52,925
Campania	140,119	123,379	147,352	154,217
Apulia	154,438	166,787	197,096	221,027
Basilicata	26,796	20,527	19,096	19,779
Calabria	76,503	79,758	50,270	50,461
Sicily	223,163	239,703	261,484	254,770
Sardinia	44,797	46,614	37,982	39,813

Available data on the sector of the economy in which the memberships of both confederations are employed (Table 5-7) show that in both 1950 and 1961 industrial workers made up the strongest group in the General Confederation, followed by agricultural workers (mostly farm laborers and sharecroppers). The service sector, both public and private, was poorly represented. In the Catholic-oriented Confederation of Free Unions the proportion of industrial workers decreased markedly between 1950 and 1961, while the proportion of agricultural workers in the membership remained fairly stable. Workers in public and private, made up about a third of the membership in 1950 and more than half in 1961. Union membership did not keep pace with the changing composition of the labor force. For instance, the representation of industrial workers dropped from nearly 2 million to 1.5 million in the General Confederation of Italian Workers between 1950 and 1961, and remained around the 600,000 mark in the Confederation of Free Unions. During the same period industrial workers in the labor force increased from 4.2 million to 6.5 million. This decline in unionization at a time of rapid industrial development and growing employment—developments generally favorable to unionization—may be the price the Italian labor movement pays for its high degree of orientation to ideologies and political parties.

TABLE 5-7. *Percentage distribution of the membership of the two leading Italian labor confederations, by employment sector, 1950 and 1961*

	1950		1961	
Employment sector	*CGIL*	*CISL*	*CGIL*	*CISL*
Industry	39.0	41.4	43.2	26.0
Agriculture	30.0	25.0	30.8	22.9
Services	9.5	14.8	6.0	23.9
Civil Service	10.4	17.8	9.5	27.2
Pensioners	—	—	10.5	—
Other	11.1	—	—	—

Further indication of the respective strength of the two confederations is shown in the returns from annual employee elections from 1952 to 1963 for grievance committees in 3,000 firms employing more than a million workers.[28] (Table 5-8) Grievance committees are legally recognized bodies, elected under rules that provide for a secret vote on competitive slates of candidates, generally identified with one of the union confederations. The comparative strength of support for the policies of the confederations can thus be gauged with precision within a single plant. However, statistical problems arise in trying to combine the results from a large number of plants to obtain an aggregate measure of the relative strength of the confederations. In fact, fairly divergent results are reached every year, not only by the two confederations but by outside observers using the same basic data. Despite these doubts about the complete relia-

28. M. Neufeld, *Labor Unions and National Politics in Italian Industrial Plants* (Ithaca, Institute of International Labor and Industrial Relations, 1954).

bility of the figures, the table does indicate trends in employee support of the competing confederations.

The share of the employees' vote going to the General Confederation dropped from more than three fourths of the total in 1952 to

TABLE 5-8. *Percentage distribution of votes cast for candidates for factory grievance committees by union confederations, 1952–63*

Year	CGIL	CISL	Other [a]
1952	78.5	16.6	4.9
1953	71.3	22.5	6.2
1954	68.3	23.9	7.8
1955	56.2	33.9	9.9
1956	51.8	36.6	11.6
1957	48.0	38.6	13.4
1958	48.5	35.9	15.6
1959	53.0	30.0	17.0
1960	52.3	29.5	18.2
1961	48.6	39.0	12.4
1962	47.6	32.9	19.5
1963	48.2	23.6	28.2

a. Generally, unions affiliated with the Italian Union of Labor.

about one half in 1963; while the share of the vote going to the Confederation of Free Unions nearly doubled, reaching a plateau at around one third of the total vote until 1963, when it dropped to less than a fourth.

THE GENERAL CONFEDERATION OF ITALIAN WORKERS AND THE COMMUNIST PARTY [29]

The extent to which the General Confederation adopts a Communist view of the socialist tradition and, moreover, the extent to which it appears dominated by the Communist Party may limit its appeal to socialist-oriented workers reluctant to accept the Communist leadership.

The secession of the Catholics from the General Confederation in 1948 and of the left-of-center lay forces in 1949 left the once-united workers' federation under Communist domination. The few top Socialist leaders who remained in the confederation in 1963, a number of whom had left the Socialist Party when it began to collaborate with the Christian Democrats in the national Cabinet, were committed in principle to the policies of the Communist Party and to

29. See Horowitz, *The Italian Labor Movement*, Chap. 7.

the left-wing socialist splinter party, which some of them joined.

Communist domination of the General Confederation is even more evident in the leadership of the major affiliated unions than in the top leadership of the confederation itself.[30] Even when policies are formulated at the top to reflect general socialist positions, they are likely to have a straight Communist interpretation at the local, operational level. In 1960–61, for example, the marked disagreements between the Socialists and the Communists in the top leadership of the confederation found very little echo among the rank and file.

The General Confederation has never taken a position opposed to that of the Communist Party, except in the evaluation in 1956 of the events in Hungary, and that represented only a reluctance by the confederation to openly endorse the party's line rather than to be in open conflict with it. The General Confederation has occasionally been critical of the USSR-dominated World Federation of Trade Unions, but so has the Italian Communist Party. The critical attitude of the General Confederation toward such developments as the Common Market and the center-left coalition followed the lead of the Communist Party rather than of the Socialist Party.

Undoubtedly the General Confederation's subordination to the Communist Party has harmed its development. The party's long-range political strategy is not responsive to such purely economic developments as changing conditions in the labor market or the pace of technological innovation in the productive process. And thus the General Confederation of Italian Workers has lagged behind in interpreting these new demands in the workers' interest and has therefore failed to widen its support among the new types of workers.

The reason the Communist Party has not changed its strategy and allowed the General Confederation of Italian Workers to function more adequately as a union organization is probably that the General Confederation, despite its deficiencies as a union organization, has been a fairly efficient machine for mobilizing the political support of the workers for the Communist Party. The party's insistence on an orthodox class ideology, for instance, strengthens the workers' sense of belonging together as a class—a feeling that naturally expresses itself in massive support for the Communists at the polls. A vote for the Communist Party is represented as the best weapon in

30. According to data supplied by the Socialist Party in the early 1960s, Socialists represent 37 percent of the leadership at the top level of the confederation, but only 29 percent and 26 percent, respectively, at the intermediate and lower levels in the affiliated unions.

the hands of the workers—better than the strike itself, better than a
cogently argued case at the collective bargaining table. The confederation does well by the party by sharpening the worker's sense of
his own inferiority in present Italian society, by creating in him a serious antagonism toward the rest of the society, and finally by presenting (more or less explicitly) the Communist Party as the committed political channel for this antagonism. In orthodox Leninist
terms, the party still views the union as a "transmission belt," and
evaluates its performance by this standard. In the present Italian situation this cannot spell total ruin for the General Confederation of
Italian Workers, since an adequate alternative in purely union
terms does not exist. The Confederation of Free Unions, oriented toward the Christian Democratic Party, has failed to provide such an
alternative.

THE ITALIAN CONFEDERATION OF FREE UNIONS AND THE CHRISTIAN DEMOCRATIC PARTY

The relationship between the Catholic party and the Italian Confederation of Free Unions, which can itself be identified as Catholic,
is very different from that between the Communist Party and its
supporting union. In the first place, the Christian Democratic Party
does not enjoy the undisputed control over all other organized forces
within the Catholic world that the Communist Party has over its
supporting organizations. Also, the Confederation of Free Unions
has officially defined itself, and has attempted to behave as, an ideologically and politically neutral labor movement rather than as a
Catholic labor union.

A first step in this direction was taken by the party as early as
1944, four years before the constitution of the Confederation of Free
Unions as an independent organization. At that time the Holy See
approved the plan to build a united confederation embracing workers of all political creeds and religious belief, which resulted in the
formation of the General Confederation of Italian Workers. Achille
Grandi, a Christian Democrat who had been one of the top leaders
of the prefascist "Catholic" union movement, signed this joint pact
with the Communist Giuseppe Di Vittorio and the Socialist Oreste
Lizzadri.

Even before unfolding events began to dispel the climate of antifascist goodwill, the Catholics found themselves no match, either in

numbers or ability, to cope with fellow unionists and union leaders from the two parties of the socialist left, particularly the Communists. At this point the Catholics could have openly met the challenge of the clearly Marxist-inspired General Confederation by organizing a union movement actively committed to a global design of society inspired by the Church. However, this solution was not adopted when the Catholic component, led by the Association of Christian Workers, left the General Confederation. The new labor confederation that was formed soon after was called the "Italian Confederation of Free Unions," to appeal to all those workers who rejected the Communist Party's tyranny over the labor movement. The term "free" signified that the new confederation was aligning itself with the bona fide labor movements of the "free world," and that it intended to model itself after the trade union movement in the United States.

These ideas may actually have shaped the Confederation of Free Unions and it may in fact be autonomous in relation to the hierarchy and the Catholic Action organizations. The hierarchy seems to have left the Confederation of Free Unions pretty much to itself in the period covered by the present study, although it may have tried to control it indirectly through the Association of Christian Workers, considered one of the Catholic Action organizations. Its relations with the Christian Democratic Party are of more interest. Broadly speaking, the confederation has followed, since its founding, policies that are either consistent with those of the party or lend them support. This result has been achieved by a very simple mechanism: the confederation is manned, at all levels, almost exclusively by Catholics, most of whom are also Christian Democrats and often party leaders.

Despite this fact, the Confederation of Free Unions is not so much an organization supporting the party as a whole, as one of the major forces in the factional strife within it. The relationship between the confederation and the party is largely determined by the position taken by the group within the party often identified as the "union wing." The many Free Union leaders who are active in the party to a large extent share a common orientation; they take a consistent position in internal party affairs as well as toward the policies of the government.

In the second half of 1953, for instance, when the Confederation of Free Unions was hostile to the government, it undertook to organize labor agitation. This was a source of trouble to the government, because the Premier, Giuseppe Pella, depended primarily on the right-of-center forces, both inside and outside the party. However, from 1954 on, the union wing, under the leadership of the confederation's general secretary, Giulio Pastore, was clearly aligned with the party majority and favorably disposed toward the successive cabinets. This exposed it to some attacks from the Association of Christian Workers, which charged the confederation with lack of zeal in the labor field and excessive friendliness toward the government. After Pastore had left the leadership of the confederation for an important cabinet post, the new leader, Bruno Storti, brought about a reconciliation between the two opposing workers' groups. Significantly, however, this operation led to the formation of a single new faction, "Rinnovamento," which was made possible, to a large extent, by the fact that the party had jettisoned Amintore Fanfani and had formed, around Aldo Moro, a new majority dominated by an opportunistic center group called *"dorotei,"* the name of the restaurant in which their founding meeting was held.

The extent to which the Confederation of Free Unions operates as a faction within the Christian Democratic Party affects not only the behavior of the confederation-supported politicians in the parliament, the national government, and the local administrations, but also its own behavior as a union movement. Its position within the party and in relation to the government affects from time to time such critical aspects of union policy as the determination with which it pushes certain claims in collective bargaining, its willingness to call strikes, and its decisions regarding agreements on joint strategy with the other two labor confederations.

This has meant that the Italian Confederation of Free Unions has failed to operate as a union devoted exclusively to the pursuit of the interests of workers as workers. Because of its close political ties, it has not been able to confront the employers with the sole intention of increasing the workers' bargaining power and exploiting it fully.

The Catholic-oriented labor union has proved as unable as the Communist-dominated union to work out a strategy that meets the demands of changing conditions in the Italian labor market and in the Italian economy. While the General Confederation of Italian Workers has remained a prisoner of Communist orthodoxy, the Confederation of Free Unions has allowed political developments—often a struggle for the levers of power, with little relationship to the evolving needs and potentialities of society—to shape and constantly alter its operations as a union. Chiefly for this reason, the Confederation of Free Unions has not become the serious challenge that a different type of union movement, not so committed politically, might have been to the Communist-dominated union.

THE PARTIES AND THE COOPERATIVE MOVEMENT

The history of the Italian cooperative movement in some ways parallels that of the labor movement. Both movements have always been characterized by a high degree of political and ideological orientation. The first cooperatives founded in Italy, even before the rise of socialism, were guided by the ideology of Giuseppe Mazzini, an ardent advocate of Italian national unity and the brotherhood of man.[31] In the last quarter of the nineteenth century the early socialist movement and the Catholics sponsored a proliferation of cooperatives within their own subcultures. Both cooperative movements sought not only to provide economic benefits to their members but also to promote ideological and political solidarity.

The fascist regime abolished the two cooperative movements and brought individual cooperatives under centralized government control. At the end of the Second World War the two competing cooperative movements were immediately revived on the old basis. They did not attempt, as had the labor unions, to organize a unified, nonpartisan movement. Even the names of the prefascist movements were used: the National Cooperative League, comprising the cooperatives controlled by the Communists, Socialists, and Republicans (who had as one of their traditional strongholds a flourishing cooperative network in Emilia-Romagna); and the Italian Cooperative Confederation, a group of Catholic cooperatives. After 1948 the cooperatives associated with the Social Democratic and the Republican parties seceded from the National Cooperative League and founded their own General Cooperative Federation. In addition to the cooperatives discussed here there were the smaller General Cooperative Federation and numerous others—mostly building cooperatives, established by prospective owner-occupants of apartment houses to obtain financial support from the state—affiliated with none of the organized federations and not politically significant.

The geographical distribution of all organized cooperatives and

31. R. Hostetter, *The Italian Socialist Movement*, Vol. I, *The Origins* (Princeton, Van Nostrand, 1958).

those affiliated with each of the two main organizations for the first quarter of 1948, the latest year for which comparable information for both movements is available, shows that the Communist-Socialist dominated league was much stronger than the Catholic-oriented confederation. (Table 5-9) By 1962 the balance had presumably shifted: the Confederation reported 10,049 affiliates in that year, compared with the League's 6,995.

TABLE 5-9. *Geographical distribution of cooperatives, first quarter, 1948*

Region	Total a	National Cooperative League		Italian Cooperative Confederation	
		Number of cooperatives	Percent	Number of cooperatives	Percent
Piedmont, Valle D'Aosta	1,240	865	77.8	50	4.0
Lombardy	4,015	2,266	56.5	555	13.8
Veneto, Trentino-Alto Adige	4,080	802	19.6	1,960	48.0
Emilia-Romagna	3,770	2,940	78.0	45	1.2
Liguria	975	468	48.0	150	15.3
Tuscany	1,795	1,140	63.5	70	4.0
Marches	450	238	52.6	30	6.6
Umbria	180	126	70.0	30	16.6
Latium	1,500	580	38.7	330	20.0
Abruzzi e Molise	500	50	10.0	20	4.0
Campania	1,300	570	43.8	180	13.8
Apulia	1,200	302	25.0	115	10.0
Basilicata	150	28	18.6	25	16.6
Calabria	535	306	57.2	35	6.5
Sicily	1,160	486	42.0	150	12.8
Sardinia	270	122	44.5	60	22.2
Total	23,120	11,289	49.0	3,805	16.5

a. Total includes cooperatives not affiliated with the League or the Confederation.

The National Cooperative League suffered a membership crisis in the middle 1950s. It lost more strength than the Italian Cooperative Confederation, which also suffered a marked membership loss between 1956 and 1962. By 1962 both groups were about even, with more than 2 million members each. (Table 5-10) (Membership figures were supplied by the cooperative organizations and are thus subject to the possibility of exaggeration. They are used here to give some indication of the comparative sizes of the two major cooperative movements.)

TABLE 5-10. *Membership (millions) in cooperatives
affiliated with the two largest federations of
cooperatives, selected years, 1945–62*

Year	National Cooperative League	Italian Cooperative Confederation
1945	1.5	1.0
1947	3.0	1.2
1952	3.1	1.8
1956	2.4	2.4
1962	2.1	2.2

The Communist Party and the Cooperative League

More detailed information is available concerning membership in the league than in the confederation. A regional breakdown for 1960 of affiliates of the league by type of cooperative unit, by number of individual members, and by value (in millions of lire) of the total volume of business in 1960 is shown in Appendix G. While the league was apparently well organized throughout the northern and central area, with nearly a third of its membership in Lombardy, around 15 percent in Piedmont and Liguria, and 37 percent in Emilia-Romagna and Tuscany, in terms of volume of business the two last-named regions accounted for more than half of the business done by league-affiliated cooperatives, and Emilia-Romagna alone accounted for 45 percent. These figures indicate that at least in these regions the cooperative movement should be considered not only as a mass organization operating to consolidate popular support for the Communist Party, but also as a source of economic power for the party.

The leadership of the Cooperative League suggests that the Communist Party is the major force controlling it. The party has regularly had solid majorities in the upper echelons of the league's leadership. The Socialist Party, too, has been well represented in the executive ranks.

Communist control has been even more marked in the lower units of the league and in the affiliated cooperatives. At the local level, where the national directives are carried out, something like two thirds of the leaders have been Communists and most of the rest have been Socialists who are deeply attached to the traditional unity of action with the Communists.

An analysis of the positions taken by the league on political questions confirms the hypothesis of the Communist Party's dominance. The findings of the present survey indicate that the league has refrained from taking any position whatever on issues on which there is dissent between Communists and Socialists, and that when it has made statements on issues on which the Communist and Socialist parties agree, the language has been that of the Communist Party.

Aside from the probable economic gain that the party derives from the league, the latter also provides the party with a mechanism for the social integration of its membership and for the spread of propaganda directed toward potential electoral supporters. The Communists can reward deserving comrades with positions in the league and in the individual cooperatives. It urges its members to become members of cooperatives, so that even the pursuit of their interests as producers or consumers will take place within an environment likely to strengthen their attachment to the party.

Consumer cooperatives provide an opportunity for the spread of propaganda on a personal basis. While most members of the Cooperative League can be expected to vote for the Communists, this may not be true of many nonmember shoppers who have access to the "people's shops" set up by the cooperative movement. (There were 8,000 such shops in 1962.) These shops provide a meeting place where possible votes can be secured for the party by the persuasion or influence of the manager, who is a member of the cooperative and of the party.

Signs have been growing both within the party and the cooperative movement that the use of the cooperatives to mobilize electoral support and to serve as niches for deserving party members is bound to impair the efficiency of both the party and the cooperatives. Some party officials have declared that the cooperatives should be encouraged to strengthen and streamline themselves to meet the double challenge of an expanding market for their services and of growing competition. To do so, however, they must enjoy some degree of autonomy. It would be difficult to pinpoint any specific change resulting from these declarations. All in all the party seems willing to countenance some loss of economic efficiency in order to make use of the league and its affiliates as a means of reaching and influencing the electorate.

The Christian Democratic Party and
the Italian Cooperative Confederation

The Catholic inspiration of the Italian Cooperative Confederation is unquestionable. The confederation was established explicitly for the purpose of organizing the Catholic cooperative movement and Catholic Action has given to it the same status as it has given to Coldiretti—that of an "adhering organization." However, it should not be assumed on these grounds that the relationship between the Italian Cooperative Confederation and the Christian Democratic Party is as close as that between the National Cooperative League and the Communist Party. The confederation's connections with the Christian Democratic Party concern more the output than the input side of political action—while it lacks the structure to influence voters in favor of the party, it can be considered a powerful pressure group influencing the government. It attempts to obtain legislation and administrative action favorable to the cooperative movement at large, and particularly to its own associates. In this kind of action its main resource is its relationship to the Christian Democratic Party, a relationship—to adopt the terminology suggested by LaPalombara—of *parentela,* that is, one founded, metaphorically, on "kinship." [32] Although this means that the confederation has an interest in having the governing party retain power, it is doubtful that it can do much, through its own resources, to help it obtain votes during or between elections. It lacks, among other things, the kind of influential structure that the network of the people's shops constitutes for the Cooperative League.

Most of the leading personnel in the confederation have been selected and promoted through internal channels, and apparently have not been, to any sizable degree, imposed (or even loaned) by the party. The key executive position in the confederation has been held since 1949 by Dr. Livio Molfettani, who is not even a member of the Christian Democratic Party.

The party, in turn, has not shown any particular interest in the cooperative movement. At the national level a party "office for cooperation" was created in 1951, but until 1962 it gave hardly any sign that the office existed. Only in that year (at the end, that is, of the period with which the present study is concerned) did the party

32. Joseph LaPalombara, *Interest Groups in Italian Politics,* Chap. 9.

seem to discover the possible political significance of the cooperatives.

This discovery seems to have been prompted by the development within the Catholic world of other cooperative ventures, actually or potentially competitive with the Italian Cooperative Confederation. In the second half of the 1950s, in fact, the Italian Association of Christian Workers, the Italian Confederation of Free Unions and Coldiretti undertook various cooperative initiatives among their respective members. Furthermore, many of the cooperatives sponsored by the agrarian reform agencies organized into an efficient National Federation of Agricultural Cooperatives. This proliferation of cooperative enterprises within its own sphere of influence has led the party to take an interest in the cooperative field in general.

Underlying the growth of Catholic cooperatives is the fact that the confederation, when it has taken positions on political issues, has tended to side with the Christian Democratic right-of-center factions. All of the Catholic-oriented cooperative undertakings, except perhaps those of Coldiretti, can be viewed as attempts to counterbalance the party's left. Like other organized groups within the Catholic world discussed earlier in this chapter, the cooperatives, when they have played any political role at all, have tended to revolve around the continuing factional struggles among the Christian Democrats.

6

The Two Parties and Local Governments

The postwar Constitution provides for four levels of government: national, regional, provincial and communal. It specifies that the regional governments shall have considerable autonomy in relation to the national government, shall coordinate the activities of local governmental bodies (provincial and communal), and shall have legislative powers, relieving the national legislature of many minor legislative responsibilities. It provides further for strengthening the autonomy of both provincial governments and communal governments. The framers of the Constitution thought that regional governments and strengthened provincial and communal governments, operating at a level less remote from the ordinary citizen than the national government, would encourage participation in governmental affairs and would make government more responsive to the individual citizen's needs and opinions. The regional governments were to have been established within a year after the Constitution became effective in 1948.[1]

This governmental framework was a main plank in the platform of the Christian Democrats for the 1946 Constituent Assembly (as it had been for the Popular Party after the First World War). In one of its earliest statements of political objectives the Christian Democratic Party had committed itself to "decentralization of state powers; autonomy and wider functions, especially on administrative and financial matters, for the regional governments." The Communist Party was critical of the Christian Democratic position as threatening to give a "federal" organization to the Republic. It insisted in-

1. They were still nonexistent as this book was being completed in late 1967, but there were indications that they might be formed by late 1969.

stead on the necessity of upholding the unitary structure of the state. It sided with "a large current of public opinion" favorable to the strengthening of communal autonomy, but recognized "the necessity for controls" over the commune's exercise of its powers. These controls, it said, should be in the hands of "an elective body," possibly at the regional level.[2] However, the Communist Party accepted, with some modifications, the constitutional provisions regarding the local governmental framework.

Because of the drastic change in the political atmosphere between the time the Constitution was framed and the time it went into effect, the anticipated widespread organization of regional governments did not take place. In 1948 cooperation between the Christian Democrats on the one hand and the Communists and the Socialists on the other was a thing of the short-lived past. On the international level the cold war was at its height; on the national level it found expression in the particularly bitter electoral campaign of 1948.

As the majority party the Christian Democrats bore the main responsibility for implementing the provisions of the Constitution. But to implement those provisions for the establishment of regional governments and the granting of new status to provinces and communes would have meant giving the Communist Party the opportunity to increase its strength through its control of a number of local governments, which the Constitution endowed with broad powers and considerable autonomy. It was easy for the governing party to win support for delaying the implementation of these provisions by stressing the antidemocratic nature of communism. To the accusation that the Christian Democrats were refusing to put the Constitution into effect, Mario Scelba, the Minister of the Interior, speaking for the government party, replied that it was the presence of the Communist Party, hoping to use the instruments of democracy in order to destroy it, that prevented full implementation of the democratic principles of the Constitution.

The Christian Democratic Party, as the government party, has had much to gain from a maximum centralization of power and would have lost much by the transfer of power and control from center to periphery. The Communist Party, on the other hand, even within the existing limitations, has been able to attain many positions of local power, especially in the larger communes, and such

2. Repubblica Italiana, Ministero della Costituente, *Atti della Seconda Sotto-com-missione dell'Assemblea Costituente* (Rome, Poligrafico dello Stato, 1947), p. 682.

positions carry considerable influence for the party that occupies them. Furthermore, the limitations themselves have been used effectively to impugn the government's goodwill, and, once the cold war had drifted into the background, they made excellent propaganda for an opposition party that was trying to achieve respectability. Also, in the late 1950s and early 1960s because of the growing cleavage between the Communists and the Socialists, the Communists feared that changes in the local governmental structure might break the pattern of local alliances between the two leftist parties, to which the Communists owed a good part of their remaining power at the local levels of government.

Thus, questions concerning the very nature of the institutions of government, which should have been among the first to be considered and solved by the national parliament, became the object of vague and intermittent discussion that has been carried on without serious commitment. The two traditional levels of local government, the province and the commune, have continued to operate within the constraints of a Napoleonic administrative system [3] that the 1948 Constitution had been intended to supersede. It is a system characterized by limited provincial and communal responsibilities; control of certain provincial and communal operations by organs of the central administration, particularly the provincial prefects; [4] and narrow local taxation powers, which lead to chronic financial weakness of local administrations at all levels and indirectly reinforce their close dependence on the central authorities.

Under these conditions the local governments fail to operate as close links between the citizenry and the national government. The political contest at the local level therefore fails to provide a meaningful stimulus to real political involvement. Pervasive as the impact of legislative and administrative decisions is, these decisions have little meaning for most of the citizens, who view them as issuing from omnipotent centers of power, distant and often obtuse or even perverse.

The failure to implement the full constitutional design has had further unfortunate consequences for the efficient functioning of government. It has made it necessary for parliament to occupy itself

3. On the general characteristics of the Napoleonic system, see B. Chapman, *Introduction to French Local Government* (London, Allen & Unwin, 1953).
4. See R. Fried, *The Italian Prefects: A Study in Administrative Politics* (New Haven, Yale University Press, 1963); and B. Chapman, *The Prefects and Provincial France* (London, Allen & Unwin, 1955).

with matters of strictly local relevance, some of which might be considered the proper province of the executive branch rather than of the legislative. The overloading of the legislature's time and energy with local concerns has promoted the growth of legislative activity by parliamentary committees [5] and has been an important factor in the failure of parliament to devote adequate attention to some of the more pressing and serious needs of the political system and of Italian society as a whole, such as the tax system, the educational system, the civil service, and urban development. The inadequacy of the political leadership, particularly the so-called "immobilism" of the Christian Democratic Party, has also been a major cause of this failure.

LOCAL FINANCIAL PROBLEMS

One of the most serious results of the failure of the government to provide for the efficient functioning of local governments has been their inability to finance their activities through their own resources and the consequent chronic near-bankruptcy of most local governmental units, particularly the communes.[6] The central government, unwilling to give them wider powers of taxation, must intervene from time to time to forestall bankruptcy and must underwrite the costs of one or more of their activities, thus reinforcing their dependency.

In presenting to the Chamber of Deputies in 1952 a draft of a law whereby the national government would undertake to finance some of the communal activities, one of the most dynamic of the Christian Democratic ministers, Ezio Vanoni stated: "This proposal . . . was not and is not intended to resolve the problems of local finance." Two years later Vanoni was the author of a plan bearing his name that was intended to ensure a balanced development of the Italian economy. Thus he obviously intended to sponsor government inter-

5. On the provisions allowing for legislative activity by parliamentary committees, see J. C. Adams and P. Barile, *The Government of Republican Italy* (Boston, Houghton Mifflin, 1961), pp. 65–66; and A. Predieri, "La pruduzione legislativa," in G. Sartori and others, *Il Parlamento Italiano: 1946–1963* (Naples, Edizioni Scientifiche Italiane, 1963), pp. 201 ff.

6. Italian communes, for instance, had total deficits of 32.8 billion lire in 1949, 376 billion in 1958, and 759 billion in 1962. Local government revenues increased from 684 billion in 1955 to 1,517 billion in 1963, while their expenditures increased from 821 billion to 2,399 billion. Minister of Finance, *Attività Fiscale tra il 1954 e il 1964* (Rome, Poligrafico dello Stato, 1964), p. 247.

vention in economic affairs. Why, then, did he not intend to "resolve the problem of local finance"?

An explanation of the Christian Democratic Party's inaction is not difficult to find. Since the autonomous organization of local finances would have reduced the dependence of the local governments on the central administration, legislation that would give some content to the idea of local autonomy was looked upon with indifference or hostility by the party in power.

But the record of the Communist Party also shows a lack of serious commitment to the resolution of local financial problems. Although their deputies have periodically introduced legislative proposals for making "local finance . . . democratic and popular," the purely symbolic character of these proposals is evident from the fact that they have usually been introduced as the legislative sessions were drawing to a close, and when they therefore had no chance of being adequately discussed.[7]

Not until 1954 did the Communists propose legislation to deal with the overall problem of external controls over local governments. Then some Communist deputies introduced a draft called "Law for Meeting the Requirements of Local Autonomy." The law was discussed in the Chamber after a delay of three years, and then only in the context of a discussion of a government proposal (later withdrawn) entitled "Amendments to the Law on Communes and Provinces," which proposed minor changes and left the system of controls substantially unaltered.

On July 25, 1957, Senator Fortunati proposed another law on local finance entitled "Provisions for the Reorganization of Local Finance." This proposal was introduced at the end of the session, and, like the proposal that Fortunati had introduced in 1952, it died with the ending of the legislative session.

The Communists' lack of fervor in pressing in parliament for legislative changes in the structure of local government hardly indicates an unequivocal dedication to the problem of local autonomy. While

7. The first such proposal was presented by a group of members of parliament led by Senator Fortunati of Bologna in February 1949, and withdrawn on January 26, 1950, two days before the Senate Committee on Finance and the Treasury presented the majority and minority reports on the proposed Vanoni law. The law was finally discussed in parliament after a delay of one and a half years. During the discussion the Communist Party did not engage in a violent battle of the type that it well knows how to set off when it seriously wants to attract public attention. Instead, on November 22, 1952, Senator Fortunati presented his second and more elaborate proposal, entitled "Provisions for Local Finance."

the Communist Party is undoubtedly interested in strengthening the local governments—which are its major centers of power—it knows that a battle with the Christian Democrats on this issue would result in an ideological contest between democracy and authoritarianism, which it prefers to avoid.

LOCAL ISSUES AND PARTY PLATFORMS

An examination of the platforms of the two leading parties during each postwar local election appears to confirm the foregoing assessment of their attitudes toward local governmental structure.

The Christian Democratic Party was the declared champion of local autonomy in 1946, insisting on the "necessity of a new law on communes which is based on the principle of the widest possible governmental freedom . . . reforms in local taxation provisions, coordination [of the latter] with tax legislation of the state, making a distinction between those expenses which are of a national character and those which have to do only with the commune; direct participation of the citizens in the life of the commune by means of the referendum." [8]

The Communist Party advocated communal taxation policies that would be less burdensome on the working classes:

The progressive family tax . . . should be the principal source of communal revenue and must be levied in such a way that low-income families are practically exempt, while those of large income are heavily taxed. . . . We must certainly fight . . . against the sales tax, which is hardest on the least well off. . . . The commune [must, to] the greatest possible extent, . . . actively intervene also in the economic life of the population in order to satisfy the needs of the popular masses. . . . It is necessary to carry out on a vast scale the municipalization of services which are indispensable to the collectivity. [9]

In the local election campaigns of 1951–52, which reflected cold war tensions, there was no stress on such issues as the failures of the Christian Democrats to carry through the measures they had earlier proposed, from tax reform to referendums, or on whether the Communist Party's espousal of family taxes was in accordance with Com-

8. Resolution of the National Council of the Christian Democrats, January 9, 1946.
9. Celeste Negarville's report to the Second National Council of the Italian Communist Party, April 10, 1945.

munist principles. Instead, the Christian Democratic campaign platform focused on "the Communist threat" and the insidious forces that were plotting the "disintegration and the betrayal of the nation." [10] The Communist Party proposed to "conduct the forthcoming electoral campaign with vigor, so that the votes of millions of Italians will condemn those who are responsible for the depression, the misery, the slavery to foreigners, and those wretched groups that are preparing a new war." [11] The language of each group was equally rhetorical and apocalyptic. Solution of the administrative problems of local governments, which had been an important issue in 1946, was totally neglected.

While the two subsequent electoral campaigns did not have the excited tone of 1951–52, the cold war having "thawed," the party platforms did not deal concretely with local administrative programs. Each party explained its continued failure to press for the implementation of the promises of earlier campaigns by blaming the opposing party for the constraints it had placed on the development of local governments. The position of the Communist Party was less difficult because, as the opposition party, it could attribute the failure to implement local autonomy to the "suffocating weight" of the Christian Democrats, that is, to the government.

But the Christian Democratic Party, in its turn, layed the blame on the kind of opposition that the Communists represented. In 1949, for instance, Alcide de Gasperi asserted: "The left, . . . now that the state is not in its hands, hopes to make the regions into a sort of catapult or mine against the central power." [12] Ten years later, at the 1959 party congress, Aldo Moro said: "Another sector of activity, today dangerously open to the encroachment of the Communist Party, is that of local government, particularly the regions . . . where there are to be found communities of interest which could give rise without warning, to political solidarity with the Communist Party and to . . . subordination to it, [due to] the pressure of local interests and other political forces." [13]

Only because of the peculiar nature of the Communist Party could the Christian Democratic Party advance this sort of argument

---

10. Editorials in the issues of April 25 and March 28, 1952, respectively, of the Christian Democratic daily, *Il Popolo.*
11. From a resolution passed by the Seventh Congress of the Italian Communist Party, April 8, 1951.
12. *Il Popolo,* June 6, 1949.
13. Ibid., October 25, 1959.

to justify its failure to create the decentralized and pluralistic order favored by the Catholic political tradition and specified by the Constitution.

PARTY CONTROL OF LOCAL GOVERNMENTS

Although their autonomy is limited, local governments are important centers of power. In the larger cities their budgets represent substantial sums, and even in the smaller communes it is possible for the parties that govern them to dispense patronage and favors in order to consolidate their positions. The exploitation of these positions of power is the goal of both parties in their periodic local election campaigns.

The local political alliances of these two parties (which together control two thirds of the popular vote) with the other six national parties (which divide the remainder) are determined by this goal. During the period when the Christian Democratic Party was governing the nation as the leading party in the "center" coalition with the Social Democratic, Liberal, and Republican parties, it was allied at the local level in the southern provinces with the right (especially the Monarchists), because the center coalition there did not have a sufficient majority. At the same time the Communist Party's alliance with the Socialists was a necessary condition of its leadership in a number of local administrations, especially in the central regions and in the North, since, with few exceptions, the Communists did not have the absolute majority necessary to govern alone.

This situation began to change with the formation of the center-left government. Beginning with the elections of 1960, the Christian Democratic Party attempted to extend its collaboration with the Socialists throughout the country. The Communists have been concerned lest the Christian Democratic-Socialist alliance might be extended from national to local politics, thus threatening the Communist-controlled local administrations. But this development, which began in 1960, has implications mainly for the future and did not have any significant effect during the period under study.

PARTY POLICIES AT THE LOCAL LEVEL

The parties try to develop a uniform policy wherever they are in power. They rely for help in advancing their policies on three types of national organizations that represent those engaged in local gov-

ernment and cater to their needs—nonpolitical and nonparty organizations, political and interparty organizations, and party organizations.

Nonpolitical and Nonparty Organizations

Included in the nonpolitical organizations are the various associations of local governments and associations of the special agencies
of local governments. Among the first type are the National Association of Italian Communes,[14] the Italian Provincial Union, and
the National Union of Mountain Communes. The second type includes the National Association of Welfare Agencies and the Confederation of Public Utility Corporations.

There are several factors of political significance in these nonpolitical associations. The Communist Party's representatives are on
an equal footing with those of other parties. Membership is open to
all local governments irrespective of their political composition, and
this type of participation in public bodies as peers of representatives
of other parties is something Communist Party representatives have
long desired. Another important factor is that the local interests that
find expression in these nonpolitical organizations are often different from and in conflict with the interests of the government and
the ruling party. Even Christian Democratic local administrators attempt to increase their autonomy and power in relation to the central government, although they stop short of creating serious problems for the party on whose ballot they were elected.

The Communist representatives attempt to induce these nonparty
organizations to criticise the central government openly. They stress
the importance of the development of local autonomy and the reduction of central controls—theses that an opposition party finds
easy to support and the Christian Democrats find difficult to attack.
In the nonpartisan atmosphere that these associations seek to main-
ain, the Christian Democratic Party can hardly use the highly political arguments that it offers elsewhere in extenuation of its failure
to implement the Constitution. Its main concern is therefore to re-
strict the scope of the pronouncements of the various organizations

---

14. This is the most important organization of this type. It was founded in 1901.
Its activities were discontinued under fascism, but it was reorganized in 1946. In 1961
more than 4,000 Italian communes, accounting for almost 64 percent of the total
population, made up the association's membership. Communes controlled by the Communist Party are much more likely than others to hold membership in the association.

on the central government's policies and to keep them as technical and politically harmless as possible. Generally the organizations manage to strike a compromise between the orientations of the two parties, in order to maintain their nonpartisan character. The Italian Communist Party has to content itself with encouraging these associations to adopt positions that contain implicit criticism of the central government, while the Christian Democratic Party tries to see that public statements are not couched in openly provocative and challenging language.

POLITICAL AND INTERPARTY ORGANIZATIONS

The superior initiative of the Communist Party is demonstrated in the politically oriented organizations. In this area of activity the Communist Party controls an old and widely respected organization, the League of Democratic Communes; while the Christian Democratic Party, or rather a sector of it, has only recently created the Italian Association of Young Administrators, a more restricted organization whose membership consists not of the communes but of representatives of local political administrations.

The League of Democratic Communes was founded in 1941 and is in a certain sense a continuation of the League of Socialist Communes, created by reformist Socialists at the beginning of the century, when the Socialists were winning their first local elections. The substitution in 1947 of the adjective "democratic" for "socialist" is indicative of the pragmatic and gradualistic policy of the Italian Communist Party. The primary goal of the league, as stated in its bylaws, is the "realization of autonomy for the communes, the provinces, and the local units with respect to their finances and their democratic development within the framework of the Constitution and the regional organization; and the coordination of the activities of the local governments."

In practice the league is more concerned with the coordination and general orientation of the "democratic" administration of local government than with the promotion of local autonomy as such. Legislation proposed by members of parliament who are connected with the league is generally very technical and does nothing to meet the need for far-reaching legislative reforms.[15]

15. The league's activity is best illustrated by the following statement (concerning the period 1954–57) of its Communist leader, Senator Spezzano, made at its second

The League of Democratic Communes

The league acts as an intermediary between the central authorities and the affiliated local administrations. Most of its some 2,000 affiliated units are communes with leftist administrations, but they also include minority groups of leftist councillors from communes governed by center or right parties. Through its central and local offices and its publications [16] the league serves as a pressure group, operating largely within the framework of local government activity.

The most important of its publications, the monthly *Il Comune Democratico,* founded in 1946 when the league was being reactivated, was merged in 1949 with *l'Amministratore Democratico,* a Communist publication devoted to problems of local government. It often advocates radical reforms of local finance and reduction of controls to which even the leftist members of parliament seem uncommitted. Since 1954 its criticism of inadequate local autonomy in Italy has been accompanied by praises of developments for local autonomy in the Soviet Union and the Eastern European people's democracies.[17]

The league is largely controlled by the Communist Party. The Communists hold an absolute majority of the posts in its secretariat (a small permanent executive body), while they hold only a plurality of the posts in its larger (and presumably less influential) bodies. Even when noncommunists outnumber Communists in these larger units they frequently take positions in support of the party line. For example, in 1964 the league's executive committee, only one third of whose thirty-five members were Communists, issued the following statement:

congress: "In the various ministries—Public Works, Finance, Interior, Agriculture— and in the various offices—Cassa per il Mezzogiorno, Social Security, Workers' Housing Agency, National Bank for Communes and Provinces—the league has supported over two thousand proposals, rarely without partial or total success. We have provided written counsel for 842 requests, and many others have been handled orally. We have published seventy-two pamphlets discussing problems of a general nature, such as the preparation of budgets, the family tax, the sales tax, subcontracting, the composition of the provincial administrative boards, etc."

16. These include the monthly, *Il Comune Democratico;* the bimonthly, *Notiziario della Lega;* and the annual, *L'Agenda dell'Amministratore Democratico.*

17. Here, for instance, are the titles of some feature articles published between 1949 and 1952: "Georghi Dimitrov, Communal Councillor," "Walking Around Moscow," "The People's Councils of the Bulgarian People's Republic at Work," "The Transformation of the Rumanian Capital."

The crisis in local government is due to the failure to introduce autonomistic reforms, to the limitations imposed on local autonomy by government controls, and to the failure to grant to the elective assemblies financial means which enable them to carry out their functions. . . . [We] denounce the danger of the breakdown of local representative bodies which is implicit in this situation. . . . The situation is aggravated:

a) by the delay in approving the 1964 budget, by the practice of systematically refusing to give the necessary approval and by the unjustified demand that deficits be kept below last year's figures.

b) by the demand that the commune revise allocations where commitments have already been made . . .

c) by the limitation of credit . . .

d) by delays in the payment of state aid. . . . [We] invite the government to take the necessary measures to stop these practices which violate the rights of the communes.[18]

As explained earlier in this chapter, "practices which violate the rights of the communes" (especially central control over local budgets) are the result of a situation that the Communist Party, which controls the league, has done practically nothing to improve.

Italian Association of Young Administrators

Although the efficacy of the Communist-oriented League of Democratic Communes as a pressure group and as an instrument of propaganda is limited, the Christian Democrats completely lack agencies offering the kind of help, coordination, and information that the league makes available to Communist communes. The only comparable Christian Democratic organization—the Italian Association of Young Administrators—was not organized until 1960 and its membership is restricted to administrators, former administrators, and persons "particularly interested in the political and administrative life of local units," all of whom must have reached a minimum age. This association was not sponsored by the Christian Democratic Party, but by factions supporting the party's collaboration with the Socialists at both the local and the national levels.

18. From statement published in *Il Comune Democratico*, October 19, 1964.

In 1962 the Association of Young Administrators, which had been cooperating with units of the Christian Democratic left, was broadened to include "all those forces and groups which, in one way or another, are sincerely committed to the triumph of an articulate democracy." These turned out to be the same political forces that gave rise to the center-left coalition. Of the forty-one members of the association's enlarged national council, nineteen were Christian Democrats, nine were Socialists, six were Social Democrats, three were Republicans, three were Liberals, and one was a "liberal democrat" (left-wing defector from the Liberal Party). Later the Christian Democratic representation was increased by the inclusion of eight members on the national board (the executive organ), giving the party 54 percent of the membership of the board.

In spite of this the association has continued to express the views of only a factional group in the party. It does not have an editorial organ comparable in frequency of publication or in circulation to *Il Commune Democratico*. Its publication, *Esperienze Amministrative*, appears three or four times a year, and is scholarly and documentary in nature rather than political. According to its directors its failure to appear more often is due to financial difficulties.

Party Organizations

The party instruments through which the two parties orient their local government activity are rather similar in structure.

The Christian Democratic Party has an Office of Local Governments, with national and provincial branches, which apparently operates with only partial success. Because of the great variety of local situations and of the shades of opinion of the local politicians elected on the Christian Democratic ballot, the central branch of this organization is able to carry out its functions of orientation and coordination to only a limited extent. Its monthly publication, *Torre Civica*, appears irregularly; its control over the nomination of candidates is almost nil, except in the major cities; and its research unit is apparently not very productive.

At the provincial level there is supposed to be a permanent panel of consultants and a full-time adviser. However, if technical assistance is provided at this level, it is provided by experts who are called upon from time to time and not by a permanent staff of consultants. The provincial director is generally the only person permanently attached to the office, and even he must often perform other tasks in the party.

The Communist Party, in turn, has its Local Government Policy Section, composed exclusively of party functionaries, who act as consultants on specific local situations. It also has a Local Government Commission, including administrators, whose duty is to outline the general administrative policy of the party with respect to taxation and public works. This structure was for some time duplicated at the provincial level, but it functioned almost exclusively in the larger provinces and was marked by inefficiency, duplication, and lack of coordination.

At the Ninth Communist Party Congress in 1960 there were criticisms of party activities in local government. These included criticism of the "lack of connection between the action of Communist officeholders and the activity of party organizations" and "the distance between those comrades who have the responsibility of public administration and those who are leaders of Communist organizations." Further, the delegates criticized the "lack of coordination between the action of elected Communists and the general struggle which the party conducts for the renewal of Italian society," and a lack of faith in the possibility of "advancing toward socialism through the democratic institutions provided for by the Constitution." The resolutions of the congress urged "all Communist groups, in all elective assemblies, to follow, both when in power and when in the opposition, a responsible policy which includes not only the necessary denunciation of the present insupportable condition of the working masses, but also indications of the solutions of problems of popular interest." [19]

At the Tenth Congress in 1962 an attempt was made to overcome the poor coordination by means of a more precise allocation of responsibility. The congress abolished the provincial local government commission and transferred its functions to an appointee of the party's provincial organ.

Even a centralized party such as the Communist Party, it seems, is able to direct and coordinate the actions of its local administrators only partially, while the Christian Democrats find such direction and coordination an almost impossible task.

19. "Tesi politiche approvate dal IX Congresso del PCI," in *IX Congresso del P.C.I. Atti e Risoluzioni* (Rome, Editori Riuniti, 1960), Vol. 2, pp. 228 ff.

PARTY POLICIES AND LOCAL BUDGETS

As a test of the extent to which the two leading parties have been able to control local situations by application of uniform criteria and policies, a study was made of the 1949–62 budgets of 13 large provincial capitals—communes of 100,000 to 200,000 population—and of the 1957 budgets of all 92 provincial capitals.

TABLE 6-1. *Party control of thirteen large communes, 1946–62*

	Party [a] in control		
Commune	*1946–52*	*1952–56*	*1956–62*
Alessandria	PCI/PSI	PCI/PSI	PCI/PSI
Bergamo	DC	DC/PSDI	DC/PSDI
Brescia	DC	DC/PSDI	DC/PSDI
Ferrara	PCI/PSI	PCI/PSI	PCI/PSI
Foggia	PCI/PSI	PNM/MSI	DC
La Spezia	PCI/PSI	PCI/PSI	PCI/PSI (1956–60) PSI/DC/PSDI (1960–62)
Modena	PCI/PSI	PCI/PSI	PCI/PSI
Padua	DC	DC	DC
Parma	PCI/PSI	PCI/PSI	PCI/PSI
Reggio Calabria	DC	DC	DC
Reggio Emilia	PCI/PSI	PCI/PSI	PCI/PSI
Salerno	DC	PNM and others	DC
Vicenza	DC	DC/PSDI	DC/PSDI

a. DC, Christian Democratic Party; PCI, Communist Party; PSI and PSDI, Socialist parties; MSI, the neofascist Movimento Sociale Italiano; PNM, National Monarchist Party.

Of the thirteen large communes Parma, Reggio Emilia, Modena, Ferrara, and Alessandria had left-wing governments from 1946–62; while Bergamo, Brescia, Vicenza, Padua, and Reggio Calabria had Christian Democratic governments. (Table 6-1) Foggia and Salerno had varied governments, from right to left; while the government of La Spezia, which had been left-controlled, was controlled by the center-left in the latter part of the period studied. The sample was thus considered representative of Italian communes in terms of political leadership.

The study indicated that differences in budgetary policies are not associated in any systematic or consistent way with political orientation of the local government administrations. The findings on communal income from sales tax (considered an instrument of con-

servative fiscal policy) and on communal income from a family income tax (considered an instrument of progressive fiscal policy) illustrate this general conclusion.[20] The proportions of income
derived from each of these sources in 1952–62 are shown in Table
6-2 (family tax) and Table 6-3 (sales tax). It is clear that a heavy
reliance on the family tax is not the prerogative of communes under
left-wing control. The tables indicate that there was less variation
between communes in percentage of revenue derived from the sales
tax than in percentage of revenue derived from family tax, but there
is no evidence that the differences in either type of revenue were related to type of political administration. Whereas a distinction between communes under Christian Democratic control and under
Communist control was discernible in 1952, ten years later these differences had disappeared. From the analysis of local revenue over
the ten-year period it was not possible to distinguish Communist
from Christian Democratic taxation policies.

TABLE 6-2. *Family tax as a percent of the total revenue of
thirteen large communes, selected years, 1952–62*

Commune	1952	1954	1956	1958	1960	1962
National average	10.0	10.9	10.9	11.2	a	a
Alessandria	6.4	14.4	14.7	13.5	11.7	12.3
Bergamo	11.1	11.9	13.9	12.4	17.9	18.3
Brescia	12.7	12.4	13.5	12.8	11.4	12.9
Ferrara	13.5	15.0	16.0	15.5	13.5	16.4
Foggia	3.7	7.1	7.9	8.8	8.7	8.7
La Spezia	4.9	9.8	9.8	10.8	11.8	11.7
Modena	13.5	12.9	11.4	10.6	18.5	16.1
Padua	16.4	11.8	10.2	18.3	14.3	16.3
Parma	16.8	15.0	13.3	12.9	13.0	16.4
Reggio Calabria	5.1	4.7	5.3	6.8	9.7	7.4
Reggio Emilia	14.0	15.3	14.1	12.5	12.6	14.0
Salerno	10.5	7.3	6.5	11.8	10.0	5.3
Vicenza	10.0	15.2	12.9	13.5	13.4	14.0

a. Not available.

These general conclusions were confirmed by the examination of
the 1957 financial records of the ninety-two capitals.[21] For example,

20. For the complete report on this study, see *Il PCI e la DC nelle amministrazioni
locale e in parlamento,* which is to be published in 1970 by Società editrice il Mulino,
Bologna, as Vol. V in the series of monographs based on the surveys conducted by the
Carlo Cattaneo Institute, described in Appendix A of this book.
21. The year 1957 was selected because it was the latest year immediately following
a local election year for which figures were available from the Bureau of Statistics.

a comparison of the shares of income derived from the family tax and the sales tax by typical Christian Democratic-controlled cities and by Bologna, the model Communist-controlled city, is illuminating. Bologna's percentage (12.7) was above the national average of around 10 percent for income derived from the family tax, but was below the percentages for other large cities with Christian Democratic administrations, such as Milan (14.2), Turin (14.1), and Rome (13.1), where the Christian Democratic Party has often been supported by votes from the right. Data on the percentages of income derived from the sales tax were also revealing. Bologna's 35 percent was above the national average (33 percent) and also more than the percentages of Turin (32.5), Rome (30.4), and Milan (30.1). The Communist Party's program for increasing the family tax and reducing the sales tax had apparently not been applied in Communist-administered cities.

TABLE 6-3. *Sales tax as a percent of the total revenue of thirteen large communes, selected years, 1952–62*

Commune	1952	1954	1956	1958	1960	1962
National average	29.8	31.0	31.0	29.6	a	a
Alessandria	39.0	37.4	38.1	37.4	34.3	25.6
Bergamo	42.0	39.1	35.4	37.0	30.8	26.5
Brescia	45.6	41.7	41.7	40.0	31.9	26.9
Ferrara	33.6	36.0	37.2	36.1	31.2	25.7
Foggia	43.2	35.4	39.9	38.6	34.4	
La Spezia	30.2	47.4	44.9	40.6	38.4	33.5
Modena	40.0	39.0	33.9	35.9	29.2	28.2
Padua	43.4	45.9	37.3	35.5	26.0	24.7
Parma	36.0	38.7	34.9	32.8	33.1	28.4
Reggio Calabria	14.2	15.0	19.6	28.1	38.1	35.2
Reggio Emilia	32.4	32.3	33.4	32.1	30.4	26.3
Salerno	27.6	36.7	25.6	29.9	31.4	30.7
Vicenza	44.1	40.2	43.5	38.4	31.4	28.6

a. Not available.

EFFECT OF INTERFERENCES FROM THE CENTRAL AUTHORITIES

The Communists have often charged that Communist-controlled local administrations are systematically hampered in the planning and execution of their policies by the representatives of the central government, particularly the prefects, while the Christian Democratic local government officials are comparatively free from interference by the central authorities.

Investigations made in connection with the present study were not extensive enough to answer this question. Considering the wide and largely discretionary powers that the central authorities enjoy in relation to the local governments, it seems likely that these powers may at times be used to discriminate in favor of local administrations manned by the party of the government. However, a search for convincing proof that it was a practice for the central authorities to annul administrative decisions when they emanated from Communist administrations and approve them when they were initiated by Christian Democratic administrations proved fruitless. No such proof of discriminatory treatment was found in Communist publications, although charges of discrimination of this kind were frequent in the party press between 1949 and 1955, when Mario Scelba was at first Minister of Interior and then Prime Minister. They were less frequent in the following years, except in the early 1960s.

An examination of the decisions of the central authority with respect to Bologna, the major Communist-controlled commune, shows that while requests for small sums of money such as a grant to the Communist-inspired National Association of Italian Partisans were turned down, resolutions of major importance were regularly approved.

The principal difference in the treatment of officials of Communist-controlled governments and of officials of governments controlled by Christian Democrats, especially between 1950 and 1955, seemed to be that frequent consultations took place between Christian Democratic-dominated local boards and officials of the prefecture. The prefects made periodic visits, during which the local boards explained the action they wished to take and obtained their opinions. The control exercised by the prefects over Christian Democratic administrations was therefore more likely to take the form of preventing resolutions from being presented to central authorities than of the central authorities' turning them down. Often decisions were annulled when pressure was brought to bear on the prefect by opposing Christian Democratic factions.

In the last half of the 1950s many Communist administrations also began to discuss proposed actions with the prefects, although Communist governments apparently sometimes passed resolutions that they knew would be annulled by the prefects, so that they could

benefit from the propaganda value of denouncing the prefects' interference. Toward the end of the period under consideration this kind
of opposition to the central authority was beginning to be replaced
by a spirit of cooperation.

Many of the observers and administrators interviewed in connection with the present study offered the opinion that a stern attitude
in regard to administrative standards on the part of the central authority toward Communist administrators had at times led to a
higher degree of competence. If this was true, the central government, by treating Christian Democratic administrators with greater
laxity, may at times have been responsible for a decrease in the
efficiency of local Christian Democratic-controlled governments.

LOCAL POLITICAL LEADERSHIP

Since the examination of budgetary policies revealed no substantial differences between Christian Democratic and Communist local
administrations, it was necessary to look elsewhere to attempt to determine whether the local policies of the two parties varied significantly. The findings indicated that the key to differences in the performance of the two parties is the types of local political personnel
that they have tended to support.[22] Local elected officials—councillors, assemblymen, members of city boards, mayors—especially in
the smaller communes, can be expected to reflect the social composition of the party's electorate better than officials elected at the national level.

By supporting attempts of the working class to gain positions of
local leadership, the Communist Party, for example, makes concrete
what Giovanni Sartori has called its "high level of proletarian mys-
tique." The Communist Party projects the image of a popular and
working class party more through its local political personnel than
through its national leaders. At this level the electorate may recognize itself not only ideologically in the party but socially in its
elected representatives.

To test this hypothesis it was necessary to compile some statistics
on the party affiliation of local elected officials. For a variety of reasons this proved difficult. In the smaller communes, where a major-

22. See Chapter 4 for a discussion of the leadership of the two parties on a national
basis. See also Giovanni Sartori, *Democrazia e Definizioni* (Bologna, il Mulino, 1958);
and Sartori et al., *Il Parlamento Italiano*.

ity rather than a proportional electoral system is used, one or more parties tend to form joint tickets. Until 1960 the proportional representation system used in Sicilian communes differed from that used in the rest of Italy. Furthermore, not all communes hold elections at the same time, which accounts for the marked variations in the absolute numbers of officials elected from year to year. Because of these difficulties, figures were compiled on the number of local officials elected not only as Christian Democratic and Communist candidates but also as candidates of alliances formed around these two parties. (Table 6-4)

TABLE 6-4. *Local officials elected by the Christian Democratic and Communist parties and the associations allied with them, selected years, 1946–60*

| | | Christian Democratic | | | | Communist | | |
| | | Party | | Associations | | Party | Associa-tions | Com-bined |
Year	Total	Number	Percent	Number	Percent	Number	Number	Percent
1946 a	106,275	36,635	34	7,048	6	1,314	38,486	38
1951–52	148,689	45,287	31	27,181	19	4,983	32,503	25
1956	134,383	50,254	38	22,818	15	5,634	28,132	25
1960	133,716	62,205	44	15,673	12	25,084	4,900	23

a. In the smaller communes a joint Communist-Socialist ticket was usual during this period.

The Ministry of the Interior classifies all officials not elected on a given party's ballot as either "Right," "Left," or "Center." This system has always been criticized by the parties of the left, as the tendency is to automatically classify officials whose affiliation is doubtful as Christian Democratic or Christian Democratic-associated. Thus the number of officials shown in the table as Christian Democratic may be inflated.

Communes of 10,000 or more inhabitants use the proportional representation system to elect local officials, whose political affiliations are therefore known. The percentage of council seats occupied by members of the Christian Democratic Party in these larger communes has progressively increased from 26 in 1946 to 44 in 1960. The position of the Communist Party in 1946 cannot be determined in these communes, since in that year the party in many central and southern areas appeared on a left coalition ballot, the Popular Bloc. The Communist Party held 20 percent of local council seats in 1951–52 and over 26 percent in 1960, the same percentage that the Christian Democrats had held in 1946.

The number of communes with under 10,000 inhabitants returning Christian Democratic and Communist majorities is shown in
Table 6-5. While the percentage of these communes controlled by
the Christian Democratic Party steadily increased from 42 in 1946 to
65 in 1960, the Communist Party suffered a marked decline in the
percentage of communes in which it held the majority—from 34.5 in
1946 to 22.5 in 1951–52, to about 20 in 1956 and 1960.

TABLE 6-5. *Communes with Christian Democratic and Communist
majorities among communes of under 10,000 inhabitants
that held elections, 1946–60*

Year	Total	Christian Democratic		Communist	
		Number	Percent	Number	Percent
1946	6,044	2,563	42	2,084	34.5
1951–52	6,044	3,394	56	1,338	22.5
1956	6,193	3,745	60	1,313	20.5
1960	6,138	4,192	65	1,235	20.0

In communes of 10,000 or more inhabitants the trend was different. In 1946, 35 percent of these communes had a Christian Democratic administration, while the Communist Party was in the majority in 54 percent. For the express purpose of changing this balance
of power, the government sponsored a "majority premium" electoral
law for the local elections of 1951–52. This law awarded "a prize"
of extra seats to those parties that, though running separately, had
previously declared themselves to be allied with the government
party and in such an alliance had won a plurality. The local elections of 1951 in the North and Center and the election of 1952 and
in the South were held under this law. In these elections the Christian Democrats succeeded in gaining control of 51 percent of the
communes with 10,000 or more inhabitants. Despite the electoral
maneuver by the government party, the elections left the Communists, allied with the Socialists, still in control of 41 percent of these
larger communes.

The government's lack of success in the national elections of 1953
led to the repeal of the majority premium law, and in 1956 the proportional system was reinstated. As a consequence, both of the leading parties lost ground. Following the 1956 elections the Christian
Democrats held controlling majorities in only 40 percent of these
large communes and the Communists in only 29 percent. Center-left
coalitions entered local elections in 1960, and the Christian Demo-

cratic Party and its coalition parties gained majorities in 70 percent of the 732 communes with 10,000 or more inhabitants. Although the creation of center-left coalitions greatly strengthened the Christian Democrats in local governments in 1960 compared with 1956, the Communist Party held most of the ground it had previously gained, with majorities in 26.5 percent of these large communes.

Many of those elected to public office on Christian Democratic or Christian Democratic-oriented tickets were active members or leaders of such organizations as Catholic Action, the Italian Association of Christian Workers, or the National Confederation of Small Farmers (Coldiretti). For example, of the 73,072 local officials elected in 1956 under the banners of the Christian Democratic Party or allied associations, 26 percent were Coldiretti members; in the 1960 elections the percentage rose to 28. In 1960 a survey of local officeholders in 50 provinces showed that of the 20,762 representatives of the party or its allied associations, 11.5 percent were workers for or leaders of local units of the Italian Association of Christian Workers.

Since information on the social characteristics of local officials elected by the Christian Democratic and the Communist parties was fragmentary, a sample survey of local officials was conducted in connection with the present study in 1963. City clerks in 502 communes were sent questionnaires about specified characteristics of city councillors holding the office of mayor during the period 1947–63 and of councillors then in office. The returns supplied information on the characteristics of 276 Communist mayors and 858 Christian Democratic mayors and of 3,148 Communist and 6,158 Christian Democratic councillors holding office in 1963. (Tables 6-6 to 6-8)

Table A-1 (Appendix A), which compares the distribution of population by size of commune in the survey sample and in all communes, indicates that the sample was representative of the population distribution in Italy as a whole at the time of the survey.

Characteristics of Mayors

A comparison of the dates of birth of the mayors from the two parties elected during 1946–63, revealed by the survey returns, indicated that the differences were negligible. (Table 6-6) Not surprisingly, there were marked differences in the occupational backgrounds of the mayors from the two parties. (Table 6-7) Of the

Communist mayors, 30 percent had held low-status jobs as manual workers, farm laborers, or artisans, for example, compared with about 11 percent of the Christian Democratic mayors. There was much less disparity in the percentages of the mayors from the two parties who had worked in middle-status occupations, such as non-professional white-collar workers and teachers—21 percent of the Communists and 27 percent of the Christian Democrats. In the more highly paid professional and managerial occupations the differences were much greater. Less than 16 percent of the Communist mayors were in this economic class, compared with more than 35 percent of the Christian Democratic mayors.

TABLE 6-6. *Percentage distribution of Communist and Christian Democratic mayors who held office from 1947–63, by date of birth, and of their communes by number of inhabitants*

Characteristic	Communist (276 = 100%)	Christian Democratic (858 = 100%)
Geographic area of communes		
North	48.0	47.3
Center	24.9	11.2
South	19.1	27.6
Islands	8.0	13.9
Population of communes		
10,000 or less	37.3	50.7
10,000–50,000	44.2	33.7
50,000–100,000	10.9	10.5
More than 100,000	7.6	5.1
Date of birth of mayors		
Before 1903	33.4	36.0
1903–12	23.3	21.7
1913–22	32.6	31.3
1923–32	10.7	10.8
After 1932	—	0.2

Analysis of the occupational data by region reveals that mayors from the professional classes were more numerous in the South and in the Islands than in the rest of Italy. Also noticeable was the greater representation in the North than in other sections of white-collar workers among the Communist mayors and of teachers, businessmen, and managers among the Christian Democratic mayors. Communist mayors from the so-called "proletarian" types of occupations were reported almost exclusively by the smaller communes. In both parties, in fact, the incidence of upper status occupations among the mayors increased with size of commune. The data showed a trend toward the election of more manual workers and white-collar employees as Communist mayors, and more teachers and fewer businessmen and managers as Christian Democratic mayors.

TABLE 6-7. *Percentage distribution of Communist and Christian Democratic mayors who held office in 1947–63 by occupational status* [a]

Occupational status	Communist (276 = 100%)	Christian Democratic (858 = 100%)
Low status	30.1	10.8
Small farmers	5.8	2.6
Farm laborers	0.7	0.1
Manual workers	9.1	1.9
Artisans, shopkeepers	14.5	6.2
Middle status	21.0	27.1
Nonprofessional white-collar	15.6	10.7
Teachers	5.4	16.4
Upper status	15.6	35.4
Professional	10.9	21.0
Businessmen, managers, rentiers, farmers	4.7	14.4
Other occupations	17.7	13.5
Retired	2.9	5.4
Political	4.3	0.8
Other	10.5	7.3
Unknown	15.6	13.2

a. The questionnaire asked for the occupations at the time the mayors held office, but in some cases the current occupations of former mayors were given.

Characteristics of Councillors

In 1963 there were 3,148 Communist and 6,158 Christian Democratic city councillors. For those whose ages were known, the age distribution was as follows:

		Percent			
	Number	60 and over	50–59	40–49	30–39	less than 30
---	---	---	---	---	---	---
Communist	3,057	3.9	13.0	39.0	33.3	10.8
Christian Democratic	6,028	7.9	18.6	32.2	30.8	10.5

While it cannot be said that either party sponsored youthful public officials at the local level these figures indicate that the Communist Party had a slight edge on youthful officials in 1963. The age differences on a regional basis were even more marked. The Communist councillors in the North were on the average younger than those in the nation as a whole and in other regions they tended to be older than the average. The distribution by region was apparently just the reverse among the Christian Democratic councillors.

Among councillors of both parties the low and middle status occupations were better represented than they were among mayors. However, the Christian Democratic Party tended to have more local representatives from the middle and upper occupations than did the Communist Party. (Table 6-8)

TABLE 6-8. *Percentage distribution of Communist and Christian Democratic councillors by occupational status, 1963*

Occupational status	Communist (3,148 = 100%)	Christian Democratic (6,158 = 100%)
Low status	43.1	34.9
Farm laborers	2.5	0.6
Small farmers	8.8	16.8
Manual workers	19.2	7.3
Artisans, shopkeepers	12.6	10.2
Middle status	28.6	37.0
Nonprofessional white-collar	22.7	23.9
Teachers	5.9	13.1
Upper status	10.8	20.5
Professionals	9.2	16.0
Businessmen, managers, rentiers, farmers	1.6	4.5
Other occupations	15.7	6.6
Retired	2.9	2.8
Political	9.8	1.1
Other	3.0	2.7
Unknown	1.8	1.0

There was a marked preponderance of white-collar employees among Communist councillors in the North and of agricultural workers in the South and the Islands. In contrast, there were more Christian Democratic councillors with rural occupations in the North and with professional and teaching occupations in the South and the Islands.

Finally, there was a tendency for the low-status occupations to be better represented in the small communes. In communes with less than 10,000 inhabitants, for example, the "proletarian" element— farm laborers (and small farmers among the Christian Democrats), manual workers, artisans, and shopkeepers—accounted for 51 percent of the Communist and about 44 percent of the Christian Democratic councillors. In communes with more than 100,000 inhabitants, on the other hand, nearly a fourth of the Communist councillors and more than a third of the Christian Democratic councillors were professionals.

In general, this analysis of the occupations of councillors holding office in 1963, as reported in the returns from survey questionnaires, tended to reinforce the conclusion that the Communist Party recruits its local leadership from lower income groups than does the Christian Democratic Party.

LOCAL GOVERNMENTS IN THE POLITICAL SYSTEM

In general, the investigation of local administrations and their relationship to the policies of the two leading parties led to the conclusion that the present organization of local government is not in harmony with the pluralistic design of the Italian state, as formulated in the Constitution. The failure to remedy this basic flaw in the system as a whole through legislative action must be attributed primarily to the parliamentary majority and the government, although the minority opposition parties have also been responsible to some extent.

Until the early 1960s no serious consideration was given to the problem of creating regional governments. The Socialist and Christian Democratic left has tended since then to make this issue a keystone of the program of the center-left; it has also been a basic Communist propaganda theme. The relationship between the regional governments and lower governmental units has generally been overlooked, however. The main theme of the debate has usually been the role of the regions in economic planning. The failure to solve this problem in harmony with the provisions of the Constitution is typical of the impasses that have resulted from the relationship that has existed between the government and the opposition.

At the local level the differences between the two parties have taken several forms, including a tendency toward a greater degree of control by the central government over Communist-dominated local administrations than over Christian Democratic local administrations, especially before 1955. At the same time the Communist Party has made a greater effort to coordinate the activities of its own administrations and to furnish its administrators with assistance of various types—participation in the National Association of Italian Communes as a platform from which to put forward the themes of Communist policy, sponsorship of the League of Democratic Communes (an organization that has no counterpart in the Christian Democratic Party), more attention to the preparation and distribution of specialized periodicals, and slightly greater efficiency of the Communist central party organ concerned with local administrative problems than of its Christian Democratic counterpart. These differences reflect general characteristics of the two parties (that is, the greater connection of the Christian Democrats with the state power and the greater organizational efficiency of the Communist Party). They have affected the relative strength of the two parties at the local level but have had no uniform identifiable impact on local administrative policies.

The lack of policy differences in the small communes may be due primarily to their financial situation, sometimes so serious as to make the purchase of stationery a grave problem. The larger communes, on the other hand, are able to project broader programs, primarily because they can contract loans, something that smaller communes are unable to do. Local officials of both parties have taken this path, even borrowing on occasion from foreign sources.[23]

Although a few communes are able to balance their budgets, the majority have conspicuous deficits. In 1964, for example, Vicenza and Piacenza, both Christian Democratic communes, anticipated deficits of 600 and 700 million lire, respectively, while Mantua anticipated a deficit of 1 billion lire. The situation was no different in the Communist communes: in Reggio Emilia, Ferrara, Parma, and Modena deficits were expected to range from 1.2 billion to 1.7 billion lire.

Confronted with this situation, all local administrations have acted in a similar manner. Financial conditions justified their slowness in facing the problems of urbanization in the 1950s, a period of

23. For example, in 1964 the communes of Milan (center-left) and Turin (center) obtained loans from sources in the United States; while Bologna, administered by the Communist Party, even while carrying on an intense propaganda campaign against the "war-mongering West German capitalists," undertook to borrow a large sum from West German banks.

intense socioeconomic transformation. The Communist Party, a severe critic of the Christian Democrats on this issue, has done no better in its own local administrations. In 1948 in Bologna, for instance, it promised to enact urgently needed zoning regulations, but
did so only at the end of the council's term in office, when the regulations had been rendered practically meaningless by chaotic urban
expansion. In Communist-controlled Rimini zoning was delayed ten
years after the city's population explosion began, with the result that
it has become a jungle of asphalt and concrete, a condition that elsewhere the Communist Party likes to blame on Christian Democratic
administration.

In reality, the local administrations of the two parties often operate in the same ways and according to similar budgetary policies. In
neither large nor small communes does the Christian Democratic
Party distinguish itself through a moderate policy, nor the Communist Party through a popular one. Thus, a vote for either of the parties cannot be justified on the basis of support for a specific orientation toward local government.

There has apparently been at least one real difference between
the two parties in the social composition of the local officials elected
in their names. The local officials selected by the Communists reflect
the composition and largely proletarian characteristics of the party's
membership and electorate more closely than the Christian Democratic local officials reflect that party's base of support and its interclass characteristics. The Communist officials represent both the
working classes and the middle classes with whom the party seeks alliances and whose votes it seeks. The local Christian Democratic
leaders, however, represent in large part the middle and upper
classes but not the wage earners, from whom they hope to receive
support.

The choice between these two parties in local elections is often
more likely to reflect a response to the differences in the images the
parties project through their candidates than to real differences between the respective administrative policies. If this conclusion continues to be verified in practice, it may have some bearing in the
long run on the nature of the political contest between the two parties and on its outcome.

7

Parliament as a Political Arena

The parliamentary crisis that paved the way for the fascist dictatorship was due to the failure of the Socialists and Catholics to support the institutions of government at that critical moment when the government could not function without the support of at least one of them. The Socialist Party's unsympathetic attitude toward the liberal-democratic state was reinforced by the wave of extremism that accompanied the Russian revolution. The Popular Party's opposition was dictated by its commitment to Catholic organic pluralism and by its effort to emphasize the claims of the "real" as against the "legal" country.

PARTY ATTITUDES TOWARD THE STATE AND PARLIAMENT [1]

With the overthrow of the fascist dictatorship, the Christian Democratic Party and the Communist Party, heirs of the prewar parties, appeared on the political scene, both with strongly critical attitudes toward the liberal-democratic tradition. In its first postwar congress in 1946 the Christian Democratic Party expressed its position as follows:

> We are ready to cooperate in any new and bold construction, so long as it is based on solid Christian foundations. . . . The more liberalism increases the freedom of the individual, the more it limits the intervention of the state. . . . [We] hold instead that

1. This chapter is based on a report on the parliamentary activity of the two major parties, *Il PCI e la DC nelle amministrazioni locale e in parlamento*, to be published in 1970 by Società editrice il Mulino, Bologna, as Vol. V in the series of monographs reporting the findings of the project conducted by the Carlo Cattaneo Institute in Bologna, described in Appendix A of this book.

there is more liberty, even for the individual, as the guardianship
of the state is more watchful and efficacious. . . . While communism extolls exclusively society, and liberalism exclusively the individual, democracy tends to synthesize the social rights and duties
of the individual, and thus to exalt a state where cooperation between classes is animated by that Christian spirit which, through
ethical legislation, is able to eliminate the defects of democracy itself.

The Communist Party had explicitly asserted in 1945 that the creation of a socialist society was not among its immediate objectives,
but its attitude toward the new state was ambivalent, since it continued to adhere to the Marxist-Leninist doctrine, which holds that
the state is an instrument of the capitalist bourgeois classes for domi-
nating the rest of society.

Although the attitude of the two parties toward the state may
have changed somewhat during the postwar period, their respective
ideologies have continued to color their views of the nature and role
of the state and its institutions. A fundamental premise of Christian
Democracy is that the state is only one among several equally necessary social groupings (all coordinated into an organic arrangement,
under the guardianship of the Church). The Catholic political leaders consider all political structures as instruments to further their
basic social values, and they cannot accept without reservation those
aspects of the modern state that embody most clearly the legacy of
Italian liberalism.

The Communist Party's unwillingness to accept liberal political
institutions flows from certain aspects of the party's self-image and
particularly from the Leninist heritage. Although the party has devoted a great deal of attention to reevaluating the significance of a
democratic political framework, particularly since 1956, it has not
given a positive answer to what, from its standpoint, is the key problem—whether or not it is possible within that political framework to
bring about the "expropriation of the expropriators," the development of a noncapitalist economy through collective ownership of the
means of production, which is viewed by Marxists as the only truly
significant transformation.

Thus, the ideologies and history of the two parties tend to set
them against the conservative values of the liberal tradition and the
institutions that embody these values. One such institution is parlia-

ment, understood in a wide sense to include election regulations and procedures, the formation of cabinets, and relationships to the executive. The paradox is that this institution in its present form was shaped by the Christian Democratic and Communist parties. Both parties agreed, though with some qualifications and reservations, to set up a representative regime basically on the liberal model. In 1946, for instance, the Christian Democratic Party recommended a broad system of representation [2] and the Communist Party gave its assent to a "representative parliamentary government," while underscoring that to be viable a democratic regime would have to undertake extensive reforms to undercut the power of reactionary groups and private monopolies.[3] Yet the Constitution, written in the year these resolutions were passed, by virtue largely of cooperation between these two parties, reflects the liberal spirit.

The qualifications and reservations are still held by both parties, however, and are reflected in the way they operate in parliament. While both parties participate in the parliamentary process, they cannot entirely share the spirit of the constitutional design of parliament. Neither Catholics nor Marxists, for instance, share the classical view of political representation as enacting the purely political will of discrete sovereign units—the individual citizens. Although Catholics and Communists disagree on which of the individual's multiple social memberships is of ultimate significance in determining his political interests, both view the individual not simply as a "citizen," but rather as a member of a social category. They tend to view the parliament not as the locus of political decisions based on majority agreement among individual representatives, but as a mirror of social forces that, though they arise outside of parliament, seek a legal sanction there.

Although both parties are committed to work through parliament in spite of their specific reservations, each party tries to use it against the other. In the first two national elections under the new Constitution in 1948 and 1953, a major issue for each party was the relationship of the other to the institution of parliament. In 1948 each party presented itself as the champion of the representative state that, they assured the public, was being threatened by the other

2. See the resolution of the 1946 Congress of the Christian Democratic Party, reprinted in *I Congressi Nazionali della DC* (Rome, SPES, 1959), pp. 57 ff.

3. See one of the motions passed at the 1946 Congress of the Communist Party, reprinted in *La Politica dei Comunisti dal Quinto al Sesto Congresso* (Rome, Rinascita, 1947), pp. 9 ff.

party. The Communists saw the Christian Democrats as the promoters of an authoritarian clerical state, while the Christian Democrats saw the Communists as attempting to introduce a totalitarian communist state. But in spite of the fact that both parties were loud in their praise of parliament, in practice they apparently viewed it as no more than a place to gain legal sanction for their own strength in the country. The Christian Democratic Party saw the election results as an expression of the influence of the Catholic tradition in the nation, of the will of the "Christian country which has answered the appeal" to defeat the enemies of religion. The Communist Party, which lost, denied the legitimacy of parliamentary representation itself:

> The results of April 18 were determined in great part by the influence of foreign imperialism, religious terrorism, illicit pressure from the government and by many cleverly planned violations of the electoral laws. The Christian Democratic "victory" is the consequence of the violation of the electoral freedom of the Italian people.[4]

This was the situation at the opening of the first republican parliament, which closed with a vote on the majority electoral law (the "swindle law," described in Chapter 2), which the governing party supported and the Communist opposition attacked, both on the same basis—that a working parliament is the essential organ of representative democracy. The Christian Democrats argued in favor of the majority law on the ground that it would provide parliament with a stable two thirds majority. At its Fourth Congress in November 1952 the party leadership stated:

> The democratic state is strong if the parliament is capable and efficient. Parliament is the bulwark of democracy, which lives if parliament lives. . . . But parliament does not mean parliamentarianism. Parliament is regulated by norms from remote and different times. Our electoral program must provide for the modernization of parliamentary procedure. . . . Not the least important task is that of putting an end to obstructionism. The right of the minority to say "no" must not threaten the right of the majority to decide "yes."[5]

4. From the text of a statement by the Communist Party Central Committee, published in *L'Unità*, April 22, 1948.
5. See *I Congressi Nazionali della DC* (Rome, SPES, 1959), pp. 350–51.

While praising a "capable and efficient" parliament, the Christian Democrats were already proposing modifications in the procedures that had governed the Italian parliament for only one legislative session, an intention that could do little to strengthen the standing of the institution. The manner of parliament's formation, as well as its method of operation, was put before the country in a plebiscite.

The parallel ambivalence of the Communist Party is expressed in its vice-secretary's comment during the debate on the majority electoral law:

The lesson which De Gasperi and his associates have taught us about "their" democracy is worth more than a hundred thousand speeches which we might have made. The real limits of political democracy in a capitalist regime have been brought starkly before the eyes of everyone, even those who have never read Lenin. . . . Is democracy then dead? Is parliament finished? Without doubt a serious blow has been dealt democracy, but freedom and constitution can be saved. With their struggle and their vote the Italians may irrevocably condemn the ignoble swindle law.[6]

Anyone who had read Lenin would have known that in orthodox ideological terms the Communist Party's evaluation of parliament must be a very negative one, and that its goal of saving the Constitution and parliament is a contradiction between its ideological principles and its political goals.

The contradictory attitudes of the two parties toward parliament tended to become less marked in the two successive legislative sessions. The referendum-type elections of 1948 and 1953 had, paradoxically, contributed to the stabilization of parliamentary democracy. The prospect of a "popular democracy," which was supposed to follow a Communist victory in 1948, and the prospect of a "safe democracy," which was to have been the consequence of the 1953 implementation of the majority electoral law, had both failed to materialize. And, in the minds of the electorate, the two parties had assumed well-defined positions within the framework of a relatively stable balance of power. Parliament could no longer be considered the place where a party "cashed in" on its predominance, since the electorate had refused to turn the parliament over to either of the two major contenders. However, both parties continued to claim as

6. Editorial in *L'Unità*, April 18, 1953.

their own responsibility the formation of political will, leaving to parliament merely the function of sanctioning it.

This had always been the attitude of the Communist Party. Increasingly it became that of the Christian Democrats as well for two reasons: the growing autonomy of the party with respect to the Catholic world and its control over the power centers, which are at the disposal of the executive branch of the government, not of parliament.

Christian Democratic Emphasis on Preeminence of the Party

Amintore Fanfani's efforts during the second legislation to strengthen the Christian Democratic Party organizationally are described in Chapters 2 and 3. He tried to make the party less dependent on the goodwill of the Catholic organizations and, indirectly, of the hierarchy itself, and to vest in the national party leadership a greater control over the designation of the party's candidates. Although the factional struggle halted Fanfani's drive in these directions, his efforts changed the party's image to that of a center for the formation of political decisions.

This increasing emphasis on the responsibilities and prerogatives of the Christian Democratic Party as a political party is loftily expressed in the following passage from Aldo Moro's speech to the party congress at Naples in 1962:

> It is above all the party that counts! The party which operates in governments and in parliamentary majorities, but does not exhaust itself there. Above all matters the party, with its complex history, its ideology, its unity, its emotional appeal, the spiritual values which it cultivates, the hopes which it lights for the future. . . . It is the party as such, in its autonomy and integrity, which speaks to the electorate and offers itself as the real and enduring point of reference in the development of civilization and in the historical evolution of the country.

One fairly obvious corollary of this passionate emphasis on the primary significance of the party has been a tendency to view parliament as a place for the legislative ratification of decisions reached through party mechanisms, rather than as a place for the making of political decisions. This tendency has expressed itself in efforts to reduce the amount of parliamentary control over the operation of other organs—from the Cabinet to the public economic agencies.

Naturally this tendency could not simply and easily enforce itself, since it had to cope with (and was repeatedly checked by) the efforts of the parliamentary groups to maintain their own autonomy in relation to the party organs. Many of the innumerable postwar Cabinet crises, discussed later in this chapter, could be interpreted as an expression of this struggle.

Importance of Parliament to the Communist Party

While the Communist Party has taken for granted the preeminence of the party with respect to parliament, it has also tended to set great value on representation in that body. It is the only major public institution in which the Communists have been on an equal footing with the other parties, even though in the role of the permanent opposition.

To this fundamental reason for its high evaluation of the parliament may be added the changes that have taken place in world communism since the Twentieth Congress of the Communist Party of the Soviet Union. Pronouncements made at that congress amounted to an official sanction of the Italian Communist Party's earlier commitment to parliamentary democracy and to what it used to call "the Italian way to socialism." This development found final expression at the Tenth Italian Communist Party Congress: "Parliament must be given full power to direct and control the activity of the executive, a function which is proper to it and which is essential to its being an effective organ of democracy."

This function of control over the executive organ, which the Italian Communist Party has emphasized in order to influence the executive branch of government (from which it is absent) through the legislative branch (where it is present) has been stressed particularly with respect to government intervention in economic affairs. The Tenth Italian Communist Congress, in fact, attributed to the Christian Democratic Party the "tendency to impose maximum limitations on Parliament's powers of intervention and control in economic life and the public sector of the economy." As an alternative the Communist Party congress suggested the possibility of working-class control over production through its representatives in parliament:

The trend toward an increased intervention of the state in economic life . . . must be supported, so long as it is accompanied by a strong and broad democratic struggle which demands that government intervention in economic life will be favorable to the interest of the great working masses; which requires and insists that these sectors be at the service, not of private interest, but of the collectivity; and which insists upon far-reaching reforms of the current economic and political structures. In these areas functions of the highest importance may be given to the parliament, whenever there is active in it a strong democratic and socialist current rooted in the people and bound up with a mass movement.

According to the Communists, they have supplied the necessary "strong democratic and socialist current," and they have therefore favored giving to parliament "functions of the highest importance."

The Communist Party's defense of parliament has increased in proportion to its fears that the Christian Democratic Party and its allies were threatening to strengthen the executive organs at the expense of the parliament. Pietro Ingrao, the secretary of the Communist group in the Chamber of Deputies, voiced these concerns in 1963, at the beginning of the first center-left government, when he said that the program of the government "favors an increase and strengthening of the powers of the executive" but there is "the danger of an extension . . . of the method of *delega legislativa* [7] and of a revision of the powers of the executive and the parliamentary committees in the direction of an enlargement of the former to the detriment of representative institutions." [8] The Communist Party has taken the position that this process should be reversed, that the powers of parliament should be expanded and those of the executive reduced.

It can be concluded that both of the parties see the basic function of parliament as that of sactioning a political will of the people that is formed outside of parliament. The locus of this political will is supposed to be in the masses—the underprivileged, in the Communist view; and, in the Christian Democratic view, the Catholic world and the responsible, moderate elements in the citizenry. In each case the task of evoking, articulating, and enforcing that will is clearly reserved to the party rather than to parliament.

7. This term signifies a procedure by which parliament enacts a law delegating to the government the power to pass legislation in certain areas, with the understanding that certain broad directives specified by parliament will be complied with. Such forms of "delegated legislation" are of course well known in other representative parliamentary systems.

8. From a speech to the Central Committee of the Communist Party, as reported in *L'Unità*, December 7, 1963.

The proper role of the party in parliament has been more of a problem for the Communists than for the Christian Democrats, since ideologically the Communist Party regards parliament as a forum for propaganda and its deputies as agitators committed to the party line. It rejects the liberal concept of parliament as a forum of open discussion, where the political will of the people is formed. Communist Party deputies have become increasingly integrated into the parliamentary body, however, and in the actual working of parliament their behavior differs little from that of the other deputies.

The experience of the popular fronts in various countries in the 1930s did much to modify the communist attitude, particularly the position taken by the French Communist Party toward the Blum government. Later, at the end of World War II, the idea that communist members could enter "bourgeois" parliaments, not to destroy them but to see that they functioned in the interest of the workers, was developed in Italy also. The domestic and international tension in which the first parliament met prevented this idea from being fully put into practice, but it found expression in succeeding parliaments.

The degree of the Communist Party's commitment to work in and through parliament is indicated by the amount of space devoted to parliamentary activities in reports to party congresses. Of a 284-page report on the Communist Party's activities distributed to the delegates at the Sixth Italian Communist Party Congress (1948), 23 pages were devoted to the activities of Communist groups in the preparation of the Constitution and 13 pages to the legislative activity of the parliamentary group and its policy toward the government. In the "Report on the Activity of Parliamentary Groups and Central Commissions," a 422-page volume distributed to the delegates at the Seventh Congress (1951), the section "Parliamentary Activity" occupies 30 pages. These figures suggest that the parliamentary tasks of the party have been seen as a minor part of its activities. The Seventh Congress report also indicates the persistence of the tendency to view parliamentary activity in terms of agitation.[9]

Describing the opposition of the Communist senators to the Atlantic alliance, the report states:

> The Communist senators, after having said no to the evil pact
> and having demonstrated once again that the Italian people will
> never participate in an imperialist war against the fatherland

9. See *Relazioni sull'Attività dei Gruppi Parlamentari e delle Commissioni Centrali* (Rome, Partito Comunista Italiano, 1951), pp. 393–94.

of socialism and the popular republics, voted against the pact, singing in a body the *International*. This new and unique fact in parliamentary history sealed the solemn agreement to fight—for the good of . . . the country—against war and in defense of peace.[10]

This language and the singing of the *International*, presented here as a "new and unique fact in parliamentary history," express the persistence into the beginning of the 1950s of the agitational interpretation of the Communist Party's role in parliament. However, Communist parliamentary activity has progressively lost some of its fire and challenge and much of its earnestness. In fact the party has organized no obstruction since the debates in the first legislature on the Atlantic Pact and the majority electoral law.

Communist Attitude on Parliamentary Salaries

An episode concerning the question of the Communists' position on the issue of the salaries of members of parliament reveals the changing attitude of the party toward the role of Communist deputies.

Historically, the workers' movement has always supported the granting of salaries to members of the legislature since only members of the higher income groups could participate in parliament without remuneration. The workers' parties, by backing the principle of paid parliamentary activity, intended to allow deputies from the lower income classes to dedicate their time to parliamentary activity without having to rely on the financial resources of the party itself.

At the beginning of the 1950s, however, parliamentary salaries in Italy and the special advantages accruing to members of parliament (such as tax exemption) made their incomes far higher than those of the workers. One can understand, therefore, the sense of outrage felt in Communist Party ranks when it was announced at the end of 1954 that the Chamber, in a secret session, had approved a law providing pensions for deputies. The Communist deputies had voted for the law, which provided for a much higher pension for deputies than that which workers would receive, at a time when the meager-

10. Ibid., p. 409.

ness of workers' pensions was a constant theme of Communist propaganda.

The position taken by Palmiro Togliatti on this question at the Fourth National Conference of the party in January 1955 represents an important development. It suggests that the Communist Party had come to share the view of the other parties that parliamentary activity should be financially rewarding and should provide some security for the future. By the same token it suggests the party's willingness to consider its own members of parliament as full-fledged members of the "parliamentary guild." Togliatti raised the issue of pensions out of context, so to speak, in that it was not the central theme of a long speech. He stressed that "political representations of the workers in parliament should be remunerated," if members of that class were to be able to serve at all as legislators. Turning to the specific issue of pensions, he said:

Should one go as far as granting pensions? One cannot forget that, even recently, there have been cases of old militants of the working class parties who, growing old in parliament and finally leaving the political struggle, have found no alternative open to them but the poorhouse. Thus, the problem exists; what we must discuss is whether it is right to solve it in the way which has been proposed, and to the advantage of whom, and what measure. In general, I feel that the awarding of a large pension to everyone is not just, since it tends to change the character of parliamentary representation and may have a dangerous influence toward the bureaucratization of the leadership of political parties. I should like, however, to add another thing, to the end of unmasking the false Catos who have come out against a proposal which they themselves had approved and tried to keep from public discussion. . . . Let us take the list of Christian Democratic, Liberal, Social Democratic and Republican deputies who have been defeated in elections, and let us find out what they are doing now. We see how great is the number of those who have received, from the government and with the means of government, a sinecure, a post in some public firm. . . . It is necessary to expose the self-styled moralizers who use the apparatus of the state to provide security for their party's defeated deputies, and then engage in an antiparliamentary campaign because the parliament has considered this question. . . . A word about this was necessary so that our comrades would not be taken unawares by the deceivers and false moralizers who have raised this question. And the question is to be faced and resolved publicly, justly, and taking into account the hard conditions of the life of such a great part of the Italian workers.[11]

Apparently the Communist parliamentarians had identified themselves with the "parliamentarians' guild" to such an extent that only the spontaneous reaction of sections of the party membership to their decision had shown them the error of their ways. In fact, those sections of the party that had reacted most strongly to the action of the comrade deputies were probably identified with the so-called "*operaista* tendency," [12] led by the party vice-secretary, Pietro Secchia. Some years earlier Secchia himself had voiced a rather critical view of the parliamentary institutions:

> The results of the parliamentary elections cannot be a decisive criterion for judging the strength of a party, and much less of its influence among the working classes. Whatever its electoral system, the parliament always reproduces the balance of forces in a distorted manner. It reproduces, greatly decreased, the strength of the oppressed popular masses, while it reproduces, greatly increased, that of the dominant classes and of the parties which represent them. . . . Only the organization and the struggle of the masses reproduce the true balance of forces. In the direct and immediate struggle both for partial goals and for more advanced political and social objectives, the working class shows a force which is much greater than its parliamentary expression.[13]

As it happened, the January 1955 conference saw the demotion of Secchia and the suppression of the *operaista* opposition. The decision to grant "a large pension" aroused no further conflict and no open and public debates.

THE CHARACTER OF PARLIAMENTARY ACTIVITY

Three aspects of the behavior of the members of the two parties in parliament have been examined, in order to evaluate the parties'

11. *Partito Comunista Italiano, IV Conferenza Nazionale* (Rome, Edizioni di Cultura Sociale, 1955), pp. 330–31.
12. This was the nucleus of a short-lived semiclandestine faction whose purpose was to emphasize the party's commitment to its working-class base.
13. *Rinascita*, April–May 1948, p. 3.

parliamentary roles: the content and style of parliamentary questions or "interrogations" [14] made by the deputies of the two parties; attendance at parliamentary sessions; and their participation in parliamentary committees compared with their behavior in the Chamber of Deputies.

Parliamentary Interrogations

Questions requesting written answers are popular among parliamentarians of all parties. Typically this type of interrogation has been used to advance a specific interest or to protest a specific action by the government. An examination of the types of questions raised furnishes a certain insight into the concerns of the individual members of parliament as well as into the concerns of the party as a whole.

Many interrogations requesting written answers have been submitted in each legislature—12,472, 28,776, and 24,195 in the first, second and third legislatures, respectively. A limited sample from each legislature was analyzed. (See Appendix A for the method used in selecting the sample.)

Interrogations submitted by Christian Democratic deputies during the first legislature accounted for 48 percent of the total (53 percent of the deputies were members of that party). In the second legislature Christian Democratic deputies, representing 44 percent of the Chamber membership, submitted about 28 percent of the interrogations, and in the third, Christian Democratic deputies (about 45 percent of the Chamber's membership) submitted 20 percent of the interrogations. The Communist deputies, representing only 23 percent of the Chamber's membership during the first legislature, submitted more than a quarter of the interrogations. In the second and third legislatures, when they still represented about 23 percent of the deputies, they submitted from 27.5 to 29 percent of the interrogations.

More than half of the interrogations from both parties came from deputies from constituencies in the South and the Islands. Although

14. Members of the Italian parliament are allowed to submit questions (interrogations) to the various ministers and to specify whether they wish a written or an oral answer. These interrogations may be submitted at any time. Although the ministers are expected to answer all interrogations, in fact only 90 percent of those requesting a written answer are regularly answered, and less than half of those requiring an oral answer.

these deputies were a minority in both parties, their interrogations accounted for 54 percent of those submitted by the Communists and 62 percent of those submitted by the Christian Democrats during the first legislature. The comparable figures were 60 percent and 69 percent, respectively, during the second legislature; and in the third legislature interrogations by these deputies fell to 59 percent of Communist interrogations, while they rose to 75 percent of Christian Democratic interrogations.

Interrogations are sent to a special office of the Chamber where deputies receive suggestions on how to compose their texts in correct parliamentary language and in the form of actual questions rather than of denunciations or protests. Interrogations may be somewhat "softened" in this process, and the fact that the Communist deputies submit theirs to this office suggests an acceptance of the forms of parliamentary procedure.

In order to analyze the type and range of interests that the interrogations have covered, they have been classified as "politically oriented" (if addressed to the Prime Minister or to the Ministers of Foreign Affairs, the Interior, Defense, or Finance) or as "nonpolitical" (if addressed to any of the other ministries).

During the three postwar legislatures usually less than half of the Communist interrogations—and a smaller proportion of the Christian Democratic—have dealt with nonpolitical questions. Deputies from the southern and island regions have submitted the greatest percentage of nonpolitical interrogations in both parties. Considering that one of these parties has regularly been the party of the opposition and the other the government party, the differences in the percentages of questions devoted to political and to nonpolitical concerns by their respective deputies have been small.

Percentages of interrogations dealing with problems of primarily local interest (single provinces, single communes, etc.) in the three successive legislatures have been 60, 87, and 81 for the Communists, and 44, 72, and 68 for the Christian Democrats. The high percentages for the Communists suggest that they employ the interrogation properly, that is, with reference to restricted spheres of interest.

During the three successive legislatures the percentages of interrogations by Communist deputies that dealt with matters exclusively of interest to their own constituencies were 61, 85, and 79. For the Christian Democrats the corresponding percentages were 59, 75, and 65. Apparently Communist deputies, particularly, looked out for

their constituents by presenting, for the most part, issues that di
rectly concerned them.

Interrogations were often presented to aid specific class interests.
For the Communists 54, 26, and 40 percent of the interrogations in
the three successive legislatures fell in this category; for the Christian Democrats the corresponding percentages were 54, 36, and 37.
Clearly, the deputies of both parties have tended to represent territorial units and their constituencies more than they have a specific
social class. This is not what would have been expected of the Communists, if they had followed the Leninist concept of the party and
parliament.

This judgment is confirmed when the interrogations to aid specific class interests are examined to determine the classes with which
they are concerned. In the first legislature 14 percent of the Communist interrogations (a quarter of those dealing with specific
classes) dealt with problems of manual workers. In the second legislature the figure was only 8.5 percent (about a third of the interrogations dealing with a specific class); and in the third, 10 percent (a
fourth of the interrogations favoring a specific class). For the Christian Democratic Party—which, after all, does not call itself the
"party of the working class"—the percentages of the interrogations
aimed at problems of manual workers were lower, ranging from 3 to
9 percent. During the three legislatures, Christian Democratic interrogations dealing with employees other than industrial workers
(white-collar, agricultural, government) ranged from 11 to 26 percent of the interrogations.

Interrogations requesting information in the three successive legislatures accounted for 51, 53, and 36 percent, respectively, of all
Communist Party interrogations and those requesting action, for 29,
30, and 64 percent. Requests for action were most frequent from
Communist deputies representing the southern and island constituencies. Requests for information or explanation tended to have
more value for the Communists as a gesture of protest or propaganda than interrogations demanding action. For the Christian
Democrats, the information type of interrogations accounted for 37,
35, and 28 percent of all interrogations in the three successive legislatures, while the action type interrogations were 47, 49 and 72 percent.

The frequency with which parliamentary interrogations tended to
judge or evaluate the behavior of public authorities was naturally

higher for the Communist Party deputies than for the Christian Democratic. The range for the Communists was from 28 to 30 percent of the interrogations in the three legislatures, compared to from 1 to 11 percent for the Christian Democrats. While evaluations made by the majority party deputies were both positive and negative, those of Communist deputies were all negative.

Of the responses to Communist Party interrogations during the three successive legislatures, 36, 33, and 24 percent were positive, while 46, 42, and 55 percent were negative. The classifications of responses to Christian Democratic interrogations were similar. The percentage of positive answers was lowest for both parties during the third legislature, possibly because of the greater frequency of interrogations demanding action (as against information) during that legislature. Obviously it is easier for a public authority to grant information than to commit itself to act in the manner requested.

In general, neither the content of the interrogations nor the nature of their responses varied markedly with the party of the deputy posing the question. There seemed to be a tendency for the actions of the Communist deputies to be similar to those of the deputies of the government party, but the tendency had not crystallized into consistent behavior during the first three legislatures.

Attendance at Parliamentary Sessions

Theoretically attendance at parliamentary sessions should be simple to determine, since at the beginning of every session each deputy present is required to sign a register. But actual attendance at the sessions is another matter. Deputies often sign the register and leave. Less frequently a deputy signs the name of an absent colleague.

For this analysis a more valid measure of attendance was used— the parliamentary records of all deputies who cast votes on the creation of such agencies as the National Hydrocarbons Trust and the National Electrical Energy Agency. The percentage of the deputies of each party attending the debates and voting on the creation of these and other public agencies is shown in Table 7-1.

The rates of attendance for all party deputies during the debates on the creation of these public boards and authorities were distinctly above average, especially during the actual voting sessions. At five of the eight sessions for which attendance is shown in the table, the percentage of Communist deputies present was larger than the percentage of deputies of any other party. The Christian Democrats had the highest percentage of deputies present at two of the eight sessions.

TABLE 7-1. *Percentage of deputies present and voting on major economic issues, three legislatures, 1948–63*

Party	First legislature, 1948–53 [a]	Second legislature, 1953–58		Third legislature, 1958–63 [d]				
		A [b]	B [c]	Vote 1	Vote 2	Vote 3	Vote 4	Vote 5
Christian Democratic	76	74	81	54	49	64	82	73
Communist	62	78	89	78	78	80	90	65
Social Democratic	69	68	69	56	42	56	72	42
Liberal	40	37	72	33	30	50	60	50
Monarchist	33	20	55	60	60	45	55	50
Republican	70	20	60	84	66	17	84	50
Neofascist	16	10	16	56	52	64	72	45
Socialist	—	60	77	80	75	52	79	62

a. Vote on creation of National Hydrocarbons Trust (ENI).
b. Creation of Ministry of State Industrial Holdings.
c. Withdrawal of Institute for Industrial Reconstruction (IRI) firms from Confindustria. On this question see J. LaPalombara, *Interest Groups in Italian Politics* (Princeton, Princeton University Press, 1964).
d. Five votes on legislation for the creation of the National Electrical Energy Board (ENEL).

Legislative Activity of the Committees [15]

In the Italian parliament some laws may be passed by committees, which thus work in a legislative as well as an advisory capacity. Only as members of committees can deputies engage in legislative activities independent of those of the government. This type of legislation is generally of a minor nature, however, since the government reserves for itself practically all major legislative action. About three fourths of the 2,427 laws passed by the first legislature, the 1,840 laws passed by the second legislature, and the 2,094 laws passed by the third legislature were passed in committee.

A law may be passed in committee unless one fifth or more of the committee's members request consideration of it on the Chamber floor. Since Communist deputies always account for at least one fifth of a committee's members, any systematic opposition on their part to

15. See J. C. Adams and P. Barile, *The Government of Republican Italy* (Boston, Houghton Mifflin, 1961), pp. 65–66.

legislative action by committee vote would virtually bring it to a halt. But far from obstructing parliamentary action by committee vote, the Communist Party strongly favors this form of legislative activity.

Each committee represents a fair sample of the whole Chamber, including the Communist members. One can assume, therefore, that any law passed with less than three dissenting votes has had the support of the majority of the Communists on the committee—that is, that the posture of opposition that has come to be expected of the Communists on the Chamber floor has not been maintained in committee. In order to determine to what extent the Communists had opposed legislation passed in committee, official records were examined to determine how many votes had been cast for and against a selected sample of such legislation. The sample included laws passed by committees in calm periods as well as during times when violent clashes between the Christian Democratic and Communist parties were taking place on the Chamber floor. This inquiry revealed that opposing positions taken by the two parties in the Chamber have often not been the positions taken in the committees. In fact, laws passed by the legislative committees have usually been the result of unanimous or large majority votes.

In the first legislature, while parliament was engaged in a heated debate on the Atlantic Pact during January, February, March, and July of 1949, 125 laws were passed in committee. More than half (52 percent) of these were passed unanimously or received only two dissenting votes, which means that they were passed with the consent of the Communist members of the legislative committee or over the dissent of no more than two of them.

During December 1952 and January and February 1953 there was another period of tension, when the first legislature discussed the majority electoral law. Yet of the laws passed in committee during that period 57.5 percent were passed without organized opposition. Similarly, in two rather uneventful periods (March and April 1950 and May, June, and July 1952) 64 and 58 percent, respectively, of the laws passed in committee had little or no opposition.

From the second legislature the sample included legislation during the tense months when the Scelba government's increasing pressure on the Communist Party culminated in the restrictive measures announced in December 1954. During this period nearly two thirds of the laws passed in committee were approved without organized dissent. In the period immediately following, when a government crisis was brewing, the percentage went down to 58 percent. In the two "normal" periods of March and April 1956 and February, March, and April of 1957 the comparable percentages were 63 and 73, respectively. The examination of the votes on 149 laws passed in committee revealed that the trend has been for the proportion of committee legislation approved without organized dissent to increase.

In the third legislature, during a period of tension when the Tambroni government was formed in April and May 1960, 95 percent of the laws passed in committee were passed with little dissent. In the two "normal" months of June 1959 and February 1960 the corresponding percentage was 93, but in May to August 1963 during another "normal" period, the percentage fell to 82. From the examination of 256 laws passed in committee it appeared that during the third legislature the tendency of the two leading parties to vote in the same way in committee was much greater than in the two previous legislatures, and that public conflict or comparative peace between the two parties made little difference in the way they voted in committee.

There may be two explanations for this harmonious relationship in the committees. The deputies working in committees may have a tacit agreement, independent of their respective parties, to look out for particular sectional interests. Also, the provisions of many of the laws passed by the legislative committees are said to be dictated by technical requirements that make alternative solutions difficult. The first explanation probably accounts for the majority of the laws passed by the committees. But the apparent acceptance of the second explanation by a party committed to an obstructionist strategy in parliament is interesting. After all, the Communist deputies could refuse to accept the validity of the so-called "technical requirements."

The important fact is that, whether through deliberate choice or under the pressure of objective conditions, the behavior of party deputies in parliamentary committees is different from that of deputies dealing with legislation on the Chamber floor. The boundaries between the various parties and between the government and the opposition become more flexible in the committees. Legislative work in committees is therefore a powerful factor in the integration of the parties into the parliamentary system. These findings support the view that the trend is toward increasing participation of the Communist Party in parliamentary activity and less use by the party of parliament as a forum for propaganda.

Changes in Orientation of the Communist Party

The foregoing discussion is not meant to deny that the orientation of the Communist Party in the Italian parliament is different in principle from that of the other parties, even though its behavior has become more like theirs and reflects a remarkable commitment to the institution. Toward its own members and supporters the Communist Party always assumes an attitude and employs a language that sets it apart as the party of opposition and as the party that makes a distinction between the "legal country," as reflected in the parliamentary balance of forces, and the "real country" of the working class, whose interests the party claims to represent.

From this point of view the party, and not the parliament, is the proper locus for the formation of the political will of the people. In a sense this viewpoint became more evident in the third legislature than in the second. During the second legislature the failure of the majority electoral law, the election of President Giovanni Gronchi, and the repercussions of the Twentieth Congress of the Communist Party of the Soviet Union all brought out the rather marked parliamentary characteristics of the Italian Communist Party. In the third legislature, however, these characteristics fell into the background, because of the necessity for strengthening the authority of the party at a time when it was going through an organizational crisis.

The foregoing conclusions—which avoid the error of positing a uniform assimilation of the Communist Party into the parliamentary system—are supported by an analysis of the party's major instrument of propaganda, its daily newspaper, L'Unità. This analysis covers the three central years of each legislature, 1950, 1955, and 1960. L'Unità's editorials for these years were classified as foreign affairs or domestic affairs. Those dealing with domestic affairs were then subdivided into articles concerning parliament, the party, or general politics outside of parliament. The percentage of the total editorial space given to each subject was then calculated. This percentage was considered indicative of the emphasis the party gives to various themes. The results of the analysis are shown in Table 7-2.

The analysis showed a marked reduction in the amount of space devoted to foreign affairs between 1950 and 1960. In 1950 the Communist Party's connection with the Soviet Union and the socialist camp was the critical component of its sense of identity; the task of "building history" fell not so much to the Italian Communist Party itself as to the whole of the international movement led by the Soviet Union. For this reason during 1950 almost half of the editorial space in *L'Unità* was devoted to foreign affairs.

TABLE 7-2. *Allocation of editorial space in the Communist newspaper,* *L'Unità, 1950, 1955, 1960*

Year	Number of issues in sample	Total	Foreign affairs	Domestic affairs		
				Parliament	Party	General
1950	310	100	46.8	14.5	7.1	31.6
1955	362	100	31.8	14.1	11.0	43.1
1960	360	100	30.8	8.3	19.5	41.4

In 1955 much less space was given this topic, while the space allotted to party affairs increased. Space for these two topics dropped from 54 percent to 43 percent of the total between 1950 and 1955, while the amount of space given to parliament remained about the same. The space occupied by discussion of foreign affairs was practically unchanged in 1960. But seven years after the death of Stalin the international communist movement was no longer the unifying element that it had been ten years earlier. For these reasons, as well as to resolve the internal organizational crisis of the party, more space was devoted to discussion of the party itself. The space for this was gained at the expense of parliamentary topics.

While the party's commitment to participation in parliament increases, the audience to which its newspaper is addressed is presented with a picture of a Communist Party that sees parliament always as a means and never as an end. If one could make a distinction between the "real" and the "apparent" party, perhaps the "real" Communist Party would be the one that operates in parliament, while the Communist Party that is presented in *L'Unità* is only the "apparent" party.

The very fact that the Communist Party presents an appearance different from reality is indicative of an internal contradiction. On the one hand the party's similarity to the other parties in its parliamentary activity has increased; on the other it is barred from engaging in the most critical parliamentary activity, for it cannot present itself as an alternative government. The "apparent" party is therefore the one that emphasizes its role as the opposition, a role that it fills in the name of the "real country," from which it seeks and receives support. But the party is equally concerned that it should not appear to be on the sidelines, that its presence in parliament should be seen as a determining factor in what goes on in the country.

This contradiction finds its clearest expression at the time of a cabinet crisis. In each of the first three legislatures Communist parliamentarians worked to provoke ministerial crisis—for this gave them the opportunity to present themselves as a determining factor. The fact that they have never been able directly to cause such a crisis or to contribute substantially to its solution is a basic contradiction.

PARTY PARLIAMENTARY GROUPS AND CABINET CRISES

The two leading parties share a view of the Italian parliament as the place where political decisions are registered and sanctioned after having been formed within the party. The two parties differ markedly, however, in the extent to which this view of parliament creates problems in the relationship between the party and its members in the two houses of parliament. While such problems are very serious in the Christian Democratic Party, they are almost nonexistent in the Communist Party. This difference is a consequence of yet another that is felt in every transaction or interaction between the two parties: the Communist Party is a centralized, authoritarian party that refuses to admit the existence of factions, while the Christian Democratic Party is essentially a party of organized factions.

This difference in structure creates an imbalance in the extent to which each of the parties can exert influence on the other in parliament. The Communist Party may exert influence by throwing the support of all of its deputies behind one or another of the Christian Democratic factions. This much was explicitly stated by Giorgio Amendola, a top Communist leader, at the beginning of the fourth legislature: "In the past we have been able to unseat several governments, but always by reaching some agreement with a Christian Democratic faction (anti-Scelba, anti-Tambroni)." [16]

The Christian Democratic Party as a whole cannot play a similar game in relation to the Communists, although its factions may per-

16. From a speech to the Central Committee, as reported in *L'Unità*, April 22, 1964.

suade the Communist deputies to help pass some motion that would otherwise have insufficient support. On balance these reciprocal influences are to the advantage of the Communist Party, in that they tend to add to its prestige by demonstrating that its votes are indeed useful and effective. That one or another Christian Democratic faction benefits from this exchange reduces the advantage that the Christian Democratic Party holds because of the fact that the Communist Party does not represent a real alternative to the party running the government.

From the standpoint of the political system as a whole, this practice of gaining Communist support in challenging a particular Cabinet combination, without having to pay for it with ministerial positions, contributes to governmental instability. Although the socioeconomic and cultural development of Italy was rapid between 1948 and 1962 and contributed to a more stable social structure, stability in government did not keep pace, as the following figures on Cabinet shifts during the first two legislatures illustrate:

> The second legislature witnessed a rapid and remarkable increase in cabinet instability. While during the first legislature the average duration of the three cabinets had been 20 months, in the second it was exactly half that figure, 10 months. There were, in fact, 6 cabinets, each with a different cabinet president; including the presidents, there were 54 ministers (20 more than during the previous legislature), 33 of whom were appointed for the first time.[17]

To understand this governmental instability, one must consider how the two major parties function and interact.

Interplay of Opposing Parliamentary Groups

It has been suggested that the distribution of party strength in the Italian parliament is analogous to that of the Weimar Republic and the Fourth French Republic.[18] However, there is a substantial difference, in that almost all of the Italian center is a single party, the Christian Democratic Party. Although this party is divided into var-

17. L. Lotti, "Il Parlamento italiano 1909–1963: raffronto storico," in G. Sartori et al., *Il Parlamento Italiano: 1946–1963* (Naples, ESI, 1963), p. 190.
18. By G. Sartori, "Dove va il Parlamento," in ibid. p. 483.

ious factions, it is more cohesive (partly because of the influence of the Catholic hierarchy) than a coalition of parties could be.

Moreover, the balance of forces within parliament is relatively stable. Because of the peculiar characteristics of the confrontation that continually takes place between the Christian Democratic and Communist parties, however, it has proved impossible to form a solid majority that would support a Cabinet for an entire legislature.

The Communists in particular promote the political instability of parliament and generally increase the difficulty with which it functions. This is not primarily because the Communist Party is "antisystem," to use Sartori's expression, but because its centralized authoritarian structure allows it to exploit to the full the centrifugal tendencies of the ruling party. Or, if one prefers, the Communist Party is "antisystem" because of its structure and ideology but not because of its political strategy and goals. These propositions are supported by an examination of the Cabinet crises of the first three postwar legislatures and the solution each of the two leading parties tried to bring about.[19]

The Communist Party, in common with every opposition party, prefers a type of government that it can oppose uninhibited by excessive restrictions and under which it can enjoy maximum maneuverability and be essentially unconstrained. This could only be a government so pressed by other problems that it could not devote itself to cutting down the influence of the Communist Party, a task that the Christian Democratic Party asserts to be its principal goal.

In a factional party such as the Christian Democratic Party one of two situations may arise: one faction may be much stronger than the others, in which case there is strong party leadership, conflicts are less marked, and the government pursues a clear and consistent set of goals; or all factions are approximately equal in strength, in which case there is only a fragile accord among them or constant conflict, which has a negative effect on the functioning of the government.

In the first situation, in which its internal problems are minimized, the Christian Democratic Party can direct its energies to external problems, among them, perhaps, the task of increasing its

19. For a more coherent and complete chronicle of events, see M. Grindrod, *The Rebuilding of Italy* (London, Royal Institute of International Affairs, 1955); and G. Mammarella, *Italy After Fascism: A Political History 1943–1963* (Montreal, Casalini, 1964). A comprehensive summary is to be found in H. S. Hughes, *The United States and Italy*, rev. ed., (Cambridge, Harvard University Press, 1965).

pressure on the Communists. In the second, the Communist parliamentary group can become the most effective agency of the Communist Party, by going as far as it can to upset the Christian Democrats' internal balance of forces. Thus the strategic problem for the Communist Party is how to maintain its opposition to a Christian Democratic government without endangering its stake in preserving a government that is plagued by internal party conflicts.

An examination of postwar Cabinet crises suggests that the logic of principled opposition often prevailed over strategy, which would have sought immediate advantage for the party. And this is because the Communist Party, although sufficiently strong to influence the majority, has not been strong enough to keep in power a cabinet only weakly supported by the Christian Democratic Party itself.

Although this has not been an easy strategy for the Communists to follow, its observance has helped to maintain the principle that the party itself, both in and out of parliament, is entitled to determine what tactic best suits a given situation. In the Christian Democratic Party the strategic problem has been aggravated by the struggle to decide who in the party is going to determine the strategy and tactics to be followed. In view of the complex and devious developments of this struggle in the postwar period, the only policy directives that have had a chance of being implemented and the only Cabinet combinations that have had a chance to stay in power are those that have avoided a head-on factional clash that would have endangered the party's hold on the government.

Crises in the First Postwar Legislature

The first legislature was marked by a sharp conflict between the majority and its left-wing opposition. To some extent this kept the factional tendencies within the ruling Christian Democratic Party under the surface and made it difficult for the Communist deputies to benefit from them. Nonetheless, the first government of the May 1948 to January 1950 legislature fell victim to conflicts among the Christian Democratic factions. The party's left wing, led by Giuseppe Dossetti, forced a crisis over the government's inadequate and weak action in meeting such commitments as agrarian reform, reform of tax legislation, and measures against unemployment, which the right-wing groups had succeeded in halting or slowing down.

The new government, formed in January 1950, undertook an en-

ergetic program of agrarian reform and created the Cassa per il
Mezzogiorno. In the vote that brought it down, however, Christian
Democratic intraparty rivalries were again involved. In February
1951, while the crisis over the Korean war was at its height, a Communist amendment to a government-sponsored bill to meet the economic difficulties of the crisis was passed, with the help of at least
twenty Christian Democratic votes and the absence of over eighty
other Christian Democratic deputies. For different reasons, each of
the party factions involved opposed the balance of forces supporting
the Cabinet.

The Cabinet did not immediately resign, due to the imminence of
the local elections, but its authority was weakened and it was clearly
on the defensive when, immediately after the elections, it was confronted with another crisis. This involved the government's administration of Marshall Plan funds. Again, among the forces challenging
the government were several Christian Democratic factions—from
Giuseppe Dossetti, who claimed that Giuseppe Pella, Minister of the
Budget, was responsible for a conservative investment policy, to
some rightist groups, whose main hope seems to have been for a re-
distribution of Cabinet posts to their benefit. Pella resigned in July
1951, but the composition of the succeeding government gave little
satisfaction to the Dossetti faction.

The Opposing Parties in the Second Legislature

By the time the second legislature met, Dossetti had retired from
politics, and a realignment of forces was taking place within the
Christian Democratic Party. The "center," which had the majority,
was strongly identified with the Premier, Alcide de Gasperi. The
party's right wing was strong in the Chamber and in the Senate; on
the left some of the followers of Dossetti were organizing a new faction, "Iniziativa Democratica."

The government coalition—the Christian Democratic Party, Social
Democratic Party, Republican Party, and Liberal Party—that went
to the country in June 1953 won a bare majority, but no party received a large enough share of the vote for the "swindle law," providing for a strong majority premium, to become operative. (See the
discussion of this law in Chapter 2.) De Gasperi proposed a cabinet
made up exclusively of Christian Democratic members, but it failed

to find support. Attilio Piccioni then tried to resurrect the four-party arrangement and again failed.

Pella succeeded in obtaining a majority for his Cabinet by getting votes from the parties of the right, particularly the Monarchists. The right wing of the Christian Democratic Party and the majority of the center were with him, but his increasing reliance on rightist forces outside the party alarmed the rest of the party, and created dissensions within it. The situation was a typical one for a factional party: a weak government, continuously threatened by conflicts within the Christian Democratic Party, and therefore unable to pursue a strong policy that might somehow threaten the Communist Party's hold on the masses.

Significantly, Pella's attempt to form a government supported mainly from the right (outside of the party), was received by the Communists with fewer harsh comments than had greeted De Gasperi and Piccioni. *L'Unità* editorials recognized, in the speech with which Pella presented his program to the Senate, a number of "echoes from our own programmatic demands" and saluted Pella's noncommittal attitude on the European Defense Community as "a reasonable gesture." Palmiro Togliatti, in announcing in the Chamber that the Communists were to vote against the new Cabinet, qualified this unavoidable decision in a number of ways.

By the end of 1953 the Pella government was under fire from the Christian Democratic center and left, and the veiled expressions of solidarity it received from the Communist Party could not save it. A new crisis opened at the beginning of 1954, bringing with it the possibility of a Fanfani premiership. The Communists saw this as a major threat and acted accordingly. Since the Pella government had resigned while parliament was not in session, *L'Unità* insisted that it should do so in parliament. In its chronicles of the political situation it emphasized the opposition to a Fanfani solution that existed within the Christian Democratic Party, ignoring the fact that such opposition came mainly from the right. When right-wing opposition prevented a Fanfani Cabinet from obtaining a majority in parliament, the Communist Party claimed credit for this failure. When a Christian Democratic deputy, Rapelli, was censured by his party for speaking against the government in the Chamber, *L'Unità* took up his defense.

As it happened, after Fanfani's defeat Mario Scelba was asked to form a Cabinet, which was to be characterized by its aggressive strategy toward the Communist Party. When this development began to take shape, the Communists fought back by again making use of the discord in the Christian Democratic ranks: "The vanquished of the June elections unmasked: Gronchi refuses a post in the cabinet. . . . Strong positions taken [against Scelba] by the Pella, Piccioni, and Togni factions within the Christian Democratic Party"; "open clash between the Christian Democratic executive and the dissenting Christian Democratic currents." [20]

Thus, in opposing the emergence of a strong government, the Communist Party was willing to play upon the animosities and the resentments of all sections of the majority party, even going so far as to support those identified with Togni, who had been one of its *bêtes noires* for his close links with large business interests.

With Scelba in power the conflict between the left opposition and the government once again became sharp. It was fought out not only in parliament but in the country as well in a series of mass agitations, during which the police on some occasions opened fire on the public. But basically the Communist Party dared not throw an open challenge to the state. It preferred instead to appeal continuously to the Constitution, to the dignity of parliament, and to the rights of the opposition. In fact it was powerless to influence the political situation significantly until its favorite tactic (the exploitation of disunity within the Christian Democratic Party) again became possible.

This chance occurred when Christian Democratic deputies became restive after Fanfani assumed the leadership of the Christian Democratic Party at the Congress of Naples in June 1954. Fanfani's ambitious attempt to strengthen the party organization in order to make it more autonomous in relation to some of its traditional supporting groups has already been commented upon. Party notables as well as the parliamentary groups felt threatened by this attempt.

Once more a coalition of disparate forces took shape within the Christian Democratic Party. It was called the "Concentrazione," was led by Gonella, and joined together a number of right-wing factions, with the followers of Gronchi on the left. When the Christian Democratic group in the Chamber elected its new chairman in January 1955, the official party candidate for this important post, Aldo Moro, won by only a narrow margin over the Concentrazione candidate, Giulio Andreotti.

20. *L'Unità*, February 6, 1954; February 9, 1954.

The Communists rejoiced in this indication that the Christian Democratic Party was again split and that many of its deputies were willing to go to some lengths to embarrass Fanfani and the Scelba government. Similar indications were not infrequent, since the government was confronted with a number of issues (such as the reform of farm contracts and the terms under which foreign firms might be admitted to drill for oil in Italy) about which feelings ran high and dissension was as marked inside the Christian Democratic Party as between parties.

The Communist Party's greatest success and the most marked split within the ruling party took place over the election of the second President of the Republic. Here is *L'Unità's* report (April 30, 1955) on this event:

> A burning defeat for the candidates supported by Fanfani and Scelba; the 308 votes of the left have been decisive for Gronchi's victory. Comrade Togliatti has thus commented: "We Communists, first of all, rejoice over the fact that the new President has a large, indeed imposing, majority of the vote. This is a symptom of the solidity of the democratic parliamentary regime, and we are happy for it. . . . In the second ballot the name of Gronchi came out as a strong challenge to the Christian Democratic Party's official candidate. We decided to vote for him, both because of his personal qualities and because, far from appearing bound to party positions, objectively he appeared to be in direct and open conflict with those positions."

By making an indispensable contribution to Gronchi's election, the Communist Party was able to proclaim its own "legitimacy." Furthermore, that election seriously weakened the Scelba government, which in June was forced to resign.

The problem of the succession caused some reshuffling within the Christian Democratic Party. Antonio Segni, whom the party had designated as the new Premier, abandoned the Concentrazione, which quickly went to pieces; Fanfani strengthened his hand against the threat represented by Guido Gonella. Faced with these signs of increasing internal difficulties in the ruling party, the Communist Party looked with some benevolence on the Segni government. That this judgment was not mistaken is shown by the developments of the next months: Segni was still Premier when the Communist Party underwent its internal crisis in 1956, and it cannot be said that the government did much to increase its difficulties. Perhaps Fanfani feared that a serious weakening of the Communist Party might strengthen the Socialists and thus confront the Christian Democrats with a stronger challenge in the next election, from which Fanfani expected a big success for his party.[21]

With this in mind, Fanfani was indifferent to the Segni government's weaknesses and to its resignation a short time later over the issue of the reform of farm contracts. It was his expectation that a succession of crises and weak governments would increase the probability of a big electoral majority for the Christian Democrats. On the other hand, such a situation was viewed with favor by the Communist Party, as was shown by the relative lack of hostility with which it greeted even the Zoli Cabinet, which followed Segni's and which was supported by Neofascist and Monarchist votes as well as by the Christian Democrats.

Instability in the Third Legislature

The Zoli government ushered in the third legislature (1958–63), which was to see a succession of five governments with three different premiers and a total of forty-seven different ministers.[22] Once more the foremost reason for governmental instability was the internal strife in the ruling party. Fanfani's majority in the party was split and the moderates within it (the so-called "dorotei") were taking an increasingly independent position.

Before the split was consummated, the Communist Party realized that in the situation that was developing one faction would be stronger than the other, with Fanfani holding simultaneously the positions of party secretary, Premier, and Foreign Minister. It reacted by taking a posture of firm and uncompromising opposition, without any of the qualifications with which its previous negative votes (when the various factions were of roughly equal strength) had been announced:

> The Communist members of parliament, on the eve of the presentation of the Fanfani cabinet to the Houses, express their opposition and their lack of confidence in this new attempt to

21. See a speech by Fanfani in July 1957, reprinted in A. Fanfani, *Da Napoli a Firenze* (Milan, Garzanti, 1958), pp. 182 ff.
22. See Lotti, "Il Parlamento italiano," in G. Sartori et al., *Il Parlamento Italiano, 1946–1963*. p. 192.

preserve the Christian Democrats' monopoly of power. . . . The working classes can only deny their confidence and oppose the program of this government—which ignores entirely the all-important problem of the rights of workers which are being seriously threatened in the industrial plants; which takes no account of the serious threat to the national economy and to employment represented by the Common Market; and which is so generously complacent toward private monopolies.[23]

Behind this stern opposition lay the Communist Party's concern that competition for popular support by the Fanfani government might seriously threaten the Communist position in the country. This concern, together with the party's adherence to dated doctrines, also accounts for the negative (and mistaken) judgment so glibly passed on the Common Market and its possible impact on the Italian economy. But if Fanfani proposed to strengthen and coordinate the public sector of the economy against the wishes of the big private concerns, a group of his own supporters—the future *"dorotei"*— as well as the Christian Democratic right wing, were unwilling to accept this program. Their reaction made the prospects for the Communists much less unfavorable.

A number of defections from the majority took place in secret ballots in parliament, and eighteen deputies, led by Scelba and Pella, went so far as to abstain publicly from giving their vote of confidence to the Fanfani government. In order to bring Fanfani down, the Communist Party allied itself with his right-wing enemies in the Sicilian regional government. *L'Unità* (December 13, 1958) had the following to say about the events in Sicily that led to the defeat of the Fanfani supporter, La Loggia:

The party line of the Christian Democrats on Sicily is opposed not only from outside, but also from inside the party by groups which do not approve of the government's policy and which feel themselves threatened by the authoritarian government of Fanfani.

At the same time, of course, the Communist Party vigorously attacked and denounced Fanfani in parliament and in its press for trying "to impose on the Italian people a socially and politically reactionary, clerical, and corporative regime." [24]

23. *L'Unità,* July 10, 1958.
24. *L'Unità,* October 21, 1958.

By the beginning of 1959, however, the Fanfani government appeared so weakened, its original élan so spent, that the Communist Party seemed to reconsider its policy toward it. While it was doing so, Fanfani resigned, thus unleashing a heightened intraparty strife over the succession. The President of the Republic refused to accept the resignation and asked Fanfani to present himself to the Houses. Fanfani wavered, but then confirmed his resignation. The "unity of command" within the Christian Democratic Party was broken by a compromise by which Segni became Premier and Moro party secretary.

On the whole the Communist Party was pleased with this compromise solution, and its declaration of opposition to the new government had a rather hollow sound, except when it pointed out that the Christian Democrats were anything but unanimously behind the new government. In fact, within less than a year, the Segni government had gone down under the joint pressure of the Christian Democratic left and the new party secretary.

The longest crisis of the postwar period began to come to an end only with the formation of the Fernando Tambroni government. This was a solution supported by Gronchi and only moderately opposed by the Communist Party, since the Christian Democratic Party accepted it unwillingly and with qualifications as to its duration and as to the types of actions it could undertake. It was brought down by a spontaneous wave of popular unrest, provoked by Tambroni's complacent policy toward the Neofascists. And while the Communist Party was certainly involved in its overthrow, it did not act until popular feeling and party dissatisfaction had made the existing arrangement untenable.

Under the leadership of Moro as the party secretary and Fanfani as President-designate the Christian Democratic Party attempted a new course after the Tambroni experience—a coalition government with the center parties, supported by the abstention of the Socialists and the Monarchists. The new Cabinet temporarily and superficially unified the party by giving key posts to Scelba (Internal Affairs) and Pella (Budget). This unity and the emergence of a new pattern of alliance between the Christian Democrats and the Socialists, the Communists' traditional ally, created a novel situation for the Communist Party. It was quick to realize, however, that the opportunity its authoritarian structure offered for exploiting the disunity of the opposing parties could be used as successfully against the

Socialists and the nascent Christian Democratic-Socialist coalition as it had been against the Christian Democratic Party alone.

In 1963, at the end of the period covered by the present study, the Communist Party was still engaged in pursuing the same strategy of exploiting conflicts in the opposition camp to further its own ends. Its main intent still appeared to be defensive, that is to minimize the possibility that the government might purposefully and consistently use its power to isolate the Communist Party and to undercut the party's hold on a sizable section of the electorate. To the extent that the Christian Democratic–Socialist coalition could curb its internal conflicts, it could keep the Communists on the defensive, thus minimizing their ability to influence major political decisions.

PARLIAMENTARY DEBATE ON GOVERNMENT INTERVENTION IN THE ECONOMY [25]

The Christian Democratic Party makes commitments for significant legislative action only through a slow and complex process of mediation and compromise, avoiding whenever possible a direct clash with the vested interests themselves. Although the party seeks a wide popular base of support, its ability to articulate and carry out popular reforms is hindered by the diversity of its electorate and membership and by the fact that some sectors of the party are opposed to these reforms. The ruling party is at a further disadvantage because some of the social reforms it is trying to promote find a much more outspoken and radical champion in the Communist Party.

The evolution of legislative policy within the Christian Democratic and Communist parties is illustrated by the history of the three major pieces of legislation that greatly extended the public sector of the economy.

The first of these, passed in the first legislature, entrusted the exclusive exploitation of natural gas and oil in the Po Valley to one public corporation, the National Hydrocarbons Trust (Ente Nationale Idrocarburi), known as ENI.

The second, passed in the second legislature, created the Ministry for State Industrial Holdings, responsible for the coordination and

25. For a rapid survey of government intervention in the Italian economy, with special reference to the role of public firms, see A. Shonfield, *Modern Capitalism* (London, Oxford University Press, 1965), pp. 176–92; also H. S. Hughes, *The United States and Italy*, pp. 223–27.

general orientation of the policies of companies wholly or mostly owned by the state, either directly or through one of its public corporations. This same legislation brought to an end the membership of such companies in the Confindustria (The Italian equivalent of the National Association of Manufacturers in the United States),[26] which was strongly opposed to public intervention in the economy. For this reason the bill is often referred to as the *"distacco"* (withdrawal).

The third bill, passed in the third legislature, created the National Agency for Electrical Energy, known as ENEL (Ente Nazionale Energia Elettrica), which was to acquire a monopoly over the production and distribution of electric power by purchasing the shares of all private or public electric power companies at a fixed price.

Although these bills significantly increased the direct control the Italian state could exercise over the economy as a whole, they did not decrease the weight of the private sector to the same extent, since during the period of their enactment the private sector was expanding rapidly.

The Christian Democratic Party embarked upon development of this legislation with neither a clear perception of its importance nor a clear commitment to it. The party gradually became more aware of the enormous "power potential" of public intervention in the economy, however, and made it a significant part of the party's ideological line.

The Communist Party, while relatively indifferent to this legislation in its earliest stages (viewing it merely as a development toward more mature forms of capitalism), began to view it in the framework of "the Italian way to socialism."

Thus both parties gradually developed an interest in public intervention in the economy.

The National Hydrocarbons Trust

The 1927 Italian law governing the exploitation of mineral resources treated these resources as part of the state's patrimony, but provided that any corporation or individual could apply for a permit to search for and exploit them. However, in 1927 it had not been foreseen that parts of the Italian subsoil might contain sub-

---

26. On the Confindustria see Joseph LaPalombara, *Interest Groups in Italian Politics* (Princeton, Princeton University Press, 1964), passim.

stantial quantities of oil and natural gas. In the postwar period the law therefore had to be revised in order to allow for the orderly exploitation of such resources. One draft law, which would have extended the provisions of the 1927 bill, was presented by the Social Democrat Ivan Matteo Lombardo, then Minister of Industry, in 1950 and had the support of private corporations; but this solution was discarded, and two years later two other laws were passed. The first (sponsored by Togni, Minister of Industry) established general norms to govern the granting of permits for exploitation in most parts of the country. The second (sponsored by Ezio Vanoni, Minister of Finance) provided for the creation of a public corporation, National Hydrocarbons Trust (ENI), and reserved to it a monopoly in the search for and exploitation of oil and natural gas in the Po Valley, as well as of the distribution of whatever oil and gas might be produced.

Since the available evidence indicated that gas and oil were most likely to be found in the Po Valley, chemical companies, acting through their pressure group, the Associazione Mineraria Italiana, opposed the second piece of legislation while it was still in the draft stage. However, the government stood by it, and the Vanoni draft was submitted to an ad hoc subcommittee of the Committee for Industry of the Chamber of Deputies, one of whose members was Enrico Mattei, a Christian Democratic deputy and vice-president of the General Italian Petroleum Agency (Azienda Generale Italiana Petrolio), known as AGIP, a public oil corporation created before the war. After this committee had examined and reported on the draft, it was sent to the floor, where the discussion lasted for only two sittings (April 23 and 24, 1952) and involved only five Christian Democratic deputies (one of them Vanoni), one Social Democratic deputy, one Socialist deputy, and one Communist deputy. The last (the economist Dami) expressed his approval of a special public corporation, but argued that its monopoly should not be limited to the Po Valley but should include the whole national territory. This was in line with a previous Communist proposal, drafted by Mario Montagnani and other Communist deputies in 1950, to nationalize all oil and natural gas resources in the country outright.

The Christian Democratic deputy Giovanni Bersani, who reported on the bill for the majority, asserted that the constitution of the new public corporation was a device by which the state could "guard against malfeasances in the exploitation of natural resources as well as against the danger of the formation of private monopolies, in the defense of the public interest." [27]

Ezio Vanoni as Minister of Finance presented similar arguments in defense of the bill and stressed the necessity of the proposed legislation in view of the inadequacy of purely fiscal controls on the profits that could be derived from exploitation of the resources in question. Only a few private companies would be able to afford to enter this field, he argued, and the formation of a near-monopoly in their hands could be prevented only by the existence of a public competitor. However this undertaking by the state was not expected to discourage private initiative in the field but rather to coordinate, discipline, and buttress it.

Another Christian Democratic deputy, Aldo Fascetti, formulated a theoretical justification of this legislative measure in the light of Catholic social principles. He complained that while politicians and economists were aware of Adam Smith's liberalism, Marx's revolutionary collectivism, and Bernstein's reformism, they unjustly neglected Ketteler and Toniolo as well as other representatives of "Christian sociology" who opposed both "liberal individualism and socialist collectivism." [28]

Because of the complex character of some of the proposed regulations, the draft was sent to the Committees for Finance and for Industry for further examination in a joint session (May 9 and June 4 and 6, 1952). Again only a few deputies—eleven Christian Democrats, four Communists, and one Socialist—took part in the discussion. No serious conflict developed and only technical amendments were considered. One Communist proposal was incorporated in the revised draft, but was voted down on the floor without much objection from the Communists. The rest of the draft was approved by the Chamber after a brief discussion in which only three Christian Democratic deputies (Vanoni among them) and one Communist (Dami) took part. The latter announced that the Communist deputies would abstain from voting, and justified this decision as follows:

> We could not vote against the bill, not only out of a feeling of loyalty toward our colleagues in the majority who have on some points accepted our suggestions and cooperated with us in improving the formulation of various provisions, but above all be-

27. Repubblica Italiana, Camera dei Deputati, *Atti Parlamentari*, April 24, 1952.
28. *Atti Parlamentari*, April 23, 1952.

cause we agree with one of the main principles of the draft, which reserves to the state the right to search for oil in the Po Valley. We feel, however, that the same principle ought to be applied in the rest of the national territory. . . . Here, since there are no Italian companies which are equipped for undertaking such searches, limiting the action of ENI gives a free hand to the American companies, thus aligning us with the few countries in the world which still allow foreigners to exploit their oil fields: Yemen, Heggiaz, the principalities of the Persian Gulf, as well as some South American republics governed by ex-sergeants at the service of Washington.[29]

Thus while the Communists took advantage of the opportunity to speak some harsh words about U.S. oil companies, they allowed the draft to stand without even seriously defending their earlier proposal. As a result, the bill passed the Chamber by a comfortable majority, 269 ayes against 53 noes, and 65 abstentions. Although the Communists voted against it in the Senate, the bill was passed.

Considering the importance of this law, which laid the foundations for the future expansion of the National Hydrocarbons Trust, what strikes the observer about the Chamber debates is how brief they were and how few deputies spoke. Most of the serious work was done in committee, but even here the discussion was limited and the speeches few. It is astounding that none of the parties to the right of the center majority took part in the debates, although they certainly voted against the law. Most serious opposition from private interests took the form of attempts to delay discussion of the bill. There was no apparent disagreement within the Christian Democratic Party about the bill's merits. And the Communists' lack of interest in this piece of legislation was striking. While they voted against it in the Senate, this was because by that time (January 1953) the "swindle law" had become the main topic of political discussion and had led the Communist Party to take an uncompromising line on all topics.

The Ministry for State Industrial Holdings

Interest in the subject of industrial holdings at first was limited to proposals that firms whose shares were wholly or mostly owned by

29. Ibid., July 8, 1952.

the state (either directly or through holding companies) discontinue their membership in the employers' association, Confindustria. A Communist motion to this end was put forward in 1948 and a Socialist proposal in 1949. In 1950 a Christian Democratic union leader, Giuseppe Rapelli, in a speech on the policy of the state-owned steel firm Dalmine, challenged the official government position that there was no reason why state-owned firms should not belong to the same organization as privately owned firms.

Later this question began to be viewed within the framework of a larger one: what was to be done about those many industrial companies that the Italian state had totally or partially purchased, particularly in the fascist period, in order to salvage them from bankruptcy, and especially those whose shares were in the hands of the huge public holding company, Institute for Industrial Reconstruction (IRI), which had been created to take over and manage such firms. A wide range of opinions could be discerned within the center majority and even in the Christian Democratic Party itself. The Liberal Party deputy Vittorio Emanuele Marzotto and the Christian Democratic deputy Mario Dosi were agreed, for instance, that economically healthy IRI firms should be returned to private ownership and all others should be liquidated; while the Christian Democrat, Danilo De Cocci, a member of the "Gronchi left," held that IRI, instead of being demobilized, should act as a restraint against the monopolistic tendencies of private firms and by means of a bold policy of expansion, assume responsibility for guiding Italian industrial development.

To settle the dispute, the government appointed a special committee (led by a Catholic legal scholar, Orio Giacchi) to inquire into the economic and legal status of IRI and of the various affiliated firms, and to make recommendations concerning their future reorganization and policy. The final report of the committee (which had been drafted by Professor Mario Romani, the leading economic consultant to the Italian Confederation of Free Unions) suggested that IRI "should engage autonomously in collective bargaining, and its membership in the private employers' association should be terminated." [30] The same position was taken by the national secretariat of the Italian Confederation of Free Unions in a letter to the Premier (January 1954).

The government, on the recommendation of the Minister of In-

30. *IRI: Progetto di Riordinamento* (Turin, UTET, 1955).

dustry, the left-wing deputy Bruno Villabruna, decided to put the matter to parliament itself. In August 1954 it was put before the Chamber in the form of three motions presented respectively by Oreste Lizzadri, a Socialist; Giulio Pastore, a Christian Democrat; and Giovanni Roberti, a Neofascist. The latter opposed the withdrawal of the IRI from Confindustria, the other two were for it. Pastore's motion stated the case for withdrawal as follows:

> Private industry, based on profits, and public industry, which ought to act in the public interest, are two entirely different matters. . . . The workers demand that IRI firms should be made autonomous in their capacity as employers so as to allow for greater worker participation in their management, in order to make them more productive. The IRI should engage in separate collective bargaining with its employees.[31]

Lizzadri withdrew his motion, and Pastore's was put to a vote and passed, with the support of both Socialists and Communists and the opposition of the Liberals. Nothing came of it, however, although it was occasionally referred to in Parliament by deputies requesting the government to act upon it.

The matter came up again when a bill calling for the creation of a new Ministry for State Industrial Holdings came to the floor of the Chamber for discussion nearly a year after it had been drafted by the Antonio Segni government in 1955. The debate on this draft took place on six days between January and April 1956 and involved forty-three deputies, of whom five were Christian Democrats and seven were Communists. The draft did not touch on the question of the withdrawal from Confindustria, but merely proposed the creation of a new ministry that would have jurisdiction over all state-owned firms and be responsible for determining the general orientation of their policy. In the course of the discussion, however, the Communist deputies Domenico Colasanto, Antonio Giolitti, and Giorgio Napolitano, citing the Pastore motion approved by the Chamber a year earlier, requested that the new bill explicitly discontinue the membership of all such firms (and particularly of the IRI firms) in the Confindustria. They insisted that this was a necessary condition for the development of a new and progressive policy of industrial relations. Napolitano also stressed that, once grouped together in the framework of a new ministry, the publicly owned

31. *Atti Parlamentari,* August 2, 1954.

firms should undertake a leading role in industrial development, particularly in the South.[32]

The Christian Democratic deputy Roberto Lucifredi, reporting on the draft on behalf of the Committee for Internal Affairs, and Premier Segni both suggested a more conservative interpretation of the role of the proposed new ministry. They did so in order to curb the disquiet in the ranks of the Christian Democratic right and the alarm in the business world, which believed that the bill was an indication that the public sector of the economy would be expanded at the expense of the private sector. The business community particularly opposed the withdrawal from Confindustria of the state-owned firms. When Christian Democratic deputies, backed by the Italian Confederation of Free Unions, proposed a new clause providing for the withdrawal of the IRI firms within a year, Vittorio Foa, a leader of the General Confederation of Italian Workers, made a counterproposal, specifying that the withdrawal was to take place as soon as the bill had passed. A right-wing Christian Democratic deputy, Francesco Maria Dominedò, proposed a rider requiring that IRI firms be managed "according to standard economic criteria." The bill, including the Foa proposal and the Dominedo rider, was approved by the Chamber, and eventually became law by the end of 1956.

The Communist Party did not play a leading role in this legislative undertaking; but it claimed much of the credit on the grounds that by taking up the Pastore motion it had embarrassed the Christian Democratic majority into acting upon it. The fact that the Christian Democrats were not united behind the "withdrawal" and that some of them (particularly the Iniziativa Democratica group) did not care to make their views known, permitted the Communists to appear to have led the movement.

The National Agency for Electrical Energy

Unlike the creation of ENI and the establishment of the Ministry for State Industrial Holdings, the nationalization of electric power was thoroughly debated in and among the parties, in the press, and on TV before it came up in parliament. Only after protracted discussion in public did the question become one of the basic points in

---

32. Ibid., March 16, 1956.

the program of the first center-left government. (This government was supported by the Socialists by their abstention on critical votes, not through a direct participation in the parliamentary majority and the Cabinet.) The decision to nationalize electric power was taken by the Cabinet on June 26, 1962, and that same day the bill was presented to the Chamber of Deputies, which decided that it should be put through the special procedure for urgent matters. This meant that it would be submitted not to the standing committees but to an ad hoc committee, a decision approved by the Chamber by a very large majority (417 for, 38 against).

The ad hoc committee of forty-five members under the chairmanship of Giuseppe Togni, a Christian Democratic member, studied the bill from July 3 to July 20. No minutes of its meetings are available, and published information consists exclusively of the short summaries printed in the "Bulletins of the Parliamentary Committees." But this information is sufficiently clear with respect to the positions of the two leading political parties, which, incidentally, closely parallel the positions they later expressed on the floor.

In the committee's discussion some Christian Democratic deputies (Lorenzo Isgrò and Ivano Curti) stressed the harmony between the bill and the principles of Catholic social thought; others (Emilio Colombo, Danilo de Cocci, and Mario Ferrari-Aggradi) presented the technical arguments for the decision to nationalize. Even Dosi, a Christian Democratic deputy whose role as a defender of private industry is well known, asserted that he had always favored cooperation between the public and private sectors of the economy and that the bill was consistent with this principle.

It was the Communist Party that most strongly insisted that elected public bodies should have supreme control over the agency, and suggested a supervisory parliamentary committee that would dictate to the agency its main lines of conduct. The Communists also requested that compensation for the expropriation of the electrical companies be paid to the individual stockholders and not to the companies themselves, but this proposal was rejected.

The draft went to the floor on July 28, 1962, after two delaying motions had been voted on and rejected—one put forward by Monarchist and Neofascist deputies asserting that the bill was unconstitutional, and another by a Monarchist and a Liberal Party member requesting that the Chamber delay its deliberation until the National Council of Labor and the Economy had expressed its opinion on the bill. The Communist deputies voted with the majority against these motions.

During the debate on the bill there were continuous references by the Christian Democratic deputies to Catholic social doctrine, and particularly to the papal encyclicals, from *Quadragesimo Anno* to *Mater et Magistra*. These were made by members of those sections of the party which, at the Naples Congress, had agreed to support the center-left policy. Dissenting speeches came only from the extreme right wing of the party: "Nationalization can be undertaken only as an exceptional solution. . . . I would not overdo the appeals to the authority of the *Mater et Magistra*, which merely admits the possibility of nationalization, and does not make a point of suggesting it." [33]

Interestingly enough, the only tensions within the Christian Democratic Party that the debate revealed were those between rival factions of the left wing. Carlo Donat Cattin, a left-wing leader of the Italian Confederation of Free Unions, asserted that the conflicts had taken place not only between left and right but also "through the position taken in the party executive organ by a leader of the Base," a left-wing faction of the Christian Democratic Party. Here the reference is to Fiorentino Sullo, who had maintained that his bill on urban zoning and planning ought to have precedence over the nationalization of electric power. Another Base leader, Ripamonti, asserted that "the most progressive democratic Catholics" are entitled to some perplexity "over a nationalization which appears an end in itself. . . . Democratic Catholics ought to show that a policy of comprehensive and exacting planning is not necessarily an aspect of Marxist doctrine, but a necessity of modern society, which may be in keeping with the principles of Christian social philosophy." [34]

The Communist Party did not miss the opportunity that the Christian Democratic Party, once more divided against itself, presented it. Communist speeches constantly reiterated that the ruling party had reluctantly decided for nationalization only under the pressure of the left parties, particularly the Communist Party; and that the bill in question appeared halfhearted because the Christian Democrats had not dared to break openly with the monopolistic economic forces:

33. Ibid., August 4, 1962.
34. Ibid.

Within the Christian Democratic Party a number of marked differences of orientation are obvious . . . among the enemies of nationalization, the *"dorotei,"* and the left wing. . . . That the decision to nationalize conflicts with the position held for many years past by the Christian Democrats is shown by the fact that some of its speakers have had to quote principles which go back to the years of the Resistance and of the Constituent Assembly. . . . That decision betrays the aspiration of the Christian Democrats to shake off the burden of a policy which for over ten years had identified it as a conservative party in the eyes of the majority of the working and popular strata. Yet the Christian Democratic Party, at the same time, tries to restrain the attack on private monopolies and the attempts at social and economic reform. . . . The parties of the left do not intend to accept the "moderate" interpretation of nationalization which the Christian Democratic Party upholds.[35]

Specifically, the Communists maintained that the bill was too generous in the compensation it provided for the nationalized property. They criticized the structure of the new state agency, which became the sole producer and distributor of electric power, and the possibility given the former private electric companies of continuing to exist as holding companes. But they concluded that in spite of all these reservations

. . . the bill shows the inspiration of that broad current of social and political opinion which views the nationalization of electric power as a democratic reform of the economy, of the society, of the state. We look with favor on the alignment responsible for this decision; and by this we mean not simply our colleagues of the democratic left, but also those members of the Christian Democratic Party who have fought a battle against the forces of the right.[36]

In the second phase of the discussion (September 6 to 21) the Communist Party insisted that the new agency should not have a traditional structure but that the unions, various local elective bodies, and a special parliamentary committee should have a voice in determining the agency's policy and should exercise a firm control

35. Ibid., August 1, 1962.
36. Ibid., August 7, 1962.

over its execution. The majority, however, rejected all of the modifications proposed by the Communists.

The bill passed with a strong majority (404 ayes to 74 noes) in the Chamber; in the Senate it was passed in a modified form which made further concessions to the private companies. It was then returned to the Chamber, where its new formulation was debated during the second half of November. The majority maintained that the modifications "are of a technical character and of marginal significance," while the Communists opposed the modifications but voted for the new text as a whole. The Communist deputy Busetto made clear his party's interpretation of the bill's development:

> From all viewpoints it appears that the support of the Communist Party has played a vital role, in that it has allowed the bill to withstand the onslaught of all the groups opposed to the nationalization. The latter have received some support also from within the government majority, and not only from the opposition of the right. The conflicts within the Christian Democratic Party and its ambivalence toward the bill have made our support of it a critical factor.[37]

The alignment of forces in the debate on this bill was illuminating. There was an all-out opposition to it on the part of some economic interests and of the political groups overtly or covertly committed to their defense. This opposition managed to delay passage of the bill, but it was unable to prevent it.

Since the nationalization bill was the critical point in the center-left coalition previously decided upon, serious attempts to defeat it from within the Christian Democratic Party were out of the question and the deputies most committed to the defense of private economic interests concentrated their efforts on securing the most favorable compensation terms possible. They were largely successful, since the solutions they proposed were technically quite defensible.

The Communist Party had previously presented, in each legislature, a draft proposal for nationalizing the production and distribution of electric power; but this was merely a formal, indeed a ritual, move. The party was so far from thinking that nationalization could actually be achieved by the third legislature that, along with its nationalization proposal, it presented a more modest proposal aimed at coordinating the management of electrical resources already in pub-

37. Ibid., November 22 and 27, 1962.

lic hands. Yet, when the nationalization measure became a concrete possibility within the framework of the center-left coalition, the Communist Party was quick to play its own part in development of the measure and to claim credit for taking the initiative.

The Christian Democrats were unable to keep the Communists from taking advantage of all the possibilities of that strategy. The majority party's claim that the nationalization measure was fully in keeping with its own ideological principles raised the embarrassing question of why it had been so slow in putting them into practice. Because of its concern over the reactions of its moderate electorate and the feelings of business interests, the Christian Democratic Party did not seize the opportunity to denounce the Communist Party for having hampered, with its party line in the years of the cold war, the development of a bolder social, economic, and political policy.

The Parliamentary Arena and the Political Process

A number of difficulties prevented the laying of a sounder empirical basis for some of the conclusions reached in the foregoing analysis. For example, the voting procedures of the Italian parliament make it impossible to compile voting indexes for the various parties, as can be done for other legislative assemblies on the basis of roll-call records. To the extent that this was possible through case analysis, the study confirmed the basic hypothesis of its authors that the parliamentary confrontation between a disciplined, centralized, authoritarian party and one that is faction-ridden allows the former to influence the latter and thereby to affect the legislative and political activity of parliament more than its position of permanent opposition would otherwise permit.

Since together the two major parties in Italy have regularly, from one legislature to another, held more than two thirds of the seats in the Chamber of Deputies, the apparently multiparty character of the Italian political system is misleading. What really seems to characterize the Italian legislature is at best an imperfect biparty relationship between the Christian Democratic Party and the Communist Party. The Italian political system has thus been operating to a considerable extent as a sort of de facto bipartisan system.

All other parties have had a political impact only to the extent that they have acted as junior partners to either the Christian Democratic Party or the Communist Party.

In spite of the instability of the Cabinet, discussed earlier in this chapter, the Christian Democratic Party has regularly controlled it, either as the holder of the majority of its posts or as the sole holder of its posts. This suggests a major qualification to the statement that the Italian system has some features of a bipartisan system: one of the two leading parties is permanently in the government, the other permanently in the opposition. The Communist Party cannot form an alternative government, because of the limited size of its support and because of its ideological commitments and international ties. On the other hand, in spite of the number and magnitude of the divisive forces at work within the Christian Democratic Party, it has managed to avoid serious splits and to stay in power as a single party.

From a legislative standpoint, this system works poorly, but it works. Some major social demands are met, although tardily and incompletely enough to give the Communist Party a strategic advantage. Because of its highly disciplined nature, the Communist Party can cause continuous difficulties in the working of the system.

This aspect of the Communist Party has been emphasized in the foregoing discussion, and the extent of its role as an antisystem element in the system has been discounted. This raises the question as to whether the Communist Party is becoming just another social democratic party, instead of one committed to the political and socioeconomic transformation of the system.

Since the Communist Party has been increasingly playing the role of "just another party" in parliament (with respect to its policies, not to its structural configuration), then this role cannot be viewed as a ruse on its part, or a mere front behind which the party imperturbably carries on a revolutionary, antisystem strategy. To the extent that it can be observed, the Communist Party's behavior in parliament inevitably suggests that it has become habituated to its present parliamentary strategy.

It may be too early, however, to suggest that the Italian Communist Party has become integrated into the existing political system—that is, that it has become a social democratic party. Its authoritarian structure and its connection with the world socialist movement and with the Soviet Union in particular hinder this process of integration. The Italian Communist Party does not allow the differences of opinion and of orientation, which are recognizable within it and which reflect the serious contradictions to which its overall policy commits it, to take shape as factions competing for power within the party. It is to some extent an abnormal unit in the Italian political system, because its political will is determined through a different process from that of the other parties. It receives and processes impulses from two different sources: that large segment of Italian public opinion, particularly among the lower economic and social groups, that forms the base of its support and the "socialist world." To some extent impulses from these two sources operate at cross purposes, the first toward a maximum of integration into the Italian political system and the second toward a minimum of integration.

The present study has attempted to suggest what avenues of action are open to a party that finds itself in this situation. An analysis dealing with a larger body of evidence would probably not alter the conclusions suggested here. The same conclusions can be drawn from the last speech of Palmiro Togliatti in the Italian parliament, on the eve of the journey to the Soviet Union from which he was not to return. In commenting upon the conclusion of the cabinet crisis of the summer of 1964, from which a new version of the center-left coalition had been born, Togliatti said:

> Thus it came about that a crisis, caused to a large extent by the demands and the actions of the left and of the people, has been solved with a defeat for socialism and other leftist forces—a lamentable solution, and one which carries on the negative aspects and the wrong directions of the policy of the previous governments and aggravates them by adding a great number of new contradictions, internal contrasts and confusion.[38]

These words sound very much like those previously spoken on similar occasions, and they truthfully express the content of the Italian Communist Party's policy. The party claims every crisis as a success for the left and laments every new government as a defeat for it. It blames the other parties for those very conflicts and confusions it so ably exploits.

38. *L'Unità*, August 5, 1964.

8

Conclusions: Participation in Italy's Anomalous Political System

The forms of political participation are largely conditioned by the historical development of the country, by the manner in which political unification took place, and by the process of industrialization. In Italy the historical development of two subcultures, the socialist and Catholic, grounded in two distinct value systems, have profoundly affected political concepts and the modes of political participation and have therefore shaped the political culture of the country. As expressed through such institutions as the family and organized labor, Catholic and socialist traditions have exerted more influence in determining the attitudes of the people than have income levels, party platforms, or a party's ability to protect or further particular social or economic interests.

The relationship between the two subcultures and their values, on the one hand, and the democratic representative system and its values on the other, as expressed by the bourgeois industrial revolution, has made Italian institutional life unstable during a century of national unification. The suffrage movement that developed too slowly, the halting of the movement toward universal suffrage by the First World War and its aftermath, the twenty-year period of fascist dictatorship, and the poor functioning of the multiparty system under the Constitution of 1948, sustained in reality by an imperfect bipartisanship as represented by the Christian Democratic Party and the Italian Communist Party—these are the consequences of the lack of cultural integration that persisted for a long period after unification of the country, a cultural integration that has perhaps begun to evolve only in very recent years.

This situation, which did not permit the rise of a large mass party that would be ideologically liberal, was complicated by the fact that between 1942 and 1945, when fascism was falling, the Catholic subculture largely absorbed the traditionally conservative political groups, while the socialist subculture was divided between social democratic and authoritarian communist groups. The Communist Party's strength in Italy cannot be understood if the party is thought of as something that began either in 1945, when it became a mass party in Italy, or in 1921, when it was founded as the consequence of a split in the old Socialist Party. The force exerted by Italian communism has its roots in the Italian socialist and labor movement subcultures of 1892, the year the Socialist Party was formed, in the First International, the Italian sections of which were inspired by Bakunin rather than by the less radical Marx.

POLITICAL STRENGTH OF OPPOSING PARTIES

The intellectuals as well as the general public have viewed the development of Italian industrial society through the ideological lenses of either Catholic sociological thought or the kind of vulgarized Marxism popular at the end of the nineteenth century. These widely divergent views have dominated political participation, from voting behavior to the choice of politics as a profession. The fact that the Christian Democratic and Communist parties together poll about two thirds of the vote is the result of the degree to which these two parties have institutionalized the subcultural traditions that have dominated Italian politics for more than a century. This they have done through the establishment of such auxiliary organizations as trade unions, clubs, and cooperatives and through control of the machinery of local government.

Political participation in postwar Italy, in the sense of party loyalty and attendance at party functions and rallies, was strongest in the immediate postwar period. Later, political zeal and commitment declined to a level characteristic of older representative democracies. Parties with diverse points of view tend to lose public interest and support when clashes of opinion between them are not highly dramatic. This is particularly true of small minor parties. Large well-organized parties are less apt to lose ground during periods lacking in drama, because they have the machinery to combat a declining interest in political participation in a variety of ways. The Catholics and Communists have succeeded in keeping the respective holds on

Italian society that they won in the immediate postwar period, because the Catholic world is something greater than the Christian Democratic Party and in the Communist world the party is essentially an expression of participation in a particular social system.

Through tradition and organization these two leading parties have played a decisive role in the electoral unification of the country. Today there is much more similarity than there was in 1945 between Calabrian and Piedmontese electoral behavior. Deviation from the average national vote is manifested more clearly in regions such as Veneto, where a particularly strong Catholic subculture exists, or Emilia-Romagna, where the socialist tradition is strong. This is further proof of the superior strength of historical cultural forces over socioeconomic changes in determining voting behavior, which is the foremost indicator of the pattern of political participation in a mass society.

The increase in the Communist vote from 19 percent to 25 percent in the two decades since the war, despite the tremendous socioeconomic growth and considerable rise in the average annual income, may give the impression of remarkable electoral mobility. The data analyzed in the present study indicate, however, that this impression is erroneous and that electoral behavior in Italy, as in other democratic systems, has tended to become essentially stable after an initial period of adjustment. In Italy today the positions of the left and right are not unlike those of the immediate postwar years. The slight differences are due to the organizational efforts of the Christian Democratic and Communist parties to reinforce their positions during a period of national electoral unification, with the result that the South has tended to vote more and more like the North.

While political participation in Italy has been carried on predominantly through the Christian Democratic and Communist parties, a third of the vote has gone regularly to six or seven other national parties and to several regional parties in the Valle d'Aosta, Tyrol, Sardinia, and sometimes Sicily. This division is not without significance in the functioning of the Italian political system. In fact, neither the Christian Democrats nor the Communists are in a position to fully exploit the interaction between tradition and progress, moderate opinions and radicalism. Such interaction, when institutionalized, results in the functioning of representative democracy at the highest level of efficiency.

Both leading parties, which like the two subcultures have developed polemically, are strongly ideological in character. Their polemics have been carried on not only with each other but also with the kind of society Italy became in the early years following unification. Furthermore, they do not have sufficient basic consensus to permit them to become a moderate party and a radical party, respectively, that could succeed each other in government.

As the ideological party of the Catholics, the Christian Democratic Party embodies the greater part of the conservative tradition and the principles of the old Liberal Party. Notwithstanding this, its Catholic character limits its ability to attract the non-Catholic voter. It has not been able to capture an absolute majority, even in the election of 1948. Since then its vote has stabilized at around 40 percent of the electorate. Likewise, the Italian Communist Party, as a highly ideological party bound to the international communist movement, has absorbed a good part of the socialist tradition. It has well-defined limitations in appealing to the social democratic voters, however, and after twenty years of expansion, it has been able to obtain only 25 percent of the vote, a level of electoral appeal that seems to make any future absolute majority impossible.

Despite its lack of an absolute majority, the Christian Democratic Party has been in power throughout the postwar period. But its years of governing have been characterized by constant delay in fulfilling the needs of a developing society. Conversely, the Communist Party has practically monopolized the opposition, but its opposing rule has been sterile and demagogic, without realism and without responsibility.

The reasons for the inability of the two leading parties, both with a strong ideological bias, to perform efficiently their respective roles of governing party and opposition party are closely connected. The Christian Democrats find it difficult to apply their aspirations to Christian principles and to Catholic social action to the formation of a political platform and a governmental program. The contentions that divide the party—along lines that have always separated the moderates from the radicals, the conservatives from the innovators—are a direct result of this situation.

Similarly, the Communist Party suffers from the vagueness of its Marxist-Leninist principles and the differences in interpretation of these principles in the Stalinist and post-Stalinist eras and in the Soviet Union and China. What remains of the Marxist-Leninist credo

—the authoritarian nature of the party and the authoritarian concept of the state and of the political process—renders the Italian Communist Party unacceptable as the opposition party of the democratic left.

To the extent that their ideological connective tissue has broken down and no longer serves to motivate political programs, the Chrisian Democratic and Communist parties tend to be transformed into conservative parties, both prisoners of their old ideological patterns and of the respective positions of power each has acquired in Italian society.

From the 1950s until the mid-1960s these two parties—one always in control of the government and the other always in opposition—have caused the Italian political system to operate according to forms and procedures that are apparently in radical contrast but in fact are in substantially conservative accord. Since the other parties are too weak to break the hegemony of the leading parties, these modalities permeate the Italian political system, including the minor parties, which have been able to express themselves only in occasional or permanent collaboration with the two major parties. The change-over of the Italian Socialist Party from systematic collaboration with the Italian Communist Party to collaboration with the Christian Democratic Party has had great political significance as evidence of the failure of Communist strategy, but it has not brought significant modifications in the way in which the political system as a whole functions.

The Italian pattern of political participation is not unlike that of other democratic industrial societies as regards electoral behavior, participation in the life of the parties and parapolitical associations, and the process of forming a government. In these respects, at least, the Christian Democrats and the Communists as the two major parties more or less enact the role of a moderate and a radical party, notwithstanding their ideological peculiarities.

IMPERFECT FUNCTIONING OF THE SYSTEM

The anomaly is in the functioning of the political system. The two parties, through their organizational structure, have succeeded in promoting participation by the electorate within the framework of Catholic and Communist subcultures that are slowly adapting to a mass industrial society. They are not successful, however, in making the political system work so that society can reap the benefits of the efforts and energies that go into it.

The findings of the present study indicate that the characteristics of participation in Italian politics are likely to prevail over the anomalous characteristics of the political system and its functioning. The tendency of postwar Italian politics has been toward a more consolidated representative democracy. The tumultuous mass participation of early postwar years has been transformed into a less widespread but more stabilized participation. The elections that at one time were anxiously awaited in the entire Western world, now result in only marginal changes. The political system, while it deviates from the general pattern of democratic systems, is no longer in danger, as it was in the early 1950s. It functions in a defective and inefficient manner, but it does function.

EFFECT OF RECENT SOCIOPOLITICAL EVENTS

The Italian political system had already been stabilized and political participation and voter behavior were also well established, when the present study began in 1962. What has transpired since then has tended to make the system more rather than less stable. In 1962 the center-left coalition had just been formed, and while the Socialist Party supported this political formula, it continued to be sharply differentiated from the Social Democratic Party. At that time the economic situation in Italy was very favorable and all Italians marveled at the "Italian miracle."

The research was concluded in 1965. During the intervening years the center-left coalition had weathered the relative electoral failure of April 28, 1963, the Socialist split of January 1964, the difficult and continuous factional struggle in the Christian Democratic Party, which resulted in the party's fragmentation on the question of the election of the President of the Republic in December 1964. The coalition has survived despite a recent unfavorable economic situation. The Socialist Party has continued in the government coalition and has taken steps toward unification with the Social Democratic Party that, despite their limitations, will have a rationalizing effect in Italian politics.

The Italian political system has demonstrated its capacity to function—though not at a high level of efficiency—even in a somewhat difficult period and under difficult circumstances. During the period of the present study the inadequacies of the system were evident—the failure of the executive to function effectively, the weak and unstable parliamentary majority, and the continuous paralyzing struggles among factions of the parties in the government majority.

Meanwhile, new developments have exerted considerable influence on both of the major political parties. In the autumn of 1962 the Vatican Council II had not yet convened and the Chinese and Russian communist parties had not yet come into open conflict, but were disputing only indirectly. Since then the Vatican Council's actions have stunned the Catholic world. It can be supposed that reconsideration of the relation between religious doctrine and political action will begin to liberate the Catholic world and the Christian Democratic Party from archaic ideological positions borrowed from what had been considered the social teachings of the Church.

But even greater innovations are taking place in the political parties aligned on the left. At the Tenth Italian Communist Party Congress in 1962 Palmiro Togliatti openly criticized for the first time the stand taken by the Chinese Communists. Immediately, the Chinese sent back an arrogant reply. By 1965 the breach in the international communist movement appeared irreparable and had jeopardized all the principles and all the strategy on which Italian communism had based its forty-five years of existence. The split has continued to widen between this party's constituency and its ideology.

The problems and the crises of recent years—perhaps even more serious for the Christian Democrats than for the Communists—have resulted in a stalemate in the contest between the two major Italian political movements, and therefore in increased political stability. But the stalemate is not necessarily a permanent one. Paradoxically, the two parties, while finding themselves stationary, feel the need to change in a rapidly changing world, but are not able to make the considerable effort required to do so. They know that to begin to change at all will require that they change very much indeed. These two political forces are the product of Italy yesterday rather than of Italy today. Italy's history, interpreted in terms of subcultures, is the basis for their success. The principal reason for their persistent influence is their continuous and massive organization in a society that does not encourage spontaneous, articulate pluralism.

Italy is older and more static politically than it is culturally, economically, and socially. The influence of politics on society as a whole is secondary to the influence of these forces. Italian politics is more a restraint than an accelerating force, an impediment rather than a stimulus to the dynamics of civilized society.

Nevertheless politics has not impeded the development of Italian society. It has indeed assured the institutional stability needed in a period of great transformation. This stability can foster still further development. It is unlikely that the present relationship between political activity and economic and social advancement will deteriorate. On the contrary, it should become more favorable to the progress and welfare of the country.

Appendixes

A. METHODOLOGY AND SOURCES

The chapters of this book are summaries of the findings of a large-scale research project carried on by the Carlo Cattaneo Institute of Bologna between 1962 and 1966.

In connection with this project twelve related research studies focused on five main aspects of political organization and behavior in Italy were undertaken: electoral behavior, summarized in Chapter 2 of this volume; organizational structure of the Communist and the Christian Democratic parties, summarized in Chapter 3; party activism in the Christian Democratic and Communist parties, Chapter 4; the relationships between the two major Italian parties and other Italian institutions, such as the Catholic Church, labor unions, cooperatives, Chapter 5; the role of the two parties in local governments (Chapter 6) and in parliament (Chapter 7).

As a result of these studies the following volumes have been published in Italian by the Società editrice il Mulino in Bologna:

Francesco Alberoni, Vittorio Capecchi, Agopik Manoukian, Franca Olivetti, and Antonio Tosi, *L'attivista di partito*, 1967.
Vittorio Capecchi, Vittoria Cioni Polacchini, Giorgio Galli, Giordano Sivini, *Il comportamento elettorale in Italia*, 1968.
Franca Cervellati Cantelli, Vittoria Cioni Polacchini, Paola de Vito Piscicelli, Stefania Guarino Cappello, Gianfranco Poggi, Giacomo Sani, Giordano Sivini, and Ada Sivini Cavazzani, *L'organizzazione partitica del PCI e della DC*, 1968.
Alfonso Prandi, *Chiesa e politica: La Gerarchia e l'impegno politico dei cattolici italiani*, 1968.
Luigi Brunelli, Umberto Canullo Gianluigi Degli Esposti, Giorgio Galli, Anna Lena, Luciana Pepa, Antonio Picchi, Alfonso Prandi, Alberto Mario Rossi, Bruno Scatassa, Ada Sivini Cavazzani, Luigi Turco, *La presenza sociale del PCI e della DC*, 1969.

One additional volume is scheduled for publication in 1970:

Silvia Adilardi Tozzi, Bianca Avanzini, Vittoria Cioni Polacchini, Stefania Guarino Cappello, Sergio Pedroli, *Il PCI e la DC nelle amministrazioni locali e in Parlamento*.

The summary below gives the following information for each of the research studies on which the project focused: the scope of the study, the research methods used, the research personnel, the kind of detailed data

313

available at the Carlo Cattaneo Institute to scholars who may want to consult them and make use of them in their own work, and the form of publication of the research findings in Italian.

1. *Ecological Study of Italian Elections from 1946 to 1963* (Summarized in the latter part of Chapter 1—1946 elections—and in Chapter 2.)

The purpose of this study was to analyze Italian elections between 1946 and 1963. The trend in party votes for all competing parties was explored and these trends were correlated with time series data on a number of ecological variables at the communal and provincial levels.

In particular the project permitted an evaluation of the character and orientation of the Italian electorate in the postwar period and the measurement of the extent of the relationship between the distribution of the vote in each commune (or province) to such important ecological characteristics as size of commune, degree of industrialization, degree of illiteracy, level of post-elementary education, percentage of the population in public employment, number of television sets in relation to the population, and the variations in the size of the electorate from one election to another.

The research was carried out in part by coding the electoral results for the 7,145 communes and 92 provinces of Italy for the elections of 1946, 1948, 1953, 1958, and 1963, as published by the Ministry of the Interior in Rome.

The data on the selected ecological variables were derived from the population censuses of 1951 and 1961 and from the Agricultural Census of 1961, published by the Central Institute of Statistics, Rome. These data—coded on IBM cards and transferred to magnetic tape—permitted four principal kinds of subsequent analysis:

(1) Cross tabulation between voting behavior and ecological variables for each commune and province.

(2) The calculation of the variations in voting patterns in the five postwar elections as related to changes in industrialization, literacy, and the number of television sets. In particular, this study was based on a calculation of the variation in the individual party vote and in votes for party groups, as related to changes in industrialization between 1951 and 1961; and on the same kind of calculation of variations in the degree of literacy or the number of television sets in relation to population for the same period.

(3) Calculation of the correlation (Pearson R) between each of the ecological variables and all of the others in order to produce a single correlation matrix. Following this, multiple correlations of the same variables were executed in order to identify the most discriminating

among them. Data thus obtained were then reordered in causal chains designed to illustrate the relative weight of these variables on electoral outcomes.

(4) Multiple regression analysis and analysis of variance for all of the communes and provinces on the basis of the following independent variables: the vote on the referendum issue of the Republic in 1946; degree of industrialization; mean level of education; degree of illiteracy; voter turnout; and level of actual versus potential voter turnout. The dependent variables in this analysis were: Italian Communist Party vote; Christian Democratic vote; vote for the left minus the Communist Party; the neofascist Italian Social Movement vote; vote for the right minus the Italian Social Movement.

All data are treated geographically and are shown for the six areas into which the Central Institute of Statistics divides Italy: Northwest, Northeast, Center-North, Center-South, Sicily, and Sardinia.

The study was directed by Vittorio Capecchi and Giorgio Galli. The collection of communal data, the coding, and basic analysis were handled by Luciano Mazzaferro. Provincial data were gathered by Giordano Sivini, who was also involved in their analysis. The format for data analysis was primarily the work of Vittorio Capecchi who was assisted by Vittoria Cioni Polacchini. The computer programming of these data was managed by Luigi Anselmi, Leandro Dall'Oglio, and Lauro D'Ascanio. The data were processed by the Computer Center of Consiglio Nazionale dell'Energia Nucleare at Bologna on an IBM 704 and later on an IBM 7094.

The Carlo Cattaneo Institute archives contain IBM 7094 tapes with the following data per commune:

Results of the Institutional Referendum of June 2, 1946; potential voters, voters, valid votes, invalid votes, and votes for each party for the Constitutional Assembly of June 2, 1946; potential voters, voters, valid votes, invalid votes, and votes for each party for the national elections of April 18, 1948; June 7, 1953; May 25, 1958; April 28, 1963; distribution of land ownership in 1946; number of owners of real property; size of landholdings belonging to private persons, to corporations, and to public agencies; areas of private and public large landholdings;

From the Census of 1951—distribution of population over twenty-one years of age by sex and age, distribution of population over six years of age by level of education, distribution of population in professional positions by occupational sectors (agriculture, fishing and hunting, mining, manufacturing, construction, electric power, gas and water services, commerce, transportation, credit, insurance, and public administration), distribution of those engaged in agriculture or other economic activity by occupational level;

From the Census of 1961—distribution of population over twenty-one years of age by age group, distribution of population over six years of age by level of education, distribution of population in professional positions by occupational sector (agriculture, fishing and hunting, mining, manufacturing, construction, electric energy, gas and water services, commerce, transportation, credit, insurance, and public administration);

From the Agricultural Census of 1961—number and area of farms cultivated under direct private ownership or sharecropping; number of owners of radios as of December 31, 1957; number of owners of radio and television sets as of December 31, 1962.

These same data, as well as figures on per capita income, membership in the Italian Communist Party and the Christian Democratic Party, the circulation of the Communist daily *L'Unità,* are available for each of the ninety-two provinces in Italy. The archives also contain copies of each of the tabulations made in connection with this study.

The findings were published in Italian in *Il comportamento elettorale in Italia* (Electoral Behavior in Italy 1946–63).

2. *Organizational Structure of the Communist and Christian Democratic Parties* (Summarized in the latter part of Chapter 3.)

This study describes the evolution of the organizational characteristics of the two leading Italian political parties—the Christian Democratic Party and the Communist Party.

It describes the local, intermediate, and national structures of these parties and their typical patterns of operation at each of these levels. Changes that occurred between 1945 and 1963, the relationship of the structural characteristics of the two parties to other variables, such as membership, position of the party in the government, the degree of voter participation, and the nature of socialization of leadership cadres are analyzed.

A systematic examination was made of party documents and publications, such as constitutions, proceedings of congresses, pamphlets, periodicals, brochures, and press releases. Party leaders were interviewed.

The study was directed by Giacomo Sani, who was assisted by Stefania Guarino Cappello.

Source materials used in this study are available in the archives of the Carlo Cattaneo Institute. Of particular interest is a collection of pamphlets and party documents and tabulations on the organizational nature and development of each party.

The results of this study are reported in detail in Part I of *L'organiz-*

zazione partitica del PCI e della DC (The Party Organization of the Communist and Christian Democratic Parties).

3. Membership and Local Participation in the Christian Democratic and Communist Parties (Summarized in Chapter 4.)

The purpose of this study was to describe Communist and Christian Democratic party membership—particularly historical trends, periods of growth and decline, and new membership—from 1945 to 1963.

Membership data were analyzed by sex, age, occupation, education, party vote, geographic location, level of development of the commune involved, educational profile, per capita income, and other variables. Membership participation at the section level was studied for each of the parties.

The research involved a systematic examination of official party data. Among the sources consulted were: party congress proceedings, party press (for the Communist Party, the daily *L'Unità* and periodicals *Rinascita, Cronache meridionale,* and *Il Quaderno dell'attivista;* for the Christian Democratic Party, the daily *Il Popolo* and the journal *La Discussione*); publications privately published by the Communist Party in connection with its party congresses, and the "Reports of the Executive Committee" published by the Christian Democratic Party for its party congresses.

The ecological analysis was made by correlating provincial data on membership with the following socioeconomic variables: percentage of male and female labor force in industry, agriculture, and services; level of education; small farmers as percent of total labor force; per capita income; Christian Democratic and Communist votes as percent of total votes cast; membership in General Confederation of Italian Workers as percent of total male and female population.

Correlations were processed on an IBM 7094 computer at the Consiglio Nazionale dell'Energia Nucleare at Bologna. Data on local participation in the Communist Party were available in that party's publications. In the absence of similar data for the Christian Democratic Party, information on the history, structure, functioning, and problems of sixty-seven of the party's sections was obtained with the help of activists of the Christian Democratic Youth Movement.

The project was carried on by Giordano Sivini and Ada Sivini Cavazzani, with the collaboration of Umberto Canullo, Paola de Vito Piscicelli, Alberto Mario Rossi, and Antonio Cassese.

The archives of the Carlo Cattaneo Institute contain documents, newspapers, the schedules for the sixty-seven Christian Democratic sections, and all other documentary materials on which the study is based.

Results of this project were published in Part II of *L'organizzazione partitica del PCI e della DC* (The Party Organization of the Communist Party and the Christian Democratic Party), 1968.

4. *Communist and Christian Democratic Activists* (Summarized in Chapter 4.)

The purpose of this study was to explore by interviews in depth the patterns of political participation in local communities among active workers of the Communist and Christian Democratic parties (the party militants in the period 1945–63. The study concentrated on four main areas of investigation:

(1) The political and socioeconomic background of militants. Through the use of respondent's subjective recall, in a series of personal interviews, it was possible to identify some of the causal factors in the development of the political-ideological orientation of active party workers. These factors were interpreted in order to relate them to the objective socioeconomic background of the individuals under study.

Of particular importance was the exploration of the primary groups to which respondents belonged. This included a study of their family backgrounds (e.g., the presence or absence of and character of ideological orientation in the family, the ideological homogeneity of parents, the role of father and mother, the extent of the family's exposure to the outside world, the presence or absence of evidence regarding definite commitments or militancy in social affairs by parents or siblings. Also explored were the effects of friendships, experiences in school and work, experiences in youth movements, and contacts with educators and other persons who might have reinforced or challenged the influences and pressures exerted by the family.

(2) The social integration of the activist. Through exploration of the respondent's everyday activities and the significance of the political activity itself, the researchers sought to understand the kind and degree of integration of the individual in his community. These patterns were then compared with the integration of each individual with local political groups and the party in general. This study included the activist's adaptation to his occupation, the nature of his rapport with family and friends, his membership and participation in social and religious associations, and the extent of his participation in the life and problems of the community. Within this context, information was also obtained regarding the attitudes of respondents toward technological developments, recreation, and aspects of mass culture.

(3) Integration with the party. The quality and significance of the respondents political activity was explored. Particular attention was paid to the kind of political activity engaged in, the intensity with which each

militant worked for the party, his rapport with party comrades and co-workers, the extent and significance of his proselytizing activities, and the frequency of attendance at party section meetings and at party congresses.

(4) The world view of the party activist. The types of value systems motivating individual respondents and their ideological frames of reference in engaging in party work were explored and analyzed. Respondents were questioned about judgments and evaluations regarding their parties, in order to discover their images of local and national party leadership, notions of the historical role of the party in Italian life, and expectations regarding future party developments. Furthermore, the activists' attitudes toward the whole of society were investigated: their perceptions and degree of acceptance of existing social structures and the changes they considered possible. This phase of the research sought to determine the extent to which such attitudes were a reflection of the party's ideology and whether there might be neutral attitudinal zones in which politics is unimportant.

This study of 108 party activists was carried out in 6 communities with populations ranging from 20,000 to 80,000. The following criteria were used in selecting the communities: the importance in the community of the Christian Democratic and Communist parties; degree of industrialization and economic development; and geographic location. The communities selected consisted of: (1) one community in Lombardy that was industrialized early and had reached an advanced stage under hegemony of the Communist Party, which received 35 percent of the vote and controlled the local government; (2) another community in Lombardy in which industrialization was more recent, under control of the Christian Democrats; rather weak Communist Party; (3) an agricultural center in Veneto, under strong Christian Democratic influence and control; (4) an agricultural community in Emilia-Romagna in which industrialization began after the Second World War; the Communist Party obtained a majority of the electoral support; very weak Christian Democratic Party; (5) a community in Campania characterized by recent and rapid industrialization; Christian Democrats dominant, but the Communists were increasing in strength; (6) an agricultural community in Apulia under the hegemony of Christian Democrats, with Communists well established but not growing.

The structural, economic, and cultural characteristics and the characteristics of the local political system, in each of the six communities was determined, as was the development of the local organizations of the two parties since 1945. A list of the sample of activists to be interviewed was then drawn up.

The sample of activists consisted of 108 males chosen according to an experimental sample design. Besides taking into account residence and party affiliation, the type of party activism engaged in during the three phases corresponding to the postwar development of each party was also considered. For the Communist Party these periods were 1945–53, 1954–58, and 1959–63; for the Christian Democratic Party, 1945–50, 1951–55, and 1956–63.

The method used was the focused nondirective interview that also included some items designed to probe through direct questioning information of a personal nature and evaluations of certain major political leaders and problems.

Each interview lasted from six to seven hours and required from three to six meetings to complete. Where possible the interviews were recorded; otherwise data were recorded in writing on the spot.

The summaries of each interview ran from fifty to sixty typed pages. They were analyzed by a team consisting of three interviewers and the research director. Through this method of interpreting the reports, the team was able to formalize the coding used in scoring the 100 items in the classification schemes or models.

Data analysis took place at two levels. First, major emphasis was placed on correlating the interview materials with a number of previously chosen independent variables included in the experimental design. Second, an effort was made to arrive at a synthesis of these findings through the use of alternative multidimensional models.

The first kind of analysis explored the linkages between characteristics, attitudes, and behavior of the respondents, on the one hand, and the three base variables: the party affiliation of the activist, his place of residence, and the three phases of party development. The subjective content of responses was illustrated by quoting extensively from the individual interview summaries.

For the second type of analysis variables were selected that were susceptible to coding by spatial intervals or on a dichotomous basis. It was then possible to subject these data to all of the models of multidimensional analysis that were useful in attempts to induce a typology of respondents. These included Guttman Scales, classification schemes based on assumptions of entropy; discriminating analytical techniques; factor analysis; and linear causal models.

The study was directed by Francesco Alberoni and carried out by a research team consisting of Vittorio Capecchi, Agopik Manoukian, Franca Olivetti, and Antonio Tosi. The multidimensional analysis was undertaken by Vittorio Capecchi.

The following persons also participated in developing the data: Ada Sivini Cavazzani, Luciano Cervone, Alberto Comerio, Mario and Giuseppe D'Aquanno, Mena Furnari, Anna Galli Guerrieri, Luigi Pacella, Giuseppe Sabatelli, and Giordano Sivini.

The archives of the Carlo Cattaneo Institute contain the 6 community studies, the records of the 108 interviews, the scoring of the interviews, and the tabulations for the analysis.

The results of this study were published in *L'attivista di partito* (The Party Activist), 1967.

5. *Leadership of the Communist and the Christian Democratic Parties* (Summarized in Chapter 4.)

The purpose of this study was to analyze the leadership of the Communist and Christian Democratic parties between 1946 and 1963. The objectives of the study were: to gather data on the socioeconomic characteristics of party leaders, including age, sex, place of birth, geographic mobility, socioeconomic status of family, and occupation; to analyze the internal stratification systems of each party with particular reference to leadership mobility and turnover; discover the degree of interlocking leadership of the party, its auxiliary organizations, and public representative bodies; to delineate typical career patterns for each party. The research was based on diachronic comparison for the period 1946–63.

The study focused on a sample of political leaders who, between 1946 and 1963, were members of the party executive groups (the Christian Democratic National Council and the Communist National Committee) elected by party congresses or were in the delegations of each party to the Constituent Assembly of 1946 or the national legislature from 1948 to 1963.

The sample therefore included current party leaders as well as others who had served at an earlier date but who may have died or withdrawn from party activity. Data were gathered primarily through mail questionnaires consisting of twenty-five brief questions limited in general to neutral and objective aspects of a person's political involvement. (These questionnaires are shown in Italian in Appendix H.)

Of the 2,011 questionnaires mailed, about 78 percent were completed and returned by respondents.

		Returned	
	Mailed	*Number*	*Percent*
Communist	728	599	82.3
Christian Democratic	1,283	966	75.3
Total	2,011	1,565	77.8

For missing data the questionnaires used by Professor Giovanni Sartori in his studies of the Italian legislature (which he made available to the research team) were used. For information about those leaders not elected to parliament, party publications were consulted. The data were coded on punched cards and analyzed mechanically.

The research study was designed by Gianfranco Poggi, who was assisted by Paola de Vito Piscicelli, Franca Cervellati Cantelli, and Vittoria Cioni Polacchini.

The archives of the Carlo Cattaneo Institute contain the 2,011 questionnaires used in this study and the IBM tabulation and the coded and punched cards used in the analysis.

The results of this study are published in Part III of *L'organizzazione partitica del PCI e della DC* (The Party Organization of the Communist Party and the Christian Democratic Party).

6. *Relationships of the Communist and Christian Democratic Parties with Trade Unions and Cooperatives* (Summarized in Chapter 5.)

The study of the trade unions, based on a historical review of the nature of and the policies followed by the trade union central organizations in Italy, was designed to examine in particular the relationships of the Communist Party and General Confederation of Italian Workers and the Christian Democratic Party and the Italian Confederation of Free Unions.

Specifically, the project explored: the nature of the national leadership of these federations and the leadership of the principal union groups within them; the relationship between these leaders and the parliamentary contingents of each party; trade union participation at the local level; the financing of Italian trade unions; and the relationship between the policies of the Communist Party and General Confederation of Italian Workers and between the Christian Democratic Party, the Italian Confederation of Free Unions and the Italian Association of Christian Workers within the Catholic world.

Research on the cooperatives had the following objectives: examination of the formation and evolution of those cooperatives associated with the two leading political parties; and the analysis of functional interdependence between the cooperative movements and the parties, particularly the top leadership of these organizations, and the relations between cooperatives and local power groups.

Research included an examination of the literature on the subject, an analysis of data published by the unions and cooperatives, and interviews with leaders of both the trade unions and the cooperative movements.

The project was directed by Giorgio Galli, who was assisted by Alberto Mario Rossi in the interviewing of trade union leaders, and by Antonio Picchi for the research on the cooperatives.

The Carlo Cattaneo Institute archives contain all of the published materials and other data gathered, as well as the original text of two very long monographs that were shortened for final publication.

The research findings are reported in Part I of *La presenza sociale del PCI e della DC* (The Social Presence of the Communist and the Christian Democratic Parties).

7. *Auxiliary Organizations Allied with the Communist Party* (Summarized in Chapter 5.)

This study explored the composition and operation of associations that support the Communist Party and are more or less directly tied to its policies, organization, and ideology. Included for each organization were its name, date of constitution, scope or ends, organizational characteristics, number of members, nature of its national leadership, and its press.

Analyses in depth were made for each of the most important associations on the basis of the nature of its membership or of its particular relationship to the party (i.e., Italian Union of Women, National Association of Italian Partisans, Italian Union of Popular Sport, Italian Recreational and Cultural Association, and Italian Union of Partisans for Peace).

These analyses included: organizational characteristics; aspects of the directive bodies to delineate any interlocking directorates with the party; and the kinds of policies followed by leaders within their areas of responsibility. The relationships of these associations to nonsupportive groups operating in the same general sector were also examined as well as the extent to which they have achieved representation on public bodies. Finally, the nature and extent of their international contacts and relationships with similar organizations and the importance given by the party to each association were studied.

Research methods included: a systematic search of the press of the groups involved; an examination of pamphlets and other documents of each organization; and an examination of the press and documents of the Communist Party. Other data were secured from interviews with group leaders and from individuals.

The project was directed by Giorgio Galli. The basic analysis of newspapers, journals and documents, as well as the interviews, were carried on by Luigi Brunelli, Alberto Mario Rossi, Ada Sivini Cavazzani, and Luigi Turco.

Materials pertaining to this project in the archives of the Carlo Cattaneo Institute include all of the pamphlets and documents consulted and detailed monographs on each of the single associations subjected to intensive analysis.

The findings of this research project are extensively reported in Part II of *La presenza sociale del PCI e della DC.*

8. *Catholic Organizations and the Christian Democratic Party* (Summarized in Chapter 5.)

The purpose of this project was to study the nature, role, and orientation of associations identified with organized Catholicism, and the relationships and ties between them and the Christian Democratic Party. The research was concentrated on two different types of influential Catholic organizations operating throughout the country: those that are organized at the diocese level, and those strictly controlled by the Catholic hierarchy, such as Catholic Action (which, with its wide range of branches, including young men, university students, college graduates, and other groups, is the largest and most influential Catholic organization); and Catholic associations that are organized on a local or provincial basis. Their leaders are elected rather than appointed, which gives them more freedom from clerical control. Chosen for study in depth in this group were the Italian Associations of Christian Workers and the Italian Confederation of Small Farmers (Coldiretti).

Research materials included all types of published documents pertaining to the Catholic organizations. An analysis and codification was made by examining their treatment by the daily and periodical press and by consulting official documents. In cases where information gaps appeared, the associations themselves supplied whatever relevant data were available in their archives.

Finally, about a score of national and local leaders of these associations were interviewed, in order to round out the information.

The project was directed by Alfonso Prandi, who was assisted by Umberto Canullo, Gianluigi Degli Esposti, Anna Lena, Luciana Pepa, and Bruno Scatassa.

The archives at the Carlo Cattaneo Institute contain the source materials gathered for this study, including published data and interviews with organization leaders. The archives also contain the basic monographs and working papers prepared for the study. These monographs include analyses of: Catholic Action in its various branches, the Catholic University Graduates' Movement, the Italian Association of Catholic Teachers, the Catholic Association of University Students, Italian Women's Center, Civic Committees, the Italian Association of Christian Workers, and the Confederation of Small Farmers.

The research findings are published in Part III of *La presenza sociale del PCI e della DC*.

9. *Position of the Catholic Hierarchy Regarding the Political Commitments of Italian Catholics* (Summarized in Chapter 5.)

This project was undertaken to explore certain aspects of the intervention of the Catholic hierarchy in the political life of the country. Specifically the project focused on: the postures of Popes Pius XII and John XXIII toward Italian political events and problems; the official political positions taken by the Italian Episcopate; the kind of teaching of the Italian Catholic faithful by the Episcopate; the way in which the political positions assumed by the hierarchy were reflected and interpreted in such clerical opinion-forming publications as *Civiltà Cattolica, Aggiornamenti Sociali, Rivista del Clero, Settimana del Clero,* and *Palestra del Clero.*

A systematic examination was made of papal documents and pastoral letters of Italian bishops concerning the political commitments and obligations of Italian Catholics. In addition, the five journals mentioned above were searched for articles containing comment on the official political positions taken by the papal and episcopal authorities.

The study was directed by Alfonso Prandi, who was assisted by Gianluigi Degli Esposti.

All of the documents examined, as well as an extensive and analytical first draft of the study, are available in the archives of the Carlo Cattaneo Institute.

The research findings are reported in *Chiesa e politica: La Gerarchia e l'impegno politico dei cattolici italiani* (Church and Politics: The Hierarchy and the Political Commitments of Italian Catholics).

10. *The Parties' Relationships with the Intellectuals and the Use of Mass Media by the Two Parties* (This study is not summarized in this book, but some of its findings are briefly touched on in Chapter 2.)

The objectives of this project were: to explore the complex relationships of the Communist and Christian Democratic parties and the world of Italian intellectuals, with particular attention focused on the position of the intellectuals regarding the role of Italian politics and political leaders; and to examine the ways in which the two parties have made use of mass media.

In pursuing the first of these objectives a study was made of the political approach and orientation of the central party organs; the kind of cultural activities carried on by each party through relevant party organs; the nature of the party press and of publications directly or indirectly connected with the parties; the nature of the parties' cultural activities and organizations at the local level; and the kind of approaches each party makes to university students, professors, intellectuals, and scholars of various disciplines.

In carrying out the second objective of the study, an analysis was made of each party's publications, its use of radio and television, and its relationships with the motion picture industry.

Research procedures included a systematic examination of official party acts and proceedings, catalogues, publications, and other literature and a census of the cultural organizations and activities of each party. In addition interviews were arranged with about a score of political leaders, intellectuals, and members of quasi-political organizations.

The project was directed by Giorgio Galli, assisted by Luigi Brunelli, Umberto Canullo, and Luigi Turco.

All of the materials utilized in this study, as well as a first and longer analytical draft of the final report, are available for study at the Carlo Cattaneo Institute.

The research findings are published in Part IV of *La presenza sociale del PCI e della DC.*

11. *Commitment of the Communist and Christian Democratic Parties in Local Government* (Summarized in Chapter 6.)

The purpose of this study was to analyze the role and orientation of the Communist and Christian Democratic parties in communal and provincial politics, as well as to gauge the orientations of each party toward the problem of local self-government. The study included: an examination and evaluation of each party's conception of local government between 1945 and 1963; an analysis of the party organs or agencies involved in delineating political strategies and policies to be followed in local governmental bodies; an examination of the actual strategies or policies followed in a sample of communes; an analysis of the nature of the local political class leaders, especially mayors and councillors.

The concept of local politics and of local governmental organizations was inferred from a systematic examination of a vast amount of documentary material. Source materials included legislative debates, records of the Constituent Assembly, legislation and legislative proposals, party publications such as by-laws, platforms, internal memoranda, party press, publications of front and auxiliary organizations, and the politically informed press. In addition, all relevant Communist and Christian Democratic speeches made at the Constituent Assembly and in parliament were analyzed.

To further the analysis of the role of party organs in forming local governmental strategy, specialized publications were consulted and interviews were held with knowledgeable persons.

The policies actually followed in communal governments in which either party held a majority, were analyzed by examining the provincial and communal budgets. The types of budgets examined included those of thirteen provincial capitals in the population range of 100,000 to 200,000 for the period 1949–62; the actual budgetary expenditures for all of Italy's 92 provinces in the fiscal year 1957; and the budgets of a sample of 197 communes—not provincial capitals—in the regions of Emilia (90 out of 336) and Veneto (107 out of 793) for the fiscal year 1957.

The study of local political leadership was drawn from a sample of

502 communes chosen on the basis of size and geographic location. (See Table A-1) Two questionnaires were sent to the town clerk of each of these places, the first pertaining to mayors elected in the postwar period, the second to the composition of the communal assembly on January 1, 1965.

TABLE A-1. *Percentage distribution of population of Italian communes by number of inhabitants, 1961 census compared with 1963 survey sample*

Geographic area	10,000 or less		10,000–50,000		50,000–100,000	
	Census	Sample	Census	Sample	Census	Sample
North	58.8	60.3	35.0	37.0	43.5	43.4
Center	11.5	11.7	20.0	20.0	19.4	20.8
South	21.3	21.4	29.6	27.9	25.8	24.5
Islands	8.4	6.6	15.4	15.1	11.3	11.3
Total	100.0	100.0	100.0	100.0	100.0	100.0

	Over 100,000		Total	
	Census	Sample	Census	Sample
North	50.0	51.9	56.5	50.4
Center	18.8	18.5	12.4	15.7
South	18.8	18.5	22.0	23.7
Islands	12.4	11.1	9.1	10.2
Total	100.0	100.0	100.0	100.0

The project was directed by Giorgio Galli and was carried out by Stefania Guarino Cappello, who was assisted by Sergio Pedroli and Vittoria Cioni Polacchini.

Available at the Carlo Cattaneo Institute are: a monograph on the budgets of the communes examined; the original code sheets relating to the mayors and the composition of the communal assemblies of the 502 communes examined; and the punch cards used in all phases of this analysis.

The research findings of this study are to be published in 1970 in Part I of *Il PCI e la DC nelle amministrazione locali e in Parlamento* (The Communist Party and the Christian Democratic Party in Local Administrations and in Parliament).

12. *Parliamentary Behavior of the Communist and Christian Democratic Parties* (Summarized in Chapter 7.)

This study analyzes certain behavioral aspects of the Communist and Christian Democratic parties in the Italian Chamber of Deputies. The major directions and policies followed by each party in parliament were delineated by a close examination of the way in which each party historically evolved its orientation to parliament; their respective concepts of the role of parliament; the behavior of each party's members in parliament; and the parliamentary policies followed by the Christian Democrats and Communists from 1945 to 1963.

The first two questions were approached through a study of the platforms of each party and of ideological treatises and similar materials to which political parties look for policy guidance. Each party's position regarding the proposed reform of the Senate was also examined.

The study of parliamentary behavior of the parties was made by examining the frequency of parliamentary participation, the style of debate, the kinds of formal questions or interrogations posed, and the differences in position taken in parliamentary sittings as opposed to committee sessions. Attendance data were obtainable from official parliamentary records. An analysis was made of Christian Democratic and Communist speeches in parliament between 1948 and 1963.

The examination of the content of legislative speeches was made with reference to two periods—one of great political tension and the other of normal legislative proceedings—in each of the three postwar legislatures. Three aspects of the legislative activity of the two parties were analyzed: the relationship of legislative intervention to the relative political weights of each party; the nature of the rapport between the two parties, as revealed by what party members of parliament say to and about each other; and the kinds of technical and ideological arguments mustered by individual speakers in support of their own party's position.

A sample of the formal questions or interrogations requiring written replies posed by the members of each party was taken for the first and last months of each of the three postwar legislatures covered by the study. The questions were then coded according to a fifteen-item matrix designed to identify the member's party affiliation, geographic constituency, the minister questioned, the local or national character of the question involved, the nature of the interests involved in the interrogation, the specific nature of the request or demand, the reply made, etc. These data were then tabulated in order to shed light on the patterns of diversity, if any, apparent between the two parties.

As for behavior in open parliament as against committee sessions, the major question posed, particularly for Communist members as representing the opposition party, was whether the party's behavior was substantially different when legislative proposals were debated and voted on in public sessions and in committee sessions. Thus, an examination was made during a normal and a tense period of each of the postwar legislatures of all party votes taken in committees empowered to enact laws. Favorable, unfavorable, and abstention votes were coded as a means of determining the degree of consensus or disagreement and whether opposing views were expressed in an organized and disciplined way. This kind of examination and coding also made it possible to gauge the degree of agreement or disagreement expressed in each time period. These committee profiles could then be compared with behavior in open parliamentary sessions during the same periods.

The actual parliamentary positions taken by the two parties were determined by focusing on three particularly important legislative issues and analyzing the content of Communist and Christian Democratic speeches concerning them. The issues chosen all involved public intervention in the economy. This focus made it possible to identify aspects of the problem and the solution that each member of parliament considered most salient, as well as to watch changes in the positions of deputies over time and their attitudes toward the parliamentary system itself. To discover similarities and differences between the Communist and Christian Democratic deputies, legislative proceedings pertaining to each issue were covered as fully as possible. In addition, the issues were followed in the daily press and summaries of each parliamentary speech were prepared and analyzed.

The research was directed by Giorgio Galli and was carried out by Silvia Tozzi, assisted by Bianca Avanzini.

The archives of the Carlo Cattaneo Institute contain all of the materials and data gathered for all parts of this study, as well as the initial calculations and analyses made in connection with it.

The research findings are to be published in 1970 in Part II of *Il PCI e la DC nelle amministrazioni locali e in Parlamento.*

B. ELECTORAL BEHAVIOR

The tables show Italian electoral behavior from 1861 to 1921.

TABLE B-1. *Registration and voting, 1861–1913*

Year	Registered voters		Percent voting	Type of electoral system [a]
	Number (thousands)	*Percent of resident population*		
1861	419	1.9	57.2	
1865	504	2.0	53.9	
1867	498	1.9	51.8	Single-member constitu-
1870	530	2.0	45.5	encies with limited fran-
1874	572	2.1	55.7	chise
1876	605	2.2	59.2	
1880	622	2.2	59.4	

TABLE B-1.—*Continued*

Registered voters

Year	Number (*thousands*)	Percent of resident population	Percent voting	Type of electoral system [a]
1882	2,018	6.9	60.7 ⎫	
1886	2,420	8.1	58.5 ⎬	List system with increased franchise
1890	2,753	9.0	53.7 ⎭	
1892	2,934	9.4	55.9 ⎫	
1895	2,120	6.7	59.2	
1897	2,121	6.6	58.5 ⎬	Single-member constituencies with increased franchise
1900	2,249	6.9	58.3	
1904	2,541	7.5	62.7	
1909	2,930	8.3	65.0 ⎭	
1913	8,443	23.2	60.4	Single-member constituencies with limited universal franchise

a. For a comprehensive up-to-date treatment of electoral systems, see W. J. M. Mac-Kenzie, *Free Elections* (Allen & Unwin, London, 1958).

TABLE B-2. *Socialist vote as percent of total vote, by region, general elections, 1895–1913*

Region	1895	1900	1904	1909	1913
North					
Piedmont	5.0	21.6	28.5	31.2	29.9
Liguria	7.9	20.4	22.9	22.9	25.8
Lombardy	10.7	18.2	26.7	21.9	28.0
Veneto	6.7	10.8	21.5	15.7	19.2
Emilia-Romagna	20.7	26.5	37.8	39.6	45.0
Total	9.5	19.4	27.8	26.2	29.6
Center					
Tuscany	9.3	16.2	24.5	21.6	29.6
Marches	3.8	6.6	20.6	10.8	13.2
Umbria	1.9	7.2	22.8	22.8	17.0
Latium	4.8	5.1	19.4	13.3	25.9
Total	6.5	11.5	22.7	18.3	24.3
South					
Abruzzi e Molise	0.2	2.0	3.7	3.9	12.1
Campania	2.0	5.9	5.9	3.6	10.8
Apulia	0.6	2.9	11.6	3.0	17.3
Basilicata	—	0.5	7.0	5.0	8.9
Calabria	—	0.5	9.0	1.6	4.9
Total	1.0	3.4	7.5	3.3	11.7

Region	1895	1900	1904	1909	1913
Islands					
Sicily	8.7	2.6	11.6	10.2	17.7
Sardinia	0.1	0.9	10.2	3.9	8.1
Total	7.2	2.3	11.3	9.0	15.8
All of Italy	6.1	13.0	21.3	19.0	22.9

TABLE B-3. *Socialist electoral influence, 1895–1913*

	Socialist votes		Socialist seats in Chamber of Deputies	
	Number	Percent of total vote	Number	Percent of all seats
1895	76,359	6.1	15	3.0
1897	108,086	8.7	16	3.1
1900	164,946	13.0	33	6.5
1904	326,016	21.3	29	5.7
1909	347,615	19.0	41	8.1
1913	1,146,948	22.8	79	15.5

TABLE B-4. *Percent of votes polled by the Popular Party and by the combined Socialist and Communist parties, by region and urban and rural areas, 1919 and 1921*

	Popular Party				Socialist and Communist parties			
	1919		1921		1919		1921	
Region	Urban	Rural	Urban	Rural	Urban	Rural	Urban	Rural
Piedmont	10.9	20.1	12.8	24.2	60.3	47.6	48.2	38.9
Liguria	15.6	22.9	16.9	29.1	34.6	29.6	29.9	33.1
Lombardy	15.9	33.9	13.0	28.8	51.2	44.7	50.8	45.0
Veneto	20.5	38.3	17.2	39.6	47.1	31.3	48.1	30.4
Emilia-Romagna	14.2	19.8	14.5	21.3	55.9	61.7	40.9	37.7
Tuscany	14.9	21.9	13.3	21.2	45.5	43.3	42.1	41.4
Umbria	13.4	17.8	8.5	17.6	56.1	44.4	33.2	23.3
Marches	18.4	28.9	19.6	31.1	30.3	34.3	23.0	25.8
Latium	22.4	27.6	15.5	25.4	27.4	23.8	29.5	28.9
Abruzzi	3.7	3.5	7.8	7.2	23.0	15.6	27.7	17.2
Campania-Molise	17.7	17.6	10.9	14.4	6.8	4.6	23.4	6.2
Basilicata	—	—	5.1	4.1	1.2	5.2	3.0	9.4
Calabria	23.8	17.9	21.0	18.7	11.8	6.8	16.7	10.8
Apulia	8.5	11.0	5.9	11.4	29.7	15.5	31.9	16.8
Sicily	10.4	12.8	9.6	14.3	5.1	6.9	8.5	8.2
Sardinia	17.2	11.8	16.0	10.9	7.3	8.7	26.8	11.3
Total	14.8	21.9	13.0	22.6	40.2	30.4	36.4	27.9

TABLE B-5. *Votes cast, by party, 1919 and 1921*

Party	Percent of valid votes		Number of seats in Chamber of Deputies	
	1919	1921	1919	1921
Official Socialists and Communists	32.3	29.3	156	138
Popular Party	20.5	20.4	100	108
Republicans	0.9	1.9	4	6
"Constitutional" lists	46.3	47.1	248	274
Slavs and Germans	—	1.3	—	9

C. ELECTION RESULTS

The table shows results by zone and by political party, for the years specified. The zones, by region, are as follows:

Zone I—Northwest (Piedmont; Liguria; the province of Piacenza; and Lombardy, excluding the provinces of Bergamo, Brescia, and Mantua).

Zone II—Northeast (the provinces of Bergamo, Brescia, Trento, and Udine; and Veneto, excluding the province of Rovigo).

Zone III—Center (the provinces of Mantua, Rovigo, and Viterbo; Emilia-Romagna, excluding the province of Ascoli Piceno).

Zone IV—South (the province of Ascoli Piceno; Latium, excluding the province of Viterbo; Campania, Abruzzi e Molise; Apulia; Basilicata; and Calabria).

Zone V—Sicily.

Zone VI—Sardinia.

TABLE C-1. *Results of national elections to Constituent Assembly, 1946, and to Chamber of Deputies, 1919, 1948, 1953, 1958, and 1963*

Zone I

Voters	1919	1946	1948	1953	1958	1963
Total electorate (thousands)	2,288 a	6,904	7,003	7,256	7,742	8,491
Number of voters (thousands)	1,524	6,200	6,528	6,878	7,402	8,109
Percent of electorate	66.6	89.8	93.2	94.8	95.6	95.5
Number of valid votes cast (thousands)	1,501	5,874	6,403	6,587	7,167	7,828
Percent of total votes	98.5	94.8	98.1	95.8	96.8	96.6
Percent of valid votes cast						
Right-wing parties	28.3 b	9.2	4.7	11.2	11.0	15.4
Neofascist (MSI and Uomo Qualunque)	—	2.4	0.9	3.3	3.0	3.3
Monarchist (PNM)	—	1.2	0.6	4.4	3.1	1.3
Liberal (PLI, UND, BN)c	—	3.9	1.6	3.5	4.8	10.3
Other	28.3 b	1.7	1.6	—	0.1	0.5

Zone I

Voters	1919	1946	1948	1953	1958	1963
Christian Democratic (DC)	21.8 d	35.6	48.4	41.2	41.0	35.5
DC plus right-wing parties	50.1	44.8	53.1	52.4	52.0	50.9
Left-wing parties	49.9	55.1	46.8	47.5	46.5	48.2
Republican (PRI)	—	1.5	1.0	1.0	1.1	0.8
Social Democratic (PSDI, US)	2.0	—	10.6	6.7	6.7	7.7
Socialist (PSIUP, PSI)	47.9 e	29.5	34.7	16.1	16.9	16.5
Communist (PCI)	—	21.9		20.9	20.3	23.2
Other left-wing parties	—	2.2	0.5	2.8	1.5	—
Other national and local parties	—	0.1	0.1	0.1	1.5	0.9

Zone II

Voters	1919	1946	1948	1953	1958	1963
Total electorate (thousands)	1,196 a	3,743	3,886	3,991	4,125	4,283
Number of voters (thousands)	699	3,418	3,620	3,738	3,862	4,038
Percent of electorate	58.5	91.3	93.1	93.7	93.6	94.3
Number of valid votes cast (thousands)	684	3,183	3,544	3,564	3,753	3,917
Percent of total votes	97.8	93.1	97.9	95.3	97.2	97.1
Percent of valid votes cast						
Right-wing parties	29.5 b	5.9	3.9	9.0	8.4	9.6
Neofascist (MSI and Uomo Qualunque)	—	2.0	1.2	4.0	3.3	3.1
Monarchist (PNM)	—	1.1	0.6	2.7	1.9	0.9
Liberal (PLI, UND, BN) c	—	2.8	1.7	2.3	3.2	5.4
Other	29.4 b	—	0.4	—	—	0.2
Christian Democratic (DC)	40.7 d	50.8	63.5	56.3	57.2	53.7
DC plus right-wing parties	70.2	56.7	67.4	65.3	65.6	63.3
Left-wing parties	29.8	43.3	31.9	34.5	34.0	36.3
Republican (PRI)	—	1.9	0.7	0.5	0.7	0.4
Social Democratic (PSDI, US)	—	—	9.9	5.8	6.4	7.3
Socialist (PSIUP, PSI)	20.8 e	26.3	20.9	14.0	15.4	15.6
Communist (PCI)	—	12.5		12.2	11.5	13.0
Other left-wing parties	—	2.6	0.4	2.0	—	—
Other national and local parties	—	—	0.7	0.2	0.4	0.4

Zone III

Voters	1919	1946	1948	1953	1958	1963
Total electorate (thousands)	2,122 a	5,918	6,090	6,331	6,588	6,760
Number of voters (thousands)	1,479	5,452	5,787	6,096	6,342	6,500
Percent of electorate	70.1	92.1	95.0	96.3	96.3	96.1
Number of valid votes cast (thousands)	1,362	5,145	5,662	5,831	6,159	6,307
Percent of total votes	92.1	94.4	97.8	95.7	97.1	97.0
Percent of valid votes cast						
Right-wing parties	25.9 b	6.4	2.6	7.0	7.2	9.2
Neofascist (MSI and Uomo Qualunque)	—	3.4	1.1	4.0	3.7	3.9
Monarchist (PNM)	—	0.7	0.3	1.2	1.2	0.5
Liberal (PLI, UND, BN) c	—	2.2	1.0	1.7	2.3	4.7
Other	25.9 b	0.1	0.2	0.1	—	0.1
Christian Democratic (DC)	19.5 d	25.9	37.0	33.1	34.2	29.9
DC plus right-wing parties	45.4	32.3	39.6	40.1	41.4	39.1
Left-wing parties	54.6	67.6	60.3	59.8	58.5	60.7
Republican (PRI)	3.9	7.3	4.8	3.2	2.7	2.2
Social Democratic (PSDI, US)	—	—	7.1	5.0	4.7	5.7
Socialist (PSIUP, PSI)	50.7 e	24.5	48.0	16.4	17.3	14.8
Communist (PCI)	—	33.5		33.3	33.7	38.0
Other left-wing parties	—	2.3	0.4	1.9	0.1	—
Other national and local parties	—	0.1	0.1	0.1	0.1	0.2

TABLE C-1.—*Continued*

Zone IV

Voters	1919	1946	1948	1953	1958	1963
Total electorate (thousands)	2,809 a	8,259	8,587	8,996	9,772	10,297
Number of voters (thousands)	1,542	7,161	7,763	8,331	8,977	9,271
Percent of electorate	79.6	86.7	90.4	92.6	91.9	90.0
Number of valid votes cast (thousands)	1,509	6,367	7,578	7,901	8,727	8,981
Percent of total votes	97.9	88.9	97.6	94.9	97.2	96.8
Percent of valid votes cast						
Right-wing parties	73.7 b	31.6	17.7	25.4	19.3	17.1
Neofascist (MSI and Uomo Qualunque)	—	9.1	3.7	8.2	6.7	7.6
Monarchist (PNM)	—	6.6	5.8	13.4	9.4	3.0
Liberal (PLI, UND, BN) c	—	13.1	7.3	3.5	3.0	6.0
Other	73.7 b	2.8	0.9	0.3	0.2	0.5
Christian Democratic (DC)	14.5 d	34.5	50.7	38.4	43.0	40.0
DC plus right-wing parties	88.2	66.1	68.4	63.8	62.3	57.1
Left-wing parties	11.8	31.5	31.3	35.9	37.5	42.5
Republican (PRI)	—	6.2	2.8	1.6	1.1	1.2
Social Democratic (PSDI, US)	—		3.7	2.5	2.5	5.1
Socialist (PSIUP, PSI)	11.8 e	10.3	24.4	8.6	10.9	11.4
Communist (PCI)	—	11.5		21.6	22.6	24.7
Other left-wing parties	—	3.5	0.4	1.6	0.4	0.1
Other national and local parties	—	2.4	0.3	0.3	0.2	0.4

Zone V

Voters	1919	1946	1948	1953	1958	1963
Total electorate (thousands)	1,607 a	2,502	2,595	2,677	2,871	2,955
Number of voters (thousands)	511	2,140	2,284	2,405	2,588	2,541
Percent of electorate	47.9	85.5	88.0	89.8	90.1	86.0
Number of valid votes cast (thousands)	500	1,913	2,221	2,282	2,514	2,446
Percent of total votes	97.9	89.4	97.3	94.9	97.1	96.3
Percent of valid votes cast						
Right-wing parties	70.8 b	29.6	20.7	28.1	20.2	19.8
Neofascist (MSI and Uomo Qualunque)	—	9.7	3.1	11.7	6.9	7.3
Monarchist (PNM)	—	4.2	8.9	11.6	7.5	2.8
Liberal (PLI, UND, BN) c	—	13.5	7.9	4.6	5.7	8.8
Other	70.8 b	2.2	0.8	0.2	0.1	0.9
Christian Democratic (DC)	12.4 d	33.6	47.9	36.4	42.9	38.8
DC plus right-wing parties	83.2	63.2	68.6	64.5	63.1	58.6
Left-wing parties	16.8	26.6	31.4	35.4	36.6	41.1
Republican (PRI)	—	4.2	2.9	1.6	1.1	2.1
Social Democratic (PSDI, US)	10.3	—	5.0	2.5	2.8	4.4
Socialist (PSIUP, PSI)	6.5 e	12.3	20.9	7.5	10.8	10.9
Communist (PCI)	—	7.9		21.8	21.9	23.7
Other left-wing parties	—	2.2	2.5	2.0	—	—
Other national and local parties	—	10.2	0.1	0.1	0.2	0.3

Zone VI

Voters	1919	1946	1948	1953	1958	1963
Total electorate (thousands)	229 a	661	684	730	796	838
Number of voters (thousands)	129	568	616	669	732	744
Percent of electorate	56.6	85.9	90.0	91.7	92.0	88.8

Zone VI

Voters	1919	1946	1948	1953	1958	1963
Number of valid votes cast (thousands)	128	526	602	645	715	724
Percent of total votes	98.5	92.7	97.6	96.3	97.6	97.3
Percent of valid votes cast						
Right-wing parties	79.2 b	20.7	13.4	21.1	14.4	15.3
Neofascist (MSI and Uomo Qualunque)	—	12.4	2.8	8.2	4.7	5.8
Monarchist (PNM)	—	—	1.6	10.1	6.5	3.7
Liberal (PLI, UND, BN) c	—	6.3	8.7	2.8	2.7	5.8
Other	79.2 b	2.0	0.3	—	0.5	—
Christian Democratic (DC)	12.2 d	41.1	51.2	41.7	47.1	42.5
DC plus right-wing parties	91.4	61.8	64.6	62.8	61.5	57.8
Left-wing parties	6.8	36.2	34.9	37.2	38.5	41.3
Republican (PRI)	—	—	0.6	0.5	0.5	4.1
Social Democratic (PSDI, US)	—	—	3.7	2.3	2.0	3.7
Socialist (PSIUP, PSI)	8.6 e	8.9	} 20.3	9.0	12.4	11.1
Communist (PCI)	—	12.5		21.2	19.7	22.4
Other left-wing parties	—	14.8	10.3	4.2	3.9	—
Other national and local parties	—	2.0	0.5	—	—	0.9

a. Excludes permanent emigrants and those on military service; includes for Zone I the province of Mantua, but not the province of Piacenza; for Zone II the province of Rovigo, but not the provinces of Udine and Trento; for Zone III the provinces of Piacenza and Ascoli Piceno, but not the provinces of Mantua and Viterbo; for Zone IV the provinces of Ascoli Piceno and Viterbo.

b. Constitutional lists.

c. Includes the Liberal Party (PLI), the National Democratic Union (UND), and the National Bloc (BN).

d. Partito Popolare (Popular Party).

e. "Official" Socialists.

D. VOTING STABILITY

TABLE D-1. *Stability of party vote at communal level, 1946–63, by degree of industrialization,*a *1951–61, by zone*

Party	Degree of stability b	Degree of industrialization a		
		Low	Medium	High
All of Italy				
Number of communes		3,608	3,135	401
Percent of communes				
Christian Democratic	Stable	32.9	32.9	26.9
	Increased	52.2	53.8	56.9
	Decreased	14.9	13.3	16.2
Communist	Stable	47.9	47.1	45.7
	Increased	43.7	45.1	47.1
	Decreased	8.4	7.8	7.2

TABLE D-1.—*Continued*

Party	Degree of stability [b]	Degree of industrialization [a]		
		Low	Medium	High
Left	Stable	25.3	27.6	23.4
	Increased	29.0	25.1	33.7
	Decreased	45.7	47.3	42.9
Zone I—Northwest				
Number of communes		1,340	804	106
Percent of communes				
Christian Democratic	Stable	39.7	38.3	25.5
	Increased	46.7	50.4	60.4
	Decreased	13.6	11.3	14.1
Communist	Stable	60.7	54.0	58.5
	Increased	26.7	33.8	29.2
	Decreased	12.6	12.2	12.3
Left	Stable	28.2	29.7	24.5
	Increased	7.7	5.9	10.4
	Decreased	64.1	64.4	65.1
Zone II—Northeast				
Number of communes		444	700	53
Percent of communes				
Christian Democratic	Stable	35.8	38.0	41.5
	Increased	55.9	53.7	47.2
	Decreased	8.3	8.3	11.3
Communist	Stable	73.4	74.8	73.6
	Increased	12.2	14.0	22.6
	Decreased	14.4	11.2	3.8
Left	Stable	29.5	30.2	32.1
	Increased	4.1	4.0	13.2
	Decreased	66.4	65.8	54.7
Zone III—Center				
Number of communes		478	485	28
Percent of communes				
Christian Democratic	Stable	38.7	43.5	39.3
	Increased	57.3	52.4	53.6
	Decreased	4.0	4.1	7.1
Communist	Stable	41.8	45.8	57.1
	Increased	48.8	46.4	28.6
	Decreased	9.4	7.8	14.3
Left	Stable	29.1	30.7	28.6
	Increased	5.0	4.8	7.1
	Decreased	65.9	64.5	64.3

Party	Degree of stability b	Degree of industrialization a		
		Low	Medium	High
Zone IV—South				
Number of communes		987	879	183
Percent of communes				
Christian Democratic	Stable	23.3	20.7	21.3
	Increased	56.0	59.6	59.0
	Decreased	20.7	19.7	19.7
Communist	Stable	29.4	27.4	30.1
	Increased	68.4	69.8	65.0
	Decreased	2.2	2.8	4.9
Left	Stable	19.1	22.2	21.3
	Increased	67.5	61.3	55.8
	Decreased	13.4	16.5	22.9
Zone V—Sicily				
Number of communes		217	135	3
Percent of communes				
Christian Democratic	Stable	18.0	19.2	33.4
	Increased	58.5	54.1	33.3
	Decreased	23.5	26.7	33.3
Communist	Stable	29.5	24.4	33.3
	Increased	69.6	74.1	66.7
	Decreased	0.9	1.5	—
Left	Stable	17.0	22.2	—
	Increased	74.2	67.4	100.0
	Decreased	8.8	10.4	—
Zone VI—Sardinia				
Number of communes		242	132	28
Percent of communes				
Christian Democratic	Stable	28.9	29.5	28.6
	Increased	40.1	41.0	53.6
	Decreased	31.0	29.5	17.8
Communist	Stable	25.4	18.2	35.7
	Increased	73.9	79.5	60.7
	Decreased	0.7	2.3	3.6
Left	Stable	27.5	30.3	14.3
	Increased	53.5	45.5	35.7
	Decreased	19.0	24.2	50.0

a. Increase in industrial employment as percent of total employment. Increases of less than 10 percent are classified as low; increases of from 10 to 25 percent as medium; and increases above 25 percent as high.

b. Variations of no more than 10 percent in the 1963 party vote compared with the 1946 vote are defined as "stable"; "increased" and "decreased" indicate variations above and below 10 percent, respectively.

TABLE D-2. *Stability of the party vote at communal level in predominantly agricultural communes,*[a] *1946–63, by type of agricultural employment, by zone*

Party	Degree of stability [b]	Farm owner	Share-cropper	Farm laborer
All of Italy				
Number of communes		3,087	556	1,181
Percent of communes				
Christian Democratic	Stable	28.1	38.3	24.6
	Increased	57.1	55.0	57.8
	Decreased	14.8	6.7	17.6
Communist	Stable	49.2	36.3	33.8
	Increased	43.7	59.4	58.6
	Decreased	7.1	4.3	8.2
Left	Stable	24.5	33.6	20.8
	Increased	33.6	9.7	45.1
	Decreased	41.9	56.7	34.1
Zone I—Northwest				
Number of communes		881	4	265
Percent of communes				
Christian Democratic	Stable	32.1	50.0	32.1
	Increased	56.2	50.0	56.6
	Decreased	11.7	—	11.3
Communist	Stable	61.2	50.0	43.8
	Increased	26.9	25.0	35.1
	Decreased	11.9	25.0	21.1
Left	Stable	27.7	50.0	24.2
	Increased	14.4	—	1.9
	Decreased	57.9	50.0	73.9
Zone II—Northeast				
Number of communes		469	60	69
Percent of communes				
Christian Democratic	Stable	38.8	35.0	20.3
	Increased	53.3	55.0	75.4
	Decreased	7.7	10.0	4.3
Communist	Stable	78.9	70.0	71.0
	Increased	12.2	18.3	18.8
	Decreased	8.9	11.7	10.2
Left	Stable	30.3	36.7	14.5
	Increased	4.7	—	4.3
	Decreased	65.0	63.3	81.2
Zone III—Center				
Number of communes		311	388	83
Percent of communes				
Christian Democratic	Stable	35.0	40.5	27.7
	Increased	59.2	56.7	71.1
	Decreased	5.8	2.8	1.2
Communist	Stable	46.6	38.6	56.6

Party	Degree of stability b	Dominant type of employment		
		Farm owner	Share-cropper	Farm laborer
	Increased	39.6	57.5	24.1
	Decreased	13.8	3.9	19.3
Left	Stable	22.2	33.5	19.3
	Increased	5.5	5.2	1.2
	Decreased	72.3	61.3	79.5
Zone IV—South				
Number of communes		1,120	104	493
Percent of communes				
Christian Democratic	Stable	19.7	31.7	20.7
	Increased	60.1	49.1	60.6
	Decreased	20.2	19.2	18.7
Communist	Stable	33.4	7.7	26.0
	Increased	64.2	91.3	71.2
	Decreased	2.4	1.0	2.8
Left	Stable	20.1	31.7	19.5
	Increased	63.4	32.7	68.9
	Decreased	16.5	35.6	11.6
Zone V—Sicily				
Number of communes		148	—	158
Percent of communes				
Christian Democratic	Stable	16.9	—	21.5
	Increased	62.2	—	50.6
	Decreased	20.9	—	27.9
Communist	Stable	31.7	—	27.2
	Increased	67.6	—	70.9
	Decreased	0.7	—	1.9
Left	Stable	20.9	—	19.6
	Increased	64.9	—	73.4
	Decreased	14.2	—	7.0
Zone VI—Sardinia				
Number of communes		158	—	113
Percent of communes				
Christian Democratic	Stable	29.7	—	29.2
	Increased	42.4	—	37.2
	Decreased	27.9	—	33.6
Communist	Stable	27.2	—	14.2
	Increased	70.9	—	84.9
	Decreased	1.9	—	0.9
Left	Stable	27.2	—	25.7
	Increased	41.8	—	60.2
	Decreased	31.6	—	14.1

a. 4,824 communes in which the majority of workers are farm owners, sharecroppers, or farm laborers.

b. Variations of no more than 10 percent in the 1963 party vote compared with the 1946 vote are defined as "stable"; "increased" and "decreased" indicate variations above and below 10 percent, respectively.

E. COMPARATIVE PARTY STRENGTH

The tables show the strength of the Communist and the Christian Democratic parties in the thirty provinces in which each was strongest, in terms of membership strength and of electoral strength, during the early 1950s and early 1960s.

TABLE E-1. *Communist Party membership strength, 1951 and 1961, and electoral strength, 1953 and 1963*

	1951		*1953*
Province	*Party membership as percent of total adult population*	*Province*	*Party vote as percent of total vote*
Siena	27.7	Siena	48.7
Reggio-Emilia	25.8	Leghorn	43.2
Modena	23.6	Modena	42.2
Bologna	23.6	Reggio-Emilia	41.5
Ferrara	21.3	Bologna	39.7
Ravenna	19.6	Ferrara	38.6
Leghorn	19.1	Grosseto	37.3
Forli	17.3	Pistoia	37.1
Rovigo	16.4	Florence	36.4
Grosseto	15.7	Pisa	36.0
Mantua	14.7	Ravenna	35.0
Florence	14.6	Forli	33.6
Arezzo	13.3	Arezzo	33.2
Pistoia	13.1	Matera	32.2
Pisa	12.9	La Spezia	31.5
La Spezia	12.1	Foggia	31.5
Pesaro	11.1	Pesaro	31.1
Savona	10.9	Agrigento	31.1
Genoa	10.6	Caltanissetta	29.8
Terni	10.4	Parma	29.3
Parma	10.3	Terni	29.2
Cremona	9.0	Rovigo	29.0
Vercelli	8.9	Taranto	28.1
Pavia	8.8	Perugia	27.7
Perugia	8.2	Teramo	27.6
Milan	8.2	Pavia	27.6
Matera	8.0	Savona	27.4
Foggia	7.7	Ragusa	27.3
Novara	7.6	Alessandria	27.3
Alessandria	7.0	Pescara	26.6

	1961		1963
Province	Party membership as percent of total adult population	Province	Party vote as percent of total vote
Siena	24.2	Siena	52.5
Reggio-Emilia	23.3	Reggio-Emilia	45.5
Modena	21.6	Modena	45.2
Bologna	19.8	Leghorn	43.6
Ravenna	17.5	Bologna	43.4
Ferrara	15.9	Pistoia	42.7
Forli	14.0	Florence	41.7
Leghorn	13.5	Ravenna	41.3
Rovigo	11.6	Ferrara	41.1
Florence	11.1	Forli	39.8
Arezzo	10.8	Pisa	39.3
Grosseto	10.8	Perugia	39.0
Mantua	10.8	Grosseto	38.8
Pistoia	10.0	Pesaro	38.6
Pesaro	9.7	Terni	38.3
Pisa	9.2	Arezzo	37.9
La Spezia	8.6	Foggia	34.9
Foggia	7.8	Parma	33.2
Parma	7.7	La Spezia	32.4
Terni	7.6	Pavia	32.2
Perugia	7.0	Ragusa	31.8
Savona	6.7	Matera	31.6
Genoa	6.0	Caltanissetta	31.5
Cremona	6.0	Teramo	31.3
Enna	5.3	Alessandria	30.3
Vercelli	5.2	Ascoli Piceno	30.0
Viterbo	5.0	Vercelli	30.0
Massa Carrara	4.9	Agrigento	30.0
Ancona	4.9	Mantua	29.7
Ragusa	4.9	Ancona	29.7

TABLE E-2. *Christian Democratic Party membership strength, 1951 and 1961, and electoral strength, 1953 and 1963*

	1951		1953
Province	Party membership as percent of total adult population	Province	Party vote as percent of total vote
Frosinone	10.8	Trento	68.0
Enna	9.5	Bergamo	64.4
Trento	7.8	Vicenza	62.2
Salerno	7.5	Treviso	59.9
Caltanissetta	7.5	Padua	59.6
Agrigento	6.8	Sondrio	59.1
Rieti	6.7	Brescia	54.8

TABLE E-2.—*Continued*

1951		1953	
Province	Party membership as percent of total adult population	Province	Party vote as percent of total vote
Ragusa	6.4	Belluno	53.7
Taranto	6.4	Como	53.6
Brescia	6.0	Verona	53.4
Latina	5.9	Lucca	51.9
Viterbo	5.6	Cuneo	51.0
Bergamo	5.5	Udine	50.4
Foggia	5.1	Nuoro	49.7
Pescara	4.8	Macerata	48.2
Potenza	4.7	Gorizia	48.0
Chieti	4.6	Imperia	47.4
Padua	4.6	Varese	46.4
Lecce	4.4	Ascoli Piceno	46.3
Benevento	4.4	Frosinone	46.3
Syracuse	4.3	Campobasso	46.0
Avellino	4.3	Cremona	44.7
Campobasso	4.2	Cosenza	44.2
Como	4.1	Lecce	44.2
Cosenza	4.1	Chieti	43.2
Teramo	4.1	Venice	42.5
Matera	4.1	Sassari	42.4
Bolzano	4.0	Potenza	41.9
Reggio Calabria	4.0	Asti	41.6
Vicenza	3.9	Piacenza	41.5

1961		1963	
Province	Party membership as percent of total adult population	Province	Party vote as percent of total vote
Frosinone	11.6	Vicenza	63.8
Caserta	10.9	Bergamo	60.8
Agrigento	10.4	Trento	60.6
Chieti	10.7	Padua	57.6
Viterbo	9.9	Treviso	57.4
Taranto	9.4	Cuneo	54.8
Campobasso	9.3	Sondrio	54.0
Catania	9.1	Verona	53.5
Cosenza	9.1	Lecce	51.9
Teramo	9.1	Campobasso	51.4
L'Aquila	8.8	Brescia	51.0
Caltanissetta	8.4	Belluno	50.9
Latina	8.3	Nuoro	50.2
Brindisi	8.0	L'Aquila	49.0
Benevento	7.9	Como	48.9

	1961		*1963*
Province	*Party membership as percent of total adult population*	*Province*	*Party vote as percent of total vote*
Potenza	7.8	Chieti	48.0
Trento	7.5	Frosinone	47.7
Cagliari	7.4	Lucca	47.2
Reggio Calabria	7.1	Udine	**47.0**
Enna	7.0	Caserta	46.7
Ascoli Piceno	6.9	Macerata	45.7
Pescara	6.8	Catanzaro	45.1
Nuoro	6.8	Salerno	44.6
Foggia	6.6	Cremona	43.9
Padua	6.4	Brindisi	43.9
Macerata	6.3	Gorizia	43.8
Matera	6.2	Benevento	43.8
Lecce	6.0	Cosenza	43.5
Avellino	5.7	Teramo	43.4
Messina	5.7	Reggio Calabria	43.0

F. PARTY ACTIVISTS

The tables are based on a survey of 54 Christian Democratic and 54 Communist Party activists.

TABLE F-1. *Socioeconomic characteristics of activists*

Characteristic	Christian Democratic	Communist
Social position [a]		
Above average	13	0
Average	32	26
Below average	8	28
No opinion	1	0
Schooling completed		
Elementary	11	33
Junior high	18	14
Senior high	14	2
University	11	5
Occupation [b]		
Agricultural worker	3	7
Industrial or service worker	8	26

TABLE F-1.—*Continued*

Characteristic	Christian Democratic	Communist
White-collar worker	20	15
Manager, teacher, professional, student, businessman	23	6

a. Based on the respondent's appraisal of his own social position in relation to the average of families in the community.

b. The distribution here is different from that shown in Appendix Table F-3 in which, in order to allow for intergenerational comparison, a category of "other" was added.

TABLE F-2. *Socioeconomic influences of families of activists*

Influencing factor	Christian Democratic	Communist
Educational level of parents		
Very low	5	10
Low	23	37
Average	21	6
Above average	2	0
Unknown	3	1
Degree of socioeconomic change from paternal grandparent to activist		
Very great improvement	4	2
Gradual improvement	28	21
None	14	25
Deterioration	4	4
Unknown	4	2

TABLE F-3. *Comparison of occupation of activists, their fathers, and paternal grandfathers*

Occupation	Activist Christian Democratic	Activist Communist	Father of Christian Democratic activist	Father of Communist activist	Grandfather of Christian Democratic activist	Grandfather of Communist activist
Agricultural worker	2	4	10	12	21	21
Farmer	2	0	4	0	5	0
Artisan or tradesman	2	6	3	17	6	16
Industrial or service worker	7	23	15	22	8	10
White-collar worker	16	11	7	1	6	0
Other [a]	25	10	15	2	8	7

a. Managers, teachers, other professions.

TABLE F-4. *Political influences of families of party activists*

Influencing factor	Christian Democratic	Communist
Degree of political agreement with father		
Very close	17	16
Fairly close	26	18
Very little	9	11
None	1	8
Unknown	1	1
Degree of political agreement between activist's mother and father		
Full	39	29
General	7	11
Some disagreement	4	4
Complete disagreement	2	1
No shared ideological orientation	1	8
Unknown	1	1
Father's relationship to corresponding party [a]		
Active	13	12
Member only	14	11
None	26	30
Unknown	1	1

a. For the Christian Democratic Party, membership in either the Catholic-oriented Popular Party or the Christian Democratic Party; for the Communist Party, membership in the Socialist Party or the Communist Party.

TABLE F-5. *Factors influencing party roles of activists*

Influencing factor	Christian Democratic	Communist
On choice of party		
Gradual conviction	46	28
Critical episodes	4	18
Specific crisis	3	7
Unknown	1	1
On decision to become active [a]		
Family	20	31
Friends	23	21
Co-workers	1	16
School	0	1
Organizational affiliations	34	7
Significant encounters	11	7
Decisive movements (such as the Resistance)	4	14
Unknown	2	2

TABLE F-5.—*Continued*

Influencing factor	Christian Democratic	Communist
Indoctrination in party ideology [a]		
Party	29	40
Organizations	19	0
Unions	7	4
Self-indoctrination	16	18
Unknown	1	0

a. Totals equal more than 54, because some respondents named more than one important source.

TABLE F-6. *Activists' political activities and attitudes toward their parties*

Activity or attitude	Christian Democratic	Communist
Frequency of reading party daily press		
Always	6	49
Often	6	2
Rarely	4	2
Never	34	1
Unknown	4	0
Frequency of proselyting for party		
Always	16	45
During elections	22	4
Never	15	5
Unknown	1	0
Principal sphere of activity		
Within the party in favor of a particular faction	2	0
Among supporters and presumably like-minded people	12	2
Among neutrals	11	16
Among adversaries	13	31
Other	16	5
Attitude toward party leaders		
Approve of all	5	35
Approve of most	14	14
Admire some, oppose others	33	4
Admire none	1	1
Unknown	1	0
Expectation of future strength		
Certain to gain	8	23
Likely to gain	22	24
Do not expect gains	24	7

TABLE F-7. *Positions held by activists in local government administrations*

Position	Christian Democratic	Communist
Magistrate or other executive	11	6
Communal councillor	10	9
Nonelected member of communal board	4	5
None	28	34
Unknown	1	0

TABLE F-8. *Attitudes of Christian Democratic activists toward communism and the Catholic Church*

Attitude	Date of recruitment			
	1945–53	*1954–58*	*1959–62*	*Total*
Toward communism				
Intolerant	7	2	1	10
Tolerant but competitive	4	4	3	11
Indifferent	6	11	10	27
Actively seeking dialogue	1	1	4	6
Total	18	18	18	54
Toward relationship of party and Church				
Autonomy of party	2	1	4	7
Autonomy of party within limits of Church principles	5	9	10	24
Dependence on Church directives	7	7	4	18
Complete subjugation of party to Church	4	1	0	5
Total	18	18	18	54

G. COOPERATIVES

TABLE G-1. *Cooperatives affiliated with the National Cooperative League, by region, type, and volume of business, December 31, 1960*

Region	Total number of cooperatives [a]	Total [b]	Percent of all cooperatives	Percent in each region	Cooperatives affiliated with the league			Total membership (thousands)	Volume of business (millions of lire)
					Total excluding building cooperatives [a]	Building cooperatives	Mutuals		
Valle D'Aosta	8	1	12.5	—	1	—	—	4	250
Piedmont	783	707	79.7	9.0	546	38	123	224	14,339
Liguria	366	329	42.0	4.2	154	52	123	106	12,308
Lombardy	2,675	1,856	54.5	23.7	1,446	200	210	653	39,775
Veneto	1,105	354	30.4	4.5	337	11	6	56	6,845
Venezia Trid.	760	4	0.5	0.1	4	—	—	1	69
Venezia Giulia	874	108	28.8	1.4	108	—	—	24	3,101
Emilia-Romagna	3,329	2,256	59.8	28.7	2,030	185	41	540	103,829
Tuscany	1,297	825	58.4	10.5	756	20	49	219	31,987
Marches	232	119	41.8	1.5	97	9	13	24	3,705
Umbria	145	100	62.2	1.3	96	2	2	45	3,511
Latium	747	194	23.8	2.5	175	15	4	42	5,636
Abruzzi e Molise	240	31	12.5	0.4	30	—	1	3	153
Campania	1,036	220	16.0	2.8	173	46	1	25	1,728
Apulia	687	127	15.2	1.6	105	20	2	12	1,233
Basilicata	214	45	21.0	0.6	45	—	—	6	127
Calabria	260	111	31.4	1.4	88	11	12	17	364
Sicily	1,116	213	18.0	2.7	202	10	1	46	1,840
Sardinia	721	244	33.5	3.1	242	2	—	14	1,734
Total	16,158	7,844	41.1	100.0	6,635	621	588	2,061	232,530

a. Excludes building cooperatives.
b. All affiliated cooperatives, including building cooperatives and mutuals.

H. QUESTIONNAIRES TO PARTY LEADERS

The questionnaires were sent to leaders of the Communist and the Christian Democratic parties during the period 1946–63 (see Appendix A, sec. 5). The questionnaires sent to the two parties differed somewhat because of organizational differences between the parties and differences in organizational affiliations. The differences are shown in bracketed portions—first, the wording of the questionnaire sent to Christian Democratic leaders, followed by the variation in wording of the questionnaire sent to Communist leaders.

ISTITUTO DI STUDI E
RICERCHE "CARLO CATTANEO"
Gruppo di studio sulla partecipazione politica e la
formazione della classe dirigente in Italia

QUESTIONARIO

COGNOME E NOME?

LUOGO E DATA DI NASCITA?

LUOGO DI RESIDENZA ATTUALE?

SE HA CAMBIATO RESIDENZA, QUALE E' O QUALI SONO STATE LE SUE RESIDENZE PRECEDENTI?

DOVE HA TRASCORSO GLI ANNI FORMATIVI *(all'incirca dai 12 ai 21 anni)*?

QUAL'ERA L'OCCUPAZIONE O LA PROFESSIONE DI SUO PADRE?

QUALORA SUO PADRE ABBIA ESERCITATO VARIE PROFESSIONI, QUALE E' STATA QUELLA PRE-VALENTE?

QUAL'ERA L'OCCUPAZIONE O LA PROFESSIONE DEL NONNO PATERNO?

NEL CORSO DELLA SUA ADOLESCENZA, IN QUALI CONDIZIONI ECONOMICHE HA VISSUTO? (*)

   a) molto disagiate ☐

   b) disagiate   ☐

   c) discrete   ☐

   d) agiate   ☐

QUAL E' IL SUO TITOLO DI STUDIO?

SE SI E' ISCRITTO ALL'UNIVERSITA', PUO' PRECISARCI, OLTRE LA FACOLTA', LA SEDE UNIVERSITARIA FREQUENTATA?

OCCUPAZIONE PRESENTE?

SE IN PRECEDENZA HA ESERCITATO ATTIVITA' O PROFESSIONI DIVERSE DALL'OCCUPAZIONE PRESENTE, PUO' PRECISARCI QUALI?

   (*) Si prega di segnare con una crocetta (×) la risposta esatta, lasciando in bianco le altre.

IN QUALE LOCALITA' ESERCITA PREVALENTEMENTE LA SUA PRESENTE ATTIVITA'?

QUANTA PARTE DEL SUO TEMPO DEDICA AD ATTIVITA' DI CARATTERE POLITICO Ó DI PARTITO?

   a) solo il tempo libero   ☐

   b) molto tempo   ☐

   c) tutto il proprio tempo ☐

QUANDO SI E' ISCRITTO [ALLA DEMOCRAZIA CRISTIANA?] [al PCI?]

E' SEMPRE STATO ISCRITTO [ALLA D. C.] [al P.C.I.] O PROVIENE DA ALTRI PARTITI?

VI SONO ALTRI MEMBRI DELLA SUA FAMIGLIA ISCRITTI [ALLA DEMOCRAZIA CRISTIANA?] [al Partito Comunista?]

   a) genitori ☐

   b) fratelli ☐

   c) coniuge ☐

   d) figli ☐

QUALI DEGLI INCARICHI SOTTO INDICATI, HA OCCUPATO O OCCUPA ATTUALMENTE NEL PARTITO?

   a) Segretario di Sezione   ☐

   b) Segretario di Comitato [comunale] [Cittadino]   ☐

   c) Membro di Comitato [provinciale] [Federale]   ☐

   d) Membro di Comitato regionale   ☐

   e) Membro del [Consiglio nazionale] [Comitato centrale] ☐

   f) Membro della Direzione   ☐

   g) Altri incarichi nel Partito   ☐

QUALI DELLE CARICHE PUBBLICHE SOTTO INDICATE (IN AMMINISTRAZIONI COMUNALI, PROVINCIALI, REGIONALI) HA OCCUPATO O OCCUPA ATTUALMENTE?

   a) in amministrazioni comunali

       Consigliere comunale ☐

       Assessore comunale ☐

       Sindaco ☐

     In quali località?

   b) in amministrazioni provinciali

       Consigliere provinciale ☐

       Assessore provinciale ☐

       Presidente ☐

     In quali località?

   c) in amministrazioni regionali

       Deputato regionale ☐

       Membro di Giunta regionale ☐

     In quale regione?

E' STATO ELETTO AL PARLAMENTO NAZIONALE?

a) alla Costituente ☐

b) alla Camera ☐

c) al Senato ☐

HA RICOPERTO O RICOPRE CARICHE IN UNA DELLE SEGUENTI [ASSOCIAZIONI DI AZIONE CATTOLICA?] [ORGANIZZAZIONI?]

a) nella [Gioventù Italiana di Azione Cattolica (o Gioventù Femminile di A. C.)] [F. G. C. I.]

 come dirigente [diocesano] [provinciale] ☐

 come dirigente nazionale ☐

Se sì, in che periodo?

b) nella [FUCI] [C.G.I.L.]

 come dirigente diocesano [provinciale] ☐

 come dirigente nazionale ☐

Se sì, in che periodo?

c) [nell'Unione Uomini di Azione Cattolica (o Unione Donne)] [nella Alleanza Contadina]

 come dirigente [diocesano] [provinciale] ☐

 come dirigente nazionale ☐

Se sì, in che periodo?

d) [nel Movimento Maestri di Azione Cattolica] [nella Lega delle Cooperative]

 come dirigente [diocesano] [provinciale] ☐

 come dirigente nazionale ☐

Se sì, in che periodo?

e) nel Movimento Laureati Cattolici [no section e) in Communist questionnaire]

 come dirigente diocesano ☐

 come dirigente nazionale ☐

Se sì, in che periodo?]

The following questions, to end of brackets, were included in the Christian Democratic questionnaire only:

[HA RICOPERTO O RICOPRE CARICHE IN UNA DELLE SEGUENTI ORGANIZZAZIONI?

a) ACLI

 come dirigente provinciale ☐

 come dirigente nazionale ☐

Se sì, in che periodo?

b) Confederazione Nazionale Coltivatori Diretti

 come dirigente provinciale ☐

come   dirigente   nazionale   ☐

Se sì, in che periodo?

c) CISL

come   dirigente   provinciale   ☐

come   dirigente   nazionale   ☐

Se sì, in che periodo?

d) Confederazione Cooperative Italiane

come   dirigente   provinciale   ☐

come   dirigente   nazionale   ☐

Se sì, in che periodo?

HA RICOPERTO O RICOPRE CARICHE IN QUALCHE ALTRA ORGANIZZAZIONE CATTOLICA (OPERE DIPENDENTI O ASSOCIAZIONI COORDINATE ALL'ACI, COME AD ESEMPIO IL CSI, L'AIMC, L'UCIIM, IL CIF, L'UCID, ECC.)? QUALI E IN CHE PERIODO?]

The following bracketed question was included in the Communist questionnaire only:

[HA FATTO O FA PARTE DI ALTRE ORGANIZZAZIONI DI MASSA (AD ESEMPIO, L'ANPI, I PARTI- GIANI DELLA PACE, L'ARCI, ECC.)? IN CHE PERIODO E CON QUALE CARICA?]

HA RICOPERTO O RICOPRE ALTRE CARICHE NON SPECIFICATE NEL QUESTIONARIO, AD ESEMPIO IN ORGANISMI DEL TIPO SOTTO INDICATO?

a) Istituzioni pubbliche di beneficenza, assistenza o previdenza?   ☐

b) Aziende municipalizzate?   ☐

c) Casse di risparmio o istituti di credito analoghi?   ☐

d) Aziende o imprese pubbliche oppure a prevalente partecipazione statale?   ☐

e) Eventuali altre

E' INSIGNITO DI QUALCHE ONORIFICENZA? (Se sì, indicarne il numero e la denominazione)

Index